W9-BXC-566

QUIETIMES

QuieTimes

*A Complete, Day-by-Day Guide
to Personal Worship and Bible Study*

Max E. Anders

Wolgemuth & Hyatt, Publishers, Inc.
Brentwood, Tennessee

Wolgemuth & Hyatt, Publishers, Inc. is a commercial information packager
whose mission is to publish and distribute books that lead individuals toward:

- A personal faith in the one true God: Father, Son, and Holy Spirit;

- A lifestyle of practical discipleship; and

- A worldview that is consistent with the historic, Christian faith.

Moreover, the company endeavors to accomplish this mission at a reasonable
profit and in a manner which glorifies God and serves His Kingdom.

Wolgemuth & Hyatt, Publishers, Inc.
P.O. Box 1941, Brentwood, Tennessee 37027.
Printed in the United States of America.

ISBN 0-943497-45-0

I dedicate this book to my mother who took me to church from my earliest days and taught me that there was a God.

ACKNOWLEDGMENTS

I want to thank four people whose heroic response to the challenge, above and beyond any call of duty, made this book a possibility: Howard Morrison, Jane Cochran, Libby Woleben, and Bill Woleben. Thank you, friends, for your sacrifice of time, and your pleasant spirits under pressure. I also want to thank my wife, Margie, for applying her prodigious editorial talents to the welfare of this work. It is written to the glory of God!

INTRODUCTION

Communication, communion, and spiritual intimacy with God are things for which we all long. It is part of the new birth—part of our new relationship with Him. The desire to search the Scriptures and the desire to pray come from deep within the regenerate heart.

Yet when we open the pages of the Word of God, or when we kneel to pray, we often feel a sense of inadequacy and uncertainty. How do we study the Scriptures; how do we pray; for what do we pray? This sense of inadequacy is as old as the Bible itself. David cried out, "Open my eyes, that I may behold wondrous things from out of Thy law." Jesus' disciples came to Him while He was praying and said, "Lord, teach us to pray just as John also taught His disciples." *Quietimes* addresses these fundamental issues in the life of today's Christian.

Quietimes is a complete guide to personal worship: Bible reading, devotional meditation, prayer, and Scripture memory.

Reading: At the manageable pace of one chapter per day, you read through 365 key chapters in the Bible, reading the major historical and theological passages of the Bible in a year.

Reflecting: A brief time of reflecting on the spiritual implications of the passage of the day is offered.

Responding: In the Lord's Prayer, Jesus instructed His disciples in prayer. As we look closely at His model prayer, we see five principles which should guide us in our prayer.

- Praise: "Our Father who art in Heaven . . ." Praising, thanking, and honoring God for who He is and what He has done.
- Confession: "Forgive us our debts . . ." Keeping our hearts cleansed from sin so we may live in unbroken fellowship and harmony with God.
- Affirmation: "Thy will be done . . ." Agreeing with God's truth and submitting to His will.
- Requests: "Give us this day . . ." Asking God for His action on behalf of those things which are of concern to us.

- Closing Prayer: "For Thine is the glory forever." Closing the time of prayer with appropriate thoughts which exalt the Lord and bring the prayer to conclusion.

Throughout the Bible, there are Scriptures which fit into each of these five categories. By praying these Scriptures back to the Lord, we have great confidence that our prayer is pleasing to Him. The categories were given by Jesus Himself, and the specific Scriptures are prayed back to the One who gave them. In this way, the Scriptures elevate and guide our prayer and stimulate our own spontaneous words to the Lord as we voice the things that are on our hearts.

This kind of "Scripture prayer" will promote the process of cleansing and transforming your mind "by the washing of water with the word" (Ephesians 5:26) and of giving you God's mind in these areas.

The *Requests* are guided, offering one prayer for yourself and one prayer for others, which, in the course of the entire month, form a comprehensive outline of prayer opportunities and responsibilities. In addition, you are encouraged to keep a prayer list of special concerns and to pray for whatever the Lord puts on your heart each day.

Memory Verse: At the pace of one verse per week, repeated daily, you learn 52 of the most vital passages in the Bible which are basic to the Christian walk. These verses are divided into 10 major categories, with five verses each.

1. Salvation
2. Assurance
3. Spiritual Life
4. Prayer
5. Bible Study
6. God's Will
7. Evangelism
8. Spiritual Gifts
9. Spiritual Warfare
10. Stewardship

By firmly memorizing these verses and meditating upon them, you will find personal benefit as your mind is transformed and renewed, and they will provide a ready source of spiritual tools as you minister to others. One should strive through daily review to keep these 52 verses permanently memorized.

Set aside a daily quiet time to read and pray. You might also consider purchasing a church hymnal if you want to add music to your time of personal worship. I do. I hope you will find this devotional a significant new addition to your life as you use it to pursue your life's aspiration: spiritual intimacy with the Lord Jesus Christ.

READING

The passage for today centers on the revelation of God as the Creator of the universe. In the first three days God forms the earth, and in the second three days He populates it.

Read Genesis 1.

REFLECTING

In the beginning, God! That is the way it must be. God first and God foremost. That is the way it is throughout the Bible. "Thou shalt have no other gods before me." "Choose this day whom you will serve." "Every knee will bow and every tongue confess that Jesus Christ is Lord." God first and God foremost.

That is the way He wants it in your life. He was the author of the first creation, and He is the author of the new creation in your heart. In the first creation, the wind and the waves obey Him. They have no choice. In the new creation, however, there is a choice—to obey or not to obey. Your way or His.

RESPONDING

1. Praise: Continue your time with the Lord by offering to the God of creation your praise:

I will bless the Lord at all times; His praise shall continually be in my mouth. My soul shall make its boast in the Lord. . . . Oh, magnify the Lord with me, and let us exalt His name together. . . . Oh, taste and see that the Lord is good; blessed is the man who trusts in Him! (Psalm 34:1-3, 8)

Now express any additional thoughts of praise or thanksgiving.

2. Confession: Pray this confession to the Lord as you seek to keep your life free from sin and in fellowship with Him:

Create in me a clean heart, O God, and renew a steadfast spirit within me. . . . then I will teach transgressors Your ways, and sinners shall be converted to You. (Psalm 51:10, 13)

Confess any personal sins which the Holy Spirit brings to your mind.

3. Affirmation: Now pray this affirmation to the Lord as you agree with and submit yourself to the will of God:

If I am wise, I will not glory in my wisdom; if I am mighty, I will not glory in my might; nor if I am rich, in my riches. But if I glory, I will only glory in the fact that I understand and know You; that You are the Lord, exercising lovingkindness, judgment, and righteousness in the earth. For in these You delight. (Jeremiah 9:23-24)

4. Requests: The Lord encourages us to come to Him with our concerns and desires. As you make your requests known to the Lord, include:

- Health and strength to serve God
- God's will to be done on earth
- Your prayer list, the concerns of your heart, and today's activities

5. Closing Prayer: Finally, offer this closing prayer to the Lord:

Now to You who are able to keep me from stumbling, and to present me faultless before the presence of Your glory with exceeding joy, to You, my God and Savior, who alone are wise, be glory and majesty, dominion and power, both now and forever. Amen. (Jude 24-25)

Memory Verse: For all have sinned and fall short of the glory of God.
Romans 3:23
Salvation Theme

JANUARY 2

READING

The passage for today centers on the rebellion of Adam and Eve against their Creator. The parents of the human race succumb to Satan's temptation to sin and are driven from the garden.

Read Genesis 3.

REFLECTING

You have heard the old saying, "For want of a nail, a shoe was lost; for want of a shoe, a horse was lost; for want of a horse, a king was lost, and for want of a king, a kingdom was lost." It is a very clever way of saying that little things are important! They matter because they lead to other larger things, often with disastrous consequences. We see the first example of that in all of history in Genesis 3:6. First, Eve "saw" the forbidden fruit. No transgression yet. Then she "desired." Still no transgression, but a step closer. Finally, she "took and ate." Transgression. The "look" seemed harmless. It was a small thing, but it led to "eating." Are there things in your life that you are "looking" at? They seem harmless now. But they lead to larger things. Spare yourself. Give them up now. "For want of a nail . . . a kingdom was lost."

RESPONDING

1. Praise: From the very beginning, no one has been without sin. Praise God with the following words for His redemption in Christ:

Blessed be the name of God forever and ever, for wisdom and might are His. . . . He gives wisdom to the wise and knowledge to those who have understanding. He reveals deep and secret things; He knows what is in the darkness, and light dwells with Him. (Daniel 2:20-21)

Take a moment to offer the Lord your personal praise and thanksgiving.

2. Confession: Pray this confession to the Lord as you seek to keep your life free from sin and in fellowship with Him:

O God, You know my foolishness; and my sins are not hidden from You. Let not those who wait for You, O Lord God of hosts, be ashamed because of me. (Psalm 69:5-6)

Confess any personal sins which the Holy Spirit may bring to your mind.

3. Affirmation: As you agree with the will of God, voice your affirmation of His word:

You, O Lord, are the portion of my inheritance and my cup; You maintain my lot. The lines have fallen to me in pleasant places; Yes, I have a good inheritance. (Psalm 16:5-6)

4. Requests: As you make your requests known to the Lord, include:

- Sensitivity to sin
- The ministry of your local church
- Your prayer list, the concerns of your heart, and today's activities

5. Closing Prayer: Finally, offer this closing prayer to the Lord:

Let the words of my mouth and the meditation of my heart be acceptable in Your sight, O Lord, my strength and my redeemer. (Psalm 19:14)

Memory Verse: For all have sinned and fall short of the glory of God.
Romans 3:23
Salvation Theme

READING

The passage for today centers on the first murder. Cain kills his brother Abel and is condemned to wander on the earth.

Read Genesis 4.

REFLECTING

Am I my brother's keeper? The answer is, "Yes." God intended for us to be social beings, to love, care for, protect each other. The mark of any society is how well it cares for those who cannot care for themselves. Elevated societies do well with this. Debased societies do not. The mark of a selfish society is that it cares well for those it likes and does not care well for those it does not like. This is a special kind of brutality. The Christian is called to have the mind of Christ on this matter. We are to do good to all men, for all men are created in the image of God. In His eyes, we all have infinite and equal value. Indeed, we are our brothers' keepers.

RESPONDING

1. Praise: Because the Lord cares for us by asking us to care for each other, offer Him your praise.

Oh, give thanks to the Lord! Call upon His name; make known His deeds among the people. Sing to Him, sing psalms to Him; talk of all his wondrous works. Glory in His holy name; let the hearts of those rejoice who seek the Lord. Seek the Lord and His strength; seek His face evermore. (Psalm 105:1-4)

Oh, give thanks to the Lord! Call upon His name; make known His deeds among the peoples. Sing to Him, sing psalms to Him; talk of all His wondrous words. Glory in His holy name; let the hearts of those rejoice who seek the Lord. Seek the Lord and His strength; seek His face evermore. (Psalm 105:1-4)

Take a moment to offer the Lord your personal praise and thanksgiving.

2. Confession: Pray this confession to the Lord as you seek to keep your life free from sin and in fellowship with Him:

Now no chastening seems to be joyful for the present, but grievous; nevertheless, afterward it yields the peaceable fruit of righteousness to those who have been trained by it. (Hebrews 12:11)

Confess any personal sins which the Holy Spirit may bring to your mind.

3. Affirmation: As you agree with the will of God, voice your affirmation of His word:

For You, O Lord, will bless the righteous; with favor You will surround me as with a shield. (Psalm 5:12)

4. Requests: As you make your requests known to the Lord, include:

- Wisdom for living life
- Needs of your immediate family
- Your prayer list, the concerns of your heart, and today's activities

5. Closing Prayer: Finally, offer this closing prayer to the Lord:

Surely goodness and mercy shall follow me all the days of my life, and I will dwell in the house of the Lord forever. (Psalm 23:6)

Memory Verse: For all have sinned and fall short of the glory of God.
Romans 3:23
Salvation Theme

JANUARY 4

READING

The passage for today centers on the wickedness of man and the judgment of God. In view of the corruption of mankind, God instructs Noah to build the ark to save him from coming judgment.

Read Genesis 6.

REFLECTING

There is great confusion over the meaning of "faith." Sometimes faith is seen as "believing in spite of the fact that there is nothing to believe." Or worse, faith is "believing in spite of the evidence to the contrary." Faith is not a matter of just believing as hard as you can, and it is not merely hoping for something. It is not like wishing upon a star.

Faith is believing the Word of God. God speaks; we believe. That is faith.

God said, "Noah, build an ark (Noah had never seen an ark) to save yourself and all these animals from the rain" (Noah had never seen rain).

But Noah believed God, and because he believed Him, he obeyed Him. That is faith: believing the Word of God and acting upon it.

RESPONDING

1. Praise: In full confidence in the character of God, offer your praise to Him.

The Lord reigns, He is clothed with majesty; the Lord is clothed, He has girded Himself with strength. Surely the world is established, so that it cannot be moved. (Psalm 93:1-2)

Take a moment to offer the Lord your personal praise and thanksgiving.

2. Confession: Pray this confession to the Lord as you seek to keep your life free from sin and in fellowship with Him:

O Lord, You ask me to return to You with all my heart. I will return to You, O Lord, for You are gracious and merciful, slow to anger, and of great kindness; and You relent from doing harm. (Joel 2:12-13)

Confess any personal sins which the Holy Spirit may bring to your mind.

3. Affirmation: As you agree with the will of God, voice your affirmation of His word:

Eye has not seen, nor ear heard, nor have entered into the heart of man the things which You, O God, have prepared for those who love You. (1 Corinthians 2:9)

4. Requests: As you make your requests known to the Lord, include:

- Insight into Scripture
- The hungry around the world
- Your prayer list, the concerns of your heart, and today's activities

5. Closing Prayer: Finally, offer this closing prayer to the Lord:

We will be of good courage, and You shall strengthen our hearts, all we who hope in the Lord. (Psalm 31:24)

Memory Verse: For all have sinned and fall short of the glory of God.
Romans 3:23
Salvation Theme

READING

The passage for today centers on the account of the flooding of the earth. God preserves Noah and his family while He judges the rest of mankind through the flood.

Read Genesis 7.

REFLECTING

God always protects his righteous ones. Always. The child of God need never fear the random blows of fate, for they will never fall. For sure, we receive blows, but they are never random, and blind fate cannot wield them. The Lord said to Noah, "Enter the ark, for you alone I have seen to be righteous before me in this time." Then He saved him and his family from a deluge that obliterated life on this earth. Romans 8:28 says, "all things work together for good to those who love God, to those who are called according to His purpose." When we feel the blows of adversity, we can take comfort in several things. There are certainly many things from which the Lord spared us (Satan would like to destroy us). Also, God will go to the ends of the earth to protect us from the things which would destroy us. In addition, whatever comes our way will be used by God to bring good from it, if we will only go through it His way.

RESPONDING

1. Praise: As you consider the protection which is yours from the hand of a loving God, offer Him these words of praise:

You are worthy, O Lord,
To receive glory and honor and power;
For You created all things,
And by Your will they exist and
*   were created. (Revelation 4:11)*

I will praise the Lord according to His righteousness,
And will sing praise to the name of
*   the Lord Most High. (Psalm 7:17)*

Take a moment to offer the Lord your personal praise and thanksgiving.

2. Confession: Pray this confession to the Lord as you seek to keep your life free from sin and in fellowship with Him:

You do not desire sacrifice, or else I would give it; You do not delight in burnt offering. The sacrifices of God are a broken spirit, a broken and a contrite heart—These, O God, You will not despise. (Psalm 51:16-17)

Confess any personal sins which the Holy Spirit may bring to your mind.

3. Affirmation: As you agree with the will of God, voice your affirmation of His word:

By this I know love, because You, Lord Jesus, laid down Your life for me. And I also ought to lay down my life for others. (1 John 3:16)

4. Requests: As you make your requests known to the Lord, include:

- Love for fellow Christians
- The work of missions in Europe and Asia
- Your prayer list, the concerns of your heart, and today's activities

5. Closing Prayer: Finally, offer this closing prayer to the Lord:

This is the day which You have made; I will rejoice and be glad in it. (Psalm 118:24)

Memory Verse: For all have sinned and fall short of the glory of God.
Romans 3:23
Salvation Theme

JANUARY 6

READING

The passage for today centers on the receding of the flood waters. As the flood subsides, Noah and his family emerge from the ark and build an altar to worship God.

Read Genesis 8.

REFLECTING

The physical world is intended to reflect the spiritual world. The resurrection is pictured throughout nature. Man falls asleep at night, but wakes up in the morning. The earth "dies" each fall, sleeps throughout the winter, but awakens in the spring. The earth died with the Great Flood, but when Noah emerged from the ark, it was to a resurrected earth. Death is a fact of nature, but God abundantly pictures to us His promise.

He will give us new life after death. When we see a rainbow in the sky, it should remind us not only of the fact that God will never again destroy the earth with water, but also that God has promised, through Christ, to give new life after death. Noah's response and ours? Worship. Thank you, Lord. Thank you.

RESPONDING

1. Praise: Think about the significance of the resurrected earth as a sign of the grace of God, and offer Him these words of praise:

Oh, the depth of the riches both of the wisdom and knowledge of God! How unsearchable are His judgments and His ways past finding out! (Romans 11:33)

Blessed are You, the God and Father of our Lord Jesus Christ, who has blessed us with every spiritual blessing in the heavenly places in Christ. (Ephesians 1:3)

Take a moment to offer the Lord your personal praise and thanksgiving.

2. Confession: Pray this confession to the Lord as you seek to keep your life free from sin and in fellowship with Him:

Deliver me from blood guiltiness,
O God, the God of my salvation,
And my tongue shall sing aloud
of Your righteousness.
O Lord, open my lips,
And my mouth
shall show forth Your praise.

(Psalm 51:14-15)

Confess any personal sins which the Holy Spirit may bring to your mind.

3. Affirmation: As you agree with the will of God, voice your affirmation of His word:

Unless You, O Lord, build my house, I labor in vain to build it; unless You, O Lord, guard my city, I stay awake watching in vain. (Psalm 127:1)

4. Requests: As you make your requests known to the Lord, include:

- Faithfulness with your time
- The president and national leaders and affairs
- Your prayer list, the concerns of your heart, and today's activities

5. Closing Prayer: Finally, offer this closing prayer to the Lord:

Oh, satisfy me early with Your mercy, that I may rejoice and be glad all my days! (Psalm 90:14)

Memory Verse: For all have sinned and fall short of the glory of God.
Romans 3:23
Salvation Theme

READING

The passage for today centers on God's covenant with Noah. God gives Noah the rainbow as a sign of His promise never to flood the earth again.

Read Genesis 9.

REFLECTING

A person is only as good as his word. If he is true to his word, he can be trusted. If he is not, he can't. It is as simple as that. God gave His word that He would never again destroy the earth with a flood. And He went even further. God said, "While the earth remains, seedtime and harvest, and cold and heat, and summer and winter, and day and night shall not cease"(Genesis 8:22). Then He set a rainbow in the sky as a sign of His promise.

For thousands of years, God has been true to His word. We sometimes get discouraged during the tough times in life because we tend to focus on circumstances rather than the promises of God. We must remember the rainbow. God is true to His word. He can be trusted.

RESPONDING

1. Praise: Use the following words to praise the power and greatness of God, who set the rainbow of promise in the sky for us:

Great and marvelous are Your works,
Lord God Almighty!
Just and true are Your ways,
O King of the saints!
Who shall not fear You, O Lord,
    and glorify Your name?
For You alone are holy.
For all nations shall come
    and worship before You,
For Your judgments

have been manifested.
(Revelation 15:3-4)

Take a moment to offer the Lord your personal praise and thanksgiving.

2. Confession: Pray this confession to the Lord as you seek to keep your life free from sin and in fellowship with Him:

I give You thanks, O Lord, that I may reason with You. Though my sins are like scarlet, they shall be as white as snow; though they are red like crimson, they shall be as wool. (Isaiah 1:18)

Confess any personal sins which the Holy Spirit may bring to your mind.

3. Affirmation: As you agree with the will of God, voice your affirmation of His word:

You who did not spare Your own Son, Jesus Christ, but delivered Him up for me, how shall You not with Him also freely give me all things? (Romans 8:32)

4. Requests: As you make your requests known to the Lord, include:

- Your financial needs
- The needs of the poor
- Your prayer list, the concerns of your heart, and today's activities

5. Closing Prayer: Finally, offer this closing prayer to the Lord:

Let the beauty of You, Lord, be upon me, and establish the work of my hands for me; yes, establish the work of my hands. (Psalm 90:17)

Memory Verse: For all have sinned and fall short of the glory of God.
Romans 3:23
Salvation Theme

JANUARY 8

READING

The passage for today centers on the construction of the tower of Babel. God overcomes man's defiance of His mandate to populate the earth by confounding the languages at Babel.

Read Genesis 11.

REFLECTING

To understand the Lord's response to the people building the tower of Babel, you must go back to a command God had given Noah and his descendants in Genesis 9:1: "And God blessed Noah and his sons and said to them: 'Be fruitful and multiply, and fill the earth.'" In apparent disobedience to this directive, the people stayed in one place and began to build a monument to themselves. God confused their languages and scattered them abroad from there over the face of the whole earth. God deals with disobedience in different ways. Sometimes, He lets us go our own way and suffer the natural consequences of our sin. At other times, the issue is a major part of His program, and it cannot be ignored. In such instances, God can tolerate no disobedience. His will will be done. Whatever the case, disobedience always has a price. And in the end, God always has his way. Therefore, while obedience is not always easy, it is always wise.

RESPONDING

1. Praise: As you consider the love of the Lord, who disciplines only for our good, offer Him these words of praise:

O Lord, our Lord, how excellent is Your name in all the earth. You who set Your glory above the heavens! When I consider Your heavens, the work of Your fingers, *what is man that You are mindful of him, and the son of man that You visit him? O Lord, our Lord, how excellent is Your name in all the earth! (Psalm 8:1, 3-4, 9)*

Take a moment to offer the Lord your personal praise and thanksgiving.

2. Confession: Pray this confession to the Lord as you seek to keep your life free from sin and in fellowship with Him:

Out of the depths I have cried to You, O Lord; Lord, hear my voice! If You, Lord, should mark iniquities, O Lord, who could stand? But there is forgiveness with You, that You may be feared. (Psalm 130:1-4)

Confess any personal sins which the Holy Spirit may bring to your mind.

3. Affirmation: As you agree with the will of God, voice your affirmation of His word:

I have believed on the Lord Jesus Christ and I am saved. (Acts 16:31)

4. Requests: As you make your requests known to the Lord, include:

- Protection from the "evil one"
- Laborers for the "harvest"
- Your prayer list, the concerns of your heart, and today's activities

5. Closing Prayer: Finally, offer this closing prayer to the Lord:

Bless the Lord, all you His hosts, you ministers of His, who do His pleasure. Bless the Lord, all His works, in all places of His dominion. (Psalm 103:21-22)

Memory Verse: For the wages of sin is death, but the gift of God is eternal life in Christ Jesus our Lord.
Romans 6:23
Salvation Theme

READING

The passage for today centers on the Abrahamic covenant. God establishes a unilateral covenant with Abraham to give him a land and descendants and to bless the world through him.

Read Genesis 12.

REFLECTING

The opposite of obedience is unbelief. The essence of obedience is belief. If you truly believe that God is totally good and all powerful, and that He never acts except for His children's benefit, you will obey whatever He asks of you. It is when you begin to doubt this that obedience becomes difficult. The New Testament tells us that Abraham believed God. Therefore, he was instantaneously and totally obedient. Genesis 12:1 reads, "Go forth!" Genesis 12:4 reads, "So Abram went forth!" And there you have it. If you have an area in your life in which you have difficulty being obedient, it could be because there is something in Scripture that you are not truly believing. Search your life, and in the tradition of the disciples, ask the Lord to increase your faith.

RESPONDING

1. Praise: In faith and obedience, offer to the Lord the praise of your lips.

Who is like You, O Lord, among the gods? Who is like You, glorious in holiness, fearful in praises, doing wonders? (Exodus 15:11)

You are great, O Lord God. For there is none like You, nor is there any God besides You, according to all that we have heard with our ears. (2 Samuel 7:22)

Take a moment to offer the Lord your personal praise and thanksgiving.

2. Confession: Pray this confession to the Lord as you seek to keep your life free from sin and in fellowship with Him:

You have not dealt with me according to my sins, nor punished me according to my iniquities. For as the heavens are high above the earth, so great is Your mercy toward those who fear You; as far as the east is from the west, so far have You removed my transgression from me. (Psalm 103:10-12)

Confess any personal sins which the Holy Spirit may bring to your mind.

3. Affirmation: As you agree with the will of God, voice your affirmation of His word:

You will keep me in perfect peace, because my mind is stayed on You, and I trust in You. (Isaiah 26:3)

4. Requests: As you make your requests known to the Lord, include:

- Commitment to the Lord
- Parachurch ministries
- Your prayer list, the concerns of your heart, and today's activities

5. Closing Prayer: Finally, offer this closing prayer to the Lord:

Lord, preserve me from all evil; preserve my soul. Lord, preserve my going out and my coming in from this time forth, and even forevermore. (Psalm 121:7-8)

Memory Verse: For the wages of sin is death, but the gift of God is eternal life in Christ Jesus our Lord.

Romans 6:23
Salvation Theme

READING

The passage for today centers on the ratification of the Abrahamic covenant. God reiterates His promise that Abraham will have an heir, and Abraham's faith is reckoned as righteousness.

Read Genesis 15.

REFLECTING

Abraham believed God, and it was reckoned to him as righteousness. Faith is central to the Christian experience. In fact, without it, there is no Christian experience. Why is it so important?

Because we cannot make ourselves righteous—any more than a cracked window can make itself uncracked. What is done is done. We have sinned. And only God can make us righteous. So, by faith, we turn to God, acknowledge our inability to restore ourselves, and ask Him to forgive us of our sin and to make us righteous. Then, by the power of a miracle, He "uncracks" the window of our lives.

RESPONDING

1. Praise: Offer your personal praise to your personal Savior in these words:

Oh, sing to the Lord a new song! Sing to the Lord, all the earth. Sing to the Lord, bless His name; proclaim the good news of His salvation from day to day. Declare His glory among the nations, His wonders among all peoples. For the Lord is great and greatly to be praised. (Psalm 96:1-4)

Take a moment to offer the Lord your personal praise and thanksgiving.

2. Confession: Pray this confession to the Lord as you seek to keep your life free from sin and in fellowship with Him:

If I sin, I have an Advocate with You, Jesus Christ the righteous. And He Himself is the propitiation for my sins, and not for mine only but also for the whole world. (1 John 2:1-2)

Confess any personal sins which the Holy Spirit may bring to your mind.

3. Affirmation: As you agree with the will of God, voice your affirmation of His word:

Before I was afflicted I went astray, but now I keep Your word. . . . It is good for me that I have been afflicted, that I may learn Your statutes. . . . I know, O Lord, that Your judgments are right, and that in faithfulness You have afflicted me. (Psalm 119:67, 71, 75)

4. Requests: As you make your requests known to the Lord, include:

- Renewing of your mind
- Needs of your extended family
- Your prayer list, the concerns of your heart, and today's activities

5. Closing Prayer: Finally, offer this closing prayer to the Lord:

May we with one mind and one mouth glorify the God and Father of our Lord Jesus Christ. (Romans 15:6)

Memory Verse: For the wages of sin is death, but the gift of God is eternal life in Christ Jesus our Lord.

Romans 6:23
Salvation Theme

READING

The passage for today centers on the promise of the birth of Isaac. Sarah laughs at God's promise to give her a son in her old age, and Abraham pleads with the messengers from God not to destroy Sodom.

Read Genesis 18.

REFLECTING

Don't you love hospitality? Isn't it a pleasant experience to enter someone's home and feel welcomed? Hospitality is a mark of an open and giving heart. The secret to hospitality is love. If you love your guests and go out of your way to make them feel loved, you will be an exceptional host or hostess.

Hospitality is such an important Christian character trait that elders in the Church must be "given to hospitality." The Bible teaches that we should be hospitable, and that in so doing, some have entertained angels without knowing it. Abraham was a man given to hospitality. Hospitality should be a mark of our lives.

RESPONDING

1. Praise: What a joy to relax in the sovereignty of God and praise Him for His goodness to us.

You who love the Lord, hate evil! He preserves the souls of His saints; He delivers them out of the hand of the wicked. Light is sown for the righteous, and gladness for the upright in heart. Rejoice in the Lord, you righteous, and give thanks at the remembrance of His holy name. (Psalm 97:10-12)

Take a moment to offer the Lord your personal praise and thanksgiving.

2. Confession: Pray this confession to the Lord as you seek to keep your life free from sin and in fellowship with Him:

Forgive me, Lord, when I am unmindful of the Rock who begot me, and forget the God who fathered me. (Deuteronomy 32:18)

Confess any personal sins which the Holy Spirit may bring to your mind.

3. Affirmation: As you agree with the will of God, voice your affirmation of His word:

Do I not know that my body is the temple of the Holy Spirit who is in me, whom I have from You, O God, and I am not my own? For I was bought at a price; therefore I should glorify You in my body and in my spirit, which are Yours. (1 Corinthians 6:19-20)

4. Requests: As you make your requests known to the Lord, include:

- The Lord's leading in your life
- Opportunities for personal evangelism
- Your prayer list, the concerns of your heart, and today's activities

5. Closing Prayer: Finally, offer this closing prayer to the Lord:

Now may the God of hope fill me with all joy and peace in believing, that I may abound in hope by the power of the Holy Spirit. (Romans 15:13)

Memory Verse: For the wages of sin is death, but the gift of God is eternal life in Christ Jesus our Lord.
Romans 6:23
Salvation Theme

JANUARY 12

READING

The passage for today centers on the birth of Isaac. Abraham and Sarah rejoice in the birth of their promised son, Isaac, and Hagar is comforted that her son Ishmael also will prosper.

Read Genesis 21.

REFLECTING

Perhaps we don't celebrate enough—often enough or grandly enough. Perhaps we don't make enough out of the good things God does for us. Abraham made a great feast on the day Isaac was weaned. Certainly, that was a cultural event. It would seem odd to celebrate the same event today. But there are other things we could celebrate within our culture that we don't. When was the last time you made a really big deal out of something important? A high school or college graduation or a successful music recital or the publishing of a book or the climbing of a mountain or the running of a marathon? God has made us with emotions which, if cultivated, would make life a richer experience for us. Perhaps we should celebrate more. In quantity and quality.

RESPONDING

1. Praise: Celebrate your relationship with the Lord Jesus Christ by offering to Him these words of praise:

You are the Rock, Your work is perfect; for all Your ways are justice, a God of truth and without injustice; righteous and upright are You. (Deuteronomy 32:4)

The Lord lives! Blessed be my Rock! Let God be exalted, the Rock of my salvation! (2 Samuel 22:47)

Take a moment to offer the Lord your personal praise and thanksgiving.

2. Confession: Pray this confession to the Lord as you seek to keep your life free from sin and in fellowship with Him:

You, O Lord, are merciful and gracious, slow to anger, and abounding in mercy. . . . As a father pities his children, so You, Lord, pity me who fears You. For You know my frame; You remember that I am dust. (Psalm 103:8, 13-14)

Confess any personal sins which the Holy Spirit may bring to your mind.

3. Affirmation: As you agree with the will of God, voice your affirmation of His word:

If I am in Christ, I am a new creation; old things have passed away; behold, all things have become new. (2 Corinthians 5:17)

4. Requests: As you make your requests known to the Lord, include:

- Love for the lost
- The work of missions in Africa
- Your prayer list, the concerns of your heart, and today's activities

5. Closing Prayer: Finally, offer this closing prayer to the Lord:

Now to You who are able to establish us according to the gospel and preaching of Jesus Christ—to You, alone wise, be glory through Jesus Christ forever. Amen. (Romans 16:25-27)

Memory Verse: For the wages of sin is death, but the gift of God is eternal life in Christ Jesus our Lord.
Romans 6:23
Salvation Theme

READING

The passage for today centers on the offering of Isaac. By asking him to offer his son Isaac, God tests Abraham's faith in His commitment to fulfill the promise of descendants.

Read Genesis 22.

REFLECTING

It is God's way to test the faith of His children. Not to try to catch them failing so He can punish them nor merely to determine genuineness, but to strengthen and increase their faith for the future. The concept of "testing" includes "refining" or "purifying." It is the same word that is used to describe the refining process through which gold is put to purify it and make it ultimately valuable. James wrote, "the testing of your faith produces endurance. And let endurance have its perfect result that you may be complete, lacking in nothing"(1:3-4). That is the purpose of testing: to yield spiritual maturity. We can take instruction from the life of Abraham to see that God's purposes behind testing are always good and we can trust Him.

RESPONDING

1. Praise: In full confidence in the character of God, offer your praise to Him through these words:

O Lord God of Israel, the One who dwells between the cherubim, You are God, You alone, of all the kingdoms of the earth. You have made heaven and earth. (2 Kings 19:15)

Lord God of Israel, there is no God in heaven like You, who keep Your covenant and mercy with Your servants who walk before You with all their heart. (1 Kings 8:23)

Offer the Lord your personal praise and thanksgiving.

2. Confession: Pray this confession to the Lord as you seek to keep your life free from sin and in fellowship with Him:

There is not a just man on earth who does good and does not sin. (Ecclesiastes 7:20)

In returning and rest I shall be saved; In quietness and confidence shall be my strength. (Isaiah 30:15)

Confess any personal sins which the Holy Spirit may bring to your mind.

3. Affirmation: As you agree with the will of God, voice your affirmation of His word:

He made Him who knew no sin to be sin for me, that I might become the righteousness of God in Him. (2 Corinthians 5:21)

4. Requests: As you make your requests known to the Lord, include:

- Faithfulness with your talents
- Your state and local leaders and affairs
- Your prayer list, the concerns of your heart, and today's activities

5. Closing Prayer: Finally, offer this closing prayer to the Lord:

The grace of the Lord Jesus Christ, and the love of God, and the communion of the Holy Spirit be with us all. Amen. (2 Corinthians 13:14)

Memory Verse: For the wages of sin is death, but the gift of God is eternal life in Christ Jesus our Lord.
Romans 6:23
Salvation Theme

READING

The passage for today centers on the marriage of Isaac. Abraham's servant is miraculously led to choose Rebekah as Isaac's future bride.

Read Genesis 24.

REFLECTING

A steward is one who is commissioned to oversee the welfare and execute the affairs of another.

The closer a steward is able to represent the mind of his superior, the better he fulfills his role. Therefore, when a steward is on assignment, ideally he has no personal mind or will. He strives to have the mind and will of his superior. Eliezer, Abraham's servant, was an excellent example of a "faithful steward." His complete mindset was to represent the will of Abraham as faithfully as possible. As Christians, we are stewards of Christ, and as such we are to strive to have the mind and will of Christ.

RESPONDING

1. Praise: Part of stewardship is offering the praise of our lips.

Give to the Lord, O kindred of the peoples, give to the Lord glory and strength. Give to the Lord the glory due His name; bring an offering, and come before Him. Oh, worship the Lord in the beauty of holiness! (1 Chronicles 16:28-29)

I will praise the Lord according to His righteousness, and will sing praise to the name of the Lord Most High. (Psalm 7:17)

Take a moment to offer the Lord your personal praise and thanksgiving.

2. Confession: Pray this confession to the Lord as you seek to keep your life free from sin and in fellowship with Him:

O Lord, You blot out my transgressions for Your own sake; and You will not remember my sins. (Isaiah 43:25)

Confess any personal sins which the Holy Spirit may bring to your mind.

3. Affirmation: As you agree with the will of God, voice your affirmation of His word:

You, Lord Jesus, are the image of the invisible God, the firstborn over all creation. For by You all things were created that are in heaven and that are on earth, visible and invisible, whether thrones or dominions or principalities or powers. All things were created through You and for You. And You are before all things, and in You all things consist. And You are the head of the body, the church; the beginning, the firstborn from the dead, that in all things You may have the preeminence. (Colossians 1:15-18)

4. Requests: As you make your requests known to the Lord, include:

- Strength for obedience
- International students in America
- Your prayer list, the concerns of your heart, and today's activities

5. Closing Prayer: Finally, offer this closing prayer to the Lord:

Now to You who are able to do exceedingly abundantly above all that I ask or think, according to the power that works in me, to You be glory in the church by Christ Jesus throughout all ages, world without end. Amen. (Ephesians 3:20-21)

Memory Verse: For the wages of sin is death, but the gift of God is eternal life in Christ Jesus our Lord.

Romans 6:23
Salvation Theme

READING

The passage for today centers on the stolen blessing. Jacob, Isaac's younger son, deceives his father into giving his blessing to him rather than to his older brother Esau.

Read Genesis 27.

REFLECTING

Chapter 27 is a pronounced low point in the life of a chosen family. It is difficult to justify the behavior of anyone. Perhaps the deepest and most helpful lesson we can learn from this is that if God was able to make a saint out of such material as Jacob, God can take our lives—with all their sin and failure—and make something out of them for His glory.

Jacob lied. We lie. Jacob deceived. We deceive. Jacob failed to trust God. We fail to trust God. Jacob took things into his own hands. We take things into our own hands. Jacob became a man of God. We can become men and women of God. We can be used significantly by the Lord.

For the child of God, there is always a future. And that future, dedicated to the Lord, can be lived to His glory and can yield significant fruit. If God can use Jacob, God can use us.

RESPONDING

1. Praise: We praise the Lord with joy because He never gives up on us, His children.

Tremble before Him, all the earth. The world also is firmly established, it shall not be moved. Let the heavens rejoice, and let the earth be glad; and let them say among the nations, "The Lord reigns.". . . Oh, give thanks to the Lord, for He is good! For His mercy endures forever. . . . Blessed be the Lord God of Israel from everlasting to everlasting! (1 Chronicles 16:30-31, 34, 36)

Take a moment to offer the Lord your personal praise and thanksgiving.

2. Confession: Pray this confession to the Lord as you seek to keep your life free from sin and in fellowship with Him:

You have blotted out, like a thick cloud, my transgressions, and like a cloud, my sins. I will return to You, for You have redeemed me. (Isaiah 44:22)

Confess any personal sins which the Holy Spirit may bring to your mind.

3. Affirmation: As you agree with the will of God, voice your affirmation of His word:

For I know the grace of my Lord Jesus Christ, that though He was rich, yet for my sake He became poor, that I through His poverty might become rich. (2 Corinthians 8:9)

4. Requests: As you make your requests known to the Lord, include:

- Your "daily bread"
- Christian education institutions
- Your prayer list, the concerns of your heart, and today's activities

5. Closing Prayer: Finally, offer this closing prayer to the Lord:

Now may You, the God of peace, sanctify me completely, and may my whole spirit, soul, and body be preserved blameless at the coming of my Lord Jesus Christ. (1 Thessalonians 5:23)

Memory Verse: For God so loved the world that He gave His only begotten Son, that whoever believes in Him should not perish but have everlasting life.

John 3:16
Salvation Theme

JANUARY 16

READING

The passage for today centers on Jacob's dream at Bethel. God appears to Jacob in a dream and extends to him the promise He had made of land and descendants to Abraham and Isaac.

Read Genesis 28.

REFLECTING

Jacob's dream, in which he saw the angels ascending and descending the ladder to heaven, seems to be a turning point in his life. It appears to be the point at which he accepted a personal relationship with the Lord. While his life after this was not flawless, nevertheless, God was able to use him in a central role in the fulfillment of ancient promises, beginning the nation of Israel with him. So too, we must have a personal relationship with God through Jesus, His son and our Savior, before we can experience the work of God in us and through us. Do you know Jesus personally?

If not, why not accept Him as your personal Savior now?

RESPONDING

1. Praise: Offer your personal praise to your personal Savior in these words:

Blessed are You, Lord God of Israel, our Father, forever and ever. Yours, O Lord, is the greatness, the power and the glory, the victory and the majesty; for all that is in heaven and in earth is Yours; Yours is the kingdom, O Lord, and You are exalted as head over all. Both riches and honor come from You, and You reign over all. In Your hand is power and might; in Your hand it is to make great and to give strength to all. Now therefore, our God, we thank you and praise Your glorious name. (1 Chronicles 29:10-13)

Take a moment to offer the Lord your personal praise and thanksgiving.

2. Confession: Pray this confession to the Lord as you seek to keep your life free from sin and in fellowship with Him:

You, O Lord, be merciful to me, and raise me up. . . . (Psalm 41:10)

Confess any personal sins which the Holy Spirit may bring to your mind.

3. Affirmation: As you agree with the will of God, voice your affirmation of His word:

Because I love you, I will keep Your commandments. (John 14:15)

4. Requests: As you make your requests known to the Lord, include:

- Passion for moral excellence
- Needs of personal friends
- Your prayer list, the concerns of your heart, and today's activities

5. Closing Prayer: Finally, offer this closing prayer to the Lord:

Now may the Lord Jesus Christ Himself, and You, my God and Father, who have loved me and given me everlasting consolation and good hope by grace, comfort my heart and establish me in every good word and work. (2 Thessalonians 2:16-17)

Memory Verse: For God so loved the world that He gave His only begotten Son, that whoever believes in Him should not perish but have everlasting life.

John 3:16
Salvation Theme

READING

The passage for today centers on the mistreatment of Joseph, Jacob's son. In response to some unsettling dreams, Joseph's brothers sell him as a slave to a caravan heading to Egypt.

Read Genesis 37.

REFLECTING

Feeling loved is one of life's greatest needs. God has given us that need, and He wants to fill it with Himself and the love of other Christians. When we don't feel loved, we will often go to great lengths to try to earn it or to retaliate against those who keep us from being loved. Joseph's brothers contemplated murder and went through with kidnapping to get rid of him whom they perceived to be a threat to them—all because Jacob let his preference for Joseph show and the brothers felt unloved. When individuals feel love, it makes it easier for them to love others in return.

RESPONDING

1. Praise: As you praise the Lord in the words of this psalm, focus on His sovereignty and goodness:

Make a joyful shout to the Lord, all you lands! Serve the Lord with gladness; come before His presence with singing. Know that the Lord, He is God; it is He who has made us, and not we ourselves; we are His people and the sheep of His pasture. Enter into His gates with thanksgiving, and into His courts with praise. Be thankful to Him, and bless His name. (Psalm 100:1-4)

Take a moment to offer the Lord your personal praise and thanksgiving.

2. Confession: Pray this confession to the Lord as you seek to keep your life free from sin and in fellowship with Him:

O Lord, You do not have as great delight in burnt offerings and sacrifices, as in our obeying Your voice. Behold, to obey is better than sacrifice, and to heed than the fat of rams. (1 Samuel 15:22)

Confess any personal sins which the Holy Spirit may bring to your mind.

3. Affirmation: As you agree with the will of God, voice your affirmation of His word:

For You are the God who commanded light to shine out of darkness, who has shone in our hearts to give the light of the knowledge of Your glory in the face of Jesus Christ. But I have this treasure in an earthen vessel, that the excellence of the power may be of God and not of me. (2 Corinthians 4:6-7)

4. Requests: As you make your requests known to the Lord, include:

* Wisdom in decision making
* Opportunities to serve the Lord
* Your prayer list, the concerns of your heart, and today's activities

5. Closing Prayer: Finally, offer this closing prayer to the Lord:

Now to You, the King eternal, immortal, invisible, to God who alone is wise, be honor and glory forever and ever. Amen. (1 Timothy 1:17)

Memory Verse: For God so loved the world that He gave His only begotten Son, that whoever believes in Him should not perish but have everlasting life.

John 3:16
Salvation Theme

JANUARY 18

READING

The passage for today centers on Joseph's rise and fall. Upon achieving success as a steward over the house of Potiphar, Joseph is unjustly imprisoned after resisting Potiphar's wife.

Read Genesis 39.

REFLECTING

Mark Twain once wrote, "Always do right. It will gratify some and astonish the rest." While we smile at that, there are greater reasons for always doing right. Joseph is a good example. When he resisted Potiphar's wife's advances, he set himself on the road to the throne of Egypt. We may never be monarchs, but God's will for our lives is the most important thing in the world for us. It is more important to be a homemaker or an employee than to be a monarch, if that is God's will. Had Joseph succumbed, he would have set himself on the road to ruin; so, too, with us. Always do right. There is more at stake than meets the eye.

RESPONDING

1. Praise: Offer the Lord your praise for His goodness through these words:

Bless the Lord, O my soul! O Lord my God, You are very great: You are clothed with honor and majesty, who cover Yourself with light as with a garment, who stretch out the heavens like a curtain. . . . May the glory of the Lord endure forever; may the Lord rejoice in His works. . . . Bless the Lord, O my soul! Praise the Lord! (Psalm 104:1-2, 31, 35)

Take a moment to offer the Lord your personal praise and thanksgiving.

2. Confession: Pray this confession to the Lord as you seek to keep your life free from sin and in fellowship with Him:

I have sinned greatly in what I have done; but now, I pray, O Lord, take away the iniquity of Your servant, for I have done very foolishly. (2 Samuel 24:10)

Confess any personal sins which the Holy Spirit may bring to your mind.

3. Affirmation: As you agree with the will of God, voice your affirmation of His word:

I will not lay up for myself treasure on earth, where moth and rust destroy and where thieves break in and steal; but I will lay up for myself treasure in heaven, where neither moth nor rust destroys and where thieves do not break in and steal. For where my treasure is, there my heart will be also. (Matthew 6:19-21)

4. Requests: As you make your requests known to the Lord, include:

- Victory over temptation
- The work of missions in North and South America
- Your prayer list, the concerns of your heart, and today's activities

5. Closing Prayer: Finally, offer this closing prayer to the Lord:

You who are the blessed and only Potentate, the King of kings and Lord of lords, who alone have immortality, dwelling in unapproachable light, whom no man has seen or can see, to You be honor and everlasting power. Amen. (1 Timothy 6:15-16)

Memory Verse: For God so loved the world that He gave His only begotten Son, that whoever believes in Him should not perish but have everlasting life.

John 3:16
Salvation Theme

READING

The passage for today centers on Joseph in prison. God gives Joseph the interpretation of the dreams of two fellow prisoners who were former servants of Pharaoh of Egypt.

Read Genesis 40.

REFLECTING

Joseph is one of the finest examples in the Bible of faithfulness in the face of tribulation. Wherever he was, Joseph viewed that place as the setting in which he was to live for the glory of God. It didn't matter if it was as a steward in the affluent household of Potiphar or as a ward in prison. Joseph bloomed where he was planted. Joseph demonstrated that he could be trusted in the tough times, thereby making himself eligible for God to use him in other settings. Joseph was faithful over small things, so God was able to set him over large things.

RESPONDING

1. Praise: Faithfulness in praise is part of our privilege as servants of God.

Blessed be Your glorious name, which is exalted above all blessing and praise! You alone are the Lord; You have made heaven, the heaven of heavens, with all their host, the earth and all things on it, the seas and all that is in them, and You preserve them all. The host of heaven worships You. (Nehemiah 9:5-6)

Take a moment to offer the Lord your personal praise and thanksgiving.

2. Confession: Pray this confession to the Lord as you seek to keep your life free from sin and in fellowship with Him:

Surely You have borne my griefs and carried my sorrows. . . . You were wounded for my transgressions, You were bruised for my iniquities; the chastisement for my peace was upon You, and by Your stripes I am healed. (Isaiah 53:4-5)

Confess any personal sins which the Holy Spirit may bring to your mind.

3. Affirmation: As you agree with the will of God, voice your affirmation of His word:

Behold, You, O Lord, are my salvation, I will trust and not be afraid; for You, the Lord, are my strength and my song; You also have become my salvation. (Isaiah 12:2)

4. Requests: As you make your requests known to the Lord, include:

- Love for your family
- Revival among Christians in America
- Your prayer list, the concerns of your heart, and today's activities

5. Closing Prayer: Finally, offer this closing prayer to the Lord:

Make me complete in every good work to do Your will, working in me what is well pleasing in Your sight, through Jesus Christ, to whom be glory forever and ever. Amen. (Hebrews 13:20-21)

Memory Verse: For God so loved the world that He gave His only begotten Son, that whoever believes in Him should not perish but have everlasting life.

John 3:16
Salvation Theme

JANUARY 20

READING

The passage for today centers on Joseph's rise to power. Joseph is divinely enabled to interpret Pharaoh's dreams, and Pharaoh responds by setting him over all the land of Egypt.

Read Genesis 41.

REFLECTING

God does the work of God. Man does the work of man. Man cannot do the work of God, and God will not do the work of men. The work of man is faithfulness to what God has called him to. The work of God is results. If we reverse those two, we can drive ourselves to an early grave. If we keep them in line, we can labor with freedom. We need not get unduly elated when things go well, puffed up with pride. Nor need we get unduly distressed when things go poorly. To Pharaoh's question, Joseph answered, "It is not in me; God will answer." What a perfect response. Our job: faithfulness. God's job: results.

RESPONDING

1. Praise: What a joy to relax in the sovereignty of God and praise Him for His goodness to me.

I will praise You, O Lord, with my whole heart; I will tell of all Your marvelous works. I will be glad and rejoice in You; I will sing praise to Your name, O Most High. . . . The Lord also will be a refuge for the oppressed, a refuge in times of trouble. And those who know Your name will put their trust in You; for You, Lord, have not forsaken those who seek You. (Psalm 9:1-2, 9-10)

Take a moment to offer the Lord your personal praise and thanksgiving.

2. Confession: Pray this confession to the Lord as you seek to keep your life free from sin and in fellowship with Him:

I, like a sheep, have gone astray; I have turned to my own way; and You, O Lord, have laid on Jesus all my iniquity. (Isaiah 53:6)

Confess any personal sins which the Holy Spirit may bring to your mind.

3. Affirmation: As you agree with the will of God, voice your affirmation of His word:

For the weapons of my warfare are not carnal but mighty in You, O God, for pulling down strongholds, casting down arguments and every high thing that exalts itself against the knowledge of You, O God, bringing every thought into captivity to the obedience of Christ. (2 Corinthians 10:4-5)

4. Requests: As you make your requests known to the Lord, include:

- Faithfulness with your treasures
- The Great Commission
- Your prayer list, the concerns of your heart, and today's activities

5. Closing Prayer: Finally, offer this closing prayer to the Lord:

May You, the God of grace, who called me to Your eternal glory by Christ Jesus, after I have suffered a while, perfect, establish, strengthen, and settle me. To You be the glory and the dominion forever and ever. Amen. (1 Peter 5:10-11)

Memory Verse: For God so loved the world that He gave His only begotten Son, that whoever believes in Him should not perish but have everlasting life.

John 3:16
Salvation Theme

READING

The passage for today centers on the visit of Joseph's brothers to Egypt. When His brothers come to Egypt to buy grain during the famine, Joseph recognizes and tests them.

Read Genesis 42.

REFLECTING

This puzzling chapter becomes more enlightening when we suggest that Joseph was testing his brothers to discover if they would treat Benjamin differently than they had treated Joseph. The issue was whether or not they could be trusted to bring Joseph's beloved brother to him without harm. While Joseph's heart cried out for reconciliation with his family, he was being cautious for Benjamin's sake. He was wise as a serpent, but harmless as a dove. So should we be.

RESPONDING

1. Praise: Wisdom falls at the feet of God to praise Him for who He is and what He has done.

I will love You, O Lord, my strength. The Lord is my rock and my fortress and my deliverer; my God, my strength, in whom I will trust; my shield and the horn of my salvation, my stronghold. I will call upon the Lord, who is worthy to be praised; so shall I be saved from my enemies. . . . The Lord lives! Blessed be my Rock! Let the God of my salvation be exalted. (Psalm 18:1-3, 46)

Take a moment to offer the Lord your personal praise and thanksgiving.

2. Confession: Pray this confession to the Lord as you seek to keep your life from sin and in fellowship with Him:

For a mere moment You have forsaken me, but with great mercies You will gather me. With a little wrath You hid Your face from me for a moment; but with everlasting kindness You will have mercy on me. (Isaiah 54:7-8)

Confess any personal sins which the Holy Spirit may bring to your mind.

3. Affirmation: As you agree with the will of God, voice your affirmation of His word:

I am not ashamed, for I know whom I have believed and am persuaded that You are able to keep what I have committed to You until that Day. (2 Timothy 1:12)

4. Requests: As you make your requests known to the Lord, include:

- Spiritual insight
- Campus ministries
- Your prayer list, the concerns of your heart, and today's activities

5. Closing Prayer: Finally, offer this closing prayer to the Lord:

May I grow in the grace and knowledge of our Lord and Savior Jesus Christ. To Him be the glory both now and forever. Amen. (2 Peter 3:18)

Memory Verse: For God so loved the world that He gave His only begotten Son, that whoever believes in Him should not perish but have everlasting life.

John 3:16
Salvation Theme

JANUARY 22

READING

The passage for today centers on the return of Joseph's brothers to Egypt. Jacob is forced to send his youngest son Benjamin to Egypt, and Joseph is moved when he sees him.

Read Genesis 43.

REFLECTING

In his commentary, F. B. Meyer regards Joseph as a type of Christ who, when his brothers come to him in fear, has only love to bestow on them. Meyer writes, "Very often we move forward with dread into the unknown; but that dread is the child of ignorance. If only we realized that love is waiting for us there, which does not ask for balm and honey, for spices and myrrh, but just for ourselves, how much happier life would become! Lift up your hearts; a feast awaits you!"

What a marvelous picture of the love of Christ for us. Many of us, like Joseph's brothers, fear because of things we have done that we ought not to have done. Nevertheless, we are children of God, and there is forgiveness with Him. Whatever you think might keep you from God, confess it to Him, receive His forgiveness, and then, like Joseph's brothers, enter into His fellowship.

RESPONDING

1. Praise: God is not unknown to us. We are free to praise Him because of what we know of Him through the Scriptures.

We have thought, O God, on Your lovingkindness, in the midst of Your temple. According to Your name, O God, so is Your praise to the ends of the earth; Your right hand is full of righteousness. (Psalm 48:9-10)

Take a moment to offer the Lord your personal praise and thanksgiving.

2. Confession: Pray this confession to the Lord as you seek to keep your life free from sin and in fellowship with Him:

Let me forsake my wicked ways, and my unrighteous thoughts; if I return to You, O Lord, You will have mercy on me; and to You, my God, for You will abundantly pardon. (Isaiah 55:7)

Confess any personal sins which the Holy Spirit may bring to your mind.

3. Affirmation: As you agree with the will of God, voice your affirmation of His word:

And this is Your commandment: that I should believe on the name of Your Son Jesus Christ and I should love others, as You gave me Your commandment. (1 John 3:23)

4. Requests: As you make your requests known to the Lord, include:

- Desire to be like Christ
- Needs in inner cities
- Your prayer list, the concerns of your heart, and today's activities

5. Closing Prayer: Finally, offer this closing prayer to the Lord:

Blessing and honor and glory and power be to You who sit on the throne, and to You, Lord, forever and ever! (Revelation 5:13)

Memory Verse: But as many as received Him, to them He gave the right to become children of God, even to those who believe in His name.

John 1:12
Salvation Theme

READING

The passage for today centers on Joseph's test of his older brothers. Joseph's brothers respond to accusations of theft as Joseph continues to probe their attitudes.

Read Genesis 44.

REFLECTING

Sometimes, we get a second chance. After a resounding failure, we get another opportunity to set it right. When we do, it is important to seize the opportunity. Judah did. Judah's nobility transcended that of his brothers. When they originally plotted to kill Joseph, it was Judah who intervened. However, he still failed in falling short of Joseph's complete delivery. Judah's second chance came when, from his perspective, Benjamin's life was in danger; Judah put his own on the line. Surely this commitment was taken into consideration in the blessings which Jacob passed on to his sons, resulting in the line of the Messiah coming through the tribe of Judah. Throughout life, we are given second chances—in large things and small. We should take them and set things right.

RESPONDING

1. Praise: Daily we have the second chance to offer praise to the God of grace.

Be exalted, O God, above the heavens; let Your glory be above all the earth. . . . I will praise You, O Lord, among the peoples; I will sing to You among the nations. For Your mercy reaches unto the heavens, and Your truth unto the clouds. Be exalted, O God, above the heavens; let Your glory be above all the earth. (Psalm 57:5, 9-11)

Take a moment to offer the Lord your personal praise and thanksgiving.

2. Confession: Pray this confession to the Lord as you seek to keep your life free from sin and in fellowship with Him:

You will again have compassion on me, and will subdue my iniquities. You will cast all my sins into the depths of the sea. (Micah 7:19)

Confess any personal sins which the Holy Spirit may bring to your mind.

3. Affirmation: As you agree with the will of God, voice your affirmation of His word:

Therefore, having been justified by faith, I have peace with You, O God, through my Lord Jesus Christ, through whom also I have access by faith into this grace in which I stand, and rejoice in hope of Your glory. (Romans 5:1-2)

4. Requests: As you make your requests known to the Lord, include:

- Personal witness for Christ
- Local churches around the nation
- Your prayer list, the concerns of your heart, and today's activities

5. Closing Prayer: Finally, offer this closing prayer to the Lord:

Amen! Blessing and glory and wisdom, thanksgiving and honor and power and might, be to You, God, forever and ever. Amen. (Revelation 7:12)

Memory Verse: But as many as received Him, to them He gave the right to become children of God, even to those who believe in His name.

John 1:12
Salvation Theme

READING

The passage for today centers on the reconciliation between Joseph and his brothers. Joseph finally reveals his true identity to his brothers, and they are warmly reunited.

Read Genesis 45.

REFLECTING

Forgiveness! Where would we be without forgiveness? Without forgiving and being forgiven? The ability to sustain any relationship depends on forgiveness, for sooner or later we will offend someone, and we must be forgiven, or someone will offend us, and we must forgive. We see in this chapter a very moving example of Joseph's being willing to forgive the very ones who some years earlier had plotted to kill him. Notice that Joseph's ability to forgive was rooted squarely in his theology: "You meant it for evil, but God meant it for good." If we lay hold of eternal rather than earthly things, we can more easily forgive when someone robs us of earthly things. Forgive, and accept forgiveness.

RESPONDING

1. Praise: Praise your God in the words of this psalm:

O Lord, how manifold are Your works! In wisdom You have made them all. The earth is full of Your possessions. . . . I will sing praise to my God while I have my being. May my meditation be sweet to Him; I will be glad in the Lord. (Psalm 104:24, 33, 34)

Take a moment to offer the Lord your personal praise and thanksgiving.

2. Confession: Pray this confession to the Lord as you seek to keep your life free from sin and in fellowship with Him:

O my God: I am too ashamed and humiliated to lift up my face to You, my God; for my iniquities have risen higher than my head, and my guilt has grown up to the heavens. (Ezra 9:6)

Confess any personal sins which the Holy Spirit may bring to your mind.

3. Affirmation: As you agree with the will of God, voice your affirmation of His word:

For my light affliction, which is but for a moment, is working for me a far more exceeding and eternal weight of glory, while I do not look at the things which are seen, but at the things which are not seen. For the things which are seen are temporary, but the things which are not seen are eternal. (2 Corinthians 4:17-18)

4. Requests: As you make your requests known to the Lord, include:

- An eternal perspective
- Needs of work or school mates
- Your prayer list, the concerns of your heart, and today's activities

5. Closing Prayer: Finally, offer this closing prayer to the Lord:

I will wait on You, the Lord; I will be of good courage, and You shall strengthen my heart; I will wait on You! (Psalm 27:14)

Memory Verse: But as many as received Him, to them He gave the right to become children of God, even to those who believe in His name.

John 1:12
Salvation Theme

READING

The passage for today centers on the burials of Jacob and Joseph. Jacob is embalmed in Egypt and buried in Canaan; Joseph requests that his remains be carried to Canaan after his death.

Read Genesis 50.

REFLECTING

God's will is often fulfilled in strange ways. Joseph was given strange childhood dreams indicating that he would rule over his brothers. Little could Joseph have imagined that that would include their trying to kill him, his spending time in prison, and eventually his ruling over the nation of Egypt. That time and those experiences were needed, however, to build into Joseph the character qualities and the wisdom needed to rule successfully. Joseph's faithfulness in the dark times allowed God to change him from the immature boy, who received the dream, into the mature man capable of ruling a nation. Never doubt in the dark what God shows us in the light.

RESPONDING

1. Praise: The Lord is worthy to receive my praise because of all that He has done for me.

Oh, give thanks to the Lord! Call upon His name; make known His deeds among the peoples. Sing to Him, sing psalms to Him; talk of all His wondrous works. Glory in His holy name; let the hearts of those rejoice who seek the Lord. Seek the Lord and His strength; seek His face evermore. (Psalm 105:1-4)

Take a moment to offer the Lord your personal praise and thanksgiving.

2. Confession: Pray this confession to the Lord as you seek to keep your life free from sin and in fellowship with Him:

O Lord, do not rebuke me in Your anger, nor chasten me in Your hot displeasure. Have mercy on me, O Lord, for I am weak; O Lord, heal me, for . . . my soul also is greatly troubled. (Psalm 6:1-3)

Confess any personal sins which the Holy Spirit may bring to your mind.

3. Affirmation: As you agree with the will of God, voice your affirmation of His word:

And He said to me, "My grace is sufficient for you, for My strength is made perfect in weakness." Therefore most gladly I will rather boast in my infirmities, that the power of Christ may rest upon me. (2 Corinthians 12:9)

4. Requests: As you make your requests known to the Lord, include:

- Personal discipline
- Christians worldwide who are persecuted for their faith
- Your prayer list, the concerns of your heart, and today's activities

5. Closing Prayer: Finally, offer this closing prayer to the Lord:

Show me the path of life; in Your presence is fullness of joy; at Your right hand are pleasures forevermore. (Psalm 16:11)

Memory Verse: But as many as received Him, to them He gave the right to become children of God, even to those who believe in His name.

John 1:12
Salvation Theme

JANUARY 26

READING

The passage for today centers on the bondage of the Israelites. After Joseph's death, a new king fears that the rapidly multiplying Israelites will be a military threat and so enslaves them.

Read Exodus 1.

REFLECTING

The success of the program of God in the world needs never be questioned. God intended to bring Israel back into the land—God had spoken it and God would do it.

At the time when that seemed least likely, it was closest to happening. In the dark hour of the people of Israel's enslavement, God was working to deliver them—through the birth and miraculous preservation of Moses. Before Moses would die, the nation of Israel would be back on the doorstep of the land which had been promised to them. Today, the fulfillment of the promises of God seem remote and unlikely. The return of Christ is scoffed at by many. But God has spoken it and God will do it. The day is drawing nearer. We must watch—and be ready.

RESPONDING

1. Praise: In the words of this psalm, praise the God of the impossible.

O God, You are my God; early will I seek You; my soul thirsts for You; my flesh longs for You in a dry and thirsty land where there is no water. So I have looked for You in the sanctuary to see Your power and Your glory. (Psalm 63:1-2)

Take a moment to offer the Lord your personal praise and thanksgiving.

2. Confession: Pray this confession to the Lord as you seek to keep your life free from sin and in fellowship with Him:

O Lord, I know my way is not in myself; it is not in me, who walks, to direct my own steps. O Lord, correct me, but with justice; not in Your anger, lest You bring me to nothing. (Jeremiah 10:23-24)

Confess any personal sins which the Holy Spirit may bring to your mind.

3. Affirmation: As you agree with the will of God, voice your affirmation of His word:

Blessed am I when I make You, O Lord, my trust, and when I do not respect the proud, nor those who turn aside to lies. (Psalm 40:4)

4. Requests: As you make your requests known to the Lord, include:

- Love for the Lord
- The work of missions in the Middle East, Australia, and the Islands
- Your prayer list, the concerns of your heart, and today's activities

5. Closing Prayer: Finally, offer this closing prayer to the Lord:

Save Your people, and bless Your inheritance; shepherd us also, and bear us up forever. (Psalm 28:9)

Memory Verse: But as many as received Him, to them He gave the right to become children of God, even to those who believe in His name.

John 1:12
Salvation Theme

READING

The passage for today centers on the birth and early life of Moses. Moses is protected as an infant and raised by Pharaoh's daughter but escapes to Midian after killing an Egyptian.

Read Exodus 2.

REFLECTING

God is sovereign in all the earth. We must never forget that. Much inner distress in life comes from losing sight of that one fact. Moses faced what appeared to be certain death. Yet God's hand was on him during the fragile time he was in the bulrushes. God lifted him from the home of a slave and put him in the palace of the king. What looked like a disaster was a triumph. The same God who cared for Moses promises to care for us—perhaps not as dramatically, but just as certainly. The "peace that passes understanding," which we are promised, is ours only if we embrace that fundamental truth.

RESPONDING

1. Praise: As you praise the Lord in the words of this psalm, focus on His sovereignty and goodness.

Because Your lovingkindness is better than life, my lips shall praise You. Thus I will bless You while I live; I will lift up my hands in Your name. My soul shall be satisfied as with marrow and fatness, and my mouth shall praise You with joyful lips. . . . Because You have been my help, therefore in the shadow of Your wings I will rejoice. (Psalm 63:3-5, 7)

Take a moment to offer the Lord your personal praise and thanksgiving.

2. Confession: Pray this confession to the Lord as you seek to keep your life free from sin and in fellowship with Him:

You will cleanse me from all my iniquity by which I have sinned against You, and You will pardon all my iniquities by which I have sinned and by which I have transgressed against You. (Jeremiah 33:8)

Confess any personal sins which the Holy Spirit may bring to your mind.

3. Affirmation: As you agree with the will of God, voice your affirmation of His word:

I will cast my burden on You, O Lord, and You will sustain me; You shall never permit me, as a righteous one, to be moved. (Psalm 55:22)

4. Requests: As you make your requests known to the Lord, include:

- Faithfulness in sharing Christ
- The Lord's work in national and world affairs
- Your prayer list, the concerns of your heart, and today's activities

5. Closing Prayer: Finally, offer this closing prayer to the Lord:

You, the Lord, will command Your lovingkindness in the daytime, and in the night Your song shall be with me—a prayer to You, the God of my life. (Psalm 42:8)

Memory Verse: But as many as received Him, to them He gave the right to become children of God, even to those who believe in His name.

John 1:12
Salvation Theme

JANUARY 28

READING

The passage for today centers on Moses' divine call. God reveals Himself to Moses in the burning bush and commissions him to deliver His people from bondage in Egypt.

Read Exodus 3.

REFLECTING

The wisdom of Egypt was not adequate to equip Moses to serve God. Luxury and ease, favor and privilege are rarely the context out of which godliness grows.

God took Moses out of the limelight, into solitude, labor, and obscurity. There, Moses met God and learned to walk with Him.

The same pattern was true for many of God's servants: Joseph, David, Daniel, Paul, John. Each one of them was taken out of the limelight for a time, into solitude, labor, and obscurity, to build into their hearts the depth, maturiy, and trustworthiness they would need to be used by God.

It is true in each life; occasionally, it will appear that we are set aside. Properly used, that time will equip the servant for the next level of ministry. Be faithful. Without deserts, there are no deliverers.

RESPONDING

1. Praise: Use the words of this psalm to offer your praise to Him who calls us.

Make a joyful shout to God, all the earth! Sing out the honor of His name; make His praise glorious. Say to God, "How awesome are Your works! Through the greatness of Your power Your enemies shall submit themselves to You. All the earth shall worship You and sing praises to You; they shall sing praises to Your name." (Psalm 66:1-4)

Take a moment to offer the Lord your personal praise and thanksgiving.

2. Confession: Pray this confession to the Lord as you seek to keep your life free from sin and in fellowship with Him:

If I say that I have no sin, I deceive myself, and the truth is not in me. If I confess my sins, You are faithful and just to forgive me my sins and to cleanse me from all unrighteousness. (1 John 1:8-9)

Confess any personal sins which the Holy Spirit may bring to your mind.

3. Affirmation: As you agree with the will of God, voice your affirmation of His word:

I will remember Your works, O Lord; surely I will remember Your wonders of old. I will also meditate on all your work, and talk of Your deeds. (Psalm 77:11-12)

4. Requests: As you make your requests known to the Lord, include:

- Compassion for others
- Missions in America
- Your prayer list, the concerns of your heart, and today's activities

5. Closing Prayer: Finally, offer this closing prayer to the Lord:

May we with one mind and one mouth glorify the God and Father of our Lord Jesus Christ. (Romans 15:6)

Memory Verse: But as many as received Him, to them He gave the right to become children of God, even to those who believe in His name.

John 1:12
Salvation Theme

READING

The passage for today centers on Moses' reluctance to accept his mission. Moses objects that he is unusable to fulfill the task to which God has called him, and Aaron is appointed to help him.

Read Exodus 4.

REFLECTING

God doesn't need any one of us. He wants us. He would like to use us, but He doesn't need us. Take away one person, and the work of God is not dimished. It goes on. When God calls us to a ministry, it is for our benefit. Should we be unwilling or impure, He can get the work done through someone else.

Serving the Lord is a privilege. Often, we do not see it as such, because we still have our own agenda for our life. We still think we know best how to run our life. We still think that the greatest fullness in life comes from our own ability to structure, guide, and fund the plans which we have for ourselves.

Only after we have been brought face to face with the barrenness of a self-run life do we see that fulfillment comes only from loving God and others. Only then do we see that serving God is a privilege. Moses is a good example of that.

RESPONDING

1. Praise: Offer the Lord your praise for His goodness through the words of this psalm.

Lord, You have been our dwelling place in all generations. Before the mountains were brought forth, or ever You had formed the earth and the world, even from everlasting to everlasting, You are God. . . . Oh, satisfy us early with Your mercy, that we may rejoice and be glad all our days! (Psalm 90:1-2, 14)

Take a moment to offer the Lord your personal praise and thanksgiving.

2. Confession: Pray this confession to the Lord as you seek to keep your life free from sin and in fellowship with Him:

No temptation has overtaken me except such as is common to man; but You are faithful, who will not allow me to be tempted beyond what I am able, but with the temptation will also make the way of escape, that I may be able to bear it. (1 Corinthians 10:13)

Confess any personal sins which the Holy Spirit may bring to your mind.

3. Affirmation: As you agree with the will of God, voice your affirmation of His word:

You have shown me what is good; and what do You, O Lord, require of me, but to do justly, to love mercy, and to walk humbly with You, O God? (Micah 6:8)

4. Requests: As you make your requests known to the Lord, include:

- Personal spiritual growth
- Military ministries
- Your prayer list, the concerns of your heart, and today's activities

5. Closing Prayer: Finally, offer this closing prayer to the Lord:

Glory to You in the highest, and on earth peace, good will toward men! (Luke 2:14)

Memory Verse: Not by works of righteousness which we have done, but according to His mercy He saved us, through the washing of regeneration and renewing of the Holy Spirit.

Titus 3:5
Salvation Theme

JANUARY 30

READING

The passage for today centers on the increase of Israel's affliction. Pharaoh responds to Moses' initial confrontation by heaping more labor upon the Israelites.

Read Exodus 5.

REFLECTING

When troubles come upon us, instinctively, the first question we ask is, "Why?" "Why me, why this, why now?" That is what Moses asked in verse 22. Yet, in retrospect, we see that the question was premature. We now know why—hindsight being better than foresight.

How long will it take the Lord to deliver us from our troubles? Usually, just a little longer than we thought we could tolerate. We must remember the example of Moses when we are tempted to ask the Lord, "Why?"

RESPONDING

1. Praise: Even in the midst of trials, we can praise the Lord who hears us and cares for us.

All Your works shall praise You, O Lord, and Your saints shall bless You. They shall speak of the glory of Your kingdom, and talk of Your power, to make known to the sons of men His mighty acts. . . . Your kingdom is an everlasting kingdom, and Your dominion endures throughout all generations. (Psalm 145:10-13)

Take a moment to offer the Lord your personal praise and thanksgiving.

2. Confession: Pray this confession to the Lord as you seek to keep your life free from sin and in fellowship with Him:

Against You, You only, have I sinned, and done this evil in Your sight—that You may be found just when You speak, and blameless when You judge. (Psalm 51:4)

Confess any personal sins which the Holy Spirit may bring to your mind.

3. Affirmation: As you agree with the will of God, voice your affirmation of His word:

You, the Father, have given me to Jesus Christ, and I have come to Him and will by no means be cast out. (John 6:37)

4. Requests: As you make your requests known to the Lord, include:

- Fruit of the Spirit in your life
- The ministry of Christian literature
- Your prayer list, the concerns of your heart, and today's activities

5. Closing Prayer: Finally, offer this closing prayer to the Lord:

Grace, mercy, and peace from You, the Father, and the Lord Jesus Christ our Savior. (Titus 1:4)

Memory Verse: Not by works of righteousness which we have done, but according to His mercy He saved us, through the washing of regeneration and renewing of the Holy Spirit.
Titus 3:5
Salvation Theme

READING

The passage for today centers on Moses' being reassured by God. God assures Moses that He will deliver Israel. The Israelites are discouraged, but God instructs Moses to confront Pharaoh again.

Read Exodus 6.

REFLECTING

Throughout the progress of revelation in the Bible, God becomes more and more personal—more and more intimate. By his official title, "El Shaddai," God made Himself known to Abraham, Isaac, and Jacob. But now, He tells Moses His name: Jehovah. Then in the Gospels, God becomes even more personal—as Jesus becomes incarnate. And finally, in Acts and the Epistles, we discover that in the Holy Spirit, God even comes to live in our hearts. The final act of intimacy will be when God brings us home, and we can fellowship with Him face to face—forever—unencumbered by sin.

RESPONDING

1. Praise: Let us praise our intimate God in the words of this psalm.

Praise the Lord! For it is good to sing praises to our God; for it is pleasant, and praise is beautiful. . . . Great is our Lord, and mighty in power. . . . The Lord takes pleasure in those who fear Him, in those who hope in His mercy. . . . He has not dealt thus with any nation; and as for His judgments, they have not known them. Praise the Lord! (Psalm 147:1, 5a, 11, 20)

Take a moment to offer the Lord your personal praise and thanksgiving.

2. Confession: Pray this confession to the Lord as you seek to keep your life free from sin and in fellowship with Him:

Purge me with hyssop, and I shall be clean; wash me, and I shall be whiter than snow. . . . Hide Your face from my sins, and blot out all my iniquities. (Psalm 51:7, 9)

Confess any personal sins which the Holy Spirit may bring to your mind.

3. Affirmation: As you agree with the will of God, voice your affirmation of His word:

Behold, God is my salvation, I will trust and not be afraid. "For YAH, the Lord is my strength and my song; He also has become my salvation." (Isaiah 12:2)

4. Requests: As you make your requests known to the Lord, include:

- Boldness in living for Christ
- God's blessing on America
- Your prayer list, the concerns of your heart, and today's activities

5. Closing Prayer: Finally, offer this closing prayer to the Lord:

Be glad in the Lord and rejoice, you righteous; and shout for joy, all you upright in heart! (Psalm 32:11)

Memory Verse: Not by works of righteousness which we have done, but according to His mercy He saved us, through the washing of regeneration and renewing of the Holy Spirit.
Titus 3:5
Salvation Theme

READING

The passage for today centers on the beginning of the ten plagues. Through Aaron and Moses, God begins afflicting Egypt with plagues because of Pharaoh's refusal to allow them to journey into the wilderness to worship Him.

Read Exodus 7.

REFLECTING

In this chapter, as the Lord speaks to Moses, we read the remarkable words, "See, I make you as God to Pharaoh." To the world God's children often stand in the place of God. We are the only Bible they will read, all of Jesus they will see.

It is important that we represent Him accurately. Of course, no mortal man can do so in any complete sense, but in a representative sense, we must. It does not mean that we must be perfect, but it does mean we are to give those around us a glimpse of who Jesus really is.

We love others as they have never been loved, or we help them as they have never been helped, or we give them truth as they have never heard before—and suddenly, by the power of God, they see God. In us. Jesus said, "Let your light shine before men in such a way that they may see your good works, and glorify your Father who is in heaven" (Matthew 5:16).

RESPONDING

1. Praise: As you continue your time with the Lord, offer to Him this praise as you dedicate your life to living before men so that they see Him in you:

Oh, the depth of the riches of both the wisdom and knowledge of God! How un-searchable are Your judgments and Your ways past finding out! Blessed are You, the God and Father of our Lord Jesus Christ, who has blessed us with every spiritual blessing in the heavenly places in Christ. (Romans 11:33; Ephesians 1:3)

Pause for personal praise and thanksgiving.

2. Confession: Pray this confession to the Lord as you seek to keep your life free from sin and in fellowship with Him:

Blessed is he whose transgression is forgiven, whose sin is covered. How blessed is the man to whom the Lord does not impute iniquity, and in whose spirit there is no guile. (Psalm 32:1-2)

Confess any personal sins which the Holy Spirit brings to mind.

3. Affirmation: Now pause to pray this affirmation to the Lord:

You have not given me a spirit of fear, but of power and of love and of a sound mind. (2 Timothy 1:7)

4. Requests: As you make your requests known to the Lord, pray for:

- Health and strength to serve God
- God's will to be done on earth
- Your prayer list, the concerns of your heart, and today's activities

5. Closing Prayer: Finally, offer this closing prayer to the Lord:

Blessed be the Lord forevermore! Amen and Amen. (Psalm 89:52)

Memory Verse: Not by works of righteousness which we have done, but according to His mercy He saved us, through the washing of regeneration and renewing of the Holy Spirit.
Titus 3:5
Salvation Theme

FEBRUARY 2

READING

The passage for today centers on additional plagues inflicted upon Egypt. Because of the Pharaoh's continued insensitivity to Moses' request, the Egyptians experience the plagues of frogs and gnats.

Read Exodus 8.

REFLECTING

In the Old Testament, God makes a distinct difference between how He treats the Jewish nation and how He treats others. God lets none of the plagues that fall on Egypt fall upon Israel.

How we wish that sometimes God would do the same for us in the Church. How we wish that because we are Christians, we would have none of the unpleasant things happen to us that happen to the world.

We must recognize that in the Old Testament, God wants the recognizable difference between Israel and the world to be physical. In the New Testament, He wants it to be spiritual. In the Old Testament, God's blessing is the fruit of the vine. In the New Testament, it is the fruit of the Spirit.

RESPONDING

1. Praise: Think about how you have been spiritually blessed by God as you offer your praise to Him:

Let my mouth be filled with Your praise and with Your glory all the day. But I will hope continually, and will praise You yet more and more. My mouth shall tell of Your righteousness and Your salvation all the day, for I do not know their limits. (Psalm 71:8, 14-17)

Now express any additional thoughts you may have of thanks or praise.

2. Confession: Pray this confession to the Lord as you seek to keep your life free from sin and in fellowship with Him:

The heart is deceitful above all things, and desperately wicked; who can know it? You, O Lord, search the heart; You test the mind. Heal me, O Lord, and I shall be healed; save me, and I shall be saved, for You are my praise. (Jeremiah 17:9-10, 14)

Confess any personal sins which the Holy Spirit brings to your mind.

3. Affirmation: Now pray this affirmation to the Lord as you agree with and submit yourself to the will of God:

You, O Lord, are good to those who wait for You, to the soul who seeks You. It is good that I should hope and wait quietly for Your salvation. (Lamentations 3:25-26)

4. Requests: The Lord encourages us to come to Him with our concerns and desires. As you make your requests known to the Lord, include:

- Sensitivity to sin
- The ministry of your local church
- Your prayer list, the concerns of your heart, and today's activities

5. Closing Prayer: Finally, offer this closing prayer to the Lord:

Let the words of my mouth and the meditation of my heart be acceptable in Your sight, O Lord, my strength and my redeemer. (Psalm 19:14)

Memory Verse: Not by works of righteousness which we have done, but according to His mercy He saved us, through the washing of regeneration and renewing of the Holy Spirit.
Titus 3:5
Salvation Theme

READING

The passage for today describes how the plagues on Egypt intensify. As the battle of wills continues between Pharaoh and Moses, God levies on Egypt the plagues of livestock pestilence, boils, and hail.

Read Exodus 9.

REFLECTING

Frogs and gnats? Boils and hail? Water into blood? Though we might not always be able to discern it, the God of omniscience does nothing without design.

The Egyptians worshiped odd and debased gods. Each plague was designed to strike at the credibility of an Egyptian god and manifest the barrenness of belief in these objects.

God does the same today. Our gods are fortune, power, beauty, talent, and intelligence. Nothing wrong with them as servants, but when we worship them, they are cruel. God shows the barrenness of worshiping them by allowing people without them to be deeply joyful while those who worship them are tortured. Again, today, God's personal mark of blessing is the fruit of the Spirit—not necessarily of the vine. Joy is found in God, not things.

RESPONDING

1. Praise: Offer the Lord praise that joy is available to us all:

It is good to give thanks to the Lord, and to sing praises to Your name, O Most High; to declare Your lovingkindness in the morning, and Your faithfulness every night. . . . To declare that the Lord is upright; He is my rock, and there is no unrighteousness in Him. (Psalm 92:1-2, 15)

Take a moment to offer the Lord your personal praise and thanksgiving.

2. Confession: Pray this confession to the Lord as you seek to keep your life free from sin and in fellowship with Him:

I return to You, O Lord my God, for I have stumbled because of my iniquity. . . . I say to You, "Take away all iniquity; receive me graciously, for I will offer the sacrifices of my lips." (Hosea 14:1-2)

Confess any personal sins which the Holy Spirit may bring to your mind.

3. Affirmation: As you agree with the will of God, voice your affirmation of His word:

Whoever drinks of the water that You shall give him will never thirst. But the water that You shall give him will become in him a fountain of water springing up into everlasting life. (John 4:14)

4. Requests: As you make your requests known to the Lord, include:

- Wisdom for living life
- Needs of your immediate family
- Your prayer list, the concerns of your heart, and today's activities

5. Closing Prayer: Finally, offer this closing prayer to the Lord:

Surely goodness and mercy shall follow me all the days of my life, and I will dwell in the house of the Lord forever. (Psalm 23:6)

Memory Verse: Not by works of righteousness which we have done, but according to His mercy He saved us, through the washing of regeneration and renewing of the Holy Spirit.
Titus 3:5
Salvation Theme

FEBRUARY 4

READING

The passage for today describes how Pharaoh's will hardens. After the eighth plague (locusts), Pharaoh warns Moses never to come back, or Pharaoh will kill him.

Read Exodus 10.

REFLECTING

God does not compromise. Moses asks Pharaoh to let the entire nation of Israel go into the wilderness to worship Him. Pharaoh refuses but says the men can go alone. But those are not God's instructions.

Pharaoh pays the price. But, while God does not compromise, He does forgive. With the hand of judgment on him, Pharaoh begs God for forgiveness. God grants it and withdraws the judgment.

Have you compromised in your walk with God? Have you followed God partially but not fully? He will not accept it. He does not compromise. But He will forgive and restore you. Ask Him.

RESPONDING

1. Praise: Offer these words of praise to our forgiving God:

Blessed be the Lord God, the God of Israel, who only does wondrous things! And blessed be His glorious name forever! And let the whole earth be filled with His glory. Amen and amen. (Psalm 72:18-19)

Take a moment to offer the Lord your personal praise and thanksgiving.

2. Confession: Pray this confession to the Lord as you seek to keep your life free from sin and in fellowship with Him:

Now no chastening seems to be joyful for the present, but grievous; nevertheless, afterward it yields the peaceable fruit of righteousness to those who have been trained by it. (Hebrews 12:11)

Confess any personal sins which the Holy Spirit may bring to your mind.

3. Affirmation: As you agree with the will of God, voice your affirmation of His word:

For You, O Lord, will bless the righteous; with favor You will surround me as with a shield. (Psalm 5:12)

4. Requests: As you make your requests known to the Lord, include:

* Insight into Scripture
* The hungry around the world
* Your prayer list, the concerns of your heart, and today's activities

5. Closing Prayer: Finally, offer this closing prayer to the Lord:

We will be of good courage, and You shall strengthen our hearts, all we who hope in the Lord. (Psalm 31:24)

Memory Verse: Not by works of righteousness which we have done, but according to His mercy He saved us, through the washing of regeneration and renewing of the Holy Spirit.
Titus 3:5
Salvation Theme

READING

The passage for today centers on the final plague on Egypt. The Lord reveals to Moses the tenth and final plague, the death of the firstborn of every household of Egypt.

Read Exodus 11.

REFLECTING

It is vain for man to enter into conflict with God. Even to say it sounds absurd. Yet how often does man shake his fist in the face of his Creator?

God's dealings with Pharaoh reveal His longsuffering attitude toward such rebellion. The plagues start out fairly minor, thus giving Pharaoh a chance to change his mind before utter calamity strikes. With each successive act of rebellion, the subsequent plague intensifies.

Analyze your own life. Have you entered into conflict with God at a small level? Abandon the conflict before it escalates.

RESPONDING

1. Praise: Rejoice in God's patience with rebellion—and praise Him:

The Lord reigns, He is clothed with majesty; the Lord is clothed, He has girded Himself with strength. Surely the world is established, so that it cannot be moved. (Psalm 93:1-2)

Take a moment to offer the Lord your personal praise and thanksgiving.

2. Confession: Pray this confession to the Lord as you seek to keep your life free from sin and in fellowship with Him:

O Lord, You ask me to return to You with all my heart. I will return to You, O Lord, for You are gracious and merciful, slow to anger,

and of great kindness; and You relent from doing harm. (Joel 2:12-13)

Confess any personal sins which the Holy Spirit may bring to your mind.

3. Affirmation: As you agree with the will of God, voice your affirmation of His word:

Eye has not seen, nor ear heard, nor have entered into the heart of man the things which You, O God, have prepared for those who love You. (1 Corinthians 2:9)

4. Requests: As you make your requests known to the Lord, include:

- Love for fellow Christians
- The work of missions in Europe and Asia
- Your prayer list, the concerns of your heart, and today's activities

5. Closing Prayer: Finally, offer this closing prayer to the Lord:

This is the day which You have made; I will rejoice and be glad in it. (Psalm 118:24)

Memory Verse: For He made Him who knew no sin to be sin for us, that we might become the righteousness of God in Him.

2 Corinthians 5:21
Salvation Theme

FEBRUARY 6

READING

The passage for today centers on the institution of the Passover. By observing the Passover, the children of Israel escape the plague of the death of the firstborn and are released by Pharaoh to leave Egypt.

Read Exodus 12.

REFLECTING

Exodus 12 is one of the most remarkable and important chapters in all of the Bible. In it we learn so many things:

1. Only God can deliver us from sin.

2. Sin's penalty is death.

3. God is willing to allow a substitute death so that we don't have to die (in this case, a lamb).

4. Faith is the basis of our salvation. Our belief results in our obedience.

5. The Old Testament Passover lamb is a foreshadowing of the New Testament Passover Lamb, Christ.

6. We are saved the same way the Israelites were saved: by faith in the substitutionary atonement of the Lamb whom God provided.

7. Not to accept this avenue of escape is to suffer the wrath of God.

The Old Testament gives us a literal picture of spiritual truth in the New Testament.

RESPONDING

1. Praise: Praise the Lord for His picture of salvation:

Oh, sing to the Lord a new song! Sing to the Lord, all the earth. Sing to the Lord, bless His name; proclaim the good news of His salvation from day to day. Declare His glory among the nations, His wonders among all peoples. For the Lord is great and greatly to be praised. (Psalm 96:1-4)

Take a moment to offer the Lord your personal praise and thanksgiving.

2. Confession: Pray this confession to the Lord as you seek to keep your life free from sin and in fellowship with Him:

If I sin, I have an Advocate with You, Jesus Christ the righteous. And He Himself is the propitiation for my sins, and not for mine only but also for the whole world. (1 John 2:1-2)

Confess any personal sins which the Holy Spirit may bring to your mind.

3. Affirmation: As you agree with the will of God, voice your affirmation of His word:

Before I was afflicted I went astray, but now I keep Your word. . . . It is good for me that I have been afflicted, that I may learn Your statutes. . . . I know, O Lord, that Your judgments are right, and that in faithfulness You have afflicted me. (Psalm 119:67, 71, 75)

4. Requests: As you make your requests known to the Lord, include:

- Faithfulness with your time
- The president and national leaders and affairs
- Your prayer list, the concerns of your heart, and today's activities

5. Closing Prayer: Finally, offer this closing prayer to the Lord:

Oh, satisfy me early with Your mercy, that I may rejoice and be glad all my days! (Psalm 90:14)

Memory Verse: For He made Him who knew no sin to be sin for us, that we might become the righteousness of God in Him.

2 Corinthians 5:21
Salvation Theme

READING

The passage for today centers on the dedication of the firstborn. The Lord instructs the Israelites to dedicate to Him the firstborn of all children and animals as a memorial to their deliverance out of Egypt.

Read Exodus 13.

REFLECTING

The spiritual truths which God wanted to ensure were never forgotten were memorialized in a ceremony, often involving a meal. The Passover meal and the Feast of Unleavened Bread were symbolic meals designed to commemorate the deliverance of Israel out of Egypt so that Israel would never forget what God had done for them. The New Testament counterpart is the Lord's Supper, in which we eat a symbolic meal to memorialize the deliverance of the Church out of sin. When we observe communion, we celebrate a meal which has been observed in unbroken succession for 2,000 years, beginning with Jesus Himself.

RESPONDING

1. Praise: Offer your praise to the Lord in these passages as you fellowship with Him:

My soul magnifies the Lord, and my spirit has rejoiced in God my savior. . . . You who are mighty have done great things for me, and holy is Your name. And Your mercy is on those who fear You from generation to generation. (Luke 1:46-47, 49-50)

Take a moment to offer the Lord your personal praise and thanksgiving.

2. Confession: Pray this confession to the Lord as you seek to keep your life free from sin and in fellowship with Him:

For you do not desire sacrifice, or else I would give it; You do not delight in burnt offering. The sacrifices of God are a broken spirit, a broken and a contrite heart—These, O God, You will not despise. (Psalm 51:16-17)

Confess any personal sins which the Holy Spirit may bring to your mind.

3. Affirmation: As you agree with the will of God, voice your affirmation of His word:

For I consider that the sufferings of this present time are not worthy to be compared with the glory which shall be revealed in us. (Romans 8:18)

4. Requests: As you make your requests known to the Lord, include:

- Your financial needs
- The needs of the poor
- Your prayer list, the concerns of your heart, and today's activities

5. Closing Prayer: Finally, offer this closing prayer to the Lord:

Let the beauty of You, Lord, be upon me, and establish the work of my hands for me; yes, establish the work of my hands. (Psalm 90:17)

> **Memory Verse:** For He made Him who knew no sin to be sin for us, that we might become the righteousness of God in Him.
>
> 2 Corinthians 5:21
> *Salvation Theme*

FEBRUARY 8

READING

The passage for today centers on the drying up of the Red Sea. The Lord parts the Red Sea, allowing the Israelites to cross over to the other shore, saving them from the Egyptian army which Pharaoh, after a change of mind, had sent to bring the Israelites back.

Read Exodus 14.

REFLECTING

When we are obedient to God, nothing can touch us that does not come through His permissive will. The armies of Egypt in the Old Testament, symbolic of the armies of Satan in the New Testament, are no match for a God who is jealous to protect and care for His beloved children.

Moses knew that his protection was in the Lord. The Israelites had no weapons, no horses, no army. He knew that God had to save them, or they would not be saved.

We must recognize that the same is true in the spiritual warfare for us today. If God does not save us, we will not be saved. Resting in God's full protection in the spiritual warfare, we may put on His full armor and stand firm, knowing that we will triumph in the Lord.

RESPONDING

1. Praise: As you continue your time with the Lord, offer Him your praise through His word.

O Lord, our Lord, how excellent is Your name in all the earth, You who set Your glory above the heavens! When I consider Your heavens, the work of Your fingers . . . what is man that You are mindful of him, and the son of man that You visit him? . . . O Lord, our Lord, How excellent is Your name in all the earth! (Psalm 8:1, 3-4, 9)

Take a moment to offer the Lord your personal praise and thanksgiving.

2. Confession: Pray this confession to the Lord as you seek to keep your life free from sin and in fellowship with Him:

For a mere moment You have forsaken me, but with great mercies You will gather me. With a little wrath You hid Your face from me for a moment; but with everlasting kindness You will have mercy on me. (Isaiah 54:7-8)

Confess any personal sins which the Holy Spirit may bring to your mind.

3. Affirmation: As you agree with the will of God, voice your affirmation of His word:

Unless the Lord builds my house, I labor in vain; Unless the Lord guards my city, I stay awake watching in vain. (Psalm 127:1)

4. Requests: As you make your requests known to the Lord, include:

- Protection from the "evil one"
- Laborers for the "harvest"
- Your prayer list, the concerns of your heart, and today's activities

5. Closing Prayer: Finally, offer this closing prayer to the Lord:

Bless the Lord, all you His hosts, you ministers of His, who do His pleasure. Bless the Lord, all His works, in all places of His dominion. (Psalm 103:21-22)

Memory Verse: For He made Him who knew no sin to be sin for us, that we might become the righteousness of God in Him.

2 Corinthians 5:21
Salvation Theme

READING

The passage for today centers on the national covenant. The Israelites migrate to Mt. Sinai where Moses meets with God, who establishes a covenant with Israel that He will be their God and they will be His people.

Read Exodus 19.

REFLECTING

God's love for us is nothing less than total. And He leaves no doubt in our minds as to His commitment to us. The Lord goes so far as to establish a covenant with Israel at Mt. Sinai and with us at Calvary as an expression of His absolute commitment to us. We should have two responses: we should love fully the God who first loved us. And, if we are to love our family as God loves us, we must leave no doubts in their minds as to the totality of our love for them.

RESPONDING

1. Praise: For His unconditional love, praise the Lord with these words:

You who love the Lord, hate evil! He preserves the souls of His saints; He delivers them out of the hand of the wicked. Light is sown for the righteous, and gladness for the upright in heart. Rejoice in the Lord, you righteous, and give thanks at the remembrance of His holy name. (Psalm 97:10-12)

Take a moment to offer the Lord your personal praise and thanksgiving.

2. Confession: Pray this confession to the Lord as you seek to keep your life free from sin and in fellowship with Him:

Forgive me, Lord, when I am unmindful of the Rock who begot me, and forget the God who fathered me. (Deuteronomy 32:18)

Confess any personal sins which the Holy Spirit may bring to your mind.

3. Affirmation: As you agree with the will of God, voice your affirmation of His word:

Do I not know that my body is the temple of the Holy Spirit who is in me, whom I have from You, O God, and I am not my own? For I was bought at a price; therefore I should glorify You in my body and in my spirit, which are Yours. (1 Corinthians 6:19-20)

4. Requests: As you make your requests known to the Lord, include:

- Commitment to the Lord
- Parachurch ministries
- Your prayer list, the concerns of your heart, and today's activities

5. Closing Prayer: Finally, offer this closing prayer to the Lord:

Lord, preserve me from all evil; preserve my soul. Lord, preserve my going out and my coming in from this time forth, and even forevermore. (Psalm 121:7-8)

Memory Verse: For He made Him who knew no sin to be sin for us, that we might become the righteousness of God in Him.

2 Corinthians 5:21
Salvation Theme

FEBRUARY 10

READING

The passage for today centers on the Ten Commandments. Moses meets with the Lord on the top of Mount Sinai, where he receives the original Ten Commandments which become the backbone of the moral law in Israel.

Read Exodus 20.

REFLECTING

The genius of God's moral system is that everything He asks of us is for our good. Often the Ten Commandments are seen by people as restrictive, keeping them from doing something that would make them happy. Initially, perhaps. But ultimately, nothing could be further from the truth. Sin is self-destructive. Righteousness is self-constructive. It makes no more sense to sin willfully than it does to become a drug addict. In both cases, the person is destroying himself. Abandon yourself to the moral law of God. It is glorifying to Him, but it is also good for you. In this light, we see the truth in the statement that anything less than the glory of God is anti-human.

RESPONDING

1. Praise: The holy God of Mount Sinai is worthy of our praise.

Make a joyful shout to the Lord, all you lands! Serve the Lord with gladness; come before His presence with singing. Know that the Lord, He is God; it is He who has made us, and not we ourselves; we are His people and the sheep of His pasture. Enter into His gates with thanksgiving, and into His courts with praise. Be thankful to Him, and bless His name. (Psalm 100:1-4)

Take a moment to offer the Lord your personal praise and thanksgiving.

2. Confession: Pray this confession to the Lord as you seek to keep your life free from sin and in fellowship with Him:

O Lord, You do not have as great delight in burnt offerings and sacrifices, as in obeying Your voice. Behold, to obey is better than sacrifice, and to heed than the fat of rams. (1 Samuel 15:22)

Confess any personal sins which the Holy Spirit may bring to your mind.

3. Affirmation: As you agree with the will of God, voice your affirmation of His word:

For You are the God who commanded light to shine out of darkness, who has shone in our hearts to give the light of the knowledge of Your glory in the face of Jesus Christ. But I have this treasure in an earthen vessel, that the excellence of the power may be of God and not of me. (2 Corinthians 4:6-7)

4. Requests: As you make your requests known to the Lord, include:

- Renewing of your mind
- Needs of your extended family
- Your prayer list, the concerns of your heart, and today's activities

5. Closing Prayer: Finally, offer this closing prayer to the Lord:

May we with one mind and one mouth glorify the God and Father of our Lord Jesus Christ. (Romans 15:6)

Memory Verse: For He made Him who knew no sin to be sin for us, that we might become the righteousness of God in Him.

2 Corinthians 5:21
Salvation Theme

READING

The passage for today centers on the sin of the people: the golden calf. While Moses is meeting with the Lord on Mount Sinai, Aaron leads the Israelites in idol worship of a golden calf, falsely commemorating their deliverance out of Egypt.

Read Exodus 32.

REFLECTING

Sin does not mind rubbing shoulders with righteousness. Even while Moses is on Mount Sinai communing with God, the children of Israel are fashioning a golden idol to worship in His place. Fueled by shamelessness and a short memory, the Israelites rush headlong into one of the most remarkable displays of indiscretion in the Bible.

Beware! Even when you are rubbing shoulders with righteousness, sin can trip you up. Even when you are basking in the light of Sinai, evil may be lurking in the shadows. Be sober, be vigilant—for "your adversary the devil walks about like a roaring lion, seeking someone to devour" (James 4:7).

RESPONDING

1. Praise: Offer praise to the Lord for His truth and light.

Bless the Lord, O my soul! O Lord my God, You are very great: You are clothed with honor and majesty, who cover Yourself with light as with a garment, who stretch out the heavens like a curtain. . . . May the glory of the Lord endure forever; may the Lord rejoice in His works. . . . Bless the Lord, O my soul! Praise the Lord! (Psalm 104:1-2, 31, 35)

Take a moment to offer the Lord your personal praise and thanksgiving.

2. Confession: Pray this confession to the Lord as you seek to keep your life free from sin and in fellowship with Him:

I have sinned greatly in what I have done; but now, I pray, O Lord, take away the iniquity of Your servant, for I have done very foolishly. (2 Samuel 24:10)

Confess any personal sins which the Holy Spirit may bring to your mind.

3. Affirmation: As you agree with the will of God, voice your affirmation of His word:

I will not lay up for myself treasure on earth, where moth and rust destroy and where thieves break in and steal; but I will lay up for myself treasure in heaven, where neither moth nor rust destroys and where thieves do not break in and steal. For where my treasure is, there my heart will be also. (Matthew 6:19-21)

4. Requests: As you make your requests known to the Lord, include:

- The Lord's leading in your life
- Opportunities for personal evangelism
- Your prayer list, the concerns of your heart, and today's activities

5. Closing Prayer: Finally, offer this closing prayer to the Lord:

Now may the God of hope fill me with all joy and peace in believing, that I may abound in hope by the power of the Holy Spirit. (Romans 15:13)

Memory Verse: For He made Him who knew no sin to be sin for us, that we might become the righteousness of God in Him.

2 Corinthians 5:21
Salvation Theme

FEBRUARY 12

READING

The passage for today centers on the Day of Atonement. The Lord gives Moses instructions on observing the Day of Atonement, the most important of all the ordinances given to Israel because on that day atonement is made for all the sins of the entire congregation.

Read Leviticus 16.

REFLECTING

In spite of God's desire that we be holy, He is fully aware that we will not remain free from sin. Isaiah writes, "There is none righteous, no not one." John writes, "If we say we have no sin, we lie. . . ." In His grace, God provides for our sins to be forgiven. Annually on the Day of Atonement in the Old Testament, the nation was cleansed from sin. Since Christ has come, we may be cleansed moment by moment. "If we confess our sins, He is faithful and just to forgive us our sins and to cleanse us from all unrighteousness" (1 John 1:9).

RESPONDING

1. Praise: Offer your praise to the God of redemption through this psalm:

O Lord, how manifold are Your works! In wisdom You have made them all. The earth is full of Your possessions . . . I will sing praise to my God while I have my being. May my meditation be sweet to Him; I will be glad in the Lord. (Psalm 104:24, 33, 34)

Take a moment to offer the Lord your personal praise and thanksgiving.

2. Confession: Pray this confession to the Lord as you seek to keep your life free from sin and in fellowship with Him:

O my God: I am too ashamed and humiliated to lift up my face to You, my God; for my iniquities have risen higher than my head, and my guilt has grown up to the heavens. (Ezra 9:6)

Confess any personal sins which the Holy Spirit may bring to your mind.

3. Affirmation: As you agree with the will of God, voice your affirmation of His word:

For my light affliction, which is but for a moment, is working for me a far more exceeding and eternal weight of glory, while I do not look at the things which are seen, but at the things which are not seen. For the things which are seen are temporary, but the things which are not seen are eternal. (2 Corinthians 4:17-18)

4. Requests: As you make your requests known to the Lord, include:

- Love for the lost
- The work of missions in Africa
- Your prayer list, the concerns of your heart, and today's activities

5. Closing Prayer: Finally, offer this closing prayer to the Lord:

Now to You who are able to establish us according to the Gospel and preaching of Jesus Christ—to You, alone wise, be glory through Jesus Christ forever. Amen. (Romans 16:25-27)

Memory Verse: Most assuredly, I say to you, he who hears My word and believes in Him who sent Me has everlasting life, and shall not come into judgment.

John 5:24
Assurance Theme

FEBRUARY 13

READING

The passage for today centers on the report of the spies. The Israelites migrate to Kadesh Barnea on their way to the promised land from Mount Sinai and hear a bad report given by their spies about the land.

Read Numbers 13.

REFLECTING

One of the most common mistakes we make in the tough times in life is to get our eyes on circumstances rather than the promises of God. The Lord had promised Israel that He would lead them into the promised land and defeat the armies that were living there. He promised that He would even send in swarms of hornets to drive out the armies so that Israel wouldn't even have to fight. One look at the giants, and every promise was forgotten. One glimpse of the armies, and God was not enough. The New Testament is full of promises for us. God will meet our physical needs, will lead us in His will, will protect us from destruction. Yet when we meet the giants of finances, questions about the future, and fear of suffering, we faint. We mut learn from Israel at Kadesh Barnea. We must keep our eyes on the promises.

RESPONDING

1. Praise: As you focus on God's promises, praise Him with this psalm:

Oh, give thanks to the Lord! Call upon His name; make known His deeds among the peoples. Sing to Him, sing psalms to Him; talk of all His wondrous works. Glory in His holy name; let the hearts of those rejoice who seek the Lord. Seek the Lord and His strength; seek His face evermore. (Psalm 105:1-4)

Take a moment to offer the Lord your personal praise and thanksgiving.

2. Confession: Pray this confession to the Lord as you seek to keep your life free from sin and in fellowship with Him:

O Lord, do not rebuke me in Your anger, nor chasten me in Your hot displeasure. Have mercy on me, O Lord, for I am weak; O Lord, heal me, for . . . my soul also is greatly troubled. (Psalm 6:1-3)

Confess any personal sins which the Holy Spirit may bring to your mind.

3. Affirmation: As you agree with the will of God, voice your affirmation of His word:

And He said to me, "My grace is sufficient for you, for My strength is made perfect in weakness." Therefore most gladly I will rather boast in my infirmities, that the power of Christ may rest upon me. (2 Corinthians 12:9)

4. Requests: As you make your requests known to the Lord, include:

- Faithfulness with your talents
- Your state and local leaders and affairs
- Your prayer list, the concerns of your heart, and today's activities

5. Closing Prayer: Finally, offer this closing prayer to the Lord:

The grace of the Lord Jesus Christ, and the love of God, and the communion of the Holy Spirit be with us all. Amen. (2 Corinthians 13:14)

Memory Verse: Most assuredly, I say to you, he who hears My word and believes in Him who sent Me has everlasting life, and shall not come into judgment.

John 5:24
Assurance Theme

FEBRUARY 14

READING

The passage for today centers on the unbelief of Israel at Kadesh Barnea. After receiving a frightening report about giants and armies in the promised land, the Israelites refuse to go in.

Read Numbers 14.

REFLECTING

By nature, we are sight-walkers, not faith-walkers. We tend to have confidence in that which we can see, that which we have known. We fear that which we can't see and haven't known. Not only do the Israelites refuse to go into the land because of the giants—they want to return to Egypt. Do they not remember that they were enslaved there? Do they not remember that they cried out to God for deliverance from Egypt? Do they not realize that they cannot go back? Neither can you go back to your old life. No matter how pleasant or safe the memory seems, it is an illusion. There is nothing there but bondage. Your hope lies in following the Lord, by faith. Walk forward.

RESPONDING

1. Praise: In the eyes of God, it is wisdom to praise Him for who He is and what He has done for us.

O God, You are my God; early will I seek You; My soul thirsts for You, my flesh longs for You in a dry and weary land where there is no water. So I have looked for You in the sanctuary, to see Your power and Your glory. (Psalm 63:1-2)

Now offer to the Lord your personal praise and thanksgiving.

2. Confession: Pray this confession to the Lord as you seek to keep your life free from sin and in fellowship with Him:

You will again have compassion on us, and will subdue our iniquities. You will cast all our sins into the depths of the sea. (Micah 7:19)

Confess any personal sins which the Holy Spirit brings to your mind.

3. Affirmation: As you agree with God's will, voice your affirmation of His word:

For I did not receive the spirit of bondage again to fear, but I received the Spirit of adoption by whom I cry out, "Abba, Father." (Romans 8:15)

4. Requests: As you make your requests known to the Lord, include:

* Strength for obedience
* International students in America
* Your prayer list, the concerns of your heart, and today's activities

5. Closing Prayer: Finally, offer this closing prayer to the Lord:

Now to You who are able to do exceedingly abundantly above all that I ask or think, according to the power that works in me, to You be glory in the church by Christ Jesus throughout all ages, world without end. Amen. (Ephesians 3:20-21)

Memory Verse: Most assuredly, I say to you, he who hears My word and believes in Him who sent Me has everlasting life, and shall not come into judgment.

John 5:24
Assurance Theme

READING

The passage for today centers on recapitulation of Israel's wandering. After moving from Kadesh Barnea to the plains of Moab, Moses retells the story of Israel's wandering from Mount Sinai to Kadesh Barnea.

Read Deuteronomy 1.

REFLECTING

Those who do not remember history are condemned to repeat it. Moses reviews the history of the wanderings of Israel to the new generation poised on the plains of Moab—ready to enter the promised land. Their fathers did not believe the promises of God. Therefore, they were not obedient to Him. They condemned themselves to a life of untold hardship. They made their own destiny. They sealed their own fate. We must be able to learn from Israel's mistakes. "Do not be deceived. God is not mocked. Whatever a man sows, that will he also reap." God is the same yesterday, today, forever. If Israel did not prosper in her disobedience, we can rest assured that neither will we. Learn from their history. Don't repeat it.

RESPONDING

1. Praise: Worship the Lord by offering Him your praise in spirit and in truth.

Praise the Lord! For it is good to sing praises to our God; for it is pleasant, and praise is beautiful. . . . Great is our Lord, and mighty in power. . . . The Lord takes pleasure in those who fear Him, in those who hope in His mercy. . . . He has not dealt thus with any nation; and as for His judgments, they have not known them. Praise the Lord! (Psalm 147:1, 5a, 11, 20)

Take a moment to offer the Lord your personal praise and thanksgiving.

2. Confession: Pray this confession to the Lord as you seek to keep your life free from sin and in fellowship with Him:

Purge me with hyssop, and I shall be clean; wash me, and I shall be whiter than snow. . . . Hide Your face from my sins, and blot out all my iniquities. (Psalm 51:7, 9)

Confess any personal sins which the Holy Spirit may bring to your mind.

3. Affirmation: As you agree with the will of God, voice your affirmation of His word:

Behold, God is my salvation, I will trust and not be afraid. "For YAH, the Lord is my strength and my song; He also has become my salvation." (Isaiah 12:2)

4. Requests: As you make your requests known to the Lord, include:

- Your "daily bread"
- Christian education institutions
- Your prayer list, the concerns of your heart, and today's activities

5. Closing Prayer: Finally, offer this closing prayer to the Lord:

Now may You, the God of peace, sanctify me completely, and may my whole spirit, soul, and body be preserved blameless at the coming of my Lord Jesus Christ. (1 Thessalonians 5:23)

Memory Verse: Most assuredly, I say to you, he who hears My word and believes in Him who sent Me has everlasting life, and shall not come into judgment.

John 5:24
Assurance Theme

FEBRUARY 16

READING

The passage for today centers on the continued chronicle of Israel's wandering. Moses details the events of the wandering of the Israelites from Kadesh Barnea to their present location, the plains of Moab.

Read Deuteronomy 2.

REFLECTING

David writes that God withholds no good thing from those who walk uprightly. But, we see that it is possible, through rebellion, to miss something good that God wants to give us. God wanted to give the Israelites the promised land. But when they refused to enter, they wandered through the wilderness until the rebellious generation died. Then, that which God had wanted to give to them, He gave to someone else. The next generation. We need not fear missing any good thing if we walk uprightly, but when we walk in rebellion, we pay a price. God's blessings often include a test. The promise is made, but an obstacle that only God can remove stands in the way. Like giants. Do we turn around? Or do we trust Him?

RESPONDING

1. Praise: We can express trust in Him with a psalm of praise.

Praise the Lord! Oh, give thanks to the Lord, for He is good! For His mercy endures forever. Who can utter the mighty acts of the Lord? Or can declare all His praise? . . . blessed be the Lord . . . from everlasting to everlasting! And let all the people say, "Amen!" Praise the Lord! (Psalm 106:1-2, 48)

Take a moment to offer the Lord your personal praise and thanksgiving.

2. Confession: Pray this confession to the Lord as you seek to keep your life free from sin and in fellowship with Him:

Who can understand his errors? Cleanse me from secret faults. Keep back Your servant also from presumptuous sins; let them not have dominion over me. Then I shall be blameless, and I shall be innocent of great transgression. (Psalm 19:12-13)

Confess any personal sins which the Holy Spirit may bring to your mind.

3. Affirmation: As you agree with the will of God, voice your affirmation of His word:

Most assuredly, You say to me, if I hear Your word and believe in Him who sent You, I have everlasting life, and shall not come into judgment, but have passed from death into life. (John 5:24)

4. Requests: As you make your requests known to the Lord, include:

- Passion for moral excellence
- Needs of personal friends
- Your prayer list, the concerns of your heart, and today's activities

5. Closing Prayer: Finally, offer this closing prayer to the Lord:

Now may the Lord Jesus Christ Himself, and You, my God and Father, who have loved me and given me everlasting consolation and good hope by grace, comfort my heart and establish me in every good word and work. (2 Thessalonians 2:16-17)

Memory Verse: Most assuredly, I say to you, he who hears My word and believes in Him who sent Me has everlasting life, and shall not come into judgment.

John 5:24
Assurance Theme

READING

The passage for today centers on the transfer of authority announced. After completing the account of the wanderings of the Israelites, Moses announces that the Lord has prohibited his entering the land and that Joshua will become their new leader.

Read Deuteronomy 3.

REFLECTING

The past is a picture of the future. When trying to determine what will be, it is important to know what has been. Throughout the wilderness journey, God reminds Israel what He has done in the past, to give them courage and hope for the future. As the reins of leadership are passed from Moses to Joshua, the Lord encourages Joshua with a review of history. "Your eyes have seen what I did to [past] kings; so the Lord shall do to all the kingdoms into which you are about to cross."

We know that the Lord is the same yesterday, today, and forever. We, too, can ponder the past for a glimpse of the future. When we face the giants in our lives, we take heart at the Lord's words to Joshua: "Do not fear, for the Lord your God is the one fighting for you."

RESPONDING

1. Praise: Use this psalm to praise the God of the past and the future.

O God, my heart is steadfast; I will sing and give praise. . . . I will praise You, O Lord, among the peoples, and I will sing praises to You among the nations. For Your mercy is great above the heavens, and Your truth reaches to the clouds. Be exalted, O God,

above the heavens, and Your glory above all the earth. (Psalm 108:1, 3-5)

Take a moment to offer the Lord your personal praise and thanksgiving.

2. Confession: Pray this confession to the Lord as you seek to keep your life free from sin and in fellowship with Him:

Show me Your ways, O Lord; teach me Your paths. Lead me in Your truth and teach me, for You are the God of my salvation; on You I wait all the day. (Psalm 25:4-5)

Confess any personal sins which the Holy Spirit may bring to your mind.

3. Affirmation: As you agree with the will of God, voice your affirmation of His word:

You are the living bread which came down from heaven. If anyone eats of this bread, he will live forever; and the bread that You shall give is Your flesh, which You shall give for the life of the world. (John 6:51)

4. Requests: As you make your requests known to the Lord, include:

- Wisdom in decision making
- Opportunities to serve the Lord
- Your prayer list, the concerns of your heart, and today's activities

5. Closing Prayer: Finally, offer this closing prayer to the Lord:

Now to You, the King eternal, immortal, invisible, to God who alone is wise, be honor and glory forever and ever. Amen. (1 Timothy 1:17)

Memory Verse: Most assuredly, I say to you, he who hears My word and believes in Him who sent Me has everlasting life, and shall not come into judgment.

John 5:24
Assurance Theme

FEBRUARY 18

READING

The passage for today centers on a call to obedience. Calling upon the Israelites to recall the greatness of God as He cared for them during their wilderness wanderings, Moses appeals to them to live a life of faithful obedience to God.

Read Deuteronomy 4.

REFLECTING

Thomas Jefferson once said, "The price of liberty is eternal vigilance." If so politically, how much more true spiritually. "Take heed," Moses says three times in chapter four. First, take heed and keep your soul diligently. Second, take heed that you not worship idols. Third, take heed that you not forget the covenant the Lord made with you. These are all dangers for us today. How easily we forget the welfare of our souls. How easily we worship the idol of money, or fame, or position. How easily we forget the promises of the Lord. We, too, must take heed. The price of our spiritual strength is eternal vigilance.

RESPONDING

1. Praise: Offer praise to the Lord for His concern for our well-being.

Praise the Lord! I will praise the Lord with my whole heart, in the assembly of the upright and in the congregation. . . . His work is honorable and glorious, and His righteousness endures forever. . . . The fear of the Lord is the beginning of wisdom; a good understanding have all those who do His commandments. His praise endures forever. (Psalm 111:1, 3, 10)

Take a moment to offer the Lord your personal praise and thanksgiving.

2. Confession: Pray this confession to the Lord as you seek to keep your life free from sin and in fellowship with Him:

Remember, O Lord, your tender mercies and Your lovingkindnesses, for they have been from of old. Do not remember the sins of my youth, nor my transgressions; according to Your mercy remember me, for Your goodness' sake, O Lord. (Psalm 25:6-7)

Confess any personal sins which the Holy Spirit may bring to your mind.

3. Affirmation: As you agree with the will of God, voice your affirmation of His word:

For Your eyes, O Lord, run to and fro throughout the whole earth, to show Yourself strong on behalf of those whose heart is loyal to You. (2 Chronicles 16:9)

4. Requests: As you make your requests known to the Lord, include:

- Victory over temptation
- The work of missions in North and South America
- Your prayer list, the concerns of your heart, and today's activities

5. Closing Prayer: Finally, offer this closing prayer to the Lord:

You who are the blessed and only Potentate, the King of kings and Lord of lords, who alone have immortality, dwelling in unapproachable light, whom no man has seen or can see, to You be honor and everlasting power. Amen. (1 Timothy 6:15-16)

Memory Verse: Most assuredly, I say to you, he who hears My word and believes in Him who sent Me has everlasting life, and shall not come into judgment.

John 5:24
Assurance Theme

FEBRUARY 19

READING

The passage for today centers on a rehearsal of Israel's law. Speaking to the new generation of Israelites, Moses reviews the account of the original giving of the Ten Commandments at Mount Sinai.

Read Deuteronomy 5.

REFLECTING

David writes that the Law of the Lord is perfect, and in keeping it there is great reward. Part of that great reward is spelled out in chapter 5. Moses says that if the children of Israel will keep God's commandments, it will go well with them and with their sons forever! In addition, the Lord promises that they will live and that they may prolong their days in the land.

Holiness is not expensive. In fact, all the deepest longings of the child of God are met only in holiness. Could we consistently believe this, our lives would be more holy. Like the Israelites, we think that we are missing something by serving God. We are missing no more than the Israelites missed of Egypt.

RESPONDING

1. Praise: Honor the holiness of God by offering Him this praise:

Praise the Lord! . . . Blessed be the name of the Lord from this time forth and forevermore! From the rising of the sun to its going down the Lord's name is to be praised. . . . Who is like the Lord our God, who dwells on high, who humbles Himself to behold the things that are in the heavens and in the earth? . . . Praise the Lord! (Psalm 113:1a, 2-3, 5-6, 9)

Take a moment to offer the Lord your personal praise and thanksgiving.

2. Confession: Pray this confession to the Lord as you seek to keep your life free from sin and in fellowship with Him:

Good and upright are You, Lord; therefore You teach sinners in the way. The humble You guide in justice, and the humble You teach Your way. All Your paths are mercy and truth, to such as keep Your covenant and Your testimonies. For Your name's sake, O Lord, pardon my iniquity, for it is great. (Psalm 25:8-11)

Confess any personal sins which the Holy Spirit may bring to your mind.

3. Affirmation: As you agree with the will of God, voice your affirmation of His word:

O Lord, You are my light and my salvation; whom shall I fear? You are the strength of my life; of whom shall I be afraid? (Psalm 27:1)

4. Requests: As you make your requests known to the Lord, include:

• Love for your family

• Revival among Christians in America

• Your prayer list, the concerns of your heart, and today's activities

5. Closing Prayer: Finally, offer this closing prayer to the Lord:

Make me complete in every good work to do Your will, working in me what is well pleasing in Your sight, through Jesus Christ, to whom be glory forever and ever. Amen. (Hebrews 13:20-21)

Memory Verse: He who has the Son has life; he who does not have the Son of God does not have life.
1 John 5:12
Assurance Theme

FEBRUARY 20

READING

The passage for today centers on the greatest commandment. During this extended time of teaching, for the benefit of the new generation of Israelites poised to enter the promised land, Moses exhorts them to obey the greatest commandment, which is to love the Lord their God with all their heart and soul and might.

Read Deuteronomy 6.

REFLECTING

There are three keys to passing your faith on to someone else. First, it must be real in your life. Moses said the words must be in your "heart," not just your "head." Second, we must impart truth and information. That is, we must teach diligently. Finally, this truth must permeate every corner of our daily lives. We must talk of it when we lie down and rise up, etc. We rarely fool anyone, and if one of these keys is missing in our lives, we will not make an impact on others. We must know the truth; it must be real to us, and it must permeate our daily lives.

RESPONDING

1. Praise: As you foster the reality of your walk with the Lord, offer to Him these words of praise:

Not unto us, O Lord, not unto us, but to Your name give glory, because of Your mercy, and because of Your truth. . . . We who fear You, O Lord, trust in You; You are our help and our shield. . . . We will bless the Lord from this time forth and forevermore. Praise the Lord! (Psalm 115:1, 11, 18)

Take a moment to offer the Lord your personal praise and thanksgiving.

2. Confession: Pray this confession to the Lord as you seek to keep your life free from sin and in fellowship with Him:

Turn Yourself to me, and have mercy on me, for I am desolate and afflicted. The troubles of my heart have enlarged; oh, bring me out of my distresses! Look on my affliction and my pain, and forgive all my sins. (Psalm 25:16-18)

Confess any personal sins which the Holy Spirit may bring to your mind.

3. Affirmation: As you agree with the will of God, voice your affirmation of His word:

I have been crucified with Christ; it is no longer I who live, but Christ lives in me; and the life which I now live in the flesh I live by faith in the Son of God, who loved me and gave Himself for me. (Galatians 2:20)

4. Requests: As you make your requests known to the Lord, include:

- Faithfulness with your treasures
- The Great Commission
- Your prayer list, the concerns of your heart, and today's activities

5. Closing Prayer: Finally, offer this closing prayer to the Lord:

May You, the God of grace, who called me to Your eternal glory by Christ Jesus, after I have suffered a while, perfect, establish, strengthen, and settle me. To You be the glory and the dominion forever and ever. Amen. (1 Peter 5:10-11)

> **Memory Verse:** He who has the Son has life; he who does not have the Son of God does not have life.
> 1 John 5:12
> *Assurance Theme*

READING

The passage for today centers on the commandment to destroy the Canaanites. Based on the principle that to bring the Canaanites into their nation would be like bringing cancer into their bodies, God commands the Israelites to destroy them.

Read Deuteronomy 7.

REFLECTING

God instructs the Israelites to remove from their land everything that would lead them to forsake their purity and commitment to the Lord. When we allow unholiness inside our walls, it seeps into our lives and corrupts us. We must remove the things from our lives that would tempt us or weaken us. Are there some things you have carried over from your earlier days that ought to be removed from your life? Why not remove them right away?

RESPONDING

1. Praise: The Lord will keep us pure and holy if we obey Him. Praise Him for His protection.

I will bless the Lord at all times; His praise shall continually be in my mouth. My soul shall make its boast in the Lord; the humble shall hear of it and be glad. Oh, magnify the Lord with me, and let us exalt His name together. . . . Oh, taste and see that the Lord is good; blessed is the man who trusts in Him! (Psalm 34:1-3, 8)

Now express any additional thoughts of praise or thanksgiving.

2. Confession: Pray this confession to the Lord as you seek to keep your life free from sin and in fellowship with Him:

Create in me a clean heart, O God, and renew a steadfast spirit within me. . . . Restore to me the joy of Your salvation, and uphold me with Your generous Spirit; then I will teach transgressors Your ways, and sinners shall be converted to You. (Psalm 51:10, 12-13)

Confess any personal sins which the Holy Spirit brings to your mind.

3. Affirmation: Now pray this affirmation to the Lord as you agree with and submit yourself to the will of God:

If I am wise, I will not glory in my wisdom; if I am mighty, I will not glory in my might; nor if I am rich, in my riches. But if I glory, I will only glory in the fact that I understand and know You; that You are the Lord, exercising lovingkindness, judgment, and righteousness in the earth. For in these You delight. (Jeremiah 9:23-24)

4. Requests: The Lord encourages us to come to Him with our concerns and desires. As you make your requests known to the Lord, include:

- Spiritual insight
- Campus ministries
- Your prayer list, the concerns of your heart, and today's activities

5. Closing Prayer: Finally, offer this closing prayer to the Lord:

May I grow in the grace and knowledge of our Lord and Savior Jesus Christ. To Him be the glory both now and forever. Amen. (2 Peter 3:18)

Memory Verse: He who has the Son has life; he who does not have the Son of God does not have life.
1 John 5:12
Assurance Theme

FEBRUARY 22

READING

The passage for today centers on an exhortation to remember the past. Moses reminds the Israelites of the Lord's blessings on them in the past 40 years and urges them not to forget the commandments of God—lest they fall under His judgment.

Read Deuteronomy 8.

REFLECTING

Following God has never been easy. God never intended for it to be. He tests us—to know what is in our hearts and to teach us that we do not live by bread alone. When things are too easy, we tend to be ungrateful. We tend not to give God the recognition for His blessing. There is inherent danger in prosperity. We begin thinking that "my power and the strength of my hand has made me this wealth." Then, once we believe that, God seems no longer necessary, and we forget Him. To keep that from happening, God often sprinkles our lives with adversity. In chapter 8, we see God's love and care, along with His tests and trials. We seem to need both to be healthy. To grow, we need sunshine and rain.

RESPONDING

1. Praise: In full confidence in the character of God, offer your praise to Him.

Blessed be Your glorious name, which is exalted above all blessing and praise! You alone are the Lord; You have made heaven, the heaven of heavens, with all their host, the earth and all things on it, the seas and all that is in them, and You preserve them all. The host of heaven worships You. (Nehemiah 9:5-6)

Take a moment to offer the Lord your personal praise and thanksgiving.

2. Confession: Pray this confession to the Lord as you seek to keep your life free from sin and in fellowship with Him:

Surely You have borne my griefs and carried my sorrows. . . . You were wounded for my transgressions, You were bruised for my iniquities; the chastisement for my peace was upon You, and by Your stripes I am healed. (Isaiah 53:4-5)

Confess any personal sins which the Holy Spirit may bring to your mind.

3. Affirmation: As you agree with the will of God, voice your affirmation of His word:

Behold, You, O Lord, are my salvation, I will trust and not be afraid; for YAH, the Lord, is my strength and my song; You also have become my salvation. (Isaiah 12:2)

4. Requests: As you make your requests known to the Lord, include:

- Desire to be like Christ
- Needs in inner cities
- Your activities for the day
- Your prayer list, the concerns of your heart, and today's activities

5. Closing Prayer: Finally, offer this closing prayer to the Lord:

Blessing and honor and glory and power be to You who sit on the throne, and to You, Lord, forever and ever! (Revelation 5:13)

Memory Verse: He who has the Son has life; he who does not have the Son of God does not have life.
1 John 5:12
Assurance Theme

READING

The passage for today centers on the curses of Mount Ebal. To dramatize the stark contrast in results between obedience and disobedience, God calls curses for disobedience from Mount Ebal.

Read Deuteronomy 27.

REFLECTING

What a drama! Mount Gerazim and Mount Ebal are two masses of limestone rock rising over 2,000 feet above sea level. Between them lies a beautiful valley, about 300 yards wide. Half the children of Israel are on one mountain, and half are on the other—with the Levites in the valley in between. Curses are called from Mount Ebal, and blessings are called from Mount Gerazim. All of this to dramatize the importance of obedience and the consequences of disobedience.

Nothing is insignificant to a holy God. Nor should it be to us. We must care about right and wrong.

RESPONDING

1. Praise: Offer praise to our holy God in these words:

Unto You I lift up my eyes, O You who dwell in the heavens. Behold, as the eyes of servants look to the hand of their master, as the eyes of a maid to the hand of her mistress, so our eyes look to the Lord our God, until He has mercy on us. (Psalm 123:1-2)

Take a moment to offer the Lord your personal praise and thanksgiving.

2. Confession: Pray this confession to the Lord as you seek to keep your life free from sin and in fellowship with Him:

I sing praise to You, O Lord; I am one of Your saints, and give thanks at the remembrance of Your holy name. For Your anger is but for a moment, Your favor is for life; weeping may endure for a night, but joy comes in the morning. (Psalm 30:4-5)

Confess any personal sins which the Holy Spirit may bring to your mind.

3. Affirmation: As you agree with the will of God, voice your affirmation of His word:

You, O Lord, are the portion of my inheritance and my cup; You maintain my lot. The lines have fallen to me in pleasant places; yes, I have a good inheritance. (Psalm 16:5-6)

4. Requests: As you make your requests known to the Lord, include:

* Personal witness for Christ
* Local churches around the nation
* Your prayer list, the concerns of your heart, and today's activities

5. Closing Prayer: Finally, offer this closing prayer to the Lord:

Amen! Blessing and glory and wisdom, thanksgiving and honor and power and might, be to You, God, forever and ever. Amen. (Revelation 7:12)

Memory Verse: He who has the Son has life; he who does not have the Son of God does not have life.
1 John 5:12
Assurance Theme

FEBRUARY 24

READING

The passage for today centers on the blessings of Mount Gerazim. From Mount Gerazim, God calls blessings upon the Israelites for obedience to His commands.

Read Deuteronomy 28.

REFLECTING

A sword and a plowshare are laid on the valley floor between Ebal and Gerazim. Blessings are piled upon blessings—until you wonder if the blessings could be contained. The Lord outdoes Himself, searching His omniscience to find ways of blessing Israel. Obviously, He takes great pleasure in doing good to them.

But in the shadow of the plowshare lies a sword. The 14 verses of blessings are followed by 52 verses of the most heart-rending curses imaginable.

How evil, how unspeakably terrible is sin. Thank God that He has delivered us from it. Thank God that, through Christ, we may taste of His blessings forever.

RESPONDING

1. Praise: Offer your praise to the Lord for His goodness in delivering us from the consequences of sin.

Praise the Lord! Praise the name of the Lord! Praise Him, O you servants of the Lord! . . . Praise the Lord, for the Lord is good; sing praises to His name, for it is pleasant. . . . For we know that the Lord is great, and our Lord is above all gods. . . . Blessed be the Lord. . . . Praise the Lord! (Psalm 135:1, 3, 5, 21)

Take a moment to offer the Lord your personal praise and thanksgiving.

2. Confession: Pray this confession to the Lord as you seek to keep your life free from sin and in fellowship with Him:

Blessed am I; my transgression is forgiven; my sin is covered. Blessed am I; the Lord does not impute iniquity to me, and in my spirit there is no guile. (Psalm 32:1-2)

Confess any personal sins which the Holy Spirit may bring to your mind.

3. Affirmation: As you agree with the will of God, voice your affirmation of His word:

I have Your commandments and when I keep them, it shows I love You. And if I love You, Lord Jesus, I will be loved by Your Father, and You will love me and manifest Yourself to me. (John 14:21)

4. Requests: As you make your requests known to the Lord, include:

- An eternal perspective
- Needs of work or school mates
- Your prayer list, the concerns of your heart, and today's activities

5. Closing Prayer: Finally, offer this closing prayer to the Lord:

I will wait on You, the Lord; I will be of good courage, and You shall strengthen my heart; I will wait on You! (Psalm 27:14)

Memory Verse: He who has the Son has life; he who does not have the Son of God does not have life.
1 John 5:12
Assurance Theme

FEBRUARY 25

READING

The passage for today centers on the covenant in Moab. God calls upon the Israelites to accept the terms of the covenant He is entering into with them.

Read Deuteronomy 29.

REFLECTING

God gives us the freedom to sin. He allows us the privilege of choice.

After laying out the options before the Israelites at Mount Ebal and Mount Gerazim, God now says, "Choose. You are free to choose." But by His grace, He makes clear the consequences of these choices.

Seeing the alternative so clearly before us, what could possibly account for our choosing the curses? The only conceivable answer is that we don't believe God. We don't really believe that the blessings will be that good—or that the curses will be that bad—or that we will be unable to control the consequences of our decisions. We trust our own judgment. We take things into our own hands.

The Old Testament was written for our instruction. We must learn to take God at His word. Period.

RESPONDING

1. Praise: Offer to the Lord this psalm of praise for giving us His blessing.

I will extol You, my God, O King; and I will bless Your name forever and ever. Every day I will bless You, and I will praise Your name forever and ever. Great is the Lord, and greatly to be praised; and His greatness is unsearchable. One generation shall praise Your works to another, and shall declare Your mighty acts. I will meditate on the glorious

splendor of Your majesty, and on Your wondrous works. (Psalm 145:1-5)

Take a moment to offer the Lord your personal praise and thanksgiving.

2. Confession: Pray this confession to the Lord as you seek to keep your life free from sin and in fellowship with Him:

I acknowledged my sin to You, and my iniquity I have not hidden. I said, "I will confess my transgressions to the Lord," and You forgave the iniquity of my sin. (Psalm 32:5)

Confess any personal sins which the Holy Spirit may bring to your mind.

3. Affirmation: As you agree with the will of God, voice your affirmation of His word:

You, O God, are Spirit, and when I worship You, I must worship in spirit and truth. (John 4:24)

4. Requests: As you make your requests known to the Lord, include:

- Personal discipline
- Christians worldwide who are persecuted for their faith
- Your prayer list, the concerns of your heart, and today's activities

5. Closing Prayer: Finally, offer this closing prayer to the Lord:

Show me the path of life; in Your presence is fullness of joy; at Your right hand are pleasures forevermore. (Psalm 16:11)

Memory Verse: He who has the Son has life; he who does not have the Son of God does not have life.
1 John 5:12
Assurance Theme

FEBRUARY 26

READING

The passage for today centers on the promised Restoration. If the Israelites should stray from the covenant and the curses of Mount Ebal fall upon them—but then they repent—God promises to restore them.

Read Deuteronomy 30.

REFLECTING

Where would we be without forgiveness? In his weakness, man is not able to sustain any relationship without eventually needing to forgive and be forgiven. This includes his relationship with God. Unless God was willing to forgive us, we could have no relationship with Him, for we are unable to be sinless before Him. What a warm and tender chapter comes on the heels of the curses.

God says, "If you turn from me, I will pour out on you the curses. But if you repent and return to me, I will forgive you and restore you." What a comfort. What a wonderful God.

RESPONDING

1. Praise: For His grace to forgive, offer the Lord these words of praise.

Men shall speak of the might of Your awesome acts, and I will declare Your greatness. They shall utter the memory of Your great goodness, and shall sing of Your righteousness. The Lord is gracious and full of compassion, slow to anger and great in mercy. The Lord is good to all, and His tender mercies are over all His works. (Psalm 145:6-9)

Take a moment to offer the Lord your personal praise and thanksgiving.

2. Confession: Pray this confession to the Lord as you seek to keep your life free from sin and in fellowship with Him:

I am righteous in Your sight, and when I cry out, You hear, O Lord, and deliver me out of all my troubles. You are near to me when I have a broken heart, and save me when I have a contrite spirit. (Psalm 34:17-18)

Confess any personal sins which the Holy Spirit may bring to your mind.

3. Affirmation: As you agree with the will of God, voice your affirmation of His word:

I delight to do Your will, O my God, and Your law is within my heart. (Psalm 40:8)

4. Requests: As you make your requests known to the Lord, include:

- Love for the Lord
- The work of missions in the Middle East, Australia, and the Islands
- Your prayer list, the concerns of your heart, and today's activities

5. Closing Prayer: Finally, offer this closing prayer to the Lord:

Save Your people, and bless Your inheritance; shepherd us also, and bear us up forever. (Psalm 28:9)

Memory Verse: I am the resurrection and the life. He who believes in Me, though he may die, he shall live. And whoever lives and believes in Me shall never die.

John 11:25-26
Assurance Theme

READING

The passage for today centers on the Song of Moses. Moses writes in poetic form a summary of everything he has taught the Israelites. Read Deuteronomy 32.

REFLECTING

Man is more than a machine. Man is more than a combination of blood vessels and bones. There is something within man that transcends his bodily functions and lifts him above the animals. It is the image of God. When the major issues of life lie before us, the image of God within demands that we sing a song or paint a picture or write a poem or perform a dance. At the end of his life, as Moses is struggling to summarize all that he needs to say to his people, he bursts out in song. Surely the thumbprint of God is seen in his crowning achievement.

RESPONDING

1. Praise: A mark of the image of God within is revealed as you offer Him your praise.

Ascribe to the Lord, O families of the peoples,
Ascribe to the Lord glory and strength.
Ascribe to the Lord the glory
due His name;
Bring an offering and come before Him;
Worship the Lord in holy array.
Indeed, the world is firmly established,
it will not be moved.
Let the heavens be glad,
and let the earth rejoice.
(2 Chronicles 16:28-31)

2. Confession: As you seek to keep your life free of sin, pray this passage of confession back to the Lord:

"Yet even now," declares the Lord,
"Return to Me with all your heart,
And with fasting, weeping, and mourning;
Rend your hearts
and not your garments."
Now return to the Lord your God,
For He is gracious and compassionate,
Slow to anger, abounding in lovingkindness,
And relenting of evil.
Joel 2:12-13

Confess any personal sins the Holy Spirit may bring to mind.

3. Affirmation: Now pause to pray this passage of affirmation back to the Lord:

Having been justified by faith, I have peace with You through my Lord Jesus Christ, through whom also I have obtained my introduction by faith into this grace in which I stand; and I exult in hope of the glory of You. (Romans 5:1-2)

4. Requests: As you make your requests known to the Lord, include:

- Faithfulness in sharing Christ
- The Lord's work in national and world affairs
- Your activities for the day
- Whatever else is on your heart

5. Closing Prayer: Finally, offer this closing prayer to the Lord.

Blessed are You, the Lord, forevermore! Amen and amen. (Psalm 89:52)

Memory Verse: I am the resurrection and the life. He who believes in Me, though he may die, he shall live. And whoever lives and believes in Me shall never die.

John 11:25-26

Assurance Theme

FEBRUARY 28

READING

The passage for today centers on the death of Moses. Moses dies atop Mount Nebo at the age of 120, and Joshua assumes command of the nation.

Read Deuteronomy 34.

REFLECTING

When a man of God dies, nothing of God dies. The will of God cannot be furthered or impeded by man. We sorrow when our spiritual leaders die or are called on to other ministries. We are concerned that the work of God may suffer. But these concerns dissolve in light of the sovereignty of God. The present work may diminish, but another work somewhere else may flourish. Overall, God's will will be done. When Moses was laid to rest, it was God who took over, not Joshua, for God was in charge with Moses. We must learn to rest in the sovereignty of God.

RESPONDING

1. Praise: Offer the sovereign God your praise as you rest in Him:

You, the Lord, will command Your lovingkindness in the daytime, and in the night Your song shall be with me—a prayer to You, the God of my life. (Psalm 42:8)

2. Confession: Pray this confession to the Lord as you seek to keep your life free from sin and in fellowship with Him:

The heart is deceitful above all things, and desperately wicked; who can know it? You, the Lord, search the heart, You test the mind, even to give every man according to his ways, and according to the fruit of his doings. . . . Heal me, O Lord, and I shall be healed; save me, and I shall be saved, for You are my praise. (Jeremiah 17:9, 10, 14)

Confess any personal sins which the Holy Spirit may bring to your mind.

3. Affirmation: As you agree with the will of God, voice your affirmation of His word:

You, the Father have given me to Jesus Christ and I have come to Him and will by no means be cast out. (John 6:37)

4. Requests: As you make your requests known to the Lord, include:

- Compassion for others
- Missions in America
- Your prayer list, the concerns of your heart, and today's activities

5. Closing Prayer: Finally, offer this closing prayer to the Lord:

This is the day the Lord has made; we will rejoice and be glad in it. (Psalm 118:24)

Oh, satisfy us in the morning with Thy lovingkindness, that we may sing for joy and be glad all our day. (Psalm 90:14)

Memory Verse: I am the resurrection and the life. He who believes in Me, though he may die, he shall live. And whoever lives and believes in Me shall never die.

John 11:25-26
Assurance Theme

READING

The passage for today centers on the birth of Jesus. After tracing Jesus' genealogy back to Abraham, Matthew records His miraculous conception and birth.

Read Matthew 1.

REFLECTING

The birth of Jesus splits the backdrop of history like a lightning bolt in a hot July sky. The stage is set for the most important event in history. It has been planned before the foundation of the world. It is promised to Abraham, Isaac, Jacob, and David. The prophets have heralded it, the people long for it, and culture is ripe for it. The Messiah is coming to establish a new relationship between God and man.

He is not just another world leader. He is God in the flesh. God, who has previously made Himself known through a nation and a law, is now to make Himself known through a man—a God-man, Jesus.

He is not coming as many had expected—in power and glory. He comes as an obscure son of an obscure carpenter. But His star is to rise, not only literally over Bethlehem, but figuratively, as He eventually becomes the most important figure in history.

RESPONDING

1. Praise: Continue your time with the Lord by offering your praise to the God of history through these words:

Tremble before Him, all the earth. The world also is firmly established, it shall not be moved. Let the heavens rejoice, and let the earth be glad. . . . Oh, give thanks to the Lord, for He is good! For His mercy endures forever. (1 Chronicles 16:30-31, 34)

Take a moment to offer the Lord your personal praise and thanksgiving.

2. Confession: Pray this confession to the Lord as you seek to keep your life free from sin and in fellowship with Him:

Lord, be merciful to me; heal my soul, for I have sinned against You. (Psalm 41:4)

Confess any personal sins which the Holy Spirit may bring to your mind.

3. Affirmation: As you agree with the will of God, voice your affirmation of His word:

I will remember the works of the Lord; surely I will remember Your wonders of old. I will also meditate on all Your work, and talk of Your deeds. (Psalm 77:11-12)

4. Requests: As you make your requests known to the Lord, include:

- Health and strength to serve God
- God's will to be done on earth
- Your prayer list, the concerns of your heart, and today's activities

5. Closing Prayer: Finally, offer this closing prayer to the Lord:

Be glad in the Lord and rejoice, you righteous; and shout for joy, all you upright in heart! (Psalm 32:11)

Memory Verse: I am the resurrection and the life. He who believes in Me, though he may die, he shall live. And whoever lives and believes in Me shall never die.

John 11:25-26
Assurance Theme

MARCH 2

READING

The passage for today centers on Jesus' early life. After the visit of the wise men, Mary and Joseph flee with Jesus to escape Herod's attempt to kill Jesus.

Read Matthew 2.

REFLECTING

When Herod asks the scholars where the Messiah is to be born, they unhesitatingly answer, "Bethlehem of Judea, for so it has been written by the prophet."

Josh McDowell writes in *Evidence That Demands a Verdict* that by using the modern science of probability in reference to all 60 major prophecies, the chances that any man might have lived down to the present time and fulfilled all 60 prophecies is 1 in 10^{157}, which is 10 followed by 157 zeros. Reason demands that we accept Jesus as the fulfillment of the Old Testament prophecies of the Messiah.

RESPONDING

1. Praise: As you rest in the security that Jesus is the Messiah, offer the Lord these words of praise:

Inasmuch as there is none like You, O Lord (You are great, and Your name is great in might), who would not fear You, O King of the nations? For this is Your rightful due, for among all the wise men of the nations, and in all their kingdoms, there is none like You. (Jeremiah 10:6-7)

Take a moment to offer the Lord your personal praise and thanksgiving.

2. Confession: Pray this confession to the Lord as you seek to keep your life free from sin and in fellowship with Him:

Have mercy upon me, O God, according to Your lovingkindness; according to the multitude of Your tender mercies, blot out my transgressions. Wash me thoroughly from my iniquity, and cleanse me from my sin. For I acknowledge my transgressions, and my sin is ever before me. (Psalm 51:1-3)

Confess any personal sins which the Holy Spirit may bring to your mind.

3. Affirmation: As you agree with the will of God, voice your affirmation of His word:

Behold what manner of love You have bestowed on me, that I should be called Your child! Therefore the world does not know me, because it did not know You. Now I am a child of God; and it has not yet been revealed what I shall be but I know that when He is revealed, I shall be like Him for I shall see Him as He is. (1 John 3:1-2)

4. Requests: As you make your requests known to the Lord, include:

- Sensitivity to sin
- The ministry of your local church
- Your prayer list, the concerns of your heart, and today's activities

5. Closing Prayer: Finally, offer this closing prayer to the Lord:

Let the words of my mouth and the meditation of my heart be acceptable in Your sight, O Lord, my strength and my redeemer. (Psalm 19:14)

Memory Verse: I am the resurrection and the life. He who believes in Me, though he may die, he shall live. And whoever lives and believes in Me shall never die.

John 11:25-26
Assurance Theme

READING

The passage for today centers on the baptism of Jesus. After being baptized by His forerunner, John, Jesus' ministry is validated by God the Father, speaking from heaven, commending Him.

Read Matthew 3.

REFLECTING

No matter when, no matter where, repentance is necessary when meeting God for the first time. To repent means to change your mind.

If you have been living your life without God, you must change your mind and live for God. If you are trusting yourself to save yourself, you must change your mind and trust Jesus.

Whether in the time of Moses or John the Baptist or today, one must repent to meet God. One must change his mind about who and what to live for.

If you were transported—just as you are—back to John's time and heard his message, would you repent? Have you repented?

RESPONDING

1. Praise: The repentant heart is one that can offer praise to the Lord:

Praise the Lord! Praise the Lord, O my soul! While I live I will praise the Lord; I will sing praises to my God while I have my being. . . . Happy is he who has the God of Jacob for his help, whose hope is in the Lord his God. . . . The Lord shall reign forever—Your God, O Zion, to all generations. Praise the Lord! (Psalm 146:1-2, 5, 10)

Take a moment to offer the Lord your personal praise and thanksgiving.

2. Confession: Pray this confession to the Lord as you seek to keep your life free from sin and in fellowship with Him:

Against You, You only, have I sinned, and done this evil in Your sight—that You may be found just when You speak and blameless when You judge. (Psalm 51:4)

Confess any personal sins which the Holy Spirit may bring to your mind.

3. Affirmation: As you agree with the will of God, voice your affirmation of His word:

You, Lord Jesus, are the resurrection and the life. If I believe in You, though I may die, I shall live. (John 11:25)

4. Requests: As you make your requests known to the Lord, include:

- Wisdom for living life
- Needs of your immediate family
- Your prayer list, the concerns of your heart, and today's activities

5. Closing Prayer: Finally, offer this closing prayer to the Lord:

Surely goodness and mercy shall follow me all the days of my life, and I will dwell in the house of the Lord forever. (Psalm 23:6)

Memory Verse: I am the resurrection and the life. He who believes in Me, though he may die, he shall live. And whoever lives and believes in Me shall never die.

John 11:25-26
Assurance Theme

MARCH 4

READING

The passage for today centers on the births of John and Jesus. The births of both John the Baptist and Jesus are foretold, followed by the account of the birth of John.

Read Luke 1.

REFLECTING

Whenever the Lord or an angel appears to men, the first words usually include, "Fear not." When Zachariah sees Gabriel in the temple, the angel says, "Do not be afraid." When Gabriel appears to Mary, he says, "Do not be afraid."

It must be frightening to come face to face with the supernatural. It seems to have a life-changing impact on whomever it is. Most of us will never have the privilege of coming face to face with an angel. We try to visualize God's presence and are transformed slowly—but just as surely—because we behold steadfastly the face of the Lord in His Word.

RESPONDING

1. Praise: Offer your praise to the Lord, who transforms us through His Word:

Praise the Lord! For it is good to sing praises to our God; for it is pleasant, and praise is beautiful. . . . Great is our Lord, and mighty in power. . . . The Lord takes pleasure in those who fear Him, in those who hope in His mercy. . . . Praise the Lord! (Psalm 147:1, 5a, 11, 20)

Take a moment to offer the Lord your personal praise and thanksgiving.

2. Confession: Pray this confession to the Lord as you seek to keep your life free from sin and in fellowship with Him:

O God, You know my foolishness; and my sins are not hidden from You. Let not those who wait for You, O Lord God of hosts, be ashamed because of me. (Psalm 69:5-6a)

Confess any personal sins which the Holy Spirit may bring to your mind.

3. Affirmation: As you agree with the will of God, voice your affirmation of His word:

You have shown me what is good; and what do You require of me, but to do justly, to love mercy, and to walk humbly with You, my God? (Micah 6:8)

4. Requests: As you make your requests known to the Lord, include:

- Insight into Scripture
- The hungry around the world
- Your prayer list, the concerns of your heart, and today's activities

5. Closing Prayer: Finally, offer this closing prayer to the Lord:

We will be of good courage, and You shall strengthen our hearts, all we who hope in the Lord. (Psalm 31:24)

Memory Verse: I am the resurrection and the life. He who believes in Me, though he may die, he shall live. And whoever lives and believes in Me shall never die.

John 11:25-26
Assurance Theme

READING

The passage for today centers on Jesus' birth and early life. Following Jesus' birth, Mary and Joseph return to Nazareth, after which they come again to Jerusalem in Jesus' twelfth year, and Jesus meets with the teachers in the temple.

Read Luke 2.

REFLECTING

To Jesus, nothing is more important than doing His Father's will. Even at the age of 12, when His parents miss Him on the trip home from the Passover, they return and find Him in the temple. "Did you not know that I had to be in My Father's house?" He asked. "My food is to do the will of Him who sent me," He later said in John 4:34. Absolute single-mindedness!

We are to have the mind in us which was also in Christ Jesus. We are to have absolute single-mindedness about doing the will of the Father. Make that your purpose and your prayer.

RESPONDING

1. Praise: Offer your praise in these words to the God who is worthy of our absolute devotion:

Praise the Lord! Praise God in His sanctuary; praise Him in His mighty firmament! Praise Him for His mighty acts; praise Him according to His excellent greatness! Praise Him with the sound of the trumpet; praise Him with the lute and harp! . . . Let everything that has breath praise the Lord. Praise the Lord! (Psalm 150:1-3, 6)

Take a moment to offer the Lord your personal praise and thanksgiving.

2. Confession: Pray this confession to the Lord as you seek to keep your life free from sin and in fellowship with Him:

Purge me with hyssop, and I shall be clean; wash me, and I shall be whiter than snow. . . . Hide Your face from my sins, and blot out all my iniquities. (Psalm 51:7, 9)

Confess any personal sins which the Holy Spirit may bring to your mind.

3. Affirmation: As you agree with the will of God, voice your affirmation of His word:

You, Lord Jesus, are the way, the truth, and the life. I cannot come to the Father except through You. (John 14:6)

4. Requests: As you make your requests known to the Lord, include:

- Love for fellow Christians
- The work of missions in Europe and Asia
- Your prayer list, the concerns of your heart, and today's activities

5. Closing Prayer: Finally, offer this closing prayer to the Lord:

This is the day which You have made; I will rejoice and be glad in it. (Psalm 118:24)

Memory Verse: There is therefore now no condemnation to those who are in Christ Jesus, who do not walk according to the flesh, but according to the Spirit.

Romans 8:1
Assurance Theme

MARCH 6

READING

The passage for today centers on the baptism of Jesus. John the Baptist's ministry gains public attention, and Jesus begins His own ministry after asking John to baptize Him. Read Luke 3.

REFLECTING

The unique contribution of each of the four gospels is very important to our understanding of the life of Christ. In the Gospel of Matthew, the genealogy takes Jesus' ancestry back to Abraham. That is because Matthew's gospel was written by a Jew to Jews and emphasizes distinctly Jewish matters. However, Luke is a Gentile, writing to Gentiles, and Luke emphasizes matters that are of concern to an audience broader than the Jewish audience.

From Matthew, we learn that, indeed, Jesus was a descendant of Abraham, and we see the fulfillment of the promises to Abraham. From Luke, we learn that, indeed, Jesus is the Son of God, and we see the fulfillment of all God's promises to those of us who are not descendants of Abraham.

RESPONDING

1. Praise: Offer your praise to the Lord who is faithful to His word:

Ah, Lord God! Behold, You have made the heavens and the earth by Your great power and outstretched arm. There is nothing too hard for You. You show lovingkindness to thousands . . . O Great and Mighty God, whose name is the Lord of hosts. You are great in counsel and mighty in work. (Jeremiah 32:17-19)

Take a moment to offer the Lord your personal praise and thanksgiving.

2. Confession: Pray this confession to the Lord as you seek to keep your life free from sin and in fellowship with Him:

Deliver me from bloodguiltiness, O God, the God of my salvation, and my tongue shall sing aloud of Your righteousness. O Lord, open my lips, and my mouth shall show forth Your praise. (Psalm 51:14-15)

Confess any personal sins which the Holy Spirit may bring to your mind.

3. Affirmation: As you agree with the will of God, voice your affirmation of His word:

You, O God, were manifested in the flesh, justified in the Spirit, seen by angels, preached among the Gentiles, believed on in the world, received up in glory. (1 Timothy 3:16)

4. Requests: As you make your requests known to the Lord, include:

- Faithfulness with your time
- The president and national leaders and affairs
- Your prayer list, the concerns of your heart, and today's activities

5. Closing Prayer: Finally, offer this closing prayer to the Lord:

Oh, satisfy me early with Your mercy, that I may rejoice and be glad all my days! (Psalm 90:14)

Memory Verse: There is therefore now no condemnation to those who are in Christ Jesus, who do not walk according to the flesh, but according to the Spirit.

Romans 8:1
Assurance Theme

READING

The passage for today centers on the temptation of Jesus. Jesus is led into the wilderness by the Holy Spirit, after which He is tempted by Satan three times.

Read Luke 4.

REFLECTING

When Satan tempts Jesus, he offers Him things which God has already promised to give to Jesus. The things are not wrong in and of themselves. But they are not offered in God's time or in God's way. Each time Jesus rebuffs Satan, He does so with Scripture. Each time Satan offers Jesus something, Jesus' reply is, "No, because it is written. . . ." And then He quotes a passage of Scripture. This is an excellent illustration of the truth that David wrote in Psalm 119: "Thy word is a lamp unto my feet and a light unto my path,"and "Thy word have I hidden in my heart that I might not sin against Thee." To be victorious, we must know Scripture well enough to use it in our spiritual warfare to see through the tricks of Satan.

RESPONDING

1. Praise: Offer your personal praise to your personal Savior in these words:

I will extol You, my God, O King; and I will bless Your name forever and ever. Every day I will bless You, and I will praise Your name forever and ever. Great is the Lord, and greatly to be praised; and His greatness is unsearchable. One generation shall praise Your works to another, and shall declare Your mighty acts. I will meditate on the glorious splendor of Your majesty, and on Your wondrous works. (Psalm 145:1-5)

Take a moment to offer the Lord your personal praise and thanksgiving.

2. Confession: Pray this confession to the Lord as you seek to keep your life free from sin and in fellowship with Him:

I acknowledged my sin to You, and my iniquity I have not hidden. I said, "I will confess my transgressions to the Lord," and You forgave the iniquity of my sin. (Psalm 32:5)

Confess any personal sins which the Holy Spirit may bring to your mind.

3. Affirmation: As you agree with the will of God, voice your affirmation of His word:

You, O God, are Spirit, and when I worship You, I must worship in spirit and truth. (John 4:24)

4. Requests: As you make your requests known to the Lord, include:

- Your financial needs
- The needs of the poor
- Your prayer list, the concerns of your heart, and today's activities

5. Closing Prayer: Finally, offer this closing prayer to the Lord:

Let the beauty of You, Lord, be upon me, and establish the work of my hands for me; yes, establish the work of my hands. (Psalm 90:17)

Memory Verse: There is therefore now no condemnation to those who are in Christ Jesus, who do not walk according to the flesh, but according to the Spirit.

Romans 8:1
Assurance Theme

MARCH 8

READING

The passage for today centers on Jesus' early life and ministry. After Jesus' baptism by John, He begins His ministry of miracles and preaching and calls His first disciples.

Read Mark 1.

REFLECTING

Mark writes that after Jesus' baptism the Spirit impels Him to go out into the wilderness where He is tempted by Satan. The next 40 days are very difficult days for Jesus. These days serve as preparation for His public ministry. He faces stress physically, emotionally, and spiritually. We know from the account in Matthew that He does not eat for 40 days and 40 nights. Satan tempts Him with goods, as well as pride. We learn from Mark that He is with wild beasts (It is uncertain whether or not the beasts posed a threat to Him), and angels minister to Him. It is not true that if you follow God's will, you will have a life of ease. Jesus stated as much when He said if men persecute us, they are actually persecuting Him. Often, the way of God involves circumstances in which we must trust in the Lord and draw on His truth and strength for perspective and persistence.

RESPONDING

1. Praise: What a joy to relax in the sovereignty of God and praise Him for His goodness to me.

Men shall speak of the might of Your awesome acts, and I will declare Your greatness. They shall utter the memory of Your great goodness, and shall sing of Your righteousness. The Lord is gracious and full of compassion, slow to anger and great in mercy. The Lord is good to all, and His tender mercies are over all His works. (Psalm 145:6-9)

Take a moment to offer the Lord your personal praise and thanksgiving.

2. Confession: Pray this confession to the Lord as you seek to keep your life free from sin and in fellowship with Him:

I am righteous in Your sight, and when I cry out, You hear, O Lord, and deliver me out of all my troubles. You are near to me when I have a broken heart, and save me when I have a contrite spirit. (Psalm 34:17-18)

Confess any personal sins which the Holy Spirit may bring to your mind.

3. Affirmation: As you agree with the will of God, voice your affirmation of His word:

I delight to do Your will, O my God, and Your law is within my heart. (Psalm 40:8)

4. Requests: As you make your requests known to the Lord, include:

- Protection from the "evil one"
- Laborers for the "harvest"
- Your prayer list, the concerns of your heart, and today's activities

5. Closing Prayer: Finally, offer this closing prayer to the Lord:

Bless the Lord, all you His hosts, you ministers of His, who do His pleasure. Bless the Lord, all His works, in all places of His dominion. (Psalm 103:21-22)

Memory Verse: There is therefore now no condemnation to those who are in Christ Jesus, who do not walk according to the flesh, but according to the Spirit.

Romans 8:1
Assurance Theme

READING

The passage for today centers on Jesus' early ministry in Capernaum. After healing a paralytic to demonstrate His power to forgive sins, Jesus calls Matthew (Levi) to be His disciple.

Read Mark 2.

REFLECTING

When a paralyzed man is brought to Jesus, He says, "My son, your sins are forgiven" (Mark 2:5). The scribes are incensed, feeling that Jesus has blasphemed since no one can forgive sin but God, and they do not believe that Jesus is God. In response, Jesus says, "Which is easier, to say to the paralytic, 'Your sins are forgiven,' or to say, 'Arise, and take up your pallet and walk'?" (Mark 2:9) Of course, it is easier to say that your sins are forgiven. After all, who can verify if it is true? So, to prove that He *is* God and has the power to forgive sins, Jesus says to the paralytic, "Rise, take up your pallet and go home" (Mark 2:11). Jesus' miracles are often timed strategically to demonstrate the validity of a central truth which He is teaching.

RESPONDING

1. Praise: Rejoice in the fact that Jesus will forgive your sin, and offer Him this praise:

Blessed be the name of God
forever and ever,
For wisdom and might are His.
He gives wisdom to the wise
And knowledge to those
who have understanding.
He reveals deep and secret things,
He knows what is in the darkness,
And light dwells with Him.
(Daniel 2:20-22)

Take a moment to offer the Lord your personal praise and thanksgiving.

2. Confession: Pray this confession to the Lord as you seek to keep your life free from sin and in fellowship with Him:

You do not desire sacrifice, or else I would give it; You do not delight in burnt offering. The sacrifices of God are a broken spirit, a broken and a contrite heart—These, O God, You will not despise. (Psalm 51:16-17)

Confess any personal sins which the Holy Spirit may bring to your mind.

3. Affirmation: As you agree with the will of God, voice your affirmation of His word:

I will not fear, for You are with me; I will not be dismayed, for You are my God. You will strengthen me, yes, You will help me; You will uphold me with Your righteous right hand. (Isaiah 41:10)

4. Requests: As you make your requests known to the Lord, include:

- Commitment to the Lord
- Parachurch ministries
- Your prayer list, the concerns of your heart, and today's activities

5. Closing Prayer: Finally, offer this closing prayer to the Lord:

Lord, preserve me from all evil; preserve my soul. Lord, preserve my going out and my coming in from this time forth, and even forevermore. (Psalm 121:7-8)

Memory Verse: There is therefore now no condemnation to those who are in Christ Jesus, who do not walk according to the flesh, but according to the Spirit.

Romans 8:1
Assurance Theme

MARCH 10

READING

The passage for today centers on the choosing of the twelve. After continuing His ministry with miracles, and encountering the Pharisees concerning the Sabbath, Jesus chooses twelve followers to be His inner circle of disciples.

Read Mark 3.

REFLECTING

God takes ordinary people and does extraordinary things through them because of their devotion to Him. A look at the twelve men Jesus chooses to be His disciples does not reveal a "Who's Who" in Judea. Rather, the men are unknown and undistinguished.

The work of God does not depend on talent or intelligence or skill. The Lord will use whatever talent, intelligence, and skill we have, whether little or a lot. But only if they are dedicated to Him

God's desire for us in service is to manifest the character of Christ in whatever circumstance we find ourselves and to share His truth with others. The results are always His through the work of His Holy Spirit.

RESPONDING

1. Praise: As you consider God's willingness to use you, no matter what your talents, offer Him your praise through this passage:

My soul magnifies the Lord, and my spirit has rejoiced in God my Savior. For He who is mighty has done great things for me, and holy is His name. And His mercy is on those who fear Him from generation to generation. (Luke 1:46b-47, 49-50)

Take a moment to offer the Lord your personal praise and thanksgiving.

2. Confession: Pray this confession to the Lord as you seek to keep your life free from sin and in fellowship with Him:

Bless the Lord, O my soul; and all that is within me, bless His holy name! Bless the Lord, O my soul, and forget not all His benefits. . . . Bless the Lord, all His works, in all places of His dominion. Bless the Lord, O my soul! (Psalm 103:1, 2, 22)

Confess any personal sins which the Holy Spirit may bring to your mind.

3. Affirmation: As you agree with the will of God, voice your affirmation of His word:

These things You have spoken to me, that in You I may have peace. In the world I will have tribulation; but I will be of good cheer. You have overcome the world. (John 16:33)

4. Requests: As you make your requests known to the Lord, include:

- Renewing of your mind
- Needs of your extended family
- Your prayer list, the concerns of your heart, and today's activities

5. Closing Prayer: Finally, offer this closing prayer to the Lord:

May we with one mind and one mouth glorify the God and Father of our Lord Jesus Christ. (Romans 15:6)

Memory Verse: There is therefore now no condemnation to those who are in Christ Jesus, who do not walk according to the flesh, but according to the Spirit.

Romans 8:1
Assurance Theme

READING

The passage for today centers on the Beatitudes. In the first of three chapters on the Sermon on the Mount, Jesus teaches on the Beatitudes and love as the basis for personal relationships.

Read Matthew 5.

REFLECTING

Love is the fundamental characteristic of all meaningful relationships. All interpersonal problems could be solved with a faithful, mutual expression of love. Wars would cease, persecution would dissolve, and discrimination and crime would be eliminated.

The question for Christians is: What would the world be like if everyone were just like me? Would there be any crime, discrimination, prejudice? Would there be adequate warmth, meaningful relationships, and concern for the welfare of others? Jesus says, "Let your light shine before men in such a way that they may see your good works, and glorify your Father who is in heaven" (Matthew 5:16).

RESPONDING

1. Praise: Offer your praise to the God who loves you and who seeks your love in return:

Great and marvelous are Your works, Lord God Almighty! Just and true are Your ways, O King of the saints! Who shall not fear Your ways, O King of the saints! Who shall not fear You, O Lord, and glorify Your name? For You alone are holy. For all nations shall come and worship before You, for Your judgments have been manifested. (Revelation 15:3-4)

Take a moment to offer the Lord your personal praise and thanksgiving.

2. Confession: Pray this confession to the Lord as you seek to keep your life free from sin and in fellowship with Him:

O Lord, you are merciful and gracious, slow to anger, and abounding in mercy. . . . As a father pities his children, so You, O Lord, pity me when I fear You. For You know my frame; You remember that I am dust. (Psalm 103:8, 13-14)

Confess any personal sins which the Holy Spirit may bring to your mind.

3. Affirmation: As you agree with the will of God, voice your affirmation of His word:

There is therefore now no condemnation of me because I am in Christ Jesus; I do not walk according to the flesh, but according to the Spirit. For the law of the Spirit of life in Christ Jesus has made me free from the law of sin and death. (Romans 8:1-2)

4. Requests: As you make your requests known to the Lord, include:

- The Lord's leading in your life
- Opportunities for personal evangelism
- Your prayer list, the concerns of your heart, and today's activities

5. Closing Prayer: Finally, offer this closing prayer to the Lord:

Now may the God of hope fill me with all joy and peace in believing, that I may abound in hope by the power of the Holy Spirit. (Romans 15:13)

Memory Verse: There is therefore now no condemnation to those who are in Christ Jesus, who do not walk according to the flesh, but according to the Spirit.

Romans 8:1
Assurance Theme

MARCH 12

READING

The passage for today centers on the Lord's Prayer. In the second chapter of the Sermon on the Mount, Jesus teaches His followers concerning prayer and the proper perspective on personal treasures. Read Matthew 6.

REFLECTING

There's no fooling God. It is impossible to put something over on One who is omniscient. We can fool all of the people some of the time and some of the people all of the time. But not God. Jesus says, "Beware of practicing your righteousness before men . . ." (Matthew 6:1).

It is easy for us to fall into the trap of living our Christian lives for the sake of other Christians. We should be living them for the sake of our relationships with the Lord. We may find ourselves going to church, singing the songs, and going through the motions but spending no time cultivating a personal relationship with the Lord. It does not come easily. It takes commitment and time.

RESPONDING

1. Praise: Ponder the fact that the Lord wants a personal relationship with us, and offer Him your praise:

Who is like You, O Lord, among the gods? Who is like You, glorious in holiness, fearful in praises, doing wonders? (Exodus 15:11)

Therefore You are great, O Lord God. For there is none like You, nor is there any God besides You, according to all that we have heard with our ears. (2 Samuel 7:22)

Take a moment to offer the Lord your personal praise and thanksgiving.

2. Confession: Pray this confession to the Lord as you seek to keep your life free from sin and in fellowship with Him:

Out of the depths I have cried to You, O Lord. . . . If You, Lord, should mark iniquities, O Lord, who could stand? But there is forgiveness with You, that You may be feared. (Psalm 130:1, 3-4)

Confess any personal sins which the Holy Spirit may bring to your mind.

3. Affirmation: As you agree with the will of God, voice your affirmation of His word:

Likewise Your Spirit also helps me in my weaknesses. For I do not know what I should pray for as I ought, but Your Spirit, Himself, makes intercession for me with groanings which cannot be uttered. (Romans 8:26)

4. Requests: As you make your requests known to the Lord, include:

- Love for the lost
- The work of missions in Africa
- Your prayer list, the concerns of your heart, and today's activities

5. Closing Prayer: Finally, offer this closing prayer to the Lord:

Now to You who are able to establish us according to the gospel and preaching of Jesus Christ—to You, alone wise, be glory through Jesus Christ forever. Amen. (Romans 16:25-27)

Memory Verse: If anyone wants to do His will, he shall know concerning the doctrine, whether it is from God or whether I speak on My own authority.

John 7:17
Assurance Theme

READING

In this third and final chapter of the Sermon on the Mount, Jesus teaches His followers concerning judging others, the need to pray, and the need to follow the Lord fully in everything.

Read Matthew 7.

REFLECTING

Love is the basis of all that God asks of us. Jesus says, "However you want people to treat you, so treat them, for this is the Law and the Prophets" (Matthew 7:12). This goes hand in hand with what Jesus teaches later in Luke 10:27, that the greatest commandment is to love God and the second greatest commandment is to love your neighbor as yourself.

All the teaching sections of the Bible tell us, in very specific terms, how to love God or how to love our fellow man. We want to be appreciated, loved, treated with dignity, cared for, and esteemed. This, then, is the way we ought to treat others.

RESPONDING

1. Praise: Praise the Lord because He has treated us with love and dignity:

You are the Rock, Your work is perfect; for all Your ways are justice, a God of truth and without injustice; righteous and upright are You. (Deuteronomy 32:4)

The Lord lives! Blessed be my Rock! Let God be exalted, the Rock of my salvation! (2 Samuel 22:47)

Take a moment to offer the Lord your personal praise and thanksgiving.

2. Confession: Pray this confession to the Lord as you seek to keep your life free from sin and in fellowship with Him:

I will praise You, for I am fearfully and wonderfully made; marvelous are Your works, and that my soul knows very well. . . . Search me, O God, and know my heart; try me, and know my anxieties; and see if there is any wicked way in me, and lead me in the way everlasting. (Psalm 139:14, 23-24)

Confess any personal sins which the Holy Spirit may bring to your mind.

3. Affirmation: As you agree with the will of God, voice your affirmation of His word:

This is Your commandment, that I love others as You have loved me. (John 15:12)

4. Requests: As you make your requests known to the Lord, include:

- Faithfulness with your talents
- Your state and local leaders and affairs
- Your prayer list, the concerns of your heart, and today's activities

5. Closing Prayer: Finally, offer this closing prayer to the Lord:

The grace of the Lord Jesus Christ, and the love of God, and the communion of the Holy Spirit be with us all. Amen. (2 Corinthians 13:14)

Memory Verse: If anyone wants to do His will, he shall know concerning the doctrine, whether it is from God or whether I speak on My own authority.

John 7:17
Assurance Theme

MARCH 14

READING

The passage for today centers on vindication of John the Baptist's ministry. After healing the centurion's servant, Jesus goes to great lengths to help the people understand the significance of John the Baptist and his ministry.

Read Luke 7.

REFLECTING

Unbelief never has enough proof. No matter how much evidence is compiled, if a person chooses not to believe, no amount of evidence will convince him. Hard hearts are self-induced. The scribes and Pharisees have already rejected God before Jesus or John ever comes on the scene. That is why they reject John when he comes preaching a message of preparation for the Messiah and Jesus when He comes. We must know in order to believe, yet we must also believe in order to know. Many truths in the Bible puzzle us. To begin mastering them, we must first rest our belief completely in the character and power of God and in the truth of His Word.

RESPONDING

1. **Praise:** As you praise the Lord in these words, focus on His sovereignty and goodness:

The Lord is righteous in all His ways, gracious in all His works. The Lord is near to all who call upon Him, to all who call upon Him in truth. He will fulfill the desire of those who fear Him; He also will hear their cry and save them. . . . My mouth shall speak the praise of the Lord, and all flesh shall bless His holy name forever and ever. (Psalm 145:17-19, 21)

Take a moment to offer the Lord your personal praise and thanksgiving.

2. **Confession:** Pray this confession to the Lord as you seek to keep your life free from sin and in fellowship with Him:

Lord, be merciful to me; heal my soul, for I have sinned against You. . . . O Lord, be merciful to me, and raise me up. . . . Blessed be You, O Lord, the God of Israel from everlasting to everlasting! Amen and amen. (Psalm 41:4, 10, 13)

Confess any personal sins which the Holy Spirit may bring to your mind.

3. **Affirmation:** As you agree with the will of God, voice your affirmation of His word:

Your word is a lamp to my feet and light to my path. (Psalm 119:105)

4. **Requests:** As you make your requests known to the Lord, include:

- Strength for obedience
- International students in America
- Your prayer list, the concerns of your heart, and today's activities

5. **Closing Prayer:** Finally, offer this closing prayer to the Lord:

Now to You who are able to do exceedingly abundantly above all that I ask or think, according to the power that works in me, to You be glory in the church by Christ Jesus throughout all ages, world without end. Amen. (Ephesians 3:20-21)

Memory Verse: If anyone wants to do His will, he shall know concerning the doctrine, whether it is from God or whether I speak on My own authority.

John 7:17
Assurance Theme

READING

The passage for today centers on the parables of Jesus. As Jesus expands His public ministry, He teaches extensively, using parables, and then calms a storm to validate the truth of His teachings.

Read Mark 4.

REFLECTING

Faith does not come to us full-blown like seedlings in a garden. It must be cultivated, nurtured. Jesus cultivates the faith of His disciples. After an extensive time of teaching, during which He emphasized the nature of faith and the need for faith, Jesus says, "Let us go over to the other side." Jesus goes out into the Sea of Galilee with the twelve, knowing that a storm will come. Then when the storm hits, Jesus is in the back, asleep on a pillow. His disciples panic and ask somewhat accusingly, "Don't you care that we are perishing?" Jesus calms the storm and then asks, rhetorically, "How is it that you have no faith?" (Mark 4:40). Has Jesus not said, "Let us go to the other side"? His disciples marvel and their faith grows. We, too, must go through the difficult process of testing to become strong.

RESPONDING

1. Praise: Offer the Lord your praise for His goodness through these words:

All Your works shall praise You, O Lord, and Your saints shall bless You. They shall speak of the glory of Your kingdom, and talk of Your power, to make known to the sons of men His mighty acts. . . . Your kingdom is an everlasting kingdom, and Your dominion endures throughout all generations. (Psalm 145:10-13)

Take a moment to offer the Lord your personal praise and thanksgiving.

2. Confession: Pray this confession to the Lord as you seek to keep your life free from sin and in fellowship with Him:

Against You, You only, have I sinned, and done this evil in Your sight—that You may be found just when You speak, and blameless when You judge. (Psalm 51:4)

Confess any personal sins which the Holy Spirit may bring to your mind.

3. Affirmation: As you agree with the will of God, voice your affirmation of His word:

You, the Father have given me to Jesus Christ and I have come to Him and will by no means be cast out. (John 6:37)

4. Requests: As you make your requests known to the Lord, include:

- Your "daily bread"
- Christian education institutions
- Your prayer list, the concerns of your heart, and today's activities

5. Closing Prayer: Finally, offer this closing prayer to the Lord:

Now may You, the God of peace, sanctify me completely, and may my whole spirit, soul, and body be preserved blameless at the coming of my Lord Jesus Christ. (1 Thessalonians 5:23)

Memory Verse: If anyone wants to do His will, he shall know concerning the doctrine, whether it is from God or whether I speak on My own authority.

John 7:17
Assurance Theme

MARCH 16

READING

The passage for today centers on the parables of Jesus. Jesus continues teaching the multitudes using parables and then returns to His hometown of Nazareth.

Read Matthew 13.

REFLECTING

Throughout His ministry, there are periods during which Jesus teaches extensively in parables. Often the multitudes do not understand the meaning of the parables, but Jesus is careful to explain them to His disciples.

This is indicative of the pattern of God's ways: to those who are the most receptive to truth, the Lord grants understanding. However, for those who are not receiving the truth, greater understanding is not given. Light received brings greater light; light rejected leaves darkness.

RESPONDING

1. Praise: Offer your praise to the God of light in these words:

O Lord God of Israel, the One who dwells between the cherubim, You are God, You alone, of all the kingdoms of the earth. You have made heaven and earth. (2 Kings 19:15)

Lord God of Israel, there is no God in heaven above or on earth below like You, who keep your covenant and mercy with Your servants who walk before You with all their heart. (1 Kings 8:23)

Take a moment to offer the Lord your personal praise and thanksgiving.

2. Confession: Pray this confession to the Lord as you seek to keep your life free from sin and in fellowship with Him:

I come to You, O Lord, to reason together with You. Though my sins are like scarlet, they shall be as white as snow; though they are red like crimson, they shall be as wool. (Isaiah 1:18)

Confess any personal sins which the Holy Spirit may bring to your mind.

3. Affirmation: As you agree with the will of God, voice your affirmation of His word:

And this is eternal life, that I may know You, the only true God, and Jesus Christ whom You have sent. (John 17:3)

4. Requests: As you make your requests known to the Lord, include:

- Passion for moral excellence
- Needs of personal friends
- Your prayer list, the concerns of your heart, and today's activities

5. Closing Prayer: Finally, offer this closing prayer to the Lord:

Now may the Lord Jesus Christ Himself, and You, my God and Father, who have loved me and given me everlasting consolation and good hope by grace, comfort my heart and establish me in every good word and work. (2 Thessalonians 2:16-17)

Memory Verse: If anyone wants to do His will, he shall know concerning the doctrine, whether it is from God or whether I speak on My own authority.

John 7:17
Assurance Theme

READING

The passage for today centers on the Gadarene demoniac. Jesus casts the demons out of a man from the country of the Gadarenes and later raises a girl from the dead.

Read Mark 5.

REFLECTING

When Jesus takes over a life, He makes a difference. The worse the life, the greater the difference He makes.

When the demoniac from Gad rushes up to Jesus, without flinching, Jesus cleanses him. Later, the man who had run naked among the tombs, howling and cutting himself, is sitting beside Jesus, clothed and in his right mind. The transformation is so startling that it is frightening to those who had known him before.

Jesus wants to make a transformation in our lives also. The transformation is not likely to be as startling as that of the demoniac. But wherever we are in our spiritual journey, the Lord wants to keep changing us ever into the image of Christ.

RESPONDING

1. **Praise:** Using this passage, offer your praise to the Lord who transforms us into the image of Christ:

Give to the Lord, O kindred of the peoples, give to the Lord glory and strength. Give to the Lord the glory due His name; bring an offering, and come before Him. Oh, worship the Lord in the beauty of holiness! (1 Chronicles 16:28-29)

I will praise the Lord according to His righteousness, and will sing praise to the name of the Lord Most High. (Psalm 7:17)

Take a moment to offer the Lord your personal praise and thanksgiving.

2. **Confession:** Pray this confession to the Lord as you seek to keep your life free from sin and in fellowship with Him:

You, even You, are He who blots out my transgressions for Your own sake; and You will not remember my sins. (Isaiah 43:25)

Confess any personal sins which the Holy Spirit may bring to your mind.

3. **Affirmation:** As you agree with the will of God, voice your affirmation of His word:

But You, O God, demonstrate Your own love toward me, in that while I was still a sinner, Christ died for me. (Romans 5:8)

4. **Requests:** As you make your requests known to the Lord, include:

- Wisdom in decision making
- Opportunities to serve the Lord
- Your prayer list, the concerns of your heart, and today's activities

5. **Closing Prayer:** Finally, offer this closing prayer to the Lord:

Now to You, the King eternal, immortal, invisible, to God who alone is wise, be honor and glory forever and ever. Amen. (1 Timothy 1:17)

Memory Verse: If anyone wants to do His will, he shall know concerning the doctrine, whether it is from God or whether I speak on My own authority.

John 7:17
Assurance Theme

MARCH 18

READING

The passage for today centers on the increase in Jesus' miracles. After returning to the area of His hometown of Nazareth, Jesus performs two of His more astounding miracles: feeding the five thousand and walking on water.

Read Mark 6.

REFLECTING

Jesus' miracles are often a double-edged sword. They are a gracious act of kindness for someone in need and, at the same time, intended as a major training experience for His disciples.

We often get discouraged when we fail to pass a test in our lives. We can be encouraged, knowing that others who have gone before us struggled with the same disappointments and difficulties but went on to spiritual maturity.

RESPONDING

1. **Praise:** We praise the Lord because He is faithful to bring us to spiritual maturity:

Tremble before Him, all the earth. The world also is firmly established. It shall not be moved. Let the heavens rejoice, and let the earth be glad; and let them say among the nations, "The Lord reigns."... Oh, give thanks to the Lord, for He is good! For His mercy endures forever.... Blessed be the Lord God of Israel from everlasting to everlasting! (1 Chronicles 16:30-31, 34, 36)

Take a moment to offer the Lord your personal praise and thanksgiving.

2. **Confession:** Pray this confession to the Lord as you seek to keep your life free from sin and in fellowship with Him:

You have blotted out, like a thick cloud, my transgressions, and like a cloud, my sins. I return to You, for You have redeemed me. (Isaiah 44:22)

Confess any personal sins which the Holy Spirit may bring to your mind.

3. **Affirmation:** As you agree with the will of God, voice your affirmation of His word:

You have delivered me from the power of darkness and translated me into the kingdom of the Son of Your love, in whom I have redemption through His blood, the forgiveness of sins. (Colossians 1:13-14)

4. **Requests:** As you make your requests known to the Lord, include:

- Victory over temptation
- The work of missions in North and South America
- Your prayer list, the concerns of your heart, and today's activities

5. **Closing Prayer:** Finally, offer this closing prayer to the Lord:

You who are the blessed and only Potentate, the King of kings and Lord of lords, who alone has immortality, dwelling in unapproachable light, whom no man has seen or can see, to You be honor and everlasting power. Amen. (1 Timothy 6:15-16)

Memory Verse: If anyone wants to do His will, he shall know concerning the doctrine, whether it is from God or whether I speak on My own authority.

John 7:17
Assurance Theme

READING

The passage for today centers on the condemnation of empty tradition. Jesus points out the hypocrisy of observing traditions while at the same time ignoring the teachings of Scripture.

Read Mark 7.

REFLECTING

Even the earnest Christian must guard against hypocrisy. Yet, there is a difference between weakness and rebellion. All of us struggle with weaknesses which we wish we didn't have and with which we wrestle in the grace of God to overcome. Rebellion expresses itself when we could overcome a sin if we wanted—but choose not to or make no attempt to overcome.

The Bible expresses compassion for us in our weaknesses as we cry out to the Lord for greater strength. It pronounces scathing rebuke for hypocrisy and rebellion. We must check our hearts to be certain that our shortcomings are weaknesses and not rebellion or hypocrisy.

RESPONDING

1. Praise: Because the Lord accepts us in spite of our weaknesses, we can praise Him:

Stand up and bless the Lord your God forever and ever! Blessed be Your glorious name, which is exalted above all blessing and praise! You alone are the Lord; You have made heaven, the heaven of heavens, with all their host, the earth and all things on it, the seas and all that is in them, and You preserve them all. The host of heaven worships You. (Nehemiah 9:5-6)

Take a moment to offer the Lord your personal praise and thanksgiving.

2. Confession: Pray this confession to the Lord as you seek to keep your life free from sin and in fellowship with Him:

Surely You have borne my griefs and carried my sorrows; yet I esteemed You stricken, smitten by God, and afflicted. But You were wounded for my transgressions, You were bruised for my iniquities; the chastisement for my peace was upon You, and by Your stripes I am healed. (Isaiah 53:4-5)

Confess any personal sins which the Holy Spirit may bring to your mind.

3. Affirmation: As you agree with the will of God, voice your affirmation of His word:

Likewise I also must reckon myself to be dead indeed to sin, but alive to You, O God, in Christ Jesus my Lord. (Romans 6:11)

4. Requests: As you make your requests known to the Lord, include:

- Love for your family
- Revival among Christians in America
- Your prayer list, the concerns of your heart, and today's activities

5. Closing Prayer: Finally, offer this closing prayer to the Lord:

Make me complete in every good work to do Your will, working in me what is well pleasing in Your sight, through Jesus Christ, to whom be glory forever and ever. Amen. (Hebrews 13:20-21)

Memory Verse: Therefore, if anyone is in Christ, he is a new creation; old things have passed away; behold, all things have become new.
2 Corinthians 5:17
Spiritual Life Theme

MARCH 20

READING

The passage for today centers on the feeding of the four thousand. Jesus feeds the four thousand as a teaching tool for instructing His disciples concerning His deity, which Peter later acknowledges.

Read Mark 8.

REFLECTING

To get a feel for Jesus' strategy in developing His disciples, it is instructive to lift the essential thread of thought from this incident. After feeding the four thousand, it is obvious that the disciples do not understand the significance of the event. Then, some days later, Jesus is along with the Twelve, and He asks them, "Who do you think I am?" Peter replies, "You are the Christ, the Son of the living God." Finally, progress!

RESPONDING

1. Praise: Offer your praise with these words to the Lord who is faithful to us when we are weak:

O Lord, our Lord,
How excellent is Your name
*   in all the earth.*
When I consider Your heavens, the
*   work of Your fingers . . .*
What is man that You are mindful of
*   him,*
*   and the son of man*
*   that You visit him? . . .*
O Lord, our Lord,
*   how excellent is Your name in all*
*   the earth!*
(Psalm 8:1, 3, 4, 9)

Take a moment to offer the Lord your personal praise and thanksgiving.

2. Confession: Pray this confession to the Lord as you seek to keep your life free from sin and in fellowship with Him:

Like a sheep, I have gone astray; I have
turned to my own way; and You, O Lord,
have laid on Jesus Christ all my iniquity.
(Isaiah 53:6)

Confess any personal sins which the Holy Spirit may bring to your mind.

3. Affirmation: As you agree with the will of God, voice your affirmation of His word:

I shall know the truth, and the truth shall
make me free. (John 8:32)

4. Requests: As you make your requests known to the Lord, include:

- Faithfulness with your treasures
- The Great Commission
- Your prayer list, the concerns of your heart, and today's activities

5. Closing Prayer: Finally, offer this closing prayer to the Lord:

May You, the God of grace, who called me
to Your eternal glory by Christ Jesus, after I
have suffered a while, perfect, establish,
strengthen, and settle me. To You be the glory
and the dominion forever and ever. Amen. (1
Peter 5:10-11)

Memory Verse: Therefore, if anyone is in Christ, he is a new creation; old things have passed away; behold, all things have become new.
2 Corinthians 5:17
Spiritual Life Theme

MARCH 21

READING

The passage for today centers on the Transfiguration. As Jesus intensifies the preparation of His disciples for His death, He takes Peter, James, and John to a mountain where He is transfigured as a validation of His deity and Messiahship.

Read Mark 9.

REFLECTING

The Transfiguration gives us an exciting glimpse into our resurrection life. From it, we may learn several things. Our physical bodies may be startlingly brilliant and beautiful, as we witness the amazing appearance of Jesus, Moses, and Elijah. We apparently will not be subject to the physical limitations of nature, since Moses and Elijah appeared and disappeared. We may know each other automatically since the disciples seemed to recognize Moses and Elijah without instruction. We will undoubtedly have an intense desire to be with and stay with the Lord as seen in Peter's question. What a joy awaits us in the kingdom and for eternity.

RESPONDING

1. Praise: Praise your God in these words:

You are my praise and You are my God, who has done these great and awesome things for me which my eyes have seen. (Deuteronomy 10:21)

*You are the rock!
Your work is perfect,
For all Your ways are just;
A God of faithfulness
and without injustice,
Righteous and upright are You.
(Deuteronomy 32:4)*

*The Lord lives,
and blessed be my rock;
And exalted be the God
of my salvation.
(2 Samuel 22:47)*

Pause for personal praise and thanksgiving.

2. Confession: As you seek to keep your life free from sin, pray this confession to the Lord:

There is not a just man on earth who does good and does not sin. (Ecclesiastes 7:20)

In returning and rest I shall be saved; in quietness and confidence shall be my strength. (Isaiah 30:15)

Confess any personal sins which the Holy Spirit may bring to your mind.

3. Affirmation: As you agree with the will of God, voice your affirmation of His word:

He made Him who knew no sin to be sin for me, that I might become the righteousness of God in Him. (2 Corinthians 5:21)

4. Requests: As you make your requests known to the Lord, include:

- Spiritual insight
- Campus ministries
- Your prayer list, the concerns of your heart, and today's activities

5. Closing Prayer: Finally, offer this closing prayer to the Lord:

May I grow in the grace and knowledge of our Lord and Savior Jesus Christ. To Him be the glory both now and forever. Amen. (2 Peter 3:18)

Memory Verse: Therefore, if anyone is in Christ, he is a new creation; old things have passed away; behold, all things have become new.
2 Corinthians 5:17
Spiritual Life Theme

MARCH 22

READING

The passage for today centers on the Good Samaritan. After sending His followers out to minister in the surrounding villages, Jesus tells the parable of the Good Samaritan, after which He spends the evening in the home of Mary and Martha.

Read Luke 10.

REFLECTING

The harsh reality of life is that we cannot help everyone in need. How do we decide whom to help? Are we responsible for every need we hear about? Christ said, "The poor you will always have with you" (Matthew 26:11). Certainly in Christ is found the balance of helping the poor with kindness and living with discernment as to whom to help. From the parable of the Good Samaritan, we can learn several things which help us evaluate when we should help: (1) whenever it is someone who comes across your path in the normal living of your life; (2) whenever someone has a legitimate need, not of his own making; (3) when he cannot help himself; (4) when you have the ability to meet the need, then (5) you are obligated to help.

RESPONDING

1. **Praise:** The Lord is worthy to receive my praise because of all that He has done for me.

Give to the Lord, O kindred of the peoples, give to the Lord glory and strength. Give to the Lord the glory due His name; bring an offering, and come before Him. Oh, worship the Lord in the beauty of holiness! (1 Chronicles 16:28-29)

I will praise the Lord according to His righteousness, and will sing praise to the name of the Lord Most High. (Psalm 7:17)

Take a moment to offer the Lord your personal praise and thanksgiving.

2. **Confession:** Pray this confession to the Lord as you seek to keep your life free from sin and in fellowship with Him:

O Lord, You blot out my transgressions for Your own sake; and You will not remember my sins. (Isaiah 43:25)

Confess any personal sins which the Holy Spirit may bring to your mind.

3. **Affirmation:** As you agree with the will of God, voice your affirmation of His word:

For to me, to live is Christ, and to die is gain. (Philippians 1:21)

4. **Requests:** As you make your requests known to the Lord, include:

- Desire to be like Christ
- Needs in inner cities
- Your prayer list, the concerns of your heart, and today's activities

5. **Closing Prayer:** Finally, offer this closing prayer to the Lord:

Blessing and honor and glory and power be to You who sit on the throne, and to You, Lord, forever and ever! (Revelation 5:13)

Memory Verse: Therefore, if anyone is in Christ, he is a new creation; old things have passed away; behold, all things have become new.

2 Corinthians 5:17
Spiritual Life Theme

READING

The passage for today centers on the parables of God's love. Jesus tells three parables to demonstrate the quality and quantity of God's love for sinners.

Read Luke 15.

REFLECTING

God earnestly longs for the lost to be saved. In the parable of the lost sheep, we see a God who is willing to leave the multitudes to seek out just one which is lost. In the parable of the lost coin, we see a God who will move heaven and earth to find a prized possession. In the parable of the prodigal son, we see a God who rejoices with unbounding joy when a lost one comes home.

One of the challenges of the Christian life is to keep that which we don't know from clouding that which we do. God loves the sinner, and on that we can rest.

RESPONDING

1. Praise: Offer to the Lord your praise for His great love for you:

I will praise You, O Lord, with my whole heart; I will tell of all Your marvelous works. I will be glad and rejoice in You; I will sing praise to Your name, O Most High. . . . The Lord also will be a refuge for the oppressed, a refuge in times of trouble. And those who know Your name will put their trust in You; for You, Lord, have not forsaken those who seek You. (Psalm 9:1-2, 9-10)

Take a moment to offer the Lord your personal praise and thanksgiving.

2. Confession: Pray this confession to the Lord as you seek to keep your life free from sin and in fellowship with Him:

For a mere moment You have forsaken me, but with great mercies You will gather me. With a little wrath You hid Your face from me for a moment; but with everlasting kindness You will have mercy on me, O Lord, my Redeemer. (Isaiah 54:7-8)

Confess any personal sins which the Holy Spirit may bring to your mind.

3. Affirmation: As you agree with the will of God, voice your affirmation of His word:

There is one God and one Mediator between You and me, the Man Christ Jesus, who gave Himself a ransom for me, to be testified in due time. (1 Timothy 2:5-6)

4. Requests: As you make your requests known to the Lord, include:

- Personal witness for Christ
- Local churches around the nation
- Your prayer list, the concerns of your heart, and today's activities

5. Closing Prayer: Finally, offer this closing prayer to the Lord:

Amen! Blessing and glory and wisdom, thanksgiving and honor and power and might, be to You, God, forever and ever. Amen. (Revelation 7:12)

Memory Verse: Therefore, if anyone is in Christ, he is a new creation; old things have passed away; behold, all things have become new.

2 Corinthians 5:17
Spiritual Life Theme

MARCH 24

READING

The passage for today centers on the parables concerning wealth. To instruct on the proper perspective on wealth, Jesus tells the parables of the unrighteous steward and of the rich man and Lazarus.

Read Luke 16.

REFLECTING

One of the great challenges of the Christian life is to let go of the temporal and grab hold of the eternal. And the strongest hold the temporal usually has on us is gained by money.

Jesus speaks a number of times about money and the Christian perspective on it. His teachings can be generally summed up by saying that we ought not to love or trust money. While we need the things money buys for us, we must be careful always to trust God who supplies the money—rather than to trust the money itself.

It is always unpleasant when we don't have enough money, but jobs don't take care of us—God does. Money doesn't meet our needs— God does. Trust Him, not money.

RESPONDING

1. Praise: Because the Lord has promised to care for our needs, offer Him these words of praise:

I will love You, O Lord, my strength. The Lord is my rock and my fortress and my deliverer; my God, my strength, in whom I will trust; my shield and the horn of my salvation, my stronghold. I will call upon the Lord, who is worthy to be praised; so shall I be saved from my enemies. . . . The Lord lives! Blessed be my rock! Let the God of my salvation be exalted. (Psalm 18:1-3, 46)

Take a moment to offer the Lord your personal praise and thanksgiving.

2. Confession: Pray this confession to the Lord as you seek to keep your life free from sin and in fellowship with Him:

I will forsake my wicked way, and my unrighteous thoughts; let me return to You, O Lord, and You will have mercy on me; and to You, my God, for You will abundantly pardon. (Isaiah 55:7)

Confess any personal sins which the Holy Spirit may bring to your mind.

3. Affirmation: As you agree with the will of God, voice your affirmation of His word:

Without faith it is impossible for me to please You, for when I come to You, I must believe that You are, and that You reward me if I diligently seek You. (Hebrews 11:6)

4. Requests: As you make your requests known to the Lord, include:

- An eternal perspective
- Needs of work or school mates
- Your prayer list, the concerns of your heart, and today's activities

5. Closing Prayer: Finally, offer this closing prayer to the Lord:

I will wait on You, the Lord; I will be of good courage, and You shall strengthen my heart; I will wait on You! (Psalm 27:14)

Memory Verse: Therefore, if anyone is in Christ, he is a new creation; old things have passed away; behold, all things have become new.
2 Corinthians 5:17
Spiritual Life Theme

READING

The passage for today centers on the foretelling of the Second Coming. In the midst of a general section of instruction, Jesus describes circumstances surrounding His second coming.

Read Luke 17.

REFLECTING

Gratitude is such a becoming characteristic. It is beautiful to witness and beautiful to experience. When we give a gift that is not appreciated, it diminishes our enjoyment. When we give a gift that is deeply appreciated, it doubles the enjoyment for us.

It is no different for the Lord. He appreciates gratitude. In Luke 17, ten lepers are healed, but only one returns to express gratitude. He is commended, but the others are indirectly chastened.

Gratitude to the Lord can be cultivated. It is a matter of envisioning the consequences of not having the Lord's grace in our lives. The consequences are indeed terrible. Our gratitude, then, can be great. Nurture an attitude of gratitude.

RESPONDING

1. Praise: Express your gratitude to the Lord by offering Him these words of praise:

I will bless the Lord at all times; His praise shall continually be in my mouth. My soul shall make its boast in the Lord; the humble shall hear of it and be glad. Oh, magnify the Lord with me, and let us exalt His name together. . . . Oh, taste and see that the Lord is good; blessed is the man who trusts in Him! (Psalm 34:1-3, 8)

Take a moment to offer the Lord your personal praise and thanksgiving.

2. Confession: Pray this confession to the Lord as you seek to keep your life free from sin and in fellowship with Him:

You will again have compassion on me, and will subdue my iniquities. You will cast all my sins into the depths of the sea. (Micah 7:19)

Confess any personal sins which the Holy Spirit may bring to your mind.

3. Affirmation: As you agree with the will of God, voice your affirmation of His word:

For the wages of sin is death, but the gift You have given, O God, is eternal life in Christ Jesus my Lord. (Romans 6:23)

4. Requests: As you make your requests known to the Lord, include:

- Personal discipline
- Christians worldwide who are persecuted for their faith
- Your prayer list, the concerns of your heart, and today's activities

5. Closing Prayer: Finally, offer this closing prayer to the Lord:

Show me the path of life; in Your presence is fullness of joy; at Your right hand are pleasures forevermore. (Psalm 16:11)

Memory Verse: Therefore, if anyone is in Christ, he is a new creation; old things have passed away; behold, all things have become new.

2 Corinthians 5:17
Spiritual Life Theme

READING

The passage for today centers on Jesus' Perean teachings. As Jesus intensifies the preparation of His disciples in view of His approaching departure from earth, He goes to Perea and teaches His disciples on a variety of subjects.

Read Mark 10.

REFLECTING

If there is anything between you and the Lord, He will pinpoint it and ask you to give it up. Whether you are a Christian or whether you are still in the process of making that decision, if you are considering a deeper relationship with the Lord, He will ask you for a total commitment.

That does not mean you cannot be committed to other things. It just means that He wants nothing to be higher on your commitment scale than He is. A husband must be committed to his wife and children. A professional must be committed to his job. An artist must be committed to his craft. But all must be committed to the Lord first.

RESPONDING

1. Praise: As an expression of your commitment to the Lord, offer Him these words of praise:

We have thought, O God, on Your lovingkindness, in the midst of Your temple. According to Your name, O God, so is Your praise to the ends of the earth; Your right hand is full of righteousness. (Psalm 48:9-10)

Take a moment to offer the Lord your personal praise and thanksgiving.

2. Confession: Pray this confession to the Lord as you seek to keep your life free from sin and in fellowship with Him:

Lord, be merciful to me; heal my soul, for I have sinned against You. . . . O Lord, be merciful to me, and raise me up. . . . Blessed be You, O Lord God of Israel, from everlasting to everlasting! Amen and Amen. (Psalm 41:10)

Confess any personal sins which the Holy Spirit may bring to your mind.

3. Affirmation: As you agree with the will of God, voice your affirmation of His word:

Every good gift and every perfect gift is from above, and comes down from You, the Father of lights; with You there is no variation or shadow of turning. (James 1:17)

4. Requests: As you make your requests known to the Lord, include:

- Love for the Lord
- The work of missions in the Middle East, Australia, and the Islands
- Your prayer list, the concerns of your heart, and today's activities

5. Closing Prayer: Finally, offer this closing prayer to the Lord:

Save Your people, and bless Your inheritance; shepherd us also, and bear us up forever. (Psalm 28:9)

Memory Verse: Abide in Me, and I in you. As the branch cannot bear fruit of itself, unless it abides in the vine, neither can you, unless you abide in Me.

John 15:4
Spiritual Life Theme

READING

The passage for today centers on the Triumphal Entry. Jesus rides into Jerusalem on a donkey to the jubilation of the crowd and cleanses the temple of the moneychangers.

Read Mark 11.

REFLECTING

When Jesus begins riding into the city of Jerusalem on a burro, why does the crowd rush out to greet Him? The answer is found in Jewish culture and history. In Old Testament times, one of the ways a king was inaugurated was to get on a burro and have a large retinue of people walk along behind him shouting, "Long live the King!"

The crowd wants to make Jesus king. That He was crucified shortly afterward indicates they were looking only for a national leader rather than a personal Savior. How do you see Him?

RESPONDING

1. Praise: Express your personal praise to the Lord in these words:

Be exalted, O God, above the heavens; let Your glory be above all the earth. . . . I will praise You, O Lord, among the peoples; I will sing to You among the nations. For Your mercy reaches unto the heavens, and Your truth unto the clouds. Be exalted, O God, above the heavens; let Your glory be above all the earth. (Psalm 57:5, 9-11)

Take a moment to offer the Lord your personal praise and thanksgiving.

2. Confession: Pray this confession to the Lord as you seek to keep your life free from sin and in fellowship with Him:

You will cleanse me from all my iniquity by which I have sinned against You, and You will pardon all my iniquities by which I have sinned and by which I have transgressed against You. (Jeremiah 33:8)

Confess any personal sins which the Holy Spirit may bring to your mind.

3. Affirmation: As you agree with the will of God, voice your affirmation of His word:

You, Lord Jesus, are the image of the invisible God, the firstborn over all creation. For by You all things were created that are in heaven and that are on earth, visible and invisible, whether thrones or dominions or principalities or powers. All things were created through You and for You. And You are before all things, and in You all things consist. And You are the head of the body, the Church; the beginning, the firstborn from the dead, that in all things You may have the preeminence. (Colossians 1:15-18)

4. Requests: As you make your requests known to the Lord, include:

- Faithfulness in sharing Christ
- The Lord's work in national and world affairs
- Your prayer list, the concerns of your heart, and today's activities

5. Closing Prayer: Finally, offer this closing prayer to the Lord:

You, the Lord, will command Your lovingkindness in the daytime, and in the night Your song shall be with me—a prayer to You, the God of my life. (Psalm 42:8)

Memory Verse: Abide in Me, and I in you. As the branch cannot bear fruit of itself, unless it abides in the vine, neither can you, unless you abide in Me.

John 15:4
Spiritual Life Theme

MARCH 28

READING

The passage for today centers on Jesus' conflict with religious leaders. The Pharisees and Sadducees attempt to discredit Jesus through treacherous questions, which Jesus answers without incident.

Read Mark 12.

REFLECTING

In today's passage, we see one of the most marvelous teachings in the New Testament. An attorney, intrigued by the quality of the answers Jesus gives to the Pharisees who are trying to discredit Him, asks Jesus what the greatest commandment is. He only asks for one; Jesus gives him two. The Lord says, "You shall love the Lord your God with all your heart . . . and your neighbor as yourself. There are no other commandments greater than these" (Mark 12:30-31). Although these two statements had been made previously in the Old Testament (Deuteronomy 6:4 and Leviticus 19:18), Jesus was the first one to link them together as the total will of God. The Christian life can be very complex, but at its heart, it is very simple: love God and others.

RESPONDING

1. Praise: Offer your praise to the Lord in these passages as you fellowship with Him:

I will extol You, my God, O King; and I will bless Your name forever and ever. Every day I will bless You, and I will praise Your name forever and ever. Great is the Lord, and greatly to be praised; and His greatness is unsearchable. One generation shall praise Your works to another, and shall declare Your mighty acts. I will meditate on the glorious splendor of Your majesty, and on Your wondrous works. (Psalm 145:1-5)

Take a moment to offer the Lord your personal praise and thanksgiving.

2. Confession: Pray this confession to the Lord as you seek to keep your life free from sin and in fellowship with Him:

I am blessed because my transgression is forgiven, and my sin is covered. I am blessed because You do not impute iniquity to me, and in my spirit there is no guile. (Psalm 32:1-2)

Confess any personal sins which the Holy Spirit may bring to your mind.

3. Affirmation: As you agree with the will of God, voice your affirmation of His word:

If I love You, I will keep Your commandments. (John 14:15)

4. Requests: As you make your requests known to the Lord, include:

- Compassion for others
- Missions in America
- Your prayer list, the concerns of your heart, and today's activities

5. Closing Prayer: Finally, offer this closing prayer to the Lord:

Blessed are You, the Lord, forevermore! Amen and amen. (Psalm 89:52)

Memory Verse: Abide in Me, and I in you. As the branch cannot bear fruit of itself, unless it abides in the vine, neither can you, unless you abide in Me.

John 15:4
Spiritual Life Theme

READING

The passage for today centers on things to come. In response to questions by Peter, James, and John, Jesus chronicles some of the future events surrounding His second coming.

Read Mark 13.

REFLECTING

The second coming of Jesus to reign is something the world and some Christians find difficult to take seriously. And, let's face it, there are so many disreputable people cloaked in religious garb, who fly the Second Coming as their only flag, that the accurate teaching becomes guilty by association. However, the Bible places great emphasis on the teaching, and it is something Christians ought to take seriously. Its reality and implications are scattered throughout the New Testament. Twice in chapter 13 of Mark, Jesus warns, "Be on the alert!" Properly understood, it should help us live righteously as we wait for that day.

RESPONDING

1. Praise: As you continue your time with the Lord, offer Him your praise through His Word.

It is good to give thanks to the Lord, and to sing praises to Your name, O Most High; to declare Your lovingkindness in the morning, and Your faithfulness every night . . . to declare that the Lord is upright; He is my rock, and there is no unrighteousness in Him. (Psalm 92:1-2, 15)

Take a moment to offer the Lord your personal praise and thanksgiving.

2. Confession: Pray this confession to the Lord as you seek to keep your life free from sin and in fellowship with Him:

I return to You, O Lord my God, for I have stumbled because of my iniquity; I take words with me, and return to You, Lord. I say to You, "Take away all iniquity; receive me graciously, for I will offer the sacrifices of my lips." (Hosea 14:1-2)

Confess any personal sins which the Holy Spirit may bring to your mind.

3. Affirmation: As you agree with the will of God, voice your affirmation of His word:

And this is eternal life, that I may know You, the only true God, and Jesus Christ whom You have sent. (John 17:3)

4. Requests: As you make your requests known to the Lord, include:

- Personal spiritual growth
- Military ministries
- Your prayer list, the concerns of your heart, and today's activities

5. Closing Prayer: Finally, offer this closing prayer to the Lord:

Glory to You in the highest, and on earth peace, good will toward men! (Luke 2:14)

Memory Verse: Abide in Me, and I in you. As the branch cannot bear fruit of itself, unless it abides in the vine, neither can you, unless you abide in Me.

John 15:4
Spiritual Life Theme

MARCH 30

READING

The passage for today centers on the Olivet Discourse. Matthew gives an expanded account of the events of Mark 13 in which Jesus urges His people to be prepared for His second coming.

Read Matthew 24.

REFLECTING

The events of chapters 24 and 25 of Matthew offer, at the same time, some of the most comforting and some of the most terrifying verses in the Bible because they detail some of the judgments to fall on mankind at the end of history. Yet they are comforting in that the events do not catch God by surprise.

These events also give us guidance. If someone comes along and says, "I am the Christ," we do not have to be confused. We know he is a false teacher, for Jesus will come boldly, in the twinkling of an eye, and there will be no time for such statements. The God of power is also the God of the future, and we can rest in His sovereign care as we trust in Him.

RESPONDING

1. Praise: As you rest in God's sovereignty, offer Him these words of praise as an expression of your trust:

Because Your lovingkindness is better than life, my lips shall praise You; thus I will bless You while I live; I will lift up my hands in Your name. My soul shall be satisfied as with marrow and fatness, and my mouth shall praise You with joyful lips. . . . Because You have been my help, therefore in the shadow of Your wings I will rejoice. (Psalm 63:3-5, 7)

Take a moment to offer the Lord your personal praise and thanksgiving.

2. Confession: Pray this confession to the Lord as you seek to keep your life free from sin and in fellowship with Him:

O Lord, I know my way is not in myself; it is not in me, who walks, to direct my own steps. O Lord, correct me, but with justice; not in Your anger, lest You bring me to nothing. (Jeremiah 10:23-24)

Confess any personal sins which the Holy Spirit may bring to your mind.

3. Affirmation: As you agree with the will of God, voice your affirmation of His word:

Jesus Christ, You are the same yesterday, today, and forever. (Hebrews 13:8)

4. Requests: As you make your requests known to the Lord, include:

- Fruit of the Spirit in your life
- The ministry of Christian literature
- Your prayer list, the concerns of your heart, and today's activities

5. Closing Prayer: Finally, offer this closing prayer to the Lord:

Grace, mercy, and peace from You, the Father, and the Lord Jesus Christ our Savior. (Titus 1:4)

Memory Verse: Abide in Me, and I in you. As the branch cannot bear fruit of itself, unless it abides in the vine, neither can you, unless you abide in Me.

John 15:4
Spiritual Life Theme

READING

The passage for today centers on the Olivet Discourse. Jesus continues His teachings concerning His Second Coming, urging faithfulness, watchfulness, and sacrifice on the part of His people.

Read Matthew 25.

REFLECTING

Christians cannot compartmentalize their lives into the secular and the sacred. All truth is God's truth, and anything done for Him—whether "religious" or not—is sacred.

Jesus equates loving your fellow man with loving Him. He equates serving those in need with serving Him. He equates caring for the suffering as caring for Him.

But we must think very carefully at this point. You can love your fellow man without loving Christ—but you cannot love Christ without loving your fellow man. Whether you are worshiping the Lord in communion or cleansing the feet of a bum on skid row, it is sacred and holy work—if it is done out of love for the Lord.

RESPONDING

1. Praise: The praise of the Lord's children is a sacred and holy work:

Make a joyful shout to God, all the earth! Sing out the honor of His name; make His praise glorious. Say to God, "How awesome are Your works! Through the greatness of Your power Your enemies shall submit themselves to You. All the earth shall worship You and sing praises to You; they shall sing praises to Your name." (Psalm 66:1-4)

Take a moment to offer the Lord your personal praise and thanksgiving.

2. Confession: Pray this confession to the Lord as you seek to keep your life free from sin and in fellowship with Him:

My heart is deceitful above all things, and desperately wicked; who can know it? You, O Lord, search the heart, You test the mind, even to give me according to my ways and according to the fruit of my doings. . . . Heal me, O Lord, and I shall be healed; save me, and I shall be saved, for You are my praise. (Jeremiah 17:9-10, 14)

Confess any personal sins which the Holy Spirit may bring to your mind.

3. Affirmation: As you agree with the will of God, voice your affirmation of His word:

Behold, You stand at the door and knock. If I hear Your voice and open the door, You will come in to me and dine with me, and I with You. (Revelation 3:20)

4. Requests: As you make your requests known to the Lord, include:

- Boldness in living for Christ
- God's blessing on America
- Your prayer list, the concerns of your heart, and today's activities

5. Closing Prayer: Finally, offer this closing prayer to the Lord:

Be glad in the Lord and rejoice, you righteous; and shout for joy, all you upright in heart! (Psalm 32:11)

Memory Verse: Abide in Me, and I in you. As the branch cannot bear fruit of itself, unless it abides in the vine, neither can you, unless you abide in Me.

John 15:4
Spiritual Life Theme

READING

The passage for today centers on the final events of Jesus' life. Jesus spends His last two days in intimate communion with His closest friends and is then arrested.

Read Mark 14.

REFLECTING

Prayer is one of the true mysteries in the Bible. It is inevitable that as we grow in our prayer life we will struggle with inadequate understanding of how to pray. At times such as these, we must concentrate on what we do know and understand rather than what we do not know and understand. The example of Jesus praying in the Garden of Gethsemane helps us with what we can know and understand about prayer. First, we can know that prayer does not automatically eliminate emotional struggling.

A second thing we can learn is that prayer can make us spiritually stronger and keep us from temptation. In all the accounts of His prayer, the Lord Jesus Christ says to His disciples, "Keep watching, and praying, that you may not come into temptation" (Mark 14:38).

RESPONDING

1. **Praise:** As you continue your time with the Lord, offer to Him this passage of praise:

Let us come before His presence with thanksgiving; let us shout joyfully to Him with psalms. For the Lord is the great God, and the great King above all gods. (Psalm 95:2-3)

Now express any additional thoughts you may have of thanks or praise.

2. **Confession:** Pray this confession to the Lord as you seek to keep your life free from sin:

If I say that I have no sin, I deceive myself, and the truth is not in me. If I confess my sins, You, O Lord, are faithful and just to forgive me of my sins and to cleanse me from all unrighteousness. (1 John 1:8-9)

Confess any personal sins which the Holy Spirit brings to your mind.

3. **Affirmation:** Now pray this affirmation to the Lord as you agree with and submit yourself to the will of God:

All Scripture is given by Your inspiration, O God, and is profitable for doctrine, for reproof, for correction, for instruction in righteousness, that the man of God may be complete, thoroughly equipped for every good work. (2 Timothy 3:16-17)

4. **Requests:** As you make your requests known to the Lord, include:

- Health and strength to serve God
- God's will to be done on earth
- Your prayer list, the concerns of your heart, and today's activities

5. **Closing Prayer:** Finally, offer this closing prayer to the Lord:

Now to You who are able to keep me from stumbling, and to present me faultless before the presence of Your glory with exceeding joy, to You, my God and Savior, who alone are wise, be glory and majesty, dominion and power, both now and forever. Amen. (Jude 24-25)

Memory Verse: Abide in Me, and I in you. As the branch cannot bear fruit of itself, unless it abides in the vine, neither can you, unless you abide in Me.

John 15:4
Spiritual Life Theme

APRIL 2

READING

The passage for today centers on the crucifixion and burial of Jesus. After the mockery of a trial before Pilate, Jesus is crucified, after which His friend, Joseph of Arimathea, buries Him in Joseph's own tomb.

Read Mark 15.

REFLECTING

Most of us have a highly developed sense of justice. We want things to be fair, and we are incensed and indignant when they aren't. From simple things, like people cutting in line ahead of us, to major things, like prejudice and bigotry, we become inflamed when we see or experience injustice. With that in mind, mentally review what happens to Jesus. He is totally righteous, without sin. Religious bigots manufacture charges against Him, take Him to a legal jellyfish who doesn't have the courage to execute justice, and release Him to be beaten, mocked, and crucified. Doesn't that inflame your sense of justice? He has the power to obliterate those who harmed Him, yet he willingly endures it *for our sakes*. Remember, Jesus does not ask us to suffer anything for Him that He was not willing to suffer for us.

RESPONDING

1. Praise: Thank the Lord and praise Him for the "great and awesome" things He has done in offering you salvation:

Let my mouth be filled with Your praise and with Your glory all the day. . . . I will hope continually, and will praise You yet more and more. My mouth shall tell of Your righteousness and Your salvation all the day, for I do not know their limits. I will go in the strength of the Lord God; I will make mention of Your righteousness, of Yours only. O God, You have taught me from my youth; and to this day I declare Your wondrous works. (Psalm 71:8, 14-17)

Take a moment to offer the Lord your personal praise and thanksgiving.

2. Confession: Pray this confession to the Lord as you seek to keep your life free from sin and in fellowship with Him:

Forgive me, Lord, when I am unmindful of You, the Rock who begot me, and when I forget you, the God who fathered me. (Deuteronomy 32:18)

Confess any personal sins which the Holy Spirit may bring to your mind.

3. Affirmation: As you agree with the will of God, voice your affirmation of His word:

You, O Lord, will instruct me and teach me in the way I should go; You will guide me with Your eye. (Psalm 32:8)

4. Requests: As you make your requests known to the Lord, include:

- Sensitivity to sin
- The ministry of your local church
- Your prayer list, the concerns of your heart, and today's activities

5. Closing Prayer: Finally, offer this closing prayer to the Lord:

Let the words of my mouth and the meditation of my heart be acceptable in Your sight, O Lord, my strength and my redeemer. (Psalm 19:14)

Memory Verse: I am the vine, you are the branches. He who abides in Me, and I in him, bears much fruit; for without Me you can do nothing.
John 15:5
Spiritual Life Theme

READING

The passage for today centers on the resurrection of Jesus. Sunday morning when Mary and Mary Magdalene go to the tomb to anoint Jesus' body, an angel announces to them that Jesus has risen from the dead.

Read Mark 16.

REFLECTING

It is a momentous morning as Mary and Mary Magdalene walk to the tomb of Joseph of Arimathea, intent on the purpose of anointing the body of Jesus, but not knowing how they will get into the tomb. They say to one another, "Who will roll away the stone for us?" Indeed, the stone probably weighs tons! Miracle number one, the stone has been rolled away. Miracle number two, an angel is sitting in the tomb, to explain to them what has happened. Miracle number three, Jesus is gone. He has risen. They have two responses. They are amazed! To say the least! And they report to the disciples all that they have seen. They expect to deal with death. They end up in the middle of more life than they can imagine. That is the way of God. He brings life from death.

RESPONDING

1. Praise: Give your praise to the Lord for offering you the gift of eternal life in the place of death:

It is good to give thanks to the Lord, and to sing praises to Your name, O Most High; to declare Your lovingkindness in the morning, and Your faithfulness every night. . . . For You, Lord, have made me glad through Your work; I will triumph in the works of Your hands. . . . To declare that the Lord is

upright; He is my rock, and there is no unrighteousness in Him. (Psalm 92:1-2, 4, 15)

Take a moment to offer the Lord your personal praise and thanksgiving.

2. Confession: Pray this confession to the Lord as you seek to keep your life free from sin and in fellowship with Him:

I have stumbled because of my iniquity; take away all iniquity; receive me graciously, for I will offer the sacrifices of my lips. (Hosea 14:1-2)

Confess any personal sins which the Holy Spirit may bring to your mind.

3. Affirmation: As you agree with the will of God, voice your affirmation of His word:

If I overcome, You, Lord Jesus, will grant to me to sit with You on Your throne, as You overcame and sat down with Your Father on His throne. (Revelation 3:21)

4. Requests: As you make your requests known to the Lord, include:

- Wisdom for living life
- Needs of your immediate family
- Your prayer list, the concerns of your heart, and today's activities

5. Closing Prayer: Finally, offer this closing prayer to the Lord:

Surely goodness and mercy shall follow me all the days of my life, and I will dwell in the house of the Lord forever. (Psalm 23:6)

Memory Verse: I am the vine, you are the branches. He who abides in Me, and I in him, bears much fruit; for without Me you can do nothing.
John 15:5
Spiritual Life Theme

APRIL 4

READING

The passage for today centers on the betrayal and arrest of Jesus. Knowing that the religious leaders are exceedingly inflamed because of Jesus' life and ministry, Judas bargains with them and betrays Jesus for thirty pieces of silver.

Read Matthew 26.

REFLECTING

Peter is living and reassuring proof that "grace is greater than all our sin." We struggle, at one time or another, with things in our lives which ought to be corrected—but aren't. We fear that our name brings a stench to the nostrils of God because we have failed Him so often. But Peter begins to curse and swear and deny that He has ever known Jesus. What a colossal sin! Yet just a matter of days later (in John 21), Peter is eating with the Lord in perfect fellowship and harmony. What a wonderful assurance we have when we see Jesus take the initiative to restore their fellowship. For the Christian, there is no sin so great that God cannot and will not forgive. "There is therefore now no condemnation for those who are in Christ Jesus" (Romans 8:1).

RESPONDING

1. Praise: In the eyes of God, it is wisdom to praise Him for who He is and what He has done for us.

Praise the Lord! Praise God in His sanctuary; praise Him in His mighty firmament! Praise Him for His mighty acts; praise Him according to His excellent greatness! Praise Him with the sound of the trumpet; praise Him with the lute and harp! . . . Let everything that has breath praise the Lord. Praise the Lord! (Psalm 150:1-3, 6)

Take a moment to offer the Lord your personal praise and thanksgiving.

2. Confession: Pray this confession to the Lord as you seek to keep your life free from sin and in fellowship with Him:

Purge me with hyssop, and I shall be clean; wash me, and I shall be whiter than snow. . . . Hide Your face from my sins, and blot out all my iniquities. (Psalm 51:7, 9)

Confess any personal sins which the Holy Spirit may bring to your mind.

3. Affirmation: As you agree with the will of God, voice your affirmation of His word:

You, Lord Jesus, are the Way, the Truth, and the Life. I cannot come to the Father except through You. (John 14:6)

4. Requests: As you make your requests known to the Lord, include:

- Insight into Scripture
- The hungry around the world
- Your prayer list, the concerns of your heart, and today's activities

5. Closing Prayer: Finally, offer this closing prayer to the Lord:

We will be of good courage, and You shall strengthen our hearts, all we who hope in the Lord. (Psalm 31:24)

Memory Verse: I am the vine, you are the branches. He who abides in Me, and I in him, bears much fruit; for without Me you can do nothing.
John 15:5
Spiritual Life Theme

APRIL 5

READING

The passage for today centers on Jesus' trial and crucifixion. Regardless of Judas' remorse over his betrayal of Jesus, Pilate tries Jesus and then hands Him over to be crucified and buried.

Read Matthew 27.

REFLECTING

Proverbs 20:17 says, "Stolen bread is sweet to a man, but afterward his mouth will be filled with gravel." If ever a man is an illustration of that truth, Judas is. Some mysterious passion burns in his breast to betray Jesus. Whether it is political ambition or mere lust for money, we do not know. But later, as he experiences the emptiness of his task, his remorse is so great that he throws the money away and hangs himself. We must remember Judas when illicit desire burns in our hearts. It always promises more than it delivers. This is an example of Satan's work of deception. The world promises us rewards, but it delivers a product that never satisfies. In fact, it always turns to gravel in our mouths.

RESPONDING

1. Praise: Worship the Lord by offering Him your praise in spirit and in truth.

Great and marvelous are Your works, Lord God Almighty! Just and true are Your ways, O King of the saints! Who shall not fear Your ways, O King of the saints! Who shall not fear You, O Lord, and glorify Your name? For You alone are holy. For all nations shall come and worship before You, for Your judgments have been manifested. (Revelation 15:3-4)

Take a moment to offer the Lord your personal praise and thanksgiving.

2. Confession: Pray this confession to the Lord as you seek to keep your life free from sin and in fellowship with Him:

O Lord, You are merciful and gracious, slow to anger, and abounding in mercy. . . . As a father pities his children, so You, O Lord, pity me when I fear You. For You know my frame; You remember that I am dust. (Psalm 103:8, 13-14)

Confess any personal sins which the Holy Spirit may bring to your mind.

3. Affirmation: As you agree with the will of God, voice your affirmation of His word:

There is therefore now no condemnation of me because I am in Christ Jesus; I do not walk according to the flesh, but according to the Spirit. For the law of the Spirit of life in Christ Jesus has made me free from the law of sin and death. (Romans 8:1-2)

4. Requests: As you make your requests known to the Lord, include:

- Love for fellow Christians
- The work of missions in Europe and Asia
- Your prayer list, the concerns of your heart, and today's activities

5. Closing Prayer: Finally, offer this closing prayer to the Lord:

This is the day which You have made; I will rejoice and be glad in it. (Psalm 118:24)

Memory Verse: I am the vine, you are the branches. He who abides in Me, and I in him, bears much fruit; for without Me you can do nothing.
John 15:5
Spiritual Life Theme

APRIL 6

READING

The passage for today centers on the resurrection of Jesus. After His resurrection, Jesus appears to His disciples and commissions them to take His message of salvation to all the world.

Read Matthew 28.

REFLECTING

Jesus' message of salvation is the greatest news on earth. It is inherent in the message that it needs to be taken to all the people of the earth. Jesus does not leave that to doubt, however. In Matthew 28, He charges His disciples with that commission— the Great Commission. Usually, a recital of that commission begins with verse 19. That is the Great Omission, because verse 18 is central to it. Verse 19 begins with the word "therefore." To fully understand it, we must go to verse 18 to see what the "therefore" is there for. "All authority is given unto Me in heaven and on earth. Therefore, go and make disciples of all the nations." On the basis of His authority, we are to go— and go in confidence that as we are obedient to His commission, He will accomplish His work through us.

RESPONDING

1. Praise: Because someone "came" to give the gospel to us, thank the Lord and give Him your praise:

The Lord reigns, he is clothed with majesty; the Lord is clothed, He has girded Himself with strength. Surely the world is established, so that it cannot be moved. Your throne is established from of old; You are from everlasting. (Psalm 93:1-2)

Take a moment to offer the Lord your personal praise and thanksgiving.

2. Confession: Pray this confession to the Lord as you seek to keep your life free from sin and in fellowship with Him:

You, O Lord, say to me, "Now, therefore, turn to Me with all your heart, with fasting, with weeping, and with mourning." You ask me to rend my heart, and not my garments; to return to You, my God; for You are gracious and merciful, slow to anger, and of great kindness; and You relent from doing harm. (Joel 2:12-13)

Confess any personal sins which the Holy Spirit may bring to your mind.

3. Affirmation: As you agree with the will of God, voice your affirmation of His word:

For You, O God, have not given me a spirit of fear, but of power and of love and of a sound mind. (2 Timothy 1:7)

4. Requests: As you make your requests known to the Lord, include:

- Faithfulness with your time
- The president and national leaders and affairs
- Your prayer list, the concerns of your heart, and today's activities

5. Closing Prayer: Finally, offer this closing prayer to the Lord:

Oh, satisfy me early with Your mercy, that I may rejoice and be glad all my days! (Psalm 90:14)

Memory Verse: I am the vine, you are the branches. He who abides in Me, and I in him, bears much fruit; for without Me you can do nothing.
John 15:5
Spiritual Life Theme

READING

The passage for today centers on the Last Supper. Jesus shares the Passover meal with His disciples and retires to the Garden of Gethsemane, where He is arrested.

Read Luke 22.

REFLECTING

Preeminence is one of the deepest longings of natural man. It is part of the fall, part of what we inherit from Adam and Eve. It is as old as the fall of Satan. He said, "I will raise my throne above the stars of God. . . . I will be like God" (Isaiah 14:14). And since the fall, man has wanted to be like God, controlling his own world. Even those who actually walked with Jesus fell prey to it, for it comes from within the human heart. During the Last Supper, which you might think would be one of the most spiritually intimate moments in the disciples' experience, an argument breaks out on who among them is the greatest.

Jesus' reply is that the greatest among them must be a servant to them all. It is unnatural, rather supernatural, but your quest must be for servanthood.

RESPONDING

1. Praise: Because Jesus gave up His preeminence for our sake and became a servant, we praise His unselfishness:

Oh, sing to the Lord a new song! Sing to the Lord, all the earth. Sing to the Lord, bless His name; proclaim the good news of His salvation from day to day. Declare His glory among the nations, His wonders among all peoples. For the Lord is great and greatly to be praised; He is to be feared above all gods. (Psalm 96:1-4)

Take a moment to offer the Lord your personal praise and thanksgiving.

2. Confession: Pray this confession to the Lord as you seek to keep your life free from sin and in fellowship with Him:

No temptation has overtaken me except such as is common to man; but You, O God, are faithful, who will not allow me to be tempted beyond what I am able, but with the temptation will also make the way of escape, that I may be able to bear it. (1 Corinthians 10:13)

Confess any personal sins which the Holy Spirit may bring to your mind.

3. Affirmation: As you agree with the will of God, voice your affirmation of His word:

The beginning of wisdom is to fear You, O Lord, and the knowledge of You, the Holy One, brings me understanding. (Proverbs 9:10)

4. Requests: As you make your requests known to the Lord, include:

- Your financial needs
- The needs of the poor
- Your prayer list, the concerns of your heart, and today's activities

5. Closing Prayer: Finally, offer this closing prayer to the Lord:

Let the beauty of You, Lord, be upon me, and establish the work of my hands for me; yes, establish the work of my hands. (Psalm 90:17)

Memory Verse: I am the vine, you are the branches. He who abides in Me, and I in him, bears much fruit; for without Me you can do nothing.
John 15:5
Spiritual Life Theme

APRIL 8

READING

The passage for today centers on Jesus' crucifixion and burial. Pilate declares Jesus' innocence, but releases Him anyway, to be crucified on the hill called Golgotha, "the skull."

Read Luke 23.

REFLECTING

Without wars, there are no heroes. The hero and coward look alike until the battle begins. Then and only then, in the face of the challenge, is their true character manifested. Many people who might be expected to be heroes are shown to be cowards, and people who might be expected to be cowards are shown to be heroes. In the time of Jesus, you would expect heroes of the faith to emerge from the ranks of the Pharisees. Some do. One of those is Joseph of Arimathea. Risking wealth, reputation, and perhaps personal safety, he bargains for the body of Jesus, takes the body in his own hands, and lays it in his own tomb. The Bible says he was a good and righteous man who did not consent to the plan to kill Jesus. Honor to you, Joseph of Arimathea!

RESPONDING

1. Praise: The sacrifice which Jesus made for us took tremendous courage, for which we praise Him:

The Lord made the heavens. Honor and majesty are before Him; strength and beauty are in His sanctuary. Give to the Lord, O kindred of the peoples, give to the Lord glory and strength. Give to the Lord the glory due His name; bring an offering, and come into His courts. Let the heavens rejoice, and let the earth be glad. (Psalm 96:5-8, 11)

Take a moment to offer the Lord your personal praise and thanksgiving.

2. Confession: Pray this confession to the Lord as you seek to keep your life free from sin and in fellowship with Him:

Now no chastening seems to be joyful for the present, but grievous; nevertheless, afterward it yields the peaceable fruit of righteousness if I have been trained by it. (Hebrews 12:11)

Confess any personal sins which the Holy Spirit may bring to your mind.

3. Affirmation: As you agree with the will of God, voice your affirmation of His word:

You, Lord Jesus, are the Bread of Life. If I come to You, I shall never hunger, and if I believe in You, I shall never thirst. (John 6:35)

4. Requests: As you make your requests known to the Lord, include:

- Protection from the "evil one"
- Laborers for the "harvest"
- Your prayer list, the concerns of your heart, and today's activities

5. Closing Prayer: Finally, offer this closing prayer to the Lord:

Bless the Lord, all you His hosts, you ministers of His, who do His pleasure. Bless the Lord, all His works, in all places of His dominion. (Psalm 103:21-22)

Memory Verse: I am the vine, you are the branches. He who abides in Me, and I in him, bears much fruit; for without Me you can do nothing.
John 15:5
Spiritual Life Theme

APRIL 9

READING

The passage for today centers on Jesus' resurrection and ascension. After Jesus rises from the dead, He appears to a number of His disciples and then ascends into heaven from the Mount of Olives.

Read Luke 24.

REFLECTING

The most reasonable explanation for the empty tomb is the resurrection. If, as some have claimed, Jesus had not been killed, but only weakened and wounded by the crucifixion, the stone and the soldiers would have prevented His escape from the tomb. If Jesus' friends had tried to steal the body, the stone and the soldiers would likewise have prevented them. Jesus' enemies would never have taken the body since absence of His body from the tomb would only serve to encourage belief in His resurrection. The simplest and easiest way to quiet claims of His resurrection would have been to *produce the body!* This they could not do. The angel said, "He is not here. He has risen, *just as He said He would.*" If Jesus predicted and experienced His own death, burial, and resurrection, we can trust Him with our lives.

RESPONDING

1. Praise: The Lord can be trusted with our lives because of His own, and we praise Him for that:

You who love the Lord, hate evil! He preserves the souls of His saints; He delivers them out of the hand of the wicked. Light is sown for the righteous, and gladness for the upright in heart. Rejoice in the Lord, you righteous, and give thanks at the remembrance of His holy name. (Psalm 97:10-12)

Take a moment to offer the Lord your personal praise and thanksgiving.

2. Confession: Pray this confession to the Lord as you seek to keep your life free from sin and in fellowship with Him:

I do not despise Your chastening, O Lord, nor am I discouraged when You rebuke me; for whom You love, O Lord, You chasten, and You scourge every son whom You receive. (Hebrews 12:5-6)

Confess any personal sins which the Holy Spirit may bring to your mind.

3. Affirmation: As you agree with the will of God, voice your affirmation of His word:

If I overcome, I shall be clothed in white garments, and You, Lord Jesus, will not blot out my name from the Book of Life; but You will confess my name before Your Father and before His angels. (Revelation 3:5)

4. Requests: As you make your requests known to the Lord, include:

- Commitment to the Lord
- Parachurch ministries
- Your prayer list, the concerns of your heart, and today's activities

5. Closing Prayer: Finally, offer this closing prayer to the Lord:

Lord, preserve me from all evil; preserve my soul. Lord, preserve my going out and my coming in from this time forth, and even forevermore. (Psalm 121:7-8)

Memory Verse: Likewise you also, reckon yourselves to be dead indeed to sin, but alive to God in Christ Jesus our Lord.
Romans 6:11
Spiritual Life Theme

APRIL 10

READING

The passage for today centers on the declaration of Christ's deity. John traces the deity of Christ from "the beginning," to His incarnation, to the testimony of John, to Jesus' early ministry.

Read John 1.

REFLECTING

The Scripture is such an intimate and personal revelation of the mind of God that there is little distance between the Word and God Himself. John writes, "In the beginning was the Word and the Word was with God, and the Word was God" (John 1:1). Of course, this is referring to Jesus, and yet, He is called the Word. In Revelation 19:13, John writes of Jesus, "He is clothed with a robe dipped in blood; and His name is called the Word of God." To know the Word is to know of God; to uphold the Word is to uphold God; to believe the Word is to believe God; and to obey the Word is to obey God.

We do not worship the written Word (that is bibliolatry), but we use the Word to worship the God who gave the Word. Hold the Word in high regard, not as an end, but as a means to the end of knowing and loving God.

RESPONDING

1. Praise: The Word of the Lord is certain, and we praise Him for that trust:

Make a joyful shout to the Lord, all you lands! Serve the Lord with gladness; come before His presence with singing. Know that the Lord, He is God; it is He who has made us, and not we ourselves; we are His people and the sheep of His pasture. Enter into His gates with thanksgiving, and into His courts with praise. . . . For the Lord is good. (Psalm 100:1-5)

Take a moment to offer the Lord your personal praise and thanksgiving.

2. Confession: Pray this confession to the Lord as you seek to keep your life free from sin and in fellowship with Him:

If I sin, I have an Advocate with You, Father, Jesus Christ the righteous. And He Himself is the propitiation for my sins, and not for mine only, but also for the whole world. (1 John 2:1-2)

Confess any personal sins which the Holy Spirit may bring to your mind.

3. Affirmation: As you agree with the will of God, voice your affirmation of His word:

If I dwell in Your secret place, O Most High, I shall abide under Your shadow, Lord Almighty. I will say of You, O Lord, "He is my refuge and my fortress; my God, in Him I will trust." (Psalm 91:1-2)

4. Requests: As you make your requests known to the Lord, include:

* Renewing of your mind
* Needs of your extended family
* Your prayer list, the concerns of your heart, and today's activities

5. Closing Prayer: Finally, offer this closing prayer to the Lord:

May we with one mind and one mouth glorify the God and Father of our Lord Jesus Christ. (Romans 15:6)

Memory Verse: Likewise you also, reckon yourselves to be dead indeed to sin, but alive to God in Christ Jesus our Lord.

Romans 6:11
Spiritual Life Theme

READING

The passage for today centers on the miracle at Cana. Jesus attends a wedding to which He was invited and, while there, turns water into wine as His first effort to demonstrate His deity to His disciples, after which He cleanses the temple the first time.

Read John 2.

REFLECTING

In verse 24 of chapter 2, we read, "But Jesus, on His part, was not entrusting Himself to them." The word entrust is the same word as is translated faith or believe in other places in the Bible. It gives us additional insight to the concept of faith in the Bible. Faith is more than just intellectual belief or understanding. Once someone understands the gospel, he must make a personal commitment to it. He must entrust himself to it. To believe in the Lord Jesus Christ is to do more than intellectually assent to His being fully God and fully man. It also includes entrusting oneself to Him for salvation and forgiveness as well as daily needs.

RESPONDING

1. Praise: The Lord is worthy of our faith and our praise.

Who is like You, O Lord, among the gods? Who is like You, glorious in holiness, fearful in praises, doing wonders? (Exodus 15:11)

Therefore You are great, O Lord God. For there is none like You, nor is there any God besides You, according to all that we have heard with our ears. (2 Samuel 7:22)

Take a moment to offer the Lord your personal praise and thanksgiving.

2. Confession: Pray this confession to the Lord as you seek to keep your life free from sin and in fellowship with Him:

Out of the depths I have cried to You, O Lord. . . . If You, Lord, should mark iniquities, O Lord, who could stand? But there is forgiveness with You, that You may be feared. (Psalm 130:1, 3-4)

Confess any personal sins which the Holy Spirit may bring to your mind.

3. Affirmation: As you agree with the will of God, voice your affirmation of His word:

Likewise Your Spirit also helps me in my weaknesses. For I do not know what I should pray for as I ought, but Your Spirit Himself makes intercession for me with groanings which cannot be uttered. (Romans 8:26)

4. Requests: As you make your requests known to the Lord, include:

- The Lord's leading in your life
- Opportunities for personal evangelism
- Your prayer list, the concerns of your heart, and today's activities

5. Closing Prayer: Finally, offer this closing prayer to the Lord:

Now may the God of hope fill me with all joy and peace in believing, that I may abound in hope by the power of the Holy Spirit. (Romans 15:13)

Memory Verse: Likewise you also, reckon yourselves to be dead indeed to sin, but alive to God in Christ Jesus our Lord.

Romans 6:11
Spiritual Life Theme

APRIL 12

READING

The passage for today centers on Jesus' teachings on the "new birth." In response to questions asked by Nicodemus, Jesus explains the spiritual nature of salvation, establishing "faith" as the basis of salvation.

Read John 3.

REFLECTING

Faith or belief is often misunderstood. Faith has been defined as "believing in spite of the fact that there is nothing to believe" or "believing in spite of the evidence to the contrary." It is often viewed as identical with wishful thinking. Still others hold that if we believe hard enough, we can make something come true (regardless of whether or not God may approve). None of these concepts is biblical. Faith is believing what God has revealed in Scripture, entrusting oneself to it, and acting upon it. This is the faith that Jesus calls for us to exercise in order to experience a new spiritual birth. The new birth occurs as we believe, trust, and act.

RESPONDING

1. Praise: In full confidence in the character of God, offer your praise to Him:

He is the Rock, His work is perfect; for all His ways are justice, a God of truth and without injustice; righteous and upright is He. (Deuteronomy 32:4)

The Lord lives! Blessed be my Rock! Let God be exalted, the Rock of my salvation! (2 Samuel 22:47)

Take a moment to offer the Lord your personal praise and thanksgiving.

2. Confession: Pray this confession to the Lord as you seek to keep your life free from sin and in fellowship with Him:

If we say we have no sin, we are deceiving ourselves, and the truth is not in us. If we confess our sins, He is faithful and just to forgive us our sins and to cleanse us from all unrighteousness. (1 John 1:8-9)

Confess any personal sins which the Holy Spirit may bring to your mind.

3. Affirmation: As you agree with the will of God, voice your affirmation of His word:

You will keep me in perfect peace; my mind is stayed on You, because I trust in You. (Isaiah 26:3)

4. Requests: As you make your requests known to the Lord, include:

- Love for the lost
- The work of missions in Africa
- Your prayer list, the concerns of your heart, and today's activities

5. Closing Prayer: Finally, offer this closing prayer to the Lord:

Now to You who are able to establish us according to the gospel and preaching of Jesus Christ—to You, alone wise, be glory through Jesus Christ forever. Amen. (Romans 16:25-27)

Memory Verse: Likewise you also, reckon yourselves to be dead indeed to sin, but alive to God in Christ Jesus our Lord.

Romans 6:11
Spiritual Life Theme

READING

The passage for today centers on the Samaritan woman. Jesus encounters a woman who believes in Him after He tells her things that no mortal could know.

Read John 4.

REFLECTING

The supreme activity of a Christian is worship. As Jesus is talking with the Samaritan woman at the well about a location of worship, Jesus proclaims that God is spirit, and those who worship Him must worship Him in spirit. God is indifferent to places, nationalities, and method. He wants us to worship. We may worship Him on a mound of dirt or in a cathedral. Neither this mountain nor that mountain is crucial now that Jesus has come.

And we must worship Him in truth. When our bodies sit in a worship service, but our minds are elsewhere, we are not worshiping. Worship is an act of the will. You can decide to worship. Personally enter into the songs that are sung, the prayers prayed, and the Scripture read. Offer Him those things as the expression of your heart, and you will enter worship.

RESPONDING

1. Praise: As an act of personal worship, offer this psalm of praise to the Lord:

Bless the Lord, O my soul! O Lord my God, You are very great: You are clothed with honor and majesty, who cover Yourself with light as with a garment, who stretch out the heavens like a curtain. . . . May the glory of the Lord endure forever; may the Lord rejoice in His works. . . . Bless the Lord, O my soul! Praise the Lord! (Psalm 104:1-2, 31, 35)

Take a moment to offer the Lord your personal praise and thanksgiving.

2. Confession: Pray this confession to the Lord as you seek to keep your life free from sin and in fellowship with Him:

O Lord, You do not have as great delight in burnt offerings and sacrifice as in obeying Your voice. Behold, to obey is better than sacrifice, and to heed than the fat of rams. (1 Samuel 15:22)

Confess any personal sins which the Holy Spirit may bring to your mind.

3. Affirmation: As you agree with the will of God, voice your affirmation of His word:

You, Lord Jesus, are the light of the world. If I follow You, I shall not walk in darkness, but have the light of life. (John 8:12)

4. Requests: As you make your requests known to the Lord, include:

- Faithfulness with your talents
- Your state and local leaders and affairs
- Your prayer list, the concerns of your heart, and today's activities

5. Closing Prayer: Finally, offer this closing prayer to the Lord:

The grace of the Lord Jesus Christ, and the love of God, and the communion of the Holy Spirit be with us all. Amen. (2 Corinthians 13:14)

Memory Verse: Likewise you also, reckon yourselves to be dead indeed to sin, but alive to God in Christ Jesus our Lord.

Romans 6:11
Spiritual Life Theme

APRIL 14

READING

The passage for today centers on Jesus' dispute with the Pharisees. After healing the man beside the pool of Bethesda, Jesus infuriates the religious leaders by claiming equality with God.

Read John 5.

REFLECTING

The penalty for blaspheming, under the Jewish Law, was death by stoning. There are people, atheists and agnostics, as well as cults, who say that Jesus never claimed to be God. This only reveals their lack of understanding of the Bible. The Gospel of John certainly dispels that claim. In chapter 5, John writes that they picked up stones to stone Him because Jesus was making Himself equal with God. Again, in chapter 11, they pick up stones to stone Him because "You, being a man, make Yourself out to be God." Whenever you see the Jews picking up stones to stone Jesus, you can be sure it is because they understand His claims, that He is presenting Himself as God.

RESPONDING

1. Praise: Offer your praise to Jesus, who, as God, offers us salvation:

O Lord, how manifold are Your works! In wisdom You have made them all. The earth is full of Your possessions. . . . I will sing praise to my God while I have my being. May my meditation be sweet to Him; I will be glad in the Lord. (Psalm 104:24, 33, 34)

Take a moment to offer the Lord your personal praise and thanksgiving.

2. Confession: Pray this confession to the Lord as you seek to keep your life free from sin and in fellowship with Him:

I have sinned greatly in what I have done; but now, I pray, O Lord, take away the iniquity of Your servant, for I have done very foolishly. (2 Samuel 24:10)

Confess any personal sins which the Holy Spirit may bring to your mind.

3. Affirmation: As you agree with the will of God, voice your affirmation of His word:

For by grace I have been saved through faith, and that faith is not from myself; it is Your gift, O God, not of my works, lest I should boast. For I am Your workmanship, created in Christ Jesus for good works, which You prepared beforehand that I should walk in them. (Ephesians 2:8-10)

4. Requests: As you make your requests known to the Lord, include:

- Strength for obedience
- International students in America
- Your prayer list, the concerns of your heart, and today's activities

5. Closing Prayer: Finally, offer this closing prayer to the Lord:

Now to You who are able to do exceedingly abundantly above all that I ask or think, according to the power that works in me, to You be glory in the church by Christ Jesus throughout all ages, world without end. Amen. (Ephesians 3:20-21)

Memory Verse: Likewise you also, reckon yourselves to be dead indeed to sin, but alive to God in Christ Jesus our Lord.

Romans 6:11
Spiritual Life Theme

APRIL 15

READING

The passage for today centers on the bread of life. After feeding the five thousand, Jesus claims that He is the "Bread of Life" and the "manna from heaven."

Read John 6.

REFLECTING

Throughout Jesus' ministry He was often misunderstood, not only by the multitudes, but even by His disciples. He often spoke on a spiritual and figurative level, but the people understood Him on a literal level. For this reason, His words went right over their heads. With the woman at the well, He promises to give her living water so she will never thirst. Her reply is, "How will you get this water? You don't have anything to draw it up with." In chapter 6, He says, "Unless you eat My flesh and drink My blood, you have no part with Me." The people understand Him to be suggesting cannibalism and leave Him in disgust. Yet Jesus is speaking figuratively of His death on the cross. He later explains to His disciples, "The words I have spoken to you are spirit and life." To the sensitive and believing heart, Jesus reveals the deeper spiritual truths.

RESPONDING

1. Praise: The sensitive and believing heart looks for opportunities to praise the Lord for His goodness:

Oh, give thanks to the Lord! Call upon His name; make known His deeds among the peoples. Sing to Him, sing psalms to Him; talk of all His wondrous works. Glory in His holy name; let the hearts of those rejoice who seek the Lord. Seek the Lord and His strength; seek His face evermore. (Psalm 105:1-4)

Take a moment to offer the Lord your personal praise and thanksgiving.

2. Confession: Pray this confession to the Lord as you seek to keep your life free from sin and in fellowship with Him:

O my God: I am too ashamed and humiliated to lift up my face to You, my God; for my iniquities have risen higher than my head, and my guilt has grown up to the heavens. (Ezra 9:6)

Confess any personal sins which the Holy Spirit may bring to your mind.

3. Affirmation: As you agree with the will of God, voice your affirmation of His word:

Now faith is the substance of things hoped for, the evidence of things not seen. (Hebrews 11:1)

4. Requests: As you make your requests known to the Lord, include:

- Your "daily bread"
- Christian education institutions
- Your prayer list, the concerns of your heart, and today's activities

5. Closing Prayer: Finally, offer this closing prayer to the Lord:

Now may You, the God of peace, sanctify me completely, and may my whole spirit, soul, and body be preserved blameless at the coming of my Lord Jesus Christ. (1 Thessalonians 5:23)

Memory Verse: Likewise you also, reckon yourselves to be dead indeed to sin, but alive to God in Christ Jesus our Lord.

Romans 6:11
Spiritual Life Theme

APRIL 16

READING

The passage for today centers on Jesus' festival teachings. At the Festival of Booths, Jesus is embroiled in controversy with religious leaders over His true identity.

Read John 7.

REFLECTING

When iron and aluminum shavings are mixed together, they are indistinguishable. To separate them, you cannot rely on sight. You must sweep a magnet through them. It attracts all the iron filings, but the aluminum filings remain undisturbed as though nothing has happened to them. Jesus has exactly the same effect on those to whom He ministers. Those whose understanding is wedded with faith are attracted to Him like iron filings to a magnet. Those who choose not to believe remain undisturbed as though nothing special has passed among them. Some of the multitude say, "This is the Christ," while others say, "Surely the Christ is not going to come from Galilee, is He?" Understanding, combined with faith, understands even more. Unbelief blinds.

RESPONDING

1. Praise: Let us praise Him, for surely this is the Christ:

Praise the Lord! Oh, give thanks to the Lord, for He is good! For His mercy endures forever. Who can utter the mighty acts of the Lord? Or can declare all His praise? . . . Blessed be the Lord . . . from everlasting to everlasting! And let all the people say, "Amen!" Praise the Lord! (Psalm 106:1-2, 48)

Take a moment to offer the Lord your personal praise and thanksgiving.

2. Confession: Pray this confession to the Lord as you seek to keep your life free from sin and in fellowship with Him:

O Lord, do not rebuke me in Your anger, nor chasten me in Your hot displeasure. Have mercy on me, O Lord, for I am weak; O Lord, heal me, for . . . my soul also is greatly troubled. (Psalm 6:1-3)

Confess any personal sins which the Holy Spirit may bring to your mind.

3. Affirmation: As you agree with the will of God, voice your affirmation of His word:

If I love You, Lord Jesus, I will keep Your word; and Your Father will love me, and You and Your Father will come to me and make Your home with me. (John 14:23)

4. Requests: As you make your requests known to the Lord, include:

- Passion for moral excellence
- Needs of personal friends
- Your prayer list, the concerns of your heart, and today's activities

5. Closing Prayer: Finally, offer this closing prayer to the Lord:

Now may the Lord Jesus Christ Himself, and You, my God and Father, who have loved me and given me everlasting consolation and good hope by grace, comfort my heart and establish me in every good word and work. (2 Thessalonians 2:16-17)

Memory Verse: But grow in the grace and knowledge of our Lord and Savior Jesus Christ. To Him be the glory both now and forever. Amen.

2 Peter 3:18
Spiritual Life Theme

APRIL 17

READING

The passage for today centers on a discussion of eternal truth. After forgiving the adulterous woman and declaring Himself to be the light of the world, Jesus teaches on "truth." Read John 8.

REFLECTING

By nature, we want absolute freedom. We want the option of being free from anything. This is not possible, however. There is no such thing as absolute freedom. To be free to sail the seven seas, we must make ourselves a slave to the compass. This irritates us. We want to be free not to brush our teeth, and we want to be free from cavities. Both options are not open to us, however. All of life is a contrast of freedoms and corresponding bondages. We can be a slave to Jesus and free from the bondage and curses of sin, or we can be free from Jesus and a slave to the bondage and curse of sin. We can make ourselves a slave to truth, and the truth can set us free.

RESPONDING

1. Praise: The heart that has been set free by truth can offer praise to the Lord of all truth:

O God, my heart is steadfast; I will sing and give praise. . . . I will awaken the dawn. I will praise You, O Lord, among the peoples, and I will sing praises to You among the nations. For Your mercy is great above the heavens, and Your truth reaches to the clouds. Be exalted, O God, above the heavens, and Your glory above all the earth. (Psalm 108:1, 3-5)

Take a moment to offer the Lord your personal praise and thanksgiving.

2. Confession: Pray this confession to the Lord as you seek to keep your life free from sin and in fellowship with Him:

Can I understand my errors? Cleanse me from secret faults, O Lord. Keep me back from presumptuous sins; let them not have dominion over me. Then I shall be blameless, and I shall be innocent of great transgression. (Psalm 19:12-13)

Confess any personal sins which the Holy Spirit may bring to your mind.

3. Affirmation: As you agree with the will of God, voice your affirmation of His word:

For You, Lord Jesus, were a Child born to us, a Son given to us; and the government will be upon Your shoulder. And Your name will be called Wonderful, Counselor, Mighty God, Everlasting Father, Prince of Peace. (Isaiah 9:6)

4. Requests: As you make your requests known to the Lord, include:

- Wisdom in decision making
- Opportunities to serve the Lord
- Your prayer list, the concerns of your heart, and today's activities

5. Closing Prayer: Finally, offer this closing prayer to the Lord:

Now to You, the King eternal, immortal, invisible, to God who alone is wise, be honor and glory forever and ever. Amen. (1 Timothy 1:17)

Memory Verse: But grow in the grace and knowledge of our Lord and Savior Jesus Christ. To Him be the glory both now and forever. Amen.

2 Peter 3:18
Spiritual Life Theme

APRIL 18

READING

The passage for today centers on the healing of the man born blind. Jesus heals a man born blind, after which a controversy rages among religious leaders as to how it could have happened.

Read John 9.

REFLECTING

While Jesus certainly has compassion for those to whom He ministers, His miracles are done not only to relieve human suffering, but also to validate His message. He claims to be the Bread of Life, and to validate that message, He feeds the four thousand. In chapter 9, Jesus says that the man's blindness is not because of sin, but for the purpose of manifesting the works of God in him. Then He heals him and manifests the work of God. The same with Lazarus. Jesus raises Lazarus, and then says that the Son is glorified. Lazarus' death was not final, but for the purpose of bringing glory to the Son of God.

RESPONDING

1. Praise: You can bring glory to God by praising Him with these words:

Tremble before Him, all the earth. The world also is firmly established. It shall not be moved. Let the heavens rejoice, and let the earth be glad; and let them say among the nations, "The Lord reigns." . . . Oh, give thanks to the Lord, for He is good! For His mercy endures forever. . . . Blessed be the Lord God of Israel from everlasting to everlasting! (1 Chronicles 16:30-31, 34, 36)

Take a moment to offer the Lord your personal praise and thanksgiving.

2. Confession: Pray this confession to the Lord as you seek to keep your life free from sin and in fellowship with Him:

You have blotted out, like a thick cloud, my transgressions, and like a cloud, my sins. I return to You, for You have redeemed me. (Isaiah 44:22)

Confess any personal sins which the Holy Spirit may bring to your mind.

3. Affirmation: As you agree with the will of God, voice your affirmation of His word:

You have delivered me from the power of darkness and translated me into the kingdom of the Son of Your love, in whom I have redemption through His blood, the forgiveness of sins. (Colossians 1:13-14)

4. Requests: As you make your requests known to the Lord, include:

- Victory over temptation
- The work of missions in North and South America
- Your prayer list, the concerns of your heart, and today's activities

5. Closing Prayer: Finally, offer this closing prayer to the Lord:

You who are the blessed and only Potentate, the King of kings and Lord of lords, who alone have immortality, dwelling in unapproachable light, whom no man has seen or can see, to You be honor and everlasting power. Amen. (1 Timothy 6:15-16)

Memory Verse: But grow in the grace and knowledge of our Lord and Savior Jesus Christ. To Him be the glory both now and forever. Amen.

2 Peter 3:18
Spiritual Life Theme

READING

The passage for today centers on the Parable of the Good Shepherd. Jesus teaches concerning His deity and salvation by grace through faith, using the imagery of a shepherd and sheep, causing the Jews to attempt to stone Him for what they consider blasphemy.

Read John 10.

REFLECTING

Whoever comes in contact with Jesus is either blinded or enlightened. They respond to Him or reject Him. They either accept Him or begin manufacturing reasons not to believe in Him. Jesus illustrates this reality with the imagery of sheep and a shepherd. He says, "My sheep hear my voice, and I know them, and they follow Me" (10:27). Make your heart tender and sensitive to hear and obey the teachings of Jesus. Demonstrate your willingness to be His disciple by following in His steps. Walk in His light, and you will not stumble. By responding to the direction of the Shepherd, you will not wander and fall prey to the enemy or find yourself in want for your needs.

RESPONDING

1. Praise: What a joy to relax in the security of the Shepherd and praise Him for His goodness.

Inasmuch as there is none like You, O Lord (You are great, and Your name is great in might), who would not fear You, O King of the nations? For this is Your rightful due, for among all the wise men of the nations, and in all their kingdoms, there is none like You. . . . The Lord is the true God; He is the living God and the everlasting King. (Jeremiah 10:6-7, 10)

Take a moment to offer the Lord your personal praise and thanksgiving.

2. Confession: Pray this confession to the Lord as you seek to keep your life free from sin and in fellowship with Him:

O Lord, You blot out my transgressions for Your own sake; and You will not remember my sins. (Isaiah 43:25)

Confess any personal sins which the Holy Spirit may bring to your mind.

3. Affirmation: As you agree with the will of God, voice your affirmation of His word:

My eye has not seen, nor my ear heard, nor have entered into my heart the things which You, O God, have prepared for me who loves You. (1 Corinthians 2:9)

4. Requests: As you make your requests known to the Lord, include:

- Love for your family
- Revival among Christians in America
- Your prayer list, the concerns of your heart, and today's activities

5. Closing Prayer: Finally, offer this closing prayer to the Lord:

Make me complete in every good work to do Your will, working in me what is well pleasing in Your sight, through Jesus Christ, to whom be glory forever and ever. Amen. (Hebrews 13:20-21)

Memory Verse: But grow in the grace and knowledge of our Lord and Savior Jesus Christ. To Him be the glory both now and forever. Amen.

2 Peter 3:18
Spiritual Life Theme

APRIL 20

READING

The passage for today centers on the death and raising of Lazarus. Jesus' close friend Lazarus dies, and Jesus raises him from the dead, after which many believe in Him.

Read John 11.

REFLECTING

Jesus is ministering on the east side of the Jordan River, about a day's walk from Bethany, when Lazarus falls sick. Messengers are sent to tell Jesus, who waits for two days before departing. When He arrives in Bethany, He learns that Lazarus has been dead for four days. This means that he must have died the same day the messengers were originally dispatched. He is dead by the time Jesus learns about his illness. Why then, does Jesus delay His return for two days? Would we not have dropped everything and run? But Jesus knows Lazarus' condition. His delay is to heighten the manifestation of the power of God.

RESPONDING

1. Praise: As God of both power and compassion, we offer Him our praise:

Praise the Lord! I will praise the Lord with my whole heart, in the assembly of the upright and in the congregation. . . . His work is honorable and glorious, and His righteousness endures forever. He has made His wonderful works to be remembered; the Lord is gracious and full of compassion. . . . The fear of the Lord is the beginning of wisdom; a good understanding have all those who do His commandments. His praise endures forever. (Psalm 111:1, 3-4, 10)

Take a moment to offer the Lord your personal praise and thanksgiving.

2. Confession: Pray this confession to the Lord as you seek to keep your life free from sin and in fellowship with Him:

Show me Your ways, O Lord; teach me your paths. Lead me in Your truth and teach me, for You are the God of my salvation; on You I wait all the day. (Psalm 25:4-5)

Confess any personal sins which the Holy Spirit may bring to your mind.

3. Affirmation: As you agree with the will of God, voice your affirmation of His word:

If I keep Your commandments, Lord Jesus, I will abide in Your love, just as You have kept Your Father's commandments and abide in His love. (John 15:10)

4. Requests: As you make your requests known to the Lord, include:

- Faithfulness with your treasures
- The Great Commission
- Your prayer list, the concerns of your heart, and today's activities

5. Closing Prayer: Finally, offer this closing prayer to the Lord:

May You, the God of grace, who called me to Your eternal glory by Christ Jesus, after I have suffered a while, perfect, establish, strengthen, and settle me. To You be the glory and the dominion forever and ever. Amen. (1 Peter 5:10-11)

Memory Verse: But grow in the grace and knowledge of our Lord and Savior Jesus Christ. To Him be the glory both now and forever. Amen.

2 Peter 3:18
Spiritual Life Theme

READING

The passage for today centers on the Triumphal Entry. As Jesus rides a donkey into the temple, the multitudes herald Him as their Messiah, after which Jesus foretells His impending death.

Read John 12.

REFLECTING

People will talk about feeling close to God, but be offended when you bring up Jesus. There is an embarrassing quality about His name. Merely mentioning His name requires a certain amount of courage. But Jesus says that if you accept Him you accept God, and conversely, that if you do not accept Him you do not accept God. When someone talks about being close to God, but wants nothing to do with Jesus, you can be sure he is not yet close to God. To know Jesus is to know God, and one cannot know God without knowing Jesus. When Philip said, "Show us the Father," Jesus replied, "Have I been so long with you, and yet you have not come to know Me? He who has seen Me has seen the Father."

RESPONDING

1. Praise: As you seek spiritual closeness with the Father and the Son, offer this psalm of praise:

Praise the Lord! Praise, O servants of the Lord, praise the name of the Lord! Blessed be the name of the Lord from this time forth and forevermore! From the rising of the sun to its going down, the Lord's name is to be praised. . . . Who is like the Lord our God, who dwells on high, who humbles Himself to behold the things that are in the heavens and in the earth? . . . Praise the Lord! (Psalm 113:1-3, 5-6, 9)

Take a moment to offer the Lord your personal praise and thanksgiving.

2. Confession: Pray this confession to the Lord as you seek to keep your life free from sin and in fellowship with Him:

Remember, O Lord, Your tender mercies and Your lovingkindnesses, for they have been from of old. Do not remember the sins of my youth, nor my transgressions; according to Your mercy remember me, for Your goodness' sake, O Lord. (Psalm 25:6-7)

Confess any personal sins which the Holy Spirit may bring to your mind.

3. Affirmation: As you agree with the will of God, voice your affirmation of His word:

For I have sinned and fall short of Your glory, O God; being justified freely by Your grace through the redemption that is in Christ Jesus. (Romans 3:23-24)

4. Requests: As you make your requests known to the Lord, include:

- Spiritual insight
- Campus ministries
- Your prayer list, the concerns of your heart, and today's activities

5. Closing Prayer: Finally, offer this closing prayer to the Lord:

May I grow in the grace and knowledge of our Lord and Savior Jesus Christ. To Him be the glory both now and forever. Amen. (2 Peter 3:18)

Memory Verse: But grow in the grace and knowledge of our Lord and Savior Jesus Christ. To Him be the glory both now and forever. Amen.

2 Peter 3:18
Spiritual Life Theme

APRIL 22

READING

The passage for today centers on the Lord's Supper. Jesus meets with His disciples in an upper room where He institutes with them the ceremonial meal which Christians are to observe until His return.

Read John 13.

REFLECTING

Historical perspective is something for which we all long. We trace our family trees as far back as we can in order to get a feel for our places in history. We conduct archaeological digs to learn about the past and our link to it. Over two thousand years ago, Jesus ate a ceremonial meal with His disciples which originated in the Passover, and pictured His own death, burial, and resurrection, and our need to receive Him personally for our salvation. Then He instructed His disciples to observe this meal until His return. Those disciples told others, and they told others who in turn told others. And today, we observe a ceremonial meal which has been observed in unbroken succession for two thousand years, going back to Jesus Himself.

RESPONDING

1. Praise: Join your heart with the saints of the ages over the last two thousand years in offering praise to the God of our salvation:

Not unto us, O Lord, not unto us, but to Your name give glory, because of Your mercy, and because of Your truth. . . . We who fear You, O Lord, trust in You; You are our help and our shield. . . . We will bless the Lord from this time forth and forevermore. Praise the Lord! (Psalm 115:1, 11, 18)

Take a moment to offer the Lord your personal praise and thanksgiving.

2. Confession: Pray this confession to the Lord as you seek to keep your life free from sin and in fellowship with Him:

Turn Yourself to me, O God, and have mercy on me, for I am desolate and afflicted. The troubles of my heart have enlarged; oh, bring me out of my distresses! Look on my affliction and my pain, and forgive all my sins. (Psalm 25:16-18)

Confess any personal sins which the Holy Spirit may bring to your mind.

3. Affirmation: As you agree with the will of God, voice your affirmation of His word:

Lord Jesus, You bid me come to You when I labor and am heavy laden, and You promise to give me rest. You ask that I take Your yoke upon me and learn from You; for You are gentle and lowly in heart, and I will find rest for my soul. (Matthew 11:28-30)

4. Requests: As you make your requests known to the Lord, include:

* Desire to be like Christ
* Needs in inner cities
* Your prayer list, the concerns of your heart, and today's activities

5. Closing Prayer: Finally, offer this closing prayer to the Lord:

Blessing and honor and glory and power be to You who sit on the throne, and to You, Lord, forever and ever! (Revelation 5:13)

Memory Verse: But grow in the grace and knowledge of our Lord and Savior Jesus Christ. To Him be the glory both now and forever. Amen.

2 Peter 3:18
Spiritual Life Theme

READING

The passage for today centers on Jesus' Farewell Discourse. Jesus comforts His disciples regarding His imminent death by reassuring them that they will see Him in heaven and that He will send them the Holy Spirit.

Read John 14.

REFLECTING

A very tender and intimate scene begins chapter 14. The disciples do not clearly understand everything that is going on, but they know that something big is about to happen and that Jesus will be leaving them. Their teacher, their mentor, their friend for the last three years is leaving, and their hearts are crushed with the burden. In this spirit, Jesus speaks softly, kindly, tenderly to them: "Do not be troubled. I am going to prepare a place for you in my father's house, and if I go and prepare a place, I will come again and receive you." Again, "I will not leave you as orphans. I will come again. And, while I am absent, I will send my Holy Spirit to comfort you." How loving, how kind and compassionate. And He loves you and me just as much.

RESPONDING

1. Praise: God's love for us is indeed cause for us to give Him our praise and adoration:

Unto You I lift up my eyes, O You who dwell in the heavens. Behold, as the eyes of servants look to the hand of their masters, as the eyes of a maid to the hand of her mistress, so our eyes look to the Lord our God, until He has mercy on us. (Psalm 123:1-2)

Take a moment to offer the Lord your personal praise and thanksgiving.

2. Confession: Pray this confession to the Lord as you seek to keep your life free from sin and in fellowship with Him:

Good and upright are You, Lord; therefore You teach me, though a sinner, in Your way. If I am humble, You will guide me in justice and teach me Your way. All Your paths for me are mercy and truth, if I keep Your covenant and Your testimonies. For Your name's sake, O Lord, pardon my iniquity, for it is great. (Psalm 25:8-11)

Confess any personal sins which the Holy Spirit may bring to your mind.

3. Affirmation: As you agree with the will of God, voice your affirmation of His word:

And now, Lord, what do I wait for? My hope is in You. (Psalm 39:7)

4. Requests: As you make your requests known to the Lord, include:

- Personal witness for Christ
- Local churches around the nation
- Your prayer list, the concerns of your heart, and today's activities

5. Closing Prayer: Finally, offer this closing prayer to the Lord:

Amen! Blessing and glory and wisdom, thanksgiving and honor and power and might, be to You, God, forever and ever. Amen. (Revelation 7:12)

Memory Verse: Ask, and it will be given to you; seek, and you will find; knock, and it will be opened to you.
Matthew 7:7
Prayer

APRIL 24

READING

The passage for today centers on Jesus' discussion of the True Vine. Jesus teaches his disciples that cultivating a personal relationship with the Lord and with each other is central to His design and purpose.

Read John 15.

REFLECTING

Sooner or later, we all become dissatisfied with our prayer lives. It is part of the ongoing growth process. There are times when our prayers are answered, and we seem "in tune" with God. At other times our prayers seem not to be answered, and we seem not to be in tune with God. Jesus gives us two directives to keep in mind as we ponder our prayer. We are to abide in Him. This, among other things, includes fostering a conscious awareness of His presence at all times, and bringing all thoughts, attitudes and actions in line with what we understand of His teachings. Second, "and my word abide in you" must involve studying, memorizing, meditating upon the word so that we pray intelligently, knowing God's will ahead of time on some things. As we grow in these two areas, more and more of our prayers will be answered.

RESPONDING

1. Praise: Part of our prayer life with which the Lord is pleased is when we offer Him our praise:

Praise the Lord! Praise the name of the Lord; praise Him, O you servants of the Lord! . . . Praise the Lord, for the Lord is good; sing praises to His name, for it is pleasant. . . . For I know that the Lord is great, and our Lord is above all gods. . . . Blessed be the Lord. . . . Praise the Lord! (Psalm 135:1, 3, 5, 21)

Take a moment to offer the Lord your personal praise and thanksgiving.

2. Confession: Pray this confession to the Lord as you seek to keep your life free from sin and in fellowship with Him:

I will sing praise to You, O Lord, as one of Your saints, and will give thanks at the remembrance of Your holy name. For Your anger is but for a moment, Your favor is for life; weeping may endure for a night, but joy comes in the morning. (Psalm 30:4-5)

Confess any personal sins which the Holy Spirit may bring to your mind.

3. Affirmation: As you agree with the will of God, voice your affirmation of His word:

I delight to do Your will, O my God, and Your law is within my heart. (Psalm 40:8)

4. Requests: As you make your requests known to the Lord, include:

- An eternal perspective
- Needs of work or school mates
- Your prayer list, the concerns of your heart, and today's activities

5. Closing Prayer: Finally, offer this closing prayer to the Lord:

I will wait on You, the Lord; I will be of good courage, and You shall strengthen my heart; I will wait on You! (Psalm 27:14)

Memory Verse: Ask, and it will be given to you; seek, and you will find; knock, and it will be opened to you.
Matthew 7:7
Prayer

READING

The passage for today centers on the promise of the Holy Spirit. Jesus promises His disciples that upon His departure, He will send the Holy Spirit to comfort and guide them, after which He predicts His own death and instructs on prayer. Read John 16.

REFLECTING

We often gain by our losses, although we often fail to recognize it at the time. The one who has suffered no loss is still a shallow person. He has yet to experience the degree of dependence learned through a loss. It was expedient for the disciples that the Lord should go because the Spirit's presence was contingent upon His physical absence. Christ's work must be complete before the Spirit can apply it to the hearts of men. He must die and be resurrected. Then the Holy Spirit will draw men to His offer of salvation. And the best news? We'll see Jesus again once the harvest is complete. The apparent loss is our gain. The temporary suffering leads to a stronger faith and a deeper understanding of how God works in the world.

RESPONDING

1. Praise: As you praise the Lord in these words, focus on His sovereignty and goodness:

Great and marvelous are Your works, Lord God Almighty! Just and true are Your ways, O King of the saints! Who shall not fear You, O Lord, and glorify Your name? For You alone are holy. For all nations shall come and worship before You, for Your judgments have been manifested. (Revelation 15:3-4)

Take a moment to offer the Lord your personal praise and thanksgiving.

2. Confession: Pray this confession to the Lord as you seek to keep your life free from sin and in fellowship with Him:

Bless the Lord, O my soul; and all that is within me, bless His holy name! Bless the Lord, O my soul, and forget not all His benefits: who forgives all your iniquities. (Psalm 103:1-3)

Confess any personal sins which the Holy Spirit may bring to your mind.

3. Affirmation: As you agree with the will of God, voice your affirmation of His word:

If I believe on the Lord Jesus Christ, I will be saved. (Acts 16:31)

4. Requests: As you make your requests known to the Lord, include:

- Personal discipline
- Christians worldwide who are persecuted for their faith
- Your prayer list, the concerns of your heart, and today's activities

5. Closing Prayer: Finally, offer this closing prayer to the Lord:

Show me the path of life; in Your presence is fullness of joy; at Your right hand are pleasures forevermore. (Psalm 16:11)

Memory Verse: Ask, and it will be given to you; seek, and you will find; knock, and it will be opened to you.
Matthew 7:7
Prayer

APRIL 26

READING

The passage for today centers on Jesus' High Priestly Prayer. Jesus prays to the Father on behalf of His disciples and those who will become disciples as a result of their ministry, asking Him to bless them, make them fruitful, and give them future glory.

Read John 17.

REFLECTING

The mark or badge of a Christian should be love. In Matthew 22 we read that the two greatest commandments are love for God and love for our neighbor. In John 13:35 Jesus says, "By this all men will know that you are my disciples, if you have love for one another." In John 17:21 Jesus says if Christians have unity (based on love), the world will believe that Christ was sent from God. A badge designates our allegiance, our stand, our purpose. When our badge is love, the world will be convinced that we are genuine disciples of Jesus (not hypocrites) and that Christ was sent from God (He was not just a man). Jesus still prays that our badge of love might be evident and active in order for love to have its intended impact on the world.

RESPONDING

1. Praise: Offer the Lord your praise for His love through these words:

O Lord God of Israel, the One who dwells between the cherubim, You are God, You alone, of all the kingdoms of the earth. You have made heaven and earth. (2 Kings 19:15)

Lord God of Israel, there is no God in heaven above or on earth below like You, who keep Your covenant and mercy with Your ser-vants who walk before You with all their heart. (1 Kings 8:23)

Take a moment to offer the Lord your personal praise and thanksgiving.

2. Confession: Pray this confession to the Lord as you seek to keep your life free from sin and in fellowship with Him:

As a father pities his children, so You, O Lord, pity those who fear You. For You know our frame; You remember that we are dust. (Psalm 103:13-14)

Confess any personal sins which the Holy Spirit may bring to your mind.

3. Affirmation: As you agree with the will of God, voice your affirmation of His word:

You are Spirit, and those who worship You must worship in spirit and truth. (John 4:24)

4. Requests: As you make your requests known to the Lord, include:

- Love for the Lord
- The work of missions in the Middle East, Australia, and the Islands
- Your prayer list, the concerns of your heart, and today's activities

5. Closing Prayer: Finally, offer this closing prayer to the Lord:

Save Your people, and bless Your inheritance; shepherd us also, and bear us up forever. (Psalm 28:9)

Memory Verse: Ask, and it will be given to you; seek, and you will find; knock, and it will be opened to you.
Matthew 7:7
Prayer

READING

The passage for today centers on Jesus' betrayal and trials. After His arrest, Jesus is taken before the religious leaders as well as Pilate in a mocking prelude to His crucifixion. Read John 18.

REFLECTING

If it were not followed up by such suffering, the account of the arrest in chapter 18 would be humorous. The power of the Creator of the universe lies veiled in human flesh in Jesus of Nazareth. And men come to this Power with torches and weapons to subdue it. The Power asks, "Whom do you seek?" The Torches and Weapons reply, "Jesus of Nazareth." The Power answers, "I am He." With the force of those words from the Power, the Torches and Weapons are knocked flat on their backs. It must have rattled their confidence to have to take that Power into custody. How much greater significance it lends to Jesus words, "No man takes my life, but I lay it down." For our sakes, the Power laid down His life that we might take it up. He became what we are so that we might become what He is. Praise and glory to God!

RESPONDING

1. Praise: Offer to the Lord your praise for His willingness to lay down His life for you:

I will extol You, my God, O King; and I will bless Your name forever and ever. Every day I will bless you, and I will praise Your name forever and ever. Great is the Lord, and greatly to be praised; and His greatness is unsearchable. One generation shall praise Your works to another, and shall declare Your mighty acts. I will meditate on the glorious splendor of Your majesty, and on Your wondrous works. (Psalm 145:1-5)

Take a moment to offer the Lord your personal praise and thanksgiving.

2. Confession: Pray this confession to the Lord as you seek to keep your life free from sin and in fellowship with Him:

I am blessed because my transgression is forgiven, and my sin is covered. I am blessed because You do not impute iniquity to me, and in my spirit there is no guile. (Psalm 32:1-2)

Confess any personal sins which the Holy Spirit may bring to your mind.

3. Affirmation: As you agree with the will of God, voice your affirmation of His word:

If I love You, I will keep Your commandments. (John 14:15)

4. Requests: As you make your requests known to the Lord, include:

- Faithfulness in sharing Christ
- The Lord's work in national and world affairs
- Your prayer list, the concerns of your heart, and today's activities

5. Closing Prayer: Finally, offer this closing prayer to the Lord:

You, the Lord, will command Your lovingkindness in the daytime, and in the night Your song shall be with me—a prayer to You, the God of my life. (Psalm 42:8)

Memory Verse: Ask, and it will be given to you; seek, and you will find; knock, and it will be opened to you.
Matthew 7:7
Prayer

APRIL 28

READING

The passage for today centers on Jesus' crucifixion. After being cruelly mistreated, Jesus is crucified and gives up His spirit.

Read John 19.

REFLECTING

John gives the most sensitive treatment of Pilate's struggle with the destiny of Jesus. At first, Pilate says, "I find no guilt in Him." Then, he scourges Jesus, hoping to placate the Jews, and says again, "I am bringing Him out to you, that you may know that I find no guilt in Him." He plies Jesus for information, perhaps in an effort to find an angle to use in freeing Him. Without success, he makes further efforts to release Him, but the Jews will not stand for it. Afraid for his political reputation back in Rome, Pilate caves in, washes his hands of the affair (which he really could not do), and releases Jesus to the Jews to be crucified. Our tendency is to be very hard on Pilate. His sin is great, but if at any point in time he had repented of his deed, Jesus Himself would have welcomed him with open arms into the kingdom of God.

RESPONDING

1. Praise: God forgives our sin and beckons us to Himself, for which we offer Him our gratitude and praise:

Men shall speak of the might of Your awesome acts; and I will declare Your greatness. They shall utter the memory of Your great goodness, and shall sing of Your righteousness. The Lord is gracious and full of compassion, slow to anger and great in mercy. The Lord is good to all, and His tender mercies are over all His works. (Psalm 145:6-9)

Take a moment to offer the Lord your personal praise and thanksgiving.

2. Confession: Pray this confession to the Lord as you seek to keep your life free from sin and in fellowship with Him:

I acknowledged my sin to You, and my iniquity I have not hidden. I said, "I will confess my transgressions to the Lord," and You forgave the iniquity of my sin. (Psalm 32:5)

Confess any personal sins which the Holy Spirit may bring to your mind.

3. Affirmation: As you agree with the will of God, voice your affirmation of His word:

For I did not receive the spirit of bondage again to fear, but the Spirit of adoption by whom I cry out to You, "Abba, Father." (Romans 8:15)

4. Requests: As you make your requests known to the Lord, include:

- Compassion for others
- Missions in America
- Your prayer list, the concerns of your heart, and today's activities

5. Closing Prayer: Finally, offer this closing prayer to the Lord:

Blessed are You, the Lord, forevermore! Amen and amen. (Psalm 89:52)

Memory Verse: Ask, and it will be given to you; seek, and you will find; knock, and it will be opened to you.
Matthew 7:7
Prayer

READING

The passage for today centers on Jesus' resurrection. After Jesus rises from the dead and appears to His disciples, He reassures Thomas of His deity.

Read John 20.

REFLECTING

Jesus never asks us to believe on the basis of nothing. He always asks us to believe on the basis of something. Neither does He resent sincere doubt. A war was waging inside Thomas who wants to believe, but does not dare to. Knowing the basic motivation of his heart, Jesus simply says, "Here, Thomas. Feel my hands. Put your hand into My side, and be not unbelieving, but believing." Jesus sees that his heart is right. He just needs more help to believe. Without any reproach, Jesus gives him that help. Thomas's response? "My Lord and my God!" You need not fear sincere doubt. Just ask the Lord for more help to believe whatever it is you are struggling with. Like the father in Mark 9:24, your prayer can be "I believe; help my unbelief!"

RESPONDING

1. Praise: In the words of this psalm, offer your praise to the Lord who is patient with us when we doubt:

All Your works shall praise You, O Lord, and Your saints shall bless You. They shall speak of the glory of Your kingdom, and talk of Your power, to make known to the sons of men His mighty acts, and the glorious majesty of His kingdom. (Psalm 145:10-12)

Take a moment to offer the Lord your personal praise and thanksgiving.

2. Confession: Pray this confession to the Lord as you seek to keep your life free from sin and in fellowship with Him:

Have mercy upon me, O God, according to Your lovingkindness; according to the multitude of Your tender mercies, blot out my transgressions. (Psalm 51:1)

Confess any personal sins which the Holy Spirit may bring to your mind.

3. Affirmation: As you agree with the will of God, voice your affirmation of His word:

For You so loved me that You gave Your only begotten Son, that if I would believe in Him, I should not perish, but have everlasting life. For You did not send Your Son into the world to condemn me, but that through Him I might be saved. (John 3:16-17)

4. Requests: As you make your requests known to the Lord, include:

- Personal spiritual growth
- Military ministries
- Your prayer list, the concerns of your heart, and today's activities

5. Closing Prayer: Finally, offer this closing prayer to the Lord:

Glory to You in the highest, and on earth peace, good will toward men! (Luke 2:14)

Memory Verse: Ask, and it will be given to you; seek, and you will find; knock, and it will be opened to you.
Matthew 7:7
Prayer

APRIL 30

READING

The passage for today centers on Jesus' appearance at the Sea of Galilee. Jesus appears to His disciples again to reassure them and build their faith.

Read John 21.

REFLECTING

Without a shepherd, the sheep scatter. After the death of Jesus, His disciples are scattered, the fishermen return to the sea. It is clear that they do know what to do next. After an evening of unfruitful fishing, they return to the shore to find Jesus there, with breakfast ready and giving them another miracle to bolster their faith. Shortly afterward, we see a picture of Peter and Jesus eating together in perfect fellowship and harmony. Recall, this is the man who cursed Jesus and denied that he ever knew Him. This lends weight to Jesus' statement that one can love greater the one who has been forgiven the greater sin. The Lord will forgive any of our sins. He is mindful of our frame and knows that we are but dust. Let no sin fester in your heart. Confess it and accept His forgiveness.

RESPONDING

1. Praise: The Lord forgives, and the Lord reigns; praise Him for His blessing on our behalf:

Lord, You have been our dwelling place in all generations. Before the mountains were brought forth, or ever You had formed the earth and the world, even from everlasting to everlasting, You are God. . . . Oh, satisfy us early with Your mercy, that we may rejoice and be glad all our days! (Psalm 90:1-2, 14)

Take a moment to offer the Lord your personal praise and thanksgiving.

2. Confession: Pray this confession to the Lord as you seek to keep your life free from sin and in fellowship with Him:

No temptation has overtaken me except such as is common to man; but You, O God, are faithful, who will not allow me to be tempted beyond what I am able, but with the temptation will also make the way of escape, that I may be able to bear it. (1 Corinthians 10:13)

Confess any personal sins which the Holy Spirit may bring to your mind.

3. Affirmation: As you agree with the will of God, voice your affirmation of His word:

By this I know love, because You, Lord Jesus, laid down Your life for me. And I also ought to lay down my life for the brethren. (1 John 3:16)

4. Requests: As you make your requests known to the Lord, include:

- Fruit of the Spirit in your life
- The ministry of Christian literature
- Your prayer list, the concerns of your heart, and today's activities

5. Closing Prayer: Finally, offer this closing prayer to the Lord:

Grace, mercy, and peace from You, the Father, and the Lord Jesus Christ our Savior. (Titus 1:4)

Memory Verse: Be anxious for nothing, but in everything by prayer and supplication, with thanksgiving, let your requests be made known to God.

Philippians 4:6
Prayer

READING

The passage for today centers on the account of Joshua assuming command. After the Lord speaks directly to Joshua, telling him to assume command of the people of Israel, the people pledge their allegiance to his leadership.

Read Joshua 1.

REFLECTING

God tells Joshua to be careful to do according to all the law—not to turn to the right or the left—so that he may have success wherever he goes (1:7). Joshua's success is dependent upon not deviating from the law. In Joshua 1:8, the Lord instructs Joshua not to let the word of the law "depart from your mouth, but you shall meditate on it day and night." The meditation is not magic, however. Meditation time does not earn favor with God so that He begins blessing our labors. Rather, the meditation is a means to an end, not the end itself. The end is, again, "that you may be careful to do according to all that is written in it" (1:8). When Joshua does "according to all that is written in it," then "you will make yourself prosperous, and then you will have success."

The genius of God's moral code is that everything He asks of us is for our own good.

RESPONDING

1. Praise: As you continue your time with the Lord, offer to Him this praise as you ponder the significance of the Word in your life:

Who is like You, O Lord, among the gods? Who is like You, glorious in holiness, fearful in praises, doing wonders? (Exodus 15:11)

Take a moment to offer the Lord your personal praise and thanksgiving.

2. Confession: Pray this confession to the Lord as you seek to keep your life free from sin and in fellowship with Him:

Against You, You only, have I sinned, and done this evil in Your sight—that You may be found just when You speak, and blameless when You judge. (Psalm 51:4)

Confess any personal sins which the Holy Spirit may bring to your mind.

3. Affirmation: As you agree with the will of God, voice your affirmation of His word:

Blessed am I when I make You, O Lord, my trust, and when I do not respect the proud, nor such as turn aside to lies. (Psalm 40:4)

4. Requests: As you make your requests known to the Lord, include:

- Health and strength to serve God
- God's will to be done on earth
- Your prayer list, the concerns of your heart, and today's activities

5. Closing Prayer: Finally, offer this closing prayer to the Lord:

Grace, mercy, and peace from You, the Father, and the Lord Jesus Christ our Savior. (Titus 1:4)

Memory Verse: Be anxious for nothing, but in everything by prayer and supplication, with thanksgiving, let your requests be made known to God.

Philippians 4:6
Prayer

READING

The passage for today centers on Rahab's sheltering of the spies. Rahab hides two spies who are sent to Jericho on a reconnaissance mission, and then she helps them escape from the city.

Read Joshua 2.

REFLECTING

God will meet any person, any time, any place. If God seems far away, it is most likely due to our having moved away from Him, not the other way around. There are few people who seem to be farther from the Lord than a harlot. Yet, in the course of living her everyday life, Rahab finds herself meeting a divine appointment with two strangers in need and, in the process, meets with God. The kinds of risks Rahab takes will not be taken without a searching heart. In her own way, she takes a step of faith. God meets her halfway. Her reward is not only eternal life, but also the honor of being included in the line of the Messiah.

Wherever you are in your life, God will meet you there.

RESPONDING

1. Praise: Thank the Lord, and praise Him that He met you at your point of need:

My soul magnifies You, Lord, and my spirit has rejoiced in You, O God my Savior. . . . You who are mighty have done great things for me; and holy is Your name. And Your mercy is on those who fear You from generation to generation. (Luke 1:46-50)

Pause for personal praise and thanksgiving.

2. Confession: Pray this confession to the Lord as you seek to keep your life free from sin and in fellowship with Him:

Remember, O Lord, Your tender mercies and Your lovingkindnesses, for they have been from of old. Do not remember the sins of my youth, nor my transgressions; according to Your mercy remember me, for Your goodness' sake, O Lord. (Psalm 25:6-7)

Confess any personal sins which the Holy Spirit brings to your mind.

3. Affirmation: Now pause to pray this affirmation to the Lord:

You are the door. If anyone enters by You he will be saved, and will go in and out and find pasture. The thief does not come except to steal, and to kill, and to destroy. You have come that we may have life, and that we may have it more abundantly. You are the Good Shepherd. The Good Shepherd gives his life for the sheep. (John 10:9-11)

4. Requests: As you make your requests known to the Lord, pray for:

- Sensitivity to sin
- The ministry of your local church
- Your prayer list, the concerns of your heart, and today's activities

5. Closing Prayer: Finally, offer this closing prayer to the Lord:

Let the words of my mouth and the meditation of my heart be acceptable in Your sight, O Lord, my strength and my redeemer. (Psalm 19:14)

Memory Verse: Be anxious for nothing, but in everything by prayer and supplication, with thanksgiving, let your requests be made known to God.

Philippians 4:6
Prayer

READING

The passage for today centers on Israel's crossing of the Jordan. God miraculously parts water a second time for the people of Israel, as they cross over the Jordan River on solid ground.

Read Joshua 3.

REFLECTING

There are two times in history that God parts water for the Israelites: once at the Red Sea as the children are fleeing from the Egyptian army in fear, not knowing how to follow God in faith; and again at the Jordan River, as they are poised to enter the promised land with confidence now that the victory belongs to them. Such confidence had been learned through the trials in the desert. The Red Sea experience certainly receives more acclaim, but the Jordan River experience is just as miraculous. The water parts for a distance of almost twenty miles as the nation passes over on dry ground during flood season. God is faithful to all generations.

RESPONDING

1. Praise: The Lord is worthy to receive our praise because of all that He has done for us:

Oh, the depth of the riches both of the wisdom and knowledge of God! How unsearchable are Your judgments and Your ways past finding out! Blessed are You, the God and Father of our Lord Jesus Christ, who has blessed us with every spiritual blessing in the heavenly places in Christ. (Ephesians 1:3)

Pause for personal praise and thanksgiving.

2. Confession: Pray this confession to the Lord as you seek to keep your life free from sin and in fellowship with Him:

Blessed is he whose transgression is forgiven, whose sin is covered. How blessed is the man to whom the Lord does not impute iniquity, and in whose spirit there is no guile. (Psalm 32:1-2)

Confess any personal sins which the Holy Spirit brings to mind.

3. Affirmation: Now pause to pray this affirmation to the Lord:

Let me not glory in my own wisdom, let me not glory in my own might, nor let me glory in my own riches; but let me glory in this, that I understand and know You, that You are the Lord, for in this You delight. (Jeremiah 9:23-24)

4. Requests: As you make your requests known to the Lord, include:

- Wisdom for living life
- Needs of your immediate family
- Your prayer list, the concerns of your heart, and today's activities

5. Closing Prayer: Finally, offer this closing prayer to the Lord:

Surely goodness and mercy shall follow me all the days of my life, and I will dwell in the house of the Lord forever. (Psalm 23:6)

Memory Verse: Be anxious for nothing, but in everything by prayer and supplication, with thanksgiving, let your requests be made known to God.

Philippians 4:6
Prayer

MAY 4

READING

The passage for today centers on the erection of the memorial stones from the Jordan. After the Israelites cross over the Jordan, they choose twelve stones from the river bed to erect as a memorial to the faithfulness of God.

Read Joshua 4.

REFLECTING

Memorials are important. We have short memories and tend to forget things we ought to remember. Memorials help us to preserve important memories. God memorializes many important things in the Old Testament, often through feasts and ceremonies. Now He uses a monument built of stones from the bottom of the river they have just walked across. "In the future, when your children ask what these stones are, tell them that here, a miraculous God was faithful." There are things in your life which God has done for your that you ought not to forget. Think of ways to memorialize them. You might have ceremonies or anniversaries of important events or a physical memorial. Either way, foster the memory of God's work in your behalf.

RESPONDING

1. Praise: Offer to the Lord this psalm of praise as you remember all He has done for you:

Praise the Lord! For it is good to sing praises to our God; for it is pleasant, and praise is beautiful. . . . Great is our Lord, and mighty in power. . . . The Lord takes pleasure in those who fear Him, in those who hope in His mercy. . . . He has not dealt thus with any nation; and as for His judgments, they have not known them. Praise the Lord! (Psalm 147:1, 5a, 11, 20)

Take a moment to offer the Lord your personal praise and thanksgiving.

2. Confession: Pray this confession to the Lord as you seek to keep your life free from sin and in fellowship with Him:

Purge me with hyssop, and I shall be clean; wash me, and I shall be whiter than snow. . . . Hide Your face from my sins, and blot out all my iniquities. (Psalm 51:7, 9)

Confess any personal sins which the Holy Spirit may bring to your mind.

3. Affirmation: As you agree with the will of God, voice your affirmation of His word:

Behold, God is my salvation, I will trust and not be afraid; "For YAH, the Lord is my strength and my song; He also has become my salvation." (Isaiah 12:2)

4. Requests: As you make your requests known to the Lord, include:

- Insight into Scripture
- The hungry around the world
- Your prayer list, the concerns of your heart, and today's activities

5. Closing Prayer: Finally, offer this closing prayer to the Lord:

We will be of good courage, and You shall strengthen our hearts, all we who hope in the Lord. (Psalm 31:24)

Memory Verse: Be anxious for nothing, but in everything by prayer and supplication, with thanksgiving, let your requests be made known to God.

Philippians 4:6
Prayer

READING

The passage for today centers on the conquest of Jericho. After the Israelites walk around the city seven times on the seventh day, the Lord fells the walls of Jericho.

Read Joshua 6.

REFLECTING

The Word of God often goes against all reason. Consider Joshua, a military strategist so brilliant that his campaigns are still studied in War College today. He is standing on a hill overlooking Jericho, pondering how to conquer it. The angel of the Lord appears to him, and says, "walk around the city seven times and shout real loud. That ought to do it!" Can you imagine the response from the standpoint of military strategy? That command is military madness. Yet Joshua obeyed the word of God, and success was his.

The New Testament often instructs us to depart from conventional reason today. Yet God has spoken, and when we obey, our success is just as assured as was Joshua's.

RESPONDING

1. Praise: Because God always honors our obedience to Him, we praise Him:

Praise the Lord! Praise God in His sanctuary; Praise Him in His mighty firmament! Praise Him for His mighty acts; Praise Him according to His excellent greatness! Praise Him with the sound of the trumpet; Praise Him with the lute and harp! . . . Let everything that has breath praise the Lord. Praise the Lord! (Psalm 150:1-3, 6)

Take a moment to offer the Lord your personal praise and thanksgiving.

2. Confession: Pray this confession to the Lord as you seek to keep your life free from sin and in fellowship with Him:

O God, You know my foolishness; and my sins are not hidden from You. Let not those who wait for You, O Lord God of hosts, be ashamed because of me. (Psalm 69:5-6)

Confess any personal sins which the Holy Spirit may bring to your mind.

3. Affirmation: As you agree with the will of God, voice your affirmation of His word:

I cast my burden on You, O Lord, and You shall sustain me; when I am righteous, You shall never permit me to be moved. (Psalm 55:22)

4. Requests: As you make your requests known to the Lord, include:

- Love for fellow Christians
- The work of missions in Europe and Asia
- Your prayer list, the concerns of your heart, and today's activities

5. Closing Prayer: Finally, offer this closing prayer to the Lord:

This is the day which You have made; I will rejoice and be glad in it. (Psalm 118:24)

Memory Verse: Be anxious for nothing, but in everything by prayer and supplication, with thanksgiving, let your requests be made known to God.

Philippians 4:6
Prayer

MAY 6

READING

The passage for today centers on Joshua's farewell address. After the promised land is subdued and Joshua is approaching his death, he charges the Israelites to be faithful to the Lord.

Read Joshua 23.

REFLECTING

After a long and brilliant career as Israel's leader, Joshua bids them farewell in a manner similar to Moses. Just as his mentor had, Joshua calls the nation to assembly and recounts the wonderful things which God has done for them since the departure of Moses. He urges them to be faithful to the Lord and not to allow themselves to be corrupted by the gods or people of the nations around them. Then, in a manner reminiscent of the incredible "blessings and curses" passages of Deuteronomy 28, Joshua encourages them that if they are faithful, the "good words of the Lord" will come upon them, and if they are not faithful, "the Lord will bring upon you all the threats until He has destroyed you from off this land." Living for the Lord is an "all or nothing" proposition.

RESPONDING

1. Praise: Offer your praise to the Lord for His offer of good to us:

My soul magnifies the Lord, and my spirit has rejoiced in God my savior. . . . You who are mighty have done great things for me, and holy is Your name. And Your mercy is on those who fear You from generation to generation. (Luke 1:46-47, 49-50)

Take a moment to offer the Lord your personal praise and thanksgiving.

2. Confession: Pray this confession to the Lord as you seek to keep your life free from sin and in fellowship with Him:

For you do not desire sacrifice, or else I would give it; You do not delight in burnt offering. The sacrifices of God are a broken spirit, a broken and a contrite heart—these, O God, You will not despise. (Psalm 51:16-17)

Confess any personal sins which the Holy Spirit may bring to your mind.

3. Affirmation: As you agree with the will of God, voice your affirmation of His word:

For I consider that the sufferings of this present time are not worthy to be compared with the glory which shall be revealed in us. (Romans 8:18)

4. Requests: As you make your requests known to the Lord, include:

- Faithfulness with your time
- The president and national leaders and affairs
- Your prayer list, the concerns of your heart, and today's activities

5. Closing Prayer: Finally, offer this closing prayer to the Lord:

Oh, satisfy me early with Your mercy, that I may rejoice and be glad all my days! (Psalm 90:14)

Memory Verse: Be anxious for nothing, but in everything by prayer and supplication, with thanksgiving, let your requests be made known to God.

Philippians 4:6
Prayer

READING

The passage for today centers on Joshua's final days. After Joshua reviews Israel's history and charges them to serve the Lord, he dies at the age of 110.

Read Joshua 24.

REFLECTING

Joshua again gathers Israel to hear a review of their history and the good things God has done for them. He sets out the benefits and consequences of faithfulness and unfaithfulness and then draws a line in the sand. "If it is disagreeable in your eyes to serve the Lord, then choose whom you will serve, but as for me and my house, we will serve the Lord." Fortunately, the Israelites accept the gauntlet thrown down and agree to serve the Lord. The Lord will, from time to time, throw down the same gauntlet in our lives, through various and often unpredictable means. When we drift from Him or when we get stale or cease growing, the Lord will often bring a circumstance into our lives which draws a line in the sand, forcing us to choose whom we will serve. At those times, we must learn from the nation of Israel and choose to serve the Lord.

RESPONDING

1. Praise: Because the Lord cares enough about us to challenge us to total commitment, we praise Him:

You who love the Lord, hate evil! He preserves the souls of His saints; He delivers them out of the hand of the wicked. Light is sown for the righteous, and gladness for the upright in heart. Rejoice in the Lord, you righteous, and give thanks at the remembrance of His holy name. (Psalm 97:10-12)

Take a moment to offer the Lord your personal praise and thanksgiving.

2. Confession: Pray this confession to the Lord as you seek to keep your life free from sin and in fellowship with Him:

Forgive me, Lord, when I am unmindful of the Rock who begot me, and forget the God who fathered me. (Deuteronomy 32:18)

Confess any personal sins which the Holy Spirit may bring to your mind.

3. Affirmation: As you agree with the will of God, voice your affirmation of His word:

For Your eyes, O Lord, run to and fro throughout the whole earth, to show Yourself strong on behalf of those whose heart is loyal to You. (2 Chronicles 16:9)

4. Requests: As you make your requests known to the Lord, include:

- Your financial needs
- The needs of the poor
- Your prayer list, the concerns of your heart, and today's activities

5. Closing Prayer: Finally, offer this closing prayer to the Lord:

Let the beauty of You, Lord, be upon me, and establish the work of my hands for me; yes, establish the work of my hands. (Psalm 90:17)

Memory Verse: If we confess our sins, He is faithful and just to forgive us our sins and to cleanse us from all unrighteousness.

1 John 1:9
Prayer

MAY 8

READING

The passage for today centers on the military activities after Joshua. After the death of Joshua, the tribes of Israel do an inadequate job of vanquishing the aliens living in the promised land.

Read Judges 1.

REFLECTING

The book of Judges is a pathetic chronicle of a weak and willful people. Joshua's body is barely cool in the grave when they begin falling short of the directives he gave them. They fail at the most crucial point and tolerate the presence of immoral idol worshipers in their midst. The story which follows is one of sexual immorality, murder, idolatry, corruption, and greed. The depths to which the Israelites plunge are truly disgusting. All of which ignore the warnings given by Moses and Joshua. Turning your back on God always has tragic consequences. When we read about the Israelites, their foolishness seems so clear. Yet when we are faced with temptations today, it doesn't seem so clear. We can learn from the past, however. The consequences can be just as grave for us. A wise man walks with the Lord and is saved.

RESPONDING

1. Praise: Because we can be delivered from bondage to sin, offer your praise for the Lord's goodness:

Inasmuch as there is none like You, O Lord (You are great, and your name is great in might), who would not fear You, O King of the nations? For this is Your rightful due, for among all the wise men of the nations, and in all their kingdoms, there is none like You. . . . The Lord is the true God; He is the living God and the everlasting King. (Jeremiah 10:6-7, 10)

Take a moment to offer the Lord your personal praise and thanksgiving.

2. Confession: Pray this confession to the Lord as you seek to keep your life free from sin and in fellowship with Him:

O Lord, You blot out my transgressions for Your own sake; and You will not remember my sins. (Isaiah 43:25)

Confess any personal sins which the Holy Spirit may bring to your mind.

3. Affirmation: As you agree with the will of God, voice your affirmation of His word:

My eye has not seen, nor my ear heard, nor have entered into my heart the things which You, O God, have prepared for me who loves You. (1 Corinthians 2:9)

4. Requests: As you make your requests known to the Lord, include:

- Protection from the "evil one"
- Laborers for the "harvest"
- Your prayer list, the concerns of your heart, and today's activities

5. Closing Prayer: Finally, offer this closing prayer to the Lord:

Bless the Lord, all you His hosts, you ministers of His, who do His pleasure. Bless the Lord, all His works, in all places of His dominion. (Psalm 103:21-22)

Memory Verse: If we confess our sins, He is faithful and just to forgive us our sins and to cleanse us from all unrighteousness.

1 John 1:9
Prayer

READING

The passage for today centers on the spiritual defection of Israel. After the death of Joshua, the Israelites begin worshiping Baal, a god of Canaan.

Read Judges 2.

REFLECTING

There is a distinct pattern of events which begins to unfold in Judges. The children of Israel fall into sin and begin worshiping other gods. Sin is followed by servitude. The Lord causes other nations to rise up in judgment and enslave Israel. Israel cries out to God for deliverance, and the Lord delivers them by raising up a judge to lead them to victory. Then the land has rest until that judge dies—when the cycle begins over again: sin, servitude, supplication, salvation, and silence.

Sin is always followed by the consequence of bondage. Repentance always frees and opens us up to God's leadership in our lives. Is there sin in your life that God wants to remove?

RESPONDING

1. Praise: Because the Lord always responds to our repentance, offer Him your praise:

Blessed be the name of God forever and ever, for wisdom and might are His. . . . He gives wisdom to the wise and knowledge to those who have understanding. He reveals deep and secret things; He knows what is in the darkness, and light dwells with Him. (Daniel 2:20-22)

Pause for personal praise and thanksgiving.

2. Confession: Pray this confession to the Lord as you seek to keep your life free from sin and in fellowship with Him:

If we say we have no sin, we are deceiving ourselves, and the truth is not in us. If we confess our sins, He if faithful and just to forgive us our sins and to cleanse us from all unrighteousness. (1 John 1:8-9)

Confess any personal sins which the Holy Spirit brings to mind.

3. Affirmation: Now pause to pray this affirmation to the Lord:

I am not ashamed of the gospel of Christ, for it is Your power to salvation for everyone who believes, for the Jew first and also for the Greek. For in it Your righteousness is revealed from faith to faith; as it is written, "the just shall live by faith." (Romans 1:16-17)

4. Requests: As you make your requests known to the Lord, include:

- Commitment to the Lord
- Parachurch ministries
- Your prayer list, the concerns of your heart, and today's activities

5. Closing Prayer: Finally, offer this closing prayer to the Lord:

Lord, preserve me from all evil; preserve my soul. Lord, preserve my going out and my coming in from this time forth, and even forevermore. (Psalm 121:7-8)

Memory Verse: If we confess our sins, He is faithful and just to forgive us our sins and to cleanse us from all unrighteousness.

1 John 1:9
Prayer

MAY 10

READING

The passage for today centers on the story of Gideon being chosen to rule Israel. Because the Israelites repented of their apostasy, the Lord delivered them through the spiritual and military leadership of Gideon.

Read Judges 6.

REFLECTING

God is a specialist at taking ordinary people and doing extraordinary things through them because of their devotion and availability to Him. This is true in times of apostasy, when from places of obscurity, God sometimes calls "unknown" servants of His and, giving them faith to believe Him, works great deliverance through them. This is certainly the case with Gideon who exclaims that he is from the least family in Manasseh and is the youngest in that family. Yet he is devoted to the Lord and therefore usable. God is always more interested in our availability than He is in our natural ability. Availability can be used when ability might otherwise get in the way.

RESPONDING

1. Praise: Offer the Lord your praise that He uses availability rather than ability:

You are worthy, O Lord, to receive glory and honor and power; for You created all things, and by Your will they exist and were created. . . . (Revelation 4:11)

I will praise You, O Lord, according to Your righteousness, and will sing praise to Your name, O Lord Most High. (Psalm 7:17)

Pause for personal praise and thanksgiving.

2. Confession: Pray this confession to the Lord as you seek to keep your life free from sin and in fellowship with Him:

I am blessed because my transgression is forgiven, and my sin is covered. I am blessed because You do not impute iniquity to me, and in my spirit there is no guile. (Psalm 32:1-2)

Confess any personal sins which the Holy Spirit brings to mind.

3. Affirmation: Now pause to pray this affirmation to the Lord:

Behold what manner of love You, O Lord, have bestowed on me, that I should be called a child of God! Therefore the world does not know me, because it did not know my Lord Jesus. Now I am a child of God; and it has not yet been revealed what I shall be, but I know that when He is revealed, I shall be like Him, for I shall see Him as He is. (1 John 3:1-2)

4. Requests: As you make your requests known to the Lord, include:

- Renewing of your mind
- Needs of your extended family
- Your prayer list, the concerns of your heart, and today's activities

5. Closing Prayer: Finally, offer this closing prayer to the Lord:

May we with one mind and one mouth glorify the God and Father of our Lord Jesus Christ. (Romans 15:6)

Memory Verse: If we confess our sins, He is faithful and just to forgive us our sins and to cleanse us from all unrighteousness.

1 John 1:9
Prayer

READING

The passage for today centers on Gideon's 300 men. After directing Gideon to select only 300 men, God uses them to rout a Midianite army "without number."

Read Judges 7.

REFLECTING

"Not by might, nor by power, but by My Spirit," is the work of the Lord done. Few stories are more illustrative of that principle than that of Gideon and his army of 300. God wants prepared men to fight His battles with His weapons in His way. His weapons are not earthly, but spiritual. His ways are higher than our ways, and His thoughts higher than our thoughts. We want to offer God our strength, our weapons, and our insight. But He does not need them. We need Him. Rather than trying to get God to accept our plans and our strategies and our goals, we ought to be striving to understand His. His way is the way of victory.

RESPONDING

1. Praise: Because the Lord is our victory, we praise Him and rest in His care:

Great and marvelous are Your works, Lord God Almighty! Just and true are Your ways, O King of the saints! Who shall not fear You, O Lord, and glorify Your name? For You alone are holy. For all nations shall come and worship before You, for Your judgments have been manifested. (Revelation 15:3-4)

Take a moment to offer the Lord your personal praise and thanksgiving.

2. Confession: Pray this confession to the Lord as you seek to keep your life free from sin and in fellowship with Him:

Let the wicked forsake his way, and the unrighteous man his thoughts; let him return to You, the Lord, and You will have mercy on him; and You, Our God, for You will abundantly pardon. (Isaiah 55:7)

Confess any personal sins which the Holy Spirit may bring to your mind.

3. Affirmation: As you agree with the will of God, voice your affirmation of His word:

If I believe on the Lord Jesus Christ, I will be saved. (Acts 16:31)

4. Requests: As you make your requests known to the Lord, include:

- The Lord's leading in your life
- Opportunities for personal evangelism
- Your prayer list, the concerns of your heart, and today's activities

5. Closing Prayer: Finally, offer this closing prayer to the Lord:

Now may the God of hope fill me with all joy and peace in believing, that I may abound in hope by the power of the Holy Spirit. (Romans 15:13)

Memory Verse: If we confess our sins, He is faithful and just to forgive us our sins and to cleanse us from all unrighteousness.

1 John 1:9
Prayer

MAY 12

READING

The passage for today centers on Samson's marriage. Samson presses for an illicit union with a Philistine bride and later kills thirty Philistines to fulfill a foolish entanglement. Read Judges 14.

REFLECTING

It is a mystery that the work of God can be done through unclean vessels. There are souls saved through the preaching of unscrupulous preachers and instruction gained through the teaching of impure teachers. This is not the rule, but the exception. Nevertheless, it happens. Some people are strongly gifted and seem to see results regardless of their personal worthiness. This is certainly true of Samson. It is difficult to find a more unworthy vessel for the work of God. It is a challenge to decide if he wantonly disregards wisdom and the word of God or whether his decision-making ability is somehow impaired. Nevertheless, in the midst of his exceedingly foolish escapades, God uses him to bring judgment on the Philistines who have flaunted their godlessness.

RESPONDING

1. Praise: Praise the Lord for His sovereignty and for the fact that He works His will regardless of the failure of His children:

Who is like You, O Lord, among the gods? Who is like You, glorious in holiness, fearful in praises, doing wonders? (Exodus 15:11)

Therefore You are great, O Lord God. For there is none like You, nor is there any God besides You, according to all that we have heard with our ears. (2 Samuel 7:22)

Take a moment to offer the Lord your personal praise and thanksgiving.

2. Confession: Pray this confession to the Lord as you seek to keep your life free from sin and in fellowship with Him:

You have not dealt with me according to my sins, nor punished me according to my iniquities. For as the heavens are high above the earth, so great is Your mercy toward those who fear You; as far as the east is from the west, so far have You removed our transgressions from us. (Psalm 103:10-12)

Confess any personal sins which the Holy Spirit may bring to your mind.

3. Affirmation: As you agree with the will of God, voice your affirmation of His word:

You did not spare Your own Son, but delivered Him up for me, how shall You not with Him also freely give me all things? (Romans 8:32)

4. Requests: As you make your requests known to the Lord, include:

- Love for the lost
- The work of missions in Africa
- Your prayer list, the concerns of your heart, and today's activities

5. Closing Prayer: Finally, offer this closing prayer to the Lord:

Now to You who are able to establish us according to the gospel and preaching of Jesus Christ—to You, alone wise, be glory through Jesus Christ forever. Amen. (Romans 16:25-27)

Memory Verse: If we confess our sins, He is faithful and just to forgive us our sins and to cleanse us from all unrighteousness.

1 John 1:9
Prayer

MAY 13

READING

The passage for today centers on the story of Samson burning the Philistine crops. As an act of revenge, Samson uses foxes to burn the crops of the Philistines and later kills a thousand men when they try to retaliate.

Read Judges 15.

REFLECTING

It is instructive to list the sins of Samson:

1. Fraternizing with the pagans of other nations.

2. Marrying an unbeliever.

3. Disobeying his parents.

4. Deliberately touching a dead animal.

5. Murdering innocent people.

6. Visiting a harlot.

7. Lying

And these are just the obvious ones. These are the consequences of a life which ignores the word and will of God. We are often tempted to disregard the Truth. We weary of being good and always fighting natural inclinations which live in our hearts. But one glimpse at Samson's life reveals the consequences of giving in to that weariness.

RESPONDING

1. Praise: Offer your praise to the Lord who renews our strength when we wait upon Him:

He is the Rock, His work is perfect; for all His ways are justice, a God of truth and without injustice; righteous and upright is He. (Deuteronomy 32:4)

The Lord lives! Blessed be my Rock! Let God be exalted, the Rock of my salvation! (2 Samuel 22:47)

Take a moment to offer the Lord your personal praise and thanksgiving.

2. Confession: Pray this confession to the Lord as you seek to keep your life free from sin and in fellowship with Him:

Out of the depths I have cried to You, O Lord. . . . If You, Lord, should mark iniquities, O Lord, who could stand? But there is forgiveness with You, that You may be feared. (Psalm 130:1, 3-4)

Confess any personal sins which the Holy Spirit may bring to your mind.

3. Affirmation: As you agree with the will of God, voice your affirmation of His word:

You will keep me in perfect peace, my mind is stayed on You, because I trust in You. (Isaiah 26:3)

4. Requests: As you make your requests known to the Lord, include:

• Faithfulness with your talents

• Your state and local leaders and affairs

• Your prayer list, the concerns of your heart, and today's activities

5. Closing Prayer: Finally, offer this closing prayer to the Lord:

The grace of the Lord Jesus Christ, and the love of God, and the communion of the Holy Spirit be with us all. Amen. (2 Corinthians 13:14)

Memory Verse: If we confess our sins, He is faithful and just to forgive us our sins and to cleanse us from all unrighteousness.

1 John 1:9
Prayer

MAY 14

READING

The passage for today centers on Samson's death. After foolishly betraying the secret of his strength, Samson is subdued and later dies in his final act of resistance.

Read Judges 16.

REFLECTING

"Do not be deceived. God is not mocked. Whatever a man sows, that shall he also reap. For the one who sows to his own flesh shall from the flesh reap corruption" (Galatians 6:7-8). This passage is a fitting epilogue to Samson's life. His wanton foolishness finally catches up with him. In a profound example of bad judgment, he discloses the secret of his strength to a woman who has betrayed him repeatedly already. His Nazirite vow is violated as a result of this indiscretion, and all power leaves him. His eyes are gouged out, and he dies, not avenging the Lord against the pagan Philistines, but avenging his own two eyes. It is a dismal and heartbreaking conclusion to a life that is tragic, not only because of what it was, but even more for what it could have been.

RESPONDING

1. Praise: Thank the Lord and give him your praise that by His grace we can escape the consequences of Samson by living for Him:

O Lord God of Israel, the One who dwells between the cherubim, You are God, You alone, of all the kingdoms of the earth. You have made heaven and earth. (2 Kings 19:15)

Lord God of Israel, there is no God in heaven above or on earth below like You, who keep Your covenant and mercy with Your ser-

vants who walk before You with all their heart. (1 Kings 8:23)

Take a moment to offer the Lord your personal praise and thanksgiving.

2. Confession: Pray this confession to the Lord as you seek to keep your life free from sin and in fellowship with Him:

As a father pities his children, so You, O Lord, pity those who fear You. For You know our frame; You remember that we are dust. (Psalm 103:13-14)

Confess any personal sins which the Holy Spirit may bring to your mind.

3. Affirmation: As you agree with the will of God, voice your affirmation of His word:

You are Spirit, and those who worship You must worship in spirit and truth. (John 4:24)

4. Requests: As you make your requests known to the Lord, include:

- Strength for obedience
- International students in America
- Your prayer list, the concerns of your heart, and today's activities

5. Closing Prayer: Finally, offer this closing prayer to the Lord:

Now to You who are able to do exceedingly abundantly above all that I ask or think, according to the power that works in me, to You be glory in the church by Christ Jesus throughout all ages, world without end. Amen. (Ephesians 3:20-21)

Memory Verse: Now this is the confidence that we have in Him, that if we ask anything according to His will, He hears us.

1 John 5:14

Prayer

MAY 15

READING

The passage for today centers on the story of Ruth's being widowed. A Jewess, Naomi, and her two daughters-in-law lose their husbands. Read Ruth 1.

REFLECTING

Loyalty is good for the soul. In Ruth, we see one of the most stirring examples of loyalty in the Bible. In spite of Naomi's urgings to the contrary, Ruth stays with her, looking not for personal fulfillment or material comfort, but longing merely to maintain the relationship with one whom she loves. This loyalty comes from a pure heart, and it is not surprising that it extends not just to Naomi, but also to the Lord. When one has a great capacity for one thing, it often can be extended to another. In stark contrast to Samson, Ruth's life of selflessness leads to beauty, fulfillment, and the good of others as well as self. May we take instruction for our own lives and live like Ruth, not like Samson.

RESPONDING

1. Praise: Because we can have the beauty of the Lord in our lives, give thanksgiving and praise to Him:

Give to the Lord, O kindreds of the peoples. . . . Give to the Lord the glory due His name; bring an offering, and come before Him. Oh, worship the Lord in the beauty of holiness! (1 Chronicles 16:28-29)

I will praise the Lord according to His righteousness, and will sing praise to the name of the Lord Most High. (Psalm 7:17)

Take a moment to offer the Lord your personal praise and thanksgiving.

2. Confession: Pray this confession to the Lord as you seek to keep your life free from sin and in fellowship with Him:

I will praise You, for I am fearfully and wonderfully made; marvelous are Your works, and that my soul knows very well. . . . Search me, O God, and know my heart; try me, and know my anxieties; and see if there is any wicked way in me, and lead me in the way everlasting. (Psalm 139:14, 23-24)

Confess any personal sins which the Holy Spirit may bring to your mind.

3. Affirmation: As you agree with the will of God, voice your affirmation of His word:

If I am in You, O Lord, I am a new creation; old things have passed away; behold, all things have become new. (2 Corinthians 5:17)

4. Requests: As you make your requests known to the Lord, include:

- Your "daily bread"
- Christian education institutions
- Your prayer list, the concerns of your heart, and today's activities

5. Closing Prayer: Finally, offer this closing prayer to the Lord:

Now may You, the God of peace, sanctify me completely, and may my whole spirit, soul, and body be preserved blameless at the coming of my Lord Jesus Christ. (1 Thessalonians 5:23)

Memory Verse: Now this is the confidence that we have in Him, that if we ask anything according to His will, He hears us.

1 John 5:14
Prayer

MAY 16

READING

The passage for today centers on Ruth's return to Bethlehem. Though the second daughter-in-law leaves them, Ruth and Naomi return to Bethlehem in hopes of fostering a livelihood.

Read Ruth 2.

REFLECTING

Water seeks its own level. When Boaz, a noble and godly man, hears of Ruth's noble and godly actions, he cannot help but be moved with appreciation for the kind of person she is. When he finds her gleaning in his fields, he bestows kindnesses on her. Ruth asks why he should take notice of her since she is a foreigner. Boaz replies that it is because of all that she has done for Naomi. The way we go about our everyday lives communicates a "life message" to others.

RESPONDING

1. Praise: The "life message" of Jesus is one for which we can praise Him:

The Lord made the heavens. Honor and majesty are before Him; strength and beauty are in His sanctuary. Give to the Lord, O kindreds of the peoples, . . . Give to the Lord the glory due His name; bring an offering, and come into His courts. Let the heavens rejoice, and let the earth be glad. (Psalm 96:5b-8, 11)

Now express any additional thoughts you may have of thanks or praise.

2. Confession: Pray this confession to the Lord as you seek to keep your life free from sin and in fellowship with Him:

The heart is deceitful above all things, and desperately wicked; who can know it? You, the Lord, search the heart; You test the mind, even to give every man according to his ways, and according to the fruit of his doings. . . . Heal me, O Lord, and I shall be healed; save me, and I shall be saved, for You are my praise. (Jeremiah 17:9, 10, 14)

Confess any personal sins which the Holy Spirit brings to your mind.

3. Affirmation: Now pray this affirmation to the Lord as you agree with and submit yourself to the will of God:

The Spirit Himself bears witness with my spirit that I am a child of Yours, O God, and if a child, then an heir—heir of Yours and joint heirs with Christ, if indeed I suffer with Him, that I may also be glorified. (Romans 8:16-17)

4. Requests: As you make your requests known to the Lord, include:

* Passion for moral excellence
* Needs of personal friends
* Your prayer list, the concerns of your heart, and today's activities

5. Closing Prayer: Finally, offer this closing prayer to the Lord:

Now may the Lord Jesus Christ Himself, and You, my God and Father, who have loved me and given me everlasting consolation and good hope by grace, comfort my heart and establish me in every good word and work. (2 Thessalonians 2:16-17)

Memory Verse: Now this is the confidence that we have in Him, that if we ask anything according to His will, He hears us.

1 John 5:14
Prayer

READING

The passage for today centers on Ruth's redemption. Boaz, a close relative of Naomi and the owner of the fields in which Ruth is gleaning, agrees to marry Ruth.

Read Ruth 3.

REFLECTING

The custom in the Old Testament is that when a relative dies without leaving a male heir, the next nearest relative who can is to marry the surviving spouse to preserve the family name and property rights. Naomi thinks Boaz is the next of kin; therefore, there is nothing forward in Ruth's actions. Boaz exercises admirable restraint, knowing that there is closer kin. His concern for Ruth's good name again shows his nobility of character, for he is surely attracted to Ruth already. God judges our motives as well as our actions. "Motives are weighed by the Lord" (Proverbs 16:2). Is your life above reproach, filled with integrity, honesty, and purity?

RESPONDING

1. Praise: Worship the Lord by offering Him your praise in spirit and in truth:

Ah, Lord God! Behold, You have made the heavens and the earth by Your great power and outstretched arm. There is nothing too hard for You. You show lovingkindness to thousands. . . . the Great, the Mighty God, whose name is the Lord of hosts. You are great in counsel and mighty in work. (Jeremiah 32:17-19)

Pause for personal praise and thanksgiving.

2. Confession: Pray this confession to the Lord as you seek to keep your life free from sin and in fellowship with Him:

Who can understand his errors? Cleanse me from secret faults. Keep back Your servant from presumptuous sins; let them not have dominion over me. Then I shall be blameless, and I shall be innocent of great transgression. (Psalm 19:12-13)

Confess any personal sins which the Holy Spirit brings to mind.

3. Affirmation: Now pause to pray this affirmation to the Lord:

For Your thoughts are not my thoughts, nor are my ways Your ways. For as the heavens are higher than the earth, so are Your ways higher than my ways, and Your thoughts than my thoughts. (Isaiah 55:8-9)

4. Requests: As you make your requests known to the Lord, pray for:

- Wisdom in decision making
- Opportunities to serve the Lord
- Your prayer list, the concerns of your heart, and today's activities

5. Closing Prayer: Finally, offer this closing prayer to the Lord:

Now to You, the King eternal, immortal, invisible, to God who alone is wise, be honor and glory forever and ever. Amen. (1 Timothy 1:17)

Memory Verse: Now this is the confidence that we have in Him, that if we ask anything according to His will, He hears us.

1 John 5:14
Prayer

MAY 18

READING

The passage for today centers on the marriage of Ruth. Fulfilling an age-old custom, Boaz marries Ruth and restores the fortunes of her and Naomi.

Read Ruth 4.

REFLECTING

What a happy ending! The gleaner need no longer tread the fields, following the reapers. Because of her faithfulness and circumspection, all the broad acres in which she once gleaned as a destitute alien are now hers, for she had become one with the owner. When we are one with Christ, we are no longer aliens in another's fields, but, being one with Christ, all that was His is now also ours. As Ruth is translated from isolation and poverty to union and wealth in Boaz, so we become fellow heirs of the riches of Christ and the grace of God. It is likely that the story of Ruth was intended by God to picture our redemption in Christ. Our story is even greater than the story of Ruth.

RESPONDING

1. Praise: Ruth is such a beautiful story of redemption; praise the Lord for His redemption of us:

Tremble before Him, all the earth. The world also is firmly established, it shall not be moved. Let the heavens rejoice, and let the earth be glad. . . . Oh, give thanks to the Lord, for He is good! For His mercy endures forever. . . . Blessed be the Lord God of Israel from everlasting to everlasting! (1 Chronicles 16:30-31, 34, 36)

Take a moment to offer the Lord your personal praise and thanksgiving.

2. Confession: Pray this confession to the Lord as you seek to keep your life free from sin and in fellowship with Him:

We give You thanks, O Lord, that we may reason with You. Though our sins are like scarlet, they shall be as white as snow; though they are red like crimson, They shall be as wool. (Isaiah 1:18)

Confess any personal sins which the Holy Spirit may bring to your mind.

3. Affirmation: As you agree with the will of God, voice your affirmation of His word:

I will remember the works of the Lord; surely I will remember Your wonders of old. I will also meditate on all Your work, and talk of Your deeds. (Psalm 77:11-12)

4. Requests: As you make your requests known to the Lord, include:

- Victory over temptation
- The work of missions in North and South America
- Your prayer list, the concerns of your heart, and today's activities

5. Closing Prayer: Finally, offer this closing prayer to the Lord:

You who are the blessed and only Potentate, the King of kings and Lord of lords, who alone has immortality, dwelling in unapproachable light, whom no man has seen or can see, to You be honor and everlasting power. Amen. (1 Timothy 6:15-16)

Memory Verse: Now this is the confidence that we have in Him, that if we ask anything according to His will, He hears us.

1 John 5:14
Prayer

READING

The passage for today centers on Samuel's birth. God gives a child to a godly couple, Hannah and Elkanah, after years of her praying for a son.

Read 1 Samuel 1.

REFLECTING

Much of life is utter mystery, and this is especially true when it comes to the matter of God's children suffering. It is often inexplicable, yet we see it turning the godly ones in the Scripture to the Lord. The grief of being childless drove Hannah to God. There she found her only resource. As a child who cries when being taken to a doctor by its parents still trusts in the parents in spite of the fear and pain, so we must still trust and cling to the Lord, even though we do not understand why He doesn't deliver us from the pain.

Just as the child will some day understand about the doctor, we will some day understand about the pain.

Until then, let the pain drive us closer to the Lord, rather than farther away.

RESPONDING

1. Praise: Even though you may be in pain, praise the Lord that He loves you and cares for you:

Blessed be Your glorious name, which is exalted above all blessing and praise! You alone are the Lord; You have made heaven, the heaven of heavens, with all their host, the earth and all things on it, the seas and all that is in them, and You preserve them all. The host of heaven worships You. (Nehemiah 9:5-6)

Take a moment to offer the Lord your personal praise and thanksgiving.

2. Confession: Pray this confession to the Lord as you seek to keep your life free from sin and in fellowship with Him:

You have blotted out, like a thick cloud, my transgressions, and like a cloud, my sins. I will return to You, for You have redeemed me. (Isaiah 44:22)

Confess any personal sins which the Holy Spirit may bring to your mind.

3. Affirmation: As you agree with the will of God, voice your affirmation of His word:

I have been crucified with Christ; it is no longer I who live, but Christ lives in me; and the life which I now live in the flesh I live by faith in the Son of God, who loved me and gave Himself for me. (Galatians 2:20)

4. Requests: As you make your requests known to the Lord, include:

- Love for your family
- Revival among Christians in America
- Your prayer list, the concerns of your heart, and today's activities

5. Closing Prayer: Finally, offer this closing prayer to the Lord:

Make me complete in every good work to do Your will, working in me what is well pleasing in Your sight, through Jesus Christ, to whom be glory forever and ever. Amen. (Hebrews 13:20-21)

Memory Verse: Now this is the confidence that we have in Him, that if we ask anything according to His will, He hears us.

1 John 5:14
Prayer

MAY 20

READING

The passage for today centers on Samuel's dedication. True to her word, Hannah dedicates Samuel to the service of the Lord, and he goes to live with Eli the priest.

Read 1 Samuel 2.

REFLECTING

The overstimulated society in which we live demands such an endless succession of thrills that we rarely give due appreciation when significant things happen to us. We rarely give God sufficient thanks and praise for the things He does for us, and we rarely give Him adequate worship for who He is and for His significant answers to prayer.

By contrast, Hannah's song of thanksgiving is especially gratifying. She prays earnestly for a child, and when the Lord gives her one, she expresses her gratitude in full-blown poetic praise. Her response is fitting to the gift. We may not be able to write poetry or express ourselves as eloquently as Hannah, but we can search our creativity for ways of expressing gratitude as well as we can.

RESPONDING

1. Praise: Use the following to express your gratitude and praise to the Lord for all He has done for you:

O Lord, our Lord, how excellent is Your name in all the earth, You who set Your glory above the heavens! When I consider Your heavens, the work of Your fingers. . . , what is man that You are mindful of him, and the son of man that You visit him? . . . O Lord, our Lord, How excellent is Your name in all the earth! (Psalm 8:1, 3-4, 9)

Take a moment to offer the Lord your personal praise and thanksgiving.

2. Confession: Pray this confession to the Lord as you seek to keep your life free from sin and in fellowship with Him:

For a mere moment You have forsaken me, but with great mercies You will gather me. With a little wrath You hid Your face from me for a moment; but with everlasting kindness You will have mercy on me. (Isaiah 54:7-8)

Confess any personal sins which the Holy Spirit may bring to your mind.

3. Affirmation: As you agree with the will of God, voice your affirmation of His word:

Unless the Lord builds my house, I labor in vain; Unless the Lord guards my city, I stay awake watching in vain. (Psalm 127:1)

4. Requests: As you make your requests known to the Lord, include:

- Faithfulness with your treasures
- The Great Commission
- Your prayer list, the concerns of your heart, and today's activities

5. Closing Prayer:

Finally, offer this closing prayer to the Lord:

May You, the God of grace, who called me to Your eternal glory by Christ Jesus, after I have suffered a while, perfect, establish, strengthen, and settle me. To You be the glory and the dominion forever and ever. Amen. (1 Peter 5:10-11)

Memory Verse: Now this is the confidence we have in Him, that if we ask anything according to His will, He hears us.

1 John 5:14
Prayer

READING

The passage for today centers on Samuel's prophetic call. The Lord speaks directly to Samuel, and all Israel recognizes Samuel as a prophet of God.

Read 1 Samuel 3.

REFLECTING

For all the glory and joy of speaking directly with the Lord, Samuel is faced with a very difficult task—that of relating to Eli the troublesome message which the Lord has given. Samuel has nothing to gain or lose by the encounter and, with a pure heart, tells Eli the truth.

We are often faced with the same task of telling people the truth, knowing that the truth will hurt. Ephesians 4:15 instructs us to speak the truth in love. Speaking in love without the truth is self-defeating, and speaking the truth without love is destructive. Samuel's example is a difficult one, but a good one. Like Samuel, we can only fulfill such a task if our hearts are pure and we do not manipulate the situation for our own benefit.

RESPONDING

1. Praise: Because we can know the truth and the truth can set us free, offer your praise to the Lord:

I will praise You, O Lord, with my whole heart; I will tell of all Your marvelous works. I will be glad and rejoice in You; I will sing praise to Your name, O Most High. . . . The Lord also will be a refuge for the oppressed, a refuge in times of trouble. And those who know Your name will put their trust in You; for You, Lord have not forsaken those who seek You. (Psalm 9:1-2, 9-10)

Take a moment to offer the Lord your personal praise and thanksgiving.

2. Confession: Pray this confession to the Lord as you seek to keep your life free from sin and in fellowship with Him:

Lord, be merciful to me; heal my soul, for I have sinned against You. . . . O Lord, be merciful to me, and raise me up. . . . Blessed be the Lord God of Israel from everlasting to everlasting! Amen and amen. (Psalm 41:4, 10, 13)

Confess any personal sins which the Holy Spirit may bring to your mind.

3. Affirmation: As you agree with the will of God, voice your affirmation of His word:

For You, O Lord, made Him who knew no sin to be sin for me, that I might become the righteousness of You in Him. (2 Corinthians 5:21)

4. Requests: As you make your requests known to the Lord, include:

- Spiritual insight
- Campus ministries
- Your prayer list, the concerns of your heart, and today's activities

5. Closing Prayer: Finally, offer this closing prayer to the Lord:

May I grow in the grace and knowledge of our Lord and Savior Jesus Christ. To Him be the glory both now and forever. Amen. (2 Peter 3:18)

Memory Verse: If any of you lacks wisdom, let him ask of God, who gives to all liberally and without reproach, and it will be given to him.

James 1:5
Prayer

MAY 22

READING

The passage for today centers on the Israelites' demand for a king. The Israelites go to Samuel and demand a king from the Lord, in spite of Samuel's counsel against it.

Read 1 Samuel 8.

REFLECTING

In 1 Samuel the Lord intends to rule Israel by "theocracy," which means that God would rule them through a man who will be His spokesman. In rejecting this method, the Israelites are not rejecting Samuel, but God. True, there is a problem with Samuel's sons not walking after the Lord, but rather than asking God for another "theocratic administrator," they demand of God a monarchy. In seeking to correct a legitimate problem, they make matters worse because their motives are not pure. They have a selfish desire for a king, wanting to be like all the other nations around them.

When we see legitimate problems, we must be careful that we do not make the situation worse by demanding a wrong solution. There is no substitute for pure motives when it comes to problem solving.

RESPONDING

1. Praise: Because the Lord will lead us in the light, we need not fear His solutions to problems, and we can praise Him:

Be exalted, O God, above the heavens; let Your glory be above all the earth. . . . I will praise You, O Lord, among the peoples; I will sing to You among the nations. For Your mercy reaches unto the heavens, and Your truth unto the clouds. Be exalted, O God, above the heavens; let Your glory be above all the earth. (Psalm 57:5, 9-11)

Take a moment to offer the Lord your personal praise and thanksgiving.

2. Confession: Pray this confession to the Lord as you seek to keep your life free from sin and in fellowship with Him:

Surely You, Lord Jesus, have borne our griefs and carried our sorrows. . . . You were wounded for our transgressions, You were bruised for our iniquities; the chastisement for our peace was upon You, and by Your stripes we are healed. (Isaiah 53:4, 5)

Confess any personal sins which the Holy Spirit may bring to your mind.

3. Affirmation: As you agree with the will of God, voice your affirmation of His word:

You, Lord Jesus, are the resurrection and the life. If I believe in You, though I may die, I shall live. (John 11:25)

4. Requests: As you make your requests known to the Lord, include:

- Desire to be like Christ
- Needs in inner cities
- Your prayer list, the concerns of your heart, and today's activities

5. Closing Prayer: Finally, offer this closing prayer to the Lord:

Blessing and honor and glory and power be to You who sit on the throne, and to You, Lord, forever and ever! (Revelation 5:13)

Memory Verse: If any of you lacks wisdom, let him ask of God, who gives to all liberally and without reproach, and it will be given to him.

James 1:5
Prayer

READING

The passage for today centers on the choice for the first king. God instructs Samuel to anoint Saul, an imposing figure of a man, to be the first king over Israel.

Read 1 Samuel 9.

REFLECTING

The sovereignty of God is a difficult concept to keep in balance. Often we find ourselves making too much or too little of it. It is true, however, that many of the events in our lives which seem to come at random—with no significance—are actually events which the Lord is using to orchestrate His purpose in our lives. Saul goes looking for donkeys and ends up discovering that he will be king of Israel. The disciples found this to be true, also, as Jesus regularly acted in an unexpected manner, whether it be through a wedding celebration, storms, bread and fish, or simple parables. We should always bathe our daily activities in prayer, for we never know what the Lord might be preparing for us.

RESPONDING

1. Praise: Rest in the Lord's sovereignty, and praise His name:

Tremble before Him, all the earth. The world also is firmly established, it shall not be moved. Let the heavens rejoice, and let the earth be glad. . . . Oh, give thanks to the Lord, for He is good! For His mercy endures forever. . . . Blessed be the Lord God . . . from everlasting to everlasting! (1 Chronicles 16:30-31, 34, 36)

Pause for personal praise and thanksgiving.

2. Confession: Pray this confession to the Lord as you seek to keep your life free from sin and in fellowship with Him:

O Lord, You do not have as much delight in burnt offerings and sacrifices, as in our obeying Your voice. Behold, to obey is better than sacrifice, and to heed than the fat of rams. (1 Samuel 15:22)

Confess any personal sins which the Holy Spirit brings to your mind.

3. Affirmation: Now pause to pray this affirmation to the Lord:

There is therefore now no condemnation for me if I am in You, Christ Jesus. For the law of the Spirit of life in You, has set me free from the law of sin and death. (Romans 8:1-2)

4. Requests: As you make your requests known to the Lord, include:

- Personal witness for Christ
- Local churches around the nation
- Your prayer list, the concerns of your heart, and today's activities

5. Closing Prayer: Finally, offer this closing prayer to the Lord:

Amen! Blessing and glory and wisdom, thanksgiving and honor and power and might, be to You, God, forever and ever. Amen. (Revelation 7:12)

Memory Verse: If any of you lacks wisdom, let him ask of God, who gives to all liberally and without reproach, and it will be given to him.

James 1:5
Prayer

MAY 24

READING

The passage for today centers on the public recognition of Saul. After he anoints Saul to be Israel's first king, Samuel publicly introduces him to the nation.

Read 1 Samuel 10.

REFLECTING

Leadership is at the same time a blessing and a curse. Leaders like to have the allegiance and esteem of all their followers, but such is rarely the case. Inherent within humanity are differences of opinion, and those differences cause some to be for certain leadership and against other leadership. The very day Saul is announced to be king over Israel, there are those "worthless men" who grumble against him. If you are a follower, God calls you to submission and trust, not bickering and complaining. If you are in a position of leadership, you should not be insensitive to dissension, but you must also realize that you will never make all the people happy all the time. Both leading and following require dependence upon God's sovereignty.

RESPONDING

1. **Praise:** Show your allegiance to the Lord by giving Him your praise:

I will bless the Lord at all times; his praise shall continually be in my mouth. My soul shall make its boast in the Lord; the humble shall hear of it and be glad. Oh, magnify the Lord with me, and let us exalt His name together. . . . Oh, taste and see that the Lord is good; blessed is the man who trusts in Him! (Psalm 34:1-3, 8)

Pause for personal praise and thanksgiving.

2. **Confession:** Pray this confession to the Lord as you seek to keep your life free from sin and in fellowship with Him:

I have sinned greatly in what I have done; but now, I pray, O Lord, take away the iniquity of Your servant, for I have done very foolishly. (2 Samuel 24:10)

Confess any personal sins which the Holy Spirit brings to mind.

3. **Affirmation:** Now pause to pray this affirmation to the Lord:

My body is the temple of the Holy Spirit who is in me, whom I have from You, O God, and I am not my own. For I have been bought with a price; therefore I will glorify God in my body and in my spirit, which are Yours. (1 Corinthians 6:19-20)

4. **Requests:** As you make your requests known to the Lord, include:

- An eternal perspective
- Needs of work or school mates
- Your prayer list, the concerns of your heart, and today's activities

5. **Closing Prayer:** Finally, offer this closing prayer to the Lord:

I will wait on You, the Lord; I will be of good courage, and You shall strengthen my heart; I will wait on You! (Psalm 27:14)

Memory Verse: If any of you lacks wisdom, let him ask of God, who gives to all liberally and without reproach, and it will be given to him.

James 1:5
Prayer

READING

The passage for today centers on Saul's disobedience. In direct disobedience to Samuel's instructions, Saul breaks the law of the Lord and offers sacrifices to the Lord.

Read 1 Samuel 15.

REFLECTING

Saul's fall is fast and far. His spiritual leadership is destroyed before he really gets a good start. Such a profound disparity between how he starts and how he ends up is difficult to explain. It stands as a warning to us all, however. None of us is above falling—no matter where we are in our spiritual walk. Probably all of us know of well-known spiritual leaders who have fallen into sin.

Part of our regular prayer ought to be the prayer which Jesus taught us to pray: "Do not lead us into temptation, but deliver us from evil." Again, Jesus says, "Keep watching and praying, that you may not enter into temptation" (Matthew 26:41). The price of our spiritual welfare is eternal vigilance.

RESPONDING

1. Praise: Offer your praise to the Lord for His protection from evil:

I will love You, O Lord, my strength. The Lord is my rock and my fortress and my deliverer; my God, my strength, in whom I will trust; I will call upon the Lord, who is worthy to be praised; so shall I be saved from my enemies. . . . Blessed be my Rock! Let the God of my salvation be exalted. (Psalm 18:1-3, 46)

Take a moment to offer the Lord your personal praise and thanksgiving.

2. Confession: Pray this confession to the Lord as you seek to keep your life free from sin and in fellowship with Him:

All we like sheep have gone astray; we have turned, every one, to his own way; and You, O Lord, have laid on Him the iniquity of us all. (Isaiah 53:6)

Confess any personal sins which the Holy Spirit may bring to your mind.

3. Affirmation: As you agree with the will of God, voice your affirmation of His word:

You, Lord Jesus, are the way, the truth, and the life. I cannot come to the Father except through You. (John 14:6)

4. Requests: As you make your requests known to the Lord, include:

- Personal discipline
- Christians worldwide who are persecuted for their faith
- Your prayer list, the concerns of your heart, and today's activities

5. Closing Prayer: Finally, offer this closing prayer to the Lord:

Show me the path of life; in Your presence is fullness of joy; at Your right hand are pleasures forevermore. (Psalm 16:11)

Memory Verse: If any of you lacks wisdom, let him ask of God, who gives to all liberally and without reproach, and it will be given to him.
James 1:5
Prayer

MAY 26

READING

The passage for today centers on the anointing of David as king. After Saul's rebellion, God rejects him and instructs Samuel to anoint David, the youngest son of Jesse, to be the next king of Israel.

Read 1 Samuel 16.

REFLECTING

David is indeed an outstanding individual. As a teenager, he is known to be a "skillful musician, a mighty man of valor, one prudent in speech, and a handsome man, and the Lord is with him" (1 Samuel 16:18). In each of these things, David is not just lucky. He might have been born with musical talent, but no one can play an instrument skillfully without much practice. No warrior is skilled without unflagging practice in the military craft. No one is prudent in speech without constant attention to his words. David works hard at all the things for which he is known, including the fact that "the Lord is with him."

Each of us has been given talents and abilities. Like David, if we are to achieve our God-given potential, we must be slaves to the things which advance those abilities.

RESPONDING

1. Praise: Praise the Lord because He fulfills our lives by giving us talents and abilities to develop:

Be exalted, O God, above the heavens; let Your glory be above all the earth. . . . I will praise You, O Lord, among the peoples; I will sing to You among the nations. For Your mercy reaches unto the heavens, and Your truth unto the clouds. Be exalted, O God, above the heavens; let Your glory be above all the earth. (Psalm 57:5, 9-11)

Take a moment to offer the Lord your personal praise and thanksgiving.

2. Confession: Pray this confession to the Lord as you seek to keep your life free from sin and in fellowship with Him:

Let the wicked forsake his way, and the unrighteous man his thoughts; let him return to You, the Lord, and You will have mercy on him; and You, our God, for You will abundantly pardon. (Isaiah 55:7)

Confess any personal sins which the Holy Spirit may bring to your mind.

3. Affirmation: As you agree with the will of God, voice your affirmation of His word:

For I know the grace of You, O Lord Jesus Christ, that though You were rich, yet for my sake You became poor, that I through Your poverty might become rich. (2 Corinthians 8:9)

4. Requests: As you make your requests known to the Lord, include:

- Love for the Lord
- The work of missions in the Middle East, Australia, and the Islands
- Your prayer list, the concerns of your heart, and today's activities

5. Closing Prayer: Finally, offer this closing prayer to the Lord:

Save Your people, and bless Your inheritance; shepherd us also, and bear us up forever. (Psalm 28:9)

Memory Verse: If any of you lacks wisdom, let him ask of God, who gives to all liberally and without reproach, and it will be given to him.
James 1:5
Prayer

READING

The passage for today centers on Goliath's challenge. After Goliath, a Philistine giant, taunts the army of God, David is divinely blessed as he confronts Goliath and slays him.

Read 1 Samuel 17.

REFLECTING

When God goes to war, there are no accidents. Just as He uses Gideon and an army of only 300 to rout the Midianite army which is "without number," so He uses a boy with a slingshot to rout the Philistine army. In 2 Chronicles 18:33, a certain man draws his bow at random, but it strikes the king of Israel in a joint of his armor. There are no accidents when God goes to war. We can take great comfort in this fact in relationship to the spiritual warfare in which we all find ourselves.

The obstacles may seem insurmountable, the adversary unconquerable. But if we are on God's side, no foe is great. Martin Luther once wrote: "Did we in our own strength confide, our striving would be losing. Were not the right man on our side, the man of God's own choosing. Dost ask Who that may be? Christ Jesus it is He. Lord Sabaoth His name, from age to age the same. And He must win the battle."

RESPONDING

1. Praise: Give praise and thanks to the Lord for giving us victory over the world:

O God, You are my God; early will I seek You; My soul thirsts for You; My flesh longs for You in a dry and thirsty land where there is no water. So I have looked for You in the sanctuary, to see Your power and Your glory. (Psalm 63:1-2)

Take a moment to offer the Lord your personal praise and thanksgiving.

2. Confession: Pray this confession to the Lord as you seek to keep your life free from sin and in fellowship with Him:

You will again have compassion on us, and will subdue our iniquities. You will cast all our sins into the depths of the sea. (Micah 7:19)

Confess any personal sins which the Holy Spirit may bring to your mind.

3. Affirmation: As you agree with the will of God, voice your affirmation of His word:

This is Your commandment, that I love others as You have loved me. (John 15:12)

4. Requests: As you make your requests known to the Lord, include:

- Faithfulness in sharing Christ
- The Lord's work in national and world affairs
- Your prayer list, the concerns of your heart, and today's activities

5. Closing Prayer: Finally, offer this closing prayer to the Lord:

You, the Lord, will command Your lovingkindness in the daytime, and in the night Your song shall be with me—a prayer to You, the God of my life. (Psalm 42:8)

Memory Verse: If any of you lacks wisdom, let him ask of God, who gives to all liberally and without reproach, and it will be given to him.
James 1:5
Prayer

MAY 28

READING

The passage for today centers on David's coronation. After a delay of many years, David finally assumes the throne over all of Israel.

Read 2 Samuel 5.

REFLECTING

Years earlier, Samuel had anointed David—then a young, inexperienced boy—to be king over Israel. Fourteen years pass between the time that Samuel anoints David to be king and the time that David actually assumes the throne over all of Israel. Instead of luxuriating in the royal palace learning how to lead parades, David spends that time running from cave to cave trying to keep Saul from lopping his head off. But it is these difficult experiences that build into David the strength of character, the convictions, the sensitivity to right and wrong, and the vision to be a great king. Without the caves, there would have been no king.

How true, even for us today. The road to transformation always goes through the tunnel of trials.

RESPONDING

1. Praise: Because the Lord uses the difficult times of life to create Christlikeness in our hearts, we can praise Him for all things:

Because Your lovingkindness is better than life, My lips shall praise You. Thus I will bless You while I live; I will lift up my hands in Your name. My soul shall be satisfied as with marrow and fatness, and my mouth shall praise You with joyful lips. . . . Because You have been my help, therefore in the shadow of Your wings I will rejoice. (Psalm 63:3-5, 7)

Take a moment to offer the Lord your personal praise and thanksgiving.

2. Confession: Pray this confession to the Lord as you seek to keep your life free from sin and in fellowship with Him:

O Lord, I know the way of man is not in himself; it is not in man who walks to direct his own steps. O Lord, correct me, but with justice; not in Your anger, lest You bring me to nothing. (Jeremiah 10:23-24)

Confess any personal sins which the Holy Spirit may bring to your mind.

3. Affirmation: As you agree with the will of God, voice your affirmation of His word:

The heart is deceitful above all things, and desperately wicked; who can know it? You, the Lord, search the heart, You test the mind, even to give every man according to the fruit of his doings. . . . Heal me, O Lord, and I shall be healed; save me, and I shall be saved, for You are my praise. (Jeremiah 17: 9-10, 14)

4. Requests: As you make your requests known to the Lord, include:

* Compassion for others
* Missions in America
* Your prayer list, the concerns of your heart, and today's activities

5. Closing Prayer: Finally, offer this closing prayer to the Lord:

Blessed are You, the Lord, forevermore! Amen and amen. (Psalm 89:52)

Memory Verse: But his delight is in the law of the Lord, and in His law he meditates day and night.

Psalm 1:2
Bible Study Theme

READING

The passage for today centers on David's plans for the temple. Out of devotion to God, David begins preparations for building a temple, but God tells him that David's son will build it.

Read 2 Samuel 7.

REFLECTING

David is a visionary and a great builder. With all his heart he wants to build the temple of God. Yet because David is a man of war, God reserves that privilege for his son, Solomon, whose very name means "peace." While David cannot actually build the temple, he does draw up the plans and begin amassing the materials necessary, and Solomon's job was much easier and perhaps much better because of David's work. While David cannot actually build the temple, it is interesting to note in a parallel passage in 2 Chronicles 6:8 that the Lord says that it is good that it is in David's heart to want to build the temple— even though he is not permitted to do so.

There may be things in your heart that you would like to do for God that you cannot do. Even so, it is good that it is in your heart to want to do it.

RESPONDING

1. Praise: Praise the Lord that He rewards us, not on our deeds, but on our motives:

Praise the Lord! Praise God in His sanctuary; praise Him in His mighty firmament! Praise Him for His mighty acts; praise Him according to His excellent greatness! Praise Him with the sound of the trumpet; praise Him with the lute and harp! . . . Let everything that has breath praise the Lord. Praise the Lord! (Psalm 150:1-3, 6)

Take a moment to offer the Lord your personal praise and thanksgiving.

2. Confession: Pray this confession to the Lord as you seek to keep your life free from sin and in fellowship with Him:

Purge me with hyssop, and I shall be clean; wash me, and I shall be whiter than snow. . . . Hide Your face from my sins, and blot out all my iniquities. (Psalm 51:7, 9)

Confess any personal sins which the Holy Spirit may bring to your mind.

3. Affirmation: As you agree with the will of God, voice your affirmation of His word:

You, Lord Jesus, are the Way, the Truth, and the Life. I cannot come to the Father except through You. (John 14:6)

4. Requests: As you make your requests known to the Lord, include:

- Personal spiritual growth
- Military ministries
- Your prayer list, the concerns of your heart, and today's activities

5. Closing Prayer: Finally, offer this closing prayer to the Lord:

Glory to You in the highest, and on earth peace, good will toward men! (Luke 2:14)

Memory Verse: But his delight is in the law of the Lord, and in His law he meditates day and night.

Psalm 1:2
Bible Study Theme

READING

The passage for today centers on David's great sin. Instead of going to war with his army, David remains in Jerusalem and commits adultery with Bathsheba, the wife of one of his loyal commanders.

Read 2 Samuel 11.

REFLECTING

There is greater pain in sin than in righteousness. If you don't believe that intellectually, you can verify its truth experientially. But it would be better to learn by example.

David clearly loves Bathsheba. His extreme actions bear that out. Certainly, it would have pained him had he turned his heart away from her before having relations with her. The temptation is very real. But that potential pain found in obedience is nothing compared to the pain he brings on himself and others by taking her as his own—adultery, murder, the death of their child, the loss of respect, the memory of the guilt. He has deceived himself in assuming he can cover up or avoid the consequences. We do, too. There is often pain in doing the right thing, but always less pain than in doing the wrong thing.

RESPONDING

1. Praise: Offering the Lord your praise is part of the "right thing" we ought to do:

You are great, O Lord God. For there is none like You, nor is there any God besides You, according to all that we have heard with our ears. (2 Samuel 7:22)

Pause for personal praise and thanksgiving.

2. Confession: Pray this confession to the Lord as you seek to keep your life free from sin and in fellowship with Him:

O my God: I am too ashamed and humiliated to lift up my face to You, my God; for my iniquity has risen higher than my head, and my guilt has grown even to the heavens. (Ezra 9:6)

Confess any personal sins which the Holy Spirit brings to your mind.

3. Affirmation: Now pause to pray this affirmation to the Lord:

If I confess with my mouth the Lord Jesus, and believe in my heart that You, O God, raised Him from the dead, I shall be saved. For with the heart I believe, resulting in righteousness, and with the mouth I confess, resulting in salvation. For the Scripture says, "Whoever believes in Him will not be disappointed." (Romans 10:9-11)

4. Requests: As you make your requests known to the Lord, include:

- Fruit of the Spirit in your life
- The ministry of Christian literature
- Your prayer list, the concerns of your heart, and today's activities

5. Closing Prayer: Finally, offer this closing prayer to the Lord:

Grace, mercy, and peace from You, the Father, and the Lord Jesus Christ our Savior. (Titus 1:4)

Memory Verse: But his delight is in the law of the Lord, and in His law he meditates day and night.
Psalm 1:2
Bible Study Theme

READING

The passage for today centers on Nathan's rebuke. God reveals David's sin to Nathan the prophet, who openly rebukes David and stirs David to repent.

Read 2 Samuel 12.

REFLECTING

When Nathan comes to the palace and accuses David of adultery and murder, it is well within David's power to shout, "Off with his head!" Had he done so, Nathan's head would have come off, no questions asked. David does not issue that order, however. Instead, his heart breaks, and he repents of his sin. The horror and magnitude of his sin is incalculable, but it is to his credit that he instantly repents. Thus, God's commendation of David as a man after God's own heart. In other words, what breaks God's heart also breaks David's heart. Rather than resisting repentance because we feel we don't deserve forgiveness, we should do as David did—repent the instant we can.

RESPONDING

1. Praise: Because the Lord is instantly ready to receive our repentance, praise His name:

O Lord God, . . . the One who dwells between the cherubim, You are God, You alone, of all the kingdoms of the earth. You have made heaven and earth. (2 Kings 19:15)

Lord God, . . . there is no God in heaven above or on earth below like You, who keep Your covenant and mercy with Your servants who walk before You with all their heart. (1 Kings 8:23)

Pause for personal praise and thanksgiving.

2. Confession: Pray this confession to the Lord as you seek to keep your life free from sin and in fellowship with Him:

O Lord, do not rebuke me in Your anger, nor chasten me in Your hot displeasure. Have mercy on me, O Lord, for I am weak; O Lord, heal me, for . . . my soul also is greatly troubled. (Psalm 6:1-3)

Confess any personal sins which the Holy Spirit brings to your mind.

3. Affirmation: Now pause to pray this affirmation to the Lord:

Having been justified by faith, I have peace with You, O God, through the Lord Jesus Christ, through whom also I have obtained my introduction by faith into this grace in which I stand; and I rejoice in hope of the glory of God. (Romans 5:1-2)

4. Requests: As you make your requests known to the Lord, pray for:

• Boldness in living for Christ
• God's blessing on America
• Your prayer list, the concerns of your heart, and today's activities

5. Closing Prayer: Finally offer this closing prayer to the Lord:

Now to You who are able to keep me from stumbling, and to present me faultless before the presence of Your glory with exceeding joy, to You, my God and Savior, who alone are wise, be glory and majesty, dominion and power, both now and forever. Amen. (Jude 24-25)

Memory Verse: But his delight is in the law of the Lord, and in His law he meditates day and night.
Psalm 1:2
Bible Study Theme

JUNE 1

READING

The passage for today centers on David's old age. As David's health begins to decline, Nathan and Bathsheba conspire to ensure that Solomon replaces David as king.

Read 1 Kings 1.

REFLECTING

Adonijah is David's oldest son at this time, and it is not unexpected that he should assume the throne. David has made no public declaration regarding his successor, and apparently only Bathsheba and Nathan know of his desire that Solomon succeed him. While it is a little ambitious, it is not unreasonable that Adonijah take steps to become king. Circumstances seemed grim to Bathsheba. Should Adonijah become king, she and Solomon would most probably lose their lives, being seen as threats to the throne. Yet God rose above it all and demonstrated again that He is in control, in spite of the foreboding nature of circumstances. As we ponder the foreboding nature of circumstances in the world today, we are tempted to lose heart, to question if God is in control. We should be reminded from this passage that, indeed, He is.

It is something we *must* believe.

RESPONDING

1. Praise: As you continue your time with the Lord, offer to Him this passage of praise:

The Lord made the heavens. Honor and majesty are before Him; strength and beauty are in His sanctuary. . . . Give to the Lord, O kindred of the peoples. . . . Give to the Lord the glory due His name; bring an offering, and come into His courts. Let the heavens rejoice, and let the earth be glad. (Psalm 96:5-8,11)

Now express any additional thoughts you may have of thanks or praise.

2. Confession: Pray this confession to the Lord as you seek to keep your life free from sin and in fellowship with Him:

Your word is a lamp to my feet and a light to my path. (Psalm 119:105)

Confess any personal sins which the Holy Spirit brings to your mind.

3. Affirmation: Now pray this affirmation to the Lord as you agree with and submit yourself to the will of God:

And this is eternal life, that I may know You, the only true God, and Jesus Christ whom You have sent. (John 17:3)

4. Requests: The Lord encourages us to come to Him with our concerns and desires. As you make your requests known to the Lord, include:

* Health and strength to serve God
* God's will to be done on earth
* Your prayer list, the concerns of your heart, and today's activities

5. Closing Prayer: Finally, offer this closing prayer to the Lord:

Be glad in the Lord and rejoice, you righteous; and shout for joy, all you upright in heart! (Psalm 32:11)

Memory Verse: But his delight is in the law of the Lord, and in His law he meditates day and night.
Psalm 1:2
Bible Study Theme

JUNE 2

READING

The passage for today centers on the death of David. David charges Solomon with the urgency of living. After charging Solomon with the importance of serving the Lord, David dies. Then Solomon consolidates his power.

Read 1 Kings 2.

REFLECTING

Parts of the Old Testament tax our understanding and our acceptance. There are simply some things that are hard to understand or hard to accept. First, we do not understand as much as we ought to about Judaism, the Law, and Old Testament culture and customs. Second, many of the events are violations of God's desires, though that fact is not explained to us. And finally, God deals with men differently in the Old Testament than He does with us in New Testament times. While not all things are easily explained, in 1 Kings 2 all the people Solomon takes vengeance upon have committed acts which, in the Old Testament, were punishable by death. It doesn't answer every problem we might have with this difficult chapter, but it is a beginning.

RESPONDING

1. Praise: To the God who now deals with us in grace, offer your praise in the words of this passage:

Blessed be the name of God forever and ever, for wisdom and might are His. . . . He gives wisdom to the wise and knowledge to those who have understanding. He reveals deep and secret things; He knows what is in the darkness, and light dwells with Him. (Daniel 2:20-22)

Pause for personal praise and thanksgiving.

2. Confession: Pray this confession to the Lord as you seek to keep your life free from sin:

If we say we have no sin, we are deceiving ourselves, and the truth is not in us. If we confess our sins, He is faithful and just to forgive us our sins and to cleanse us from all unrighteousness. (1 John 1:8-9)

Confess any personal sins which the Holy Spirit brings to mind.

3. Affirmation: Now pause to pray this affirmation to the Lord:

I am not ashamed of the gospel of Christ, for it is Your power to salvation for everyone who believes, for the Jew first and also for the Greek. For in it Your righteousness is revealed from faith to faith; as it is written, "the just shall live by faith." (Romans 1:16-17)

4. Requests: As you make your requests known to the Lord, include:

- Sensitivity to sin
- The ministry of your local church
- Your prayer list, the concerns of your heart, and today's activities

5. Closing Prayer: Finally, offer this closing prayer to the Lord:

Let the words of my mouth and the meditation of my heart be acceptable in Your sight, O Lord, my strength and my redeemer. (Psalm 19:14)

Memory Verse: But his delight is in the law of the Lord, and in His law he meditates day and night.
Psalm 1:2
Bible Study Theme

READING

The passage for today centers on Solomon's early reign. Solomon prays for wisdom, which God grants, and he astounds the people with his judgment.

Read 1 Kings 3.

REFLECTING

Solomon's heart is manifested by the purity of his prayer. He could have asked for a long life, he could have asked for riches and honor. But instead, he asks simply for wisdom. He acknowledges his inadequacies before God in a disarmingly transparent manner. What an honest and unselfish prayer. Being honest with God is not as easy as we might think. We all tend to live life with masks on, behind which the real "us" hides, so as to make a better impression on people. And we find it not always easy to take the masks off when we talk with God. How foolish! God sees behind the mask, as do most people. We can learn from Solomon. God is pleased with honest, transparent prayers.

RESPONDING

1. Praise: The Lord knows us totally, and loves us completely, and for this we offer Him our praise:

My soul magnifies You, Lord, and my spirit has rejoiced in You, O God my Savior. . . . You who are mighty have done great things for me; and holy is Your name. And Your mercy is on those who fear You from generation to generation. (Luke 1:46-50)

Pause for personal praise and thanksgiving.

2. Confession: Pray this confession to the Lord as you seek to keep your life free from sin and in fellowship with Him:

Remember, O Lord, Your tender mercies and Your lovingkindnesses, for they have been from of old. Do not remember the sins of my youth, nor my transgressions; according to Your mercy remember me, for Your goodness' sake, O Lord. (Psalm 25:6-7)

Confess any personal sins which the Holy Spirit brings to your mind.

3. Affirmation: Now pause to pray this affirmation to the Lord:

You are the door. If anyone enters by You he will be saved, and will go in and out and find pasture. The thief does not come except to steal, and to kill, and to destroy. You have come that we may have life, and that we may have it more abundantly. You are the good shepherd. The good shepherd gives his life for the sheep. (John 10:9-11)

4. Requests: As you make your requests known to the Lord, include:

- Wisdom for living life
- Needs of your immediate family
- Your prayer list, the concerns of your heart, and today's activities

5. Closing Prayer: Finally, offer this closing prayer to the Lord:

Surely goodness and mercy shall follow me all the days of my life, and I will dwell in the house of the Lord forever. (Psalm 23:6)

Memory Verse: But his delight is in the law of the Lord, and in His law he meditates day and night.

Psalm 1:2
Bible Study Theme

JUNE 4

READING

The passage for today centers on God's blessing on Solomon. Solomon's wealth, power, and wisdom exceed all before him, and his fame spreads throughout the world.

Read 1 Kings 4.

REFLECTING

To understand the significance of Solomon's wealth, power, and wisdom, we must go back to Deuteronomy 28, where God gave Israel the consequences for obedience and disobedience. During the latter part of David's reign and the early part of Solomon's reign, Israel follows the Lord in righteousness for a longer period of time than any other. The results are a greater blessing than at any other time in Israel's history. It is a glaring and tragic reality that shortly after Solomon's reign, Israel follows her kings in unrighteousness, and the curses in Deuteronomy begin to come upon them. The welfare of Israel was always related to her righteousness.

RESPONDING

1. Praise: Offer your praise to the Lord who is holy, and in whose holiness we can share:

Oh, the depth of the riches both of the wisdom and knowledge of God! How unsearchable are Your judgments and Your ways past finding out! Blessed are You, the God and Father of our Lord Jesus Christ, who has blessed us with every spiritual blessing in the heavenly places in Christ. (Ephesians 1:3)

Pause for personal praise and thanksgiving.

2. Confession: Pray this confession to the Lord as you seek to keep your life free from sin and in fellowship with Him:

Blessed is he whose transgression is forgiven, whose sin is covered. How blessed is the man to whom the Lord does not impute iniquity, and in whose spirit there is no guile. (Psalm 32:1-2)

Confess any personal sins which the Holy Spirit brings to mind.

3. Affirmation: Now pause to pray this affirmation to the Lord:

Let me not glory in my own wisdom, let me not glory in my own might, nor let me glory in my own riches; but let me glory in this, that I understand and know You. That You are the Lord, for in this You delight. (Jeremiah 9:23-24)

4. Requests: As you make your requests known to the Lord, pray for:

• Insight into Scripture

• The hungry around the world

• Your prayer list, the concerns of your heart, and today's activities

5. Closing Prayer: Finally, offer this closing prayer to the Lord:

We will be of good courage, and You shall strengthen our hearts, all we who hope in the Lord. (Psalm 31:24)

Memory Verse: But be doers of the word, and not hearers only, deceiving yourselves.

James 1:22
Bible Study Theme

READING

The passage for today centers on preparations for building the temple. Solomon forms an alliance with Hiram, king of Tyre, for help in building the temple.

Read 1 Kings 5.

REFLECTING

David had built an excellent reputation with the noble leaders who lived around him. He was known as a fair, just, and righteous man. It was David who had established the initial relationship with Hiram early in his reign (2 Samuel 5:11), and 1 Kings 5:1 says "Hiram had always been a friend of David." It was perhaps the observation of these things that prompted Solomon to write in Proverbs 22:1, "A good name is to be more desired than great riches," and "A good name is better than fine perfume" (Ecclesiastes 7:1). Each of us must take Scripture to heart at this point and dedicate ourselves to the development of a spotless reputation by being fair, just, and righteous, and by being utterly true to our word.

RESPONDING

1. Praise: Offer your praise to the Lord whose reputation we share when we live for Him:

Ah, Lord God! Behold, You have made the heavens and the earth by Your great power and outstretched arm. There is nothing too hard for You. You show lovingkindness to thousands . . . the Great, the Mighty God, whose name is the Lord of hosts. You are great in counsel and mighty in work. (Jeremiah 32:17-19)

Pause for personal praise and thanksgiving.

2. Confession: Pray this confession to the Lord as you seek to keep your life free from sin and in fellowship with Him:

Who can understand his errors? Cleanse me from secret faults. Keep back Your servant from presumptuous sins; Let them not have dominion over me. Then I shall be blameless, and I shall be innocent of great transgression. (Psalm 19:12-13)

Confess any personal sins which the Holy Spirit brings to mind.

3. Affirmation: Now pause to pray this affirmation to the Lord:

For Your thoughts are not my thoughts, nor are my ways Your ways. For as the heavens are higher than the earth, so are Your ways higher than my ways, and Your thoughts than my thoughts. (Isaiah 55:8-9)

4. Requests: As you make your requests known to the Lord, pray for:

- Love for fellow Christians
- The work of missions in Europe and Asia
- Your prayer list, the concerns of your heart, and today's activities

5. Closing Prayer: Finally, offer this closing prayer to the Lord:

This is the day which You have made; I will rejoice and be glad in it. (Psalm 118:24)

Memory Verse: But be doers of the word, and not hearers only, deceiving yourselves.

James 1:22
Bible Study Theme

JUNE 6

READING

The passage for today centers on the building of the temple. Solomon oversees the temple construction, making it a work of art glorifying God.

Read 1 Kings 6.

REFLECTING

The temple which Solomon builds for the Lord is a spectacle to behold. Not only is the size ominous, but the craftsmanship is beyond comparison. The stonework is magnificent; the tapestry work is glorious, and nearly everything inside is overlaid with gold. Why such opulence? It was not beauty for beauty's sake, but because the temple was to be a physical representation of the beauty and glory of God. God's presence now resides in the "temple" of believers. Our lives are to reflect His glory with equal impact as we stand out in bold relief from the world around us.

RESPONDING

1. Praise: Focus on the glory of the Lord as you praise Him with these words:

Let my mouth be filled with Your praise and with Your glory all the day. . . . I will hope continually, and will praise You yet more and more. My mouth shall tell of Your righteousness and Your salvation all the day, for I do not know their limits. I will go in the strength of the Lord God; I will make mention of Your righteousness, of Yours only. O God, You have taught me from my youth; and to this day I declare Your wondrous works. (Psalm 71:8, 14-17)

Now express any additional thoughts of praise or thanksgiving.

2. Confession: Pray this confession to the Lord to keep your life

free from sin and in fellowship with Him:

"Now, therefore," says the Lord, "Turn to Me with all your heart. . . ." return to the Lord your God, for He is gracious and merciful, slow to anger, and of great kindness; and He relents from doing harm. (Joel 2:12-13)

Confess any personal sins which the Holy Spirit brings to your mind.

3. Affirmation: Now pray this affirmation to the Lord as you agree with and submit yourself to the will of God:

Yes, if I cry out for discernment, and lift up my voice for understanding, if I seek her as silver, and search for her as for hidden treasures; then I will understand the fear of You, O Lord, and find the knowledge of You, O God. For You, O Lord, give wisdom; from Your mouth come knowledge and understanding; You store up sound wisdom for me and are a shield to me when I walk uprightly. (Proverbs 2:3-7)

4. Requests: As you make your requests known to the Lord, include:

- Faithfulness with your time
- The president and national leaders and affairs
- Your prayer list, the concerns of your heart, and today's activities

5. Closing Prayer: Finally, offer this closing prayer to the Lord:

Oh, satisfy me early with Your mercy, that I may rejoice and be glad all my days! (Psalm 90:14)

Memory Verse: But be doers of the word, and not hearers only, deceiving yourselves.

James 1:22
Bible Study Theme

JUNE 7

READING

The passage for today centers on the completion of the temple. King Hiram of Tyre supplies artisans and craftsmen to finalize the glorious appointments in the temple.

Read 1 Kings 7.

REFLECTING

Not only is the work of the temple designed to reflect the splendor and glory of God, but also the layout of the temple is designed to reflect His work in atoning for our sin. The bronze laver, the candlesticks, the table of shewbread, the holy of holies are all designed to picture for us the atoning work of Christ. The central focus rests on the ark and its mercy seat, depicting the holiness of God and the necessity of a blood sacrifice to establish a relationship or restore fellowship with God. All this is in keeping with what Paul wrote in Romans 15:4: "Whatever was written in earlier times was written for our instruction, that through perseverance and the encouragement of the Scriptures we might have hope."

RESPONDING

1. Praise: Offer the Lord your praise for His goodness through these words:

Lord, You have been our dwelling place in all generations. Before the mountains were brought forth, or ever You had formed the earth and the world, even from everlasting to everlasting, You are God. O satisfy us early with Your mercy, that we may rejoice and be glad all our days! (Psalm 90:1-2, 14)

Take a moment to offer the Lord your personal praise and thanksgiving.

2. Confession: Pray this confession to the Lord as you seek to keep your life free from sin and in fellowship with Him:

You will cleanse me from all my iniquity by which I have sinned against You, and You will pardon all my iniquities by which I have sinned and by which I have transgressed against You. (Jeremiah 33:8)

Confess any personal sins which the Holy Spirit may bring to your mind.

3. Affirmation: As you agree with the will of God, voice your affirmation of His word:

I am not ashamed, for I know You, in whom I have believed, and am persuaded that You are able to keep what I have committed to You until that Day. (2 Timothy 1:12)

4. Requests: As you make your requests known to the Lord, include:

● Your financial needs

● The needs of the poor

● Your prayer list, the concerns of your heart, and today's activities

5. Closing Prayer: Finally, offer this closing prayer to the Lord:

Let the beauty of You, Lord, be upon me, and establish the work of my hands for me; yes, establish the work of my hands. (Psalm 90:17)

Memory Verse: But be doers of the word, and not hearers only, deceiving yourselves.

James 1:22
Bible Study Theme

JUNE 8

READING

The passage for today centers on the temple dedication. After bringing the ark into the temple, Solomon leads the Israelites in a grandiose dedication ceremony.

Read 1 Kings 8.

REFLECTING

The Lord did not choose Israel to the exclusion of all the other people in the world. He chose Israel in order to reach all the other people in the world. Even the phenomenal blessings which He pours out on righteous Israel have a purpose beyond the blessing of those people. In addition, God intends that the other nations of the world will see the favor upon Israel and desire to know God because of what they see of Him in Israel. This truth is reflected when Solomon prays that "the Lord be with us, so that all the peoples of the earth may know that the Lord is God; there is no one else." David understood this principle also when he wrote in Psalm 67, "God blesses us, that all the ends of the earth may fear Him."

And today, God wants to bless us, spiritually, that others may see Christ in us and be drawn to Him.

RESPONDING

1. Praise: Praise the Lord who blesses us that we might become one who draws others to Him because of His mark in our lives:

You are worthy, O Lord, to receive glory and honor and power; for You created all things, and by Your will they exist and were created. . . . I will praise You, O Lord, according to Your righteousness, and will sing praise to Your name, O Lord Most High. (Revelation 4:11, Psalm 7:17)

Pause for personal praise and thanksgiving.

2. Confession: Pray this confession to the Lord as you seek to keep your life free from sin:

Forgive us, Lord, when we are unmindful of You, the Rock who begot us, and have forgotten You, the God who fathered us. (Deuteronomy 32:18)

Confess any personal sins which the Holy Spirit brings to mind.

3. Affirmation: Now pause to pray this affirmation to the Lord:

Behold what manner of love You, O Lord, have bestowed on me, that I should be called a child of God! Therefore the world does not know me, because it did not know my Lord Jesus. Now I am a child of God; and it has not yet been revealed what I shall be, but I know that when You are revealed, I shall be like You, for I shall see You as You are. (1 John 3:1-2)

4. Requests: As you make your requests known to the Lord, include:

- Protection from the "evil one"
- Laborers for the "harvest"
- Your prayer list, the concerns of your heart, and today's activities

5. Closing Prayer: Finally, offer this closing prayer to the Lord:

Bless the Lord, all you His hosts, you ministers of His, who do His pleasure. Bless the Lord, all His works, in all places of His dominion. (Psalm 103:21-22)

Memory Verse: But be doers of the word, and not hearers only, deceiving yourselves.

James 1:22
Bible Study Theme

READING

The passage for today centers on Solomon's second divine encounter. The Lord appears to Solomon a second time and reiterates His promise to bless Israel for faithfulness and judge her for sin.

Read 1 Kings 9.

REFLECTING

Three things happen when Israel lives in a righteous relationship with the Lord. First, God is glorified, and a true picture of who He is is given to the world. Second, the Israelites are blessed and satisfied, receiving the fullness of life for which they long. Third, the unsaved world is drawn to want to know God because of the magnificent picture they get of Him from looking at blessed Israel. Because so much is hinging on Israel's standing before God, the Lord makes it clear to them how serious is their position. If they will trust and obey Him, He will bless them forever. However, if they live in sin, He will utterly destroy them. It is all or nothing.

RESPONDING

1. Praise: The Lord longs to bless us, and for His goodness and mercy, offer Him this psalm of praise:

Tremble before Him, all the earth. The world also is firmly established, it shall not be moved. Let the heavens rejoice, and let the earth be glad. . . . Oh, give thanks to the Lord, for He is good! For His mercy endures forever. . . . Blessed be the Lord God . . . from everlasting to everlasting! (1 Chronicles 16:30-31, 34, 36)

Pause for personal praise and thanksgiving.

2. Confession: Pray this confession to the Lord as you seek to keep your life free from sin and in fellowship with Him:

O Lord, You do not have as much delight in burnt offerings and sacrifices, as in obeying Your voice. Behold, to obey is better than sacrifice, and to heed than the fat of rams. (1 Samuel 15:22)

Confess any personal sins which the Holy Spirit brings to your mind.

3. Affirmation: Now pause to pray this affirmation to the Lord:

There is therefore now no condemnation for me if I am in You, Christ Jesus. For the law of the Spirit of life in You, has set me free from the law of sin and death. (Romans 8:1-2)

4. Requests: As you make your requests known to the Lord, include:

- Commitment to the Lord
- Parachurch ministries
- Your prayer list, the concerns of your heart, and today's activities

5. Closing Prayer: Finally, offer this closing prayer to the Lord:

Lord, preserve me from all evil; preserve my soul. Lord, preserve my going out and my coming in from this time forth, and even forevermore. (Psalm 121:7-8)

Memory Verse: But be doers of the word, and not hearers only, deceiving yourselves.

James 1:22
Bible Study Theme

JUNE 10

READING

The passage for today centers on a royal visit. The Queen of Sheba visits Solomon to see if the reports about his wealth and wisdom have been exaggerated.

Read 1 Kings 10.

REFLECTING

Solomon leads Israel in righteousness, and God pours out His blessing on the nation to such an extent that the reports of Israel's prosperity spread throughout the world. The Queen of Sheba visits Solomon because she cannot believe the reports she has been hearing. After Solomon meets with her and shows her around Jerusalem, she is overwhelmed. She cries out, "the half has not been told!" Then, she breaks out in spontaneous eulogy to God: "You exceed in wisdom and prosperity the report which I heard. Blessed be the Lord your God. . . ." That is how it was supposed to work. The blessing of Israel was to draw attention, not to Israel, but to the God of Israel. Today, as the Lord blesses us spiritually for our faithfulness to Him, attention will be drawn, not to us, but to the Lord.

RESPONDING

1. Praise: As the Queen of Sheba blessed the Lord, so we praise Him in the words of this psalm:

I will bless the Lord at all times; His praise shall continually be in my mouth. My soul shall make its boast in the Lord; The humble shall hear of it and be glad. Oh, magnify the Lord with me, and let us exalt His name together. . . . Oh, taste and see that the Lord is good; blessed is the man who trusts in Him! (Psalm 34:1-3, 8)

Pause for personal praise and thanksgiving.

2. Confession: Pray this confession to the Lord as you seek to keep your life free from sin and in fellowship with Him:

I have sinned greatly in what I have done; but now, I pray, O Lord, take away the iniquity of Your servant, for I have done very foolishly. (2 Samuel 24:10)

Confess any personal sins which the Holy Spirit brings to mind.

3. Affirmation: Now pause to pray this affirmation to the Lord:

My body is the temple of the Holy Spirit who is in me, whom I have from You, O God, and I am not my own. For I have been bought with a price; therefore I will glorify God in my body and in my spirit, which are Yours. (1 Corinthians 6:19-20)

4. Requests: As you make your requests known to the Lord, include:

- Renewing of your mind
- Needs of your extended family
- Your prayer list, the concerns of your heart, and today's activities

5. Closing Prayer: Finally, offer this closing prayer to the Lord:

May we with one mind and one mouth glorify the God and Father of our Lord Jesus Christ. (Romans 15:6)

Memory Verse: But be doers of the word, and not hearers only, deceiving yourselves.

James 1:22
Bible Study Theme

READING

The passage for today centers on Solomon's sin. In disobedience to God's commands, Solomon takes wives from and makes allegiances with foreigners, and God judges him.

Read 1 Kings 11.

REFLECTING

Unbelievable as it seems, not long after the Lord reiterates to Solomon the wonderful blessings of obedience and the cataclysmic consequences of disobedience, Solomon disobeys. He is not to take for himself foreign wives. The danger is that they would turn his heart from following the Lord. Surely enough, he begins worshiping Ashtoreth and Milcom and builds a "high place" of worship for Chemosh and for Molech, which are detestable pagan gods. True to His word, the Lord raises up an adversary, Hadad, to plague Solomon. God's purpose is not to punish. He wants the adversity to turn Solomon's heart back to Him. When you suffer adversity, ask yourself if there is some sin from which you should turn.

Sin will not always be the cause, but it is something to which we must be sensitive.

RESPONDING

1. Praise: Bless the Lord because He forgives any sin upon the asking, and praise Him for His goodness to us:

Who is like You, O Lord, among the gods? Who is like You, glorious in holiness, fearful in praises, doing wonders? (Exodus 15:11)

You are great, O Lord God. For there is none like You, nor is there any God besides You, according to all that we have heard with our ears. (2 Samuel 7:22)

Pause for personal praise and thanksgiving.

2. Confession: Pray this confession to the Lord as you seek to keep your life free from sin:

O my God: I am too ashamed and humiliated to lift up my face to You, my God; for my iniquity has risen higher than my head, and my guilt has grown even to the heavens. (Ezra 9:6)

Confess any personal sins which the Holy Spirit brings to your mind.

3. Affirmation: Now pause to pray this affirmation to the Lord:

Having been justified by faith, I have peace with You, O God, through the Lord Jesus Christ, through whom also I have obtained my introduction by faith into this grace in which I stand; and I rejoice in hope of the glory of God. (Romans 5:1-2)

4. Requests: As you make your requests known to the Lord, include:

- The Lord's leading in your life
- Opportunities for personal evangelism
- Your prayer list, the concerns of your heart, and today's activities

5. Closing Prayer: Finally, offer this closing prayer to the Lord:

Now may the God of hope fill me with all joy and peace in believing, that I may abound in hope by the power of the Holy Spirit. (Romans 15:13)

Memory Verse: This Book of the Law shall not depart from your mouth, but you shall meditate in it day and night, that you may observe to do according to all that is written in it. For then you will make your way prosperous, and then you will have good success.

Joshua 1:8
Bible Study Theme

JUNE 12

READING

The passage for today centers on the division of the kingdom. After the death of Solomon, Rehoboam and Jeroboam contend for supremacy and split the kingdom. Read 1 Kings 12.

REFLECTING

Because Solomon drifts from the Lord during the latter portion of his reign, he does not leave to his successor a healthy, vibrant nation. Israel is struggling for moral and political leadership. Rehoboam inherits the throne, but places foolish and inordinate financial demands on the nation on the heels of what Solomon had demanded to build the temple and his palace. The people rebel, and the nation splits. The northern part of the kingdom follows after Jeroboam, while Rehoboam retains control over the southern part. Neither man leads the nation in righteousness, and the disintegration that began with Solomon continues. Sin is taking its toll. It always does.

RESPONDING

1. Praise: Praise the Lord that when we confess our sin, He removes the eternal penalty:

O Lord God . . . , the One who dwells between the cherubim, You are God, You alone, of all the kingdoms of the earth. You have made heaven and earth. (2 Kings 19:15)

Lord God . . . , there is no God in heaven above or on earth below like You, who keep Your covenant and mercy with Your servants who walk before You with all their heart. (1 Kings 8:23)

Pause for personal praise and thanksgiving.

2. Confession: Pray this confession to the Lord as you seek to keep your life free from sin and in fellowship with Him:

O Lord, do not rebuke me in Your anger, nor chasten me in Your hot displeasure. Have mercy on me, O Lord, for I am weak; O Lord, heal me, for . . . my soul also is greatly troubled. (Psalm 6:1-3)

Confess any personal sins which the Holy Spirit brings to your mind.

3. Affirmation: Now pause to pray this affirmation to the Lord:

If I confess with my mouth the Lord Jesus, and believe in my heart that You, O God, raised Him from the dead, I shall be saved. For with the heart I believe, resulting in righteousness, and with the mouth I confess, resulting in salvation. For the Scripture says, "Whoever believes in Him will not be disappointed." (Romans 10:9-11)

4. Requests: As you make your requests known to the Lord, pray for:

- Love for the lost
- The work of missions in Africa
- Your prayer list, the concerns of your heart, and today's activities

5. Closing Prayer: Finally offer this closing prayer to the Lord:

Now to You who are able to establish us according to the gospel and preaching of Jesus Christ—to You, alone wise, be glory through Jesus Christ forever. Amen. (Romans 16:25-27)

Memory Verse: This Book of the Law shall not depart from your mouth, but you shall meditate in it day and night, that you may observe to do according to all that is written in it. For then you will make your way prosperous, and then you will have good success.

Joshua 1:8
Bible Study Theme

READING

The passage for today centers on Elijah's miraculous ministry. After Elijah prophesies drought, the Lord hides him and later uses him to heal a child.

Read 1 Kings 17.

REFLECTING

Drought is a devastating natural disaster, and when it comes to the children of Israel, it does not come by accident. It is always divine judgment as a consequence of disobedience. From the beginning of his reign, Ahab, who is king when Elijah begins his ministry, violates the Lord's name. He encourages idolatry and the worship of Baal, a pagan god. "He did evil in the sight of the Lord, more than all who were before him" (1 Kings 16:30). The nation suffers as a result of Ahab's leadership. Elijah's name means "Jehovah is my strength," and the Lord sets about to prove the significance of Elijah's name as He brings judgment on Israel and destroys the worshipers of Baal.

RESPONDING

1. Praise: Praise your God in the words of this psalm:

It is good to give thanks to the Lord, and to sing praises to Your name, O Most High; to declare Your lovingkindness in the morning, and Your faithfulness every night . . . to declare that the Lord is upright; He is my Rock, and there is no unrighteousness in Him. (Psalm 92:1-2, 15)

Take a moment to offer the Lord your personal praise and thanksgiving.

2. Confession: Pray this confession to the Lord as you seek to keep your life free from sin and in fellowship with Him:

I return to You, O Lord my God, for I have stumbled because of my iniquity; I take words with me, and return to You, Lord. I say to You, "Take away all iniquity; receive me graciously, for I will offer the sacrifices of my lips." (Hosea 14:1-2)

Confess any personal sins which the Holy Spirit may bring to your mind.

3. Affirmation: As you agree with the will of God, voice your affirmation of His word:

The Spirit Himself bears witness with my spirit that I am a child of Yours, O God, and if a child, then an heir—heir of Yours and joint heirs with Christ, if indeed I suffer with Him, that I may also be glorified. (Romans 8:16-17)

4. Requests: As you make your requests known to the Lord, include:

- Faithfulness with your talents
- Your state and local leaders and affairs
- Your prayer list, the concerns of your heart, and today's activities

5. Closing Prayer: Finally, offer this closing prayer to the Lord:

The grace of the Lord Jesus Christ, and the love of God, and the communion of the Holy Spirit be with us all. Amen. (2 Corinthians 13:14)

Memory Verse: This Book of the Law shall not depart from your mouth, but you shall meditate in it day and night, that you may observe to do according to all that is written in it. For then you will make your way prosperous, and then you will have good success.

Joshua 1:8
Bible Study Theme

JUNE 14

READING

The passage for today centers on the confrontation on Mount Carmel. The prophets of Baal challenge Elijah and the power of God and are defeated, after which it rains.

Read 1 Kings 18.

REFLECTING

The confrontation of Elijah and the prophets of Baal is one of the most exciting chapters in the Bible. Fire raining down from heaven consuming meat, water, and stone, all in the name of Yahweh! Then, after Baal worship is defeated, it rains, signifying an end to that judgment. Elijah prays, "Answer me, O Lord, answer me, that this people may know that Thou, O Lord, art God, and that Thou hast turned their heart back again" (18:37). God does not punish His children for sin, but rather chastens them in the hope that they will repent and return to Him.

RESPONDING

1. Praise: The Lord is worthy to receive my praise because of all that He has done for me:

Let us come before His presence with thanksgiving; let us shout joyfully to Him with psalms. For the Lord is the great God, and the great King above all gods. . . . Oh come, let us worship and bow down; let us kneel before the Lord our Maker. For He is our God, and we are the people of His pasture, and the sheep of His hand. (Psalm 95:2-3, 6-7)

Take a moment to offer the Lord your personal praise and thanksgiving.

2. Confession: Pray this confession to the Lord as you seek to keep your life free from sin and in fellowship with Him:

No temptation has overtaken me except such as is common to man; but You are faithful, O God, who will not allow me to be tempted beyond what I am able, but with the temptation will also make the way of escape, that I may be able to bear it. (1 Corinthians 10:13)

Confess any personal sins which the Holy Spirit may bring to your mind.

3. Affirmation: As you agree with the will of God, voice your affirmation of His word:

But You, O God, demonstrate Your own love toward me, in that while I was still a sinner, Christ died for me. (Romans 5:8)

4. Requests: As you make your requests known to the Lord, include:

- Strength for obedience
- International students in America
- Your prayer list, the concerns of your heart, and today's activities

5. Closing Prayer: Finally, offer this closing prayer to the Lord:

Now to You who are able to do exceedingly abundantly above all that I ask or think, according to the power that works in me, to You be glory in the Church by Christ Jesus throughout all ages, world without end. Amen. (Ephesians 3:20-21)

Memory Verse: This Book of the Law shall not depart from your mouth, but you shall meditate in it day and night, that you may observe to do according to all that is written in it. For then you will make your way prosperous, and then you will have good success.

Joshua 1:8
Bible Study Theme

READING

The passage for today centers on Elijah in the cave at Horeb. Elijah flees for his life from Jezebel, and the Lord ministers to him after saving him.

Read 1 Kings 19.

REFLECTING

On the heels of his stupendous victory over the prophets of Baal, Elijah falls into abject despair. He fears for his own life in the face of Jezebel's threat and flees to a lonely mountain for safety, there to lick his wounds and mourn his fate. How ignominious that this great prophet would call down fire from heaven one day and flee for his life the next. We all have feet of clay. Notice, though, that God does not berate him. Rather, He ministers to him quietly, reassures Elijah that He is still in control, and restores his spirit and strength. Then, once restored, God calls Elijah back into His service again. God cares when we hurt and are discouraged, and He gently calls us to Himself for new strength.

RESPONDING

1. Praise: Offer to the Lord your praise for His lovingkindness on your behalf:

Because Your lovingkindness is better than life, My lips shall praise You. Thus will I bless You while I live; I will lift up my hands in Your name. . . . When I remember You on my bed, I meditate on You in the night watches. Because You have been my help, therefore in the shadow of Your wings I will rejoice. (Psalm 63:3-5, 7)

Pause for personal praise and thanksgiving.

2. Confession: Pray this confession to the Lord as you seek to keep your life free from sin and in fellowship with Him:

Indeed I have sinned against You, O Lord God. (Joshua 7:20)

Show me Your ways, O Lord; teach my Your paths. Lead me in Your truth and teach me, for You are the God of my salvation; on You I wait all the day. (Psalm 25:4-5)

Confess any personal sins which the Holy Spirit brings to your mind.

3. Affirmation: Now pause to pray this affirmation to the Lord:

The wages of sin is death, but my free gift from You, O Lord, is eternal life in Christ Jesus my Lord. (Romans 6:23)

4. Requests: As you make your requests known to the Lord, pray for:

- Your "daily bread"
- Christian education institutions
- Your prayer list, the concerns of your heart, and today's activities

5. Closing Prayer: Finally, offer this closing prayer to the Lord:

Now may You, the God of peace, sanctify me completely, and may my whole spirit, soul, and body be preserved blameless at the coming of my Lord Jesus Christ. (1 Thessalonians 5:23)

Memory Verse: This Book of the Law shall not depart from your mouth, but you shall meditate in it day and night, that you may observe to do according to all that is written in it. For then you will make your way prosperous, and then you will have good success.

Joshua 1:8
Bible Study Theme

JUNE 16

READING

The passage for today centers on the death of Ahaziah. Because Ahaziah sought a pagan god for advice, the Lord sent Elijah to inform him that he would die.

Read 2 Kings 1.

REFLECTING

Ahab and Jezebel have become famous for their irreverence and disregard for the Law of the Lord. Yet Ahaziah, the son of Ahab went beyond them in his blatant disregard for the Lord. After an accident, he sent to inquire of Baal-Zebub, the pagan God of Ekron, whether or not he would recover from his accident. To reach Ekron, the messengers must pass Jerusalem. What a direct insult to Jehovah! In the interests of the whole nation, this insult could not be passed over in silence, and at God's bidding, Elijah informs the messengers that Ahaziah would die. No longer afraid, Elijah has been strengthened from his previous failure. We must always look at failure as an opportunity to grow, to become wiser, stronger. Indeed, failure is the back door to success.

RESPONDING

1. Praise: Thank the Lord that He can turn our failures into success, and offer Him your praise in this psalm:

Be glad in the Lord and rejoice, you righteous; and shout for joy, all you upright in heart! (Psalm 32:11).

Pause for personal praise and thanksgiving.

2. Confession: Pray this confession to the Lord as you seek to keep your life free from sin and in fellowship with Him:

Good and upright is the Lord; therefore He teaches sinners in the way. The humble He guides in justice, and the humble He teaches His way. . . . For Your name's sake, O Lord, pardon my iniquity, for it is great. (Psalm 25:8-9, 11)

Confess any personal sins which the Holy Spirit brings to your mind.

3. Affirmation: Now pause to pray this affirmation to the Lord:

You are the living bread which came down from heaven. If I eat of this bread, I will live forever; and the bread that You shall give is Your flesh, which You shall give for the life of the world. (John 6:51)

4. Requests: As you make your requests known to the Lord, include:

- Passion for moral excellence
- Needs of personal friends
- Your prayer list, the concerns of your heart, and today's activities

5. Closing Prayer: Finally, offer this closing prayer to the Lord:

Now may the Lord Jesus Christ Himself, and You, my God and Father, who have loved me and given me everlasting consolation and good hope by grace, comfort my heart and establish me in every good word and work. (2 Thessalonians 2:16-17)

Memory Verse: This Book of the Law shall not depart from your mouth, but you shall meditate in it day and night, that you may observe to do according to all that is written in it. For then you will make your way prosperous, and then you will have good success.

Joshua 1:8
Bible Study Theme

READING

The passage for today centers on Elijah being taken to heaven. After Elijah passes his mantle to his successor, Elisha, the Lord takes Elijah into heaven in a whirlwind.

Read 2 Kings 2.

REFLECTING

We tend to think that miracles permeate the entire time of the Bible. They don't. They tend to be concentrated primarily during the time of Moses, the time of the prophets, and the time of Jesus. Of course, they occur during other times, but these are the times of greatest concentration, and Elijah and Elisha represent one of the strongest of all periods—Chariots of fire, whirlwinds, parted water, floating ax heads, fire from heaven, sight into the future, recovery from the dead. While these things have little overlap with our everyday lives, they do give us an appreciation for the power of God. Today, God seems rather silent and inactive in comparison. Yet that is not because He is unable to act, but rather because He has chosen not to. The power is still there, and we can rest in the confidence that He still has all things under control.

RESPONDING

1. Praise: Confident of His control, praise the Lord with these words:

Be exalted, O Lord, in Your own strength! We will sing and praise Your power. (Psalm 21:13)

Rejoice in the Lord, O you righteous! For praise from the upright is beautiful. Praise the Lord with the harp; make melody to Him with an instrument of ten strings. (Psalm 33:1-2)

Pause for personal praise and thanksgiving.

2. Confession: Pray this confession to the Lord as you seek to keep your life free from sin:

Sing praise to the Lord, you saints of His, and give thanks at the remembrance of His holy name. For His anger is but for a moment, His favor is for a life; weeping may endure for a night, but joy comes in the morning. (Psalm 30:4-5)

Confess any personal sins which the Holy Spirit brings to your mind.

3. Affirmation: Now pause to pray this affirmation to the Lord:

O God, You are Spirit, and I must worship in spirit and truth. (John 4:24)

4. Requests: As you make your requests known to the Lord, include:

- Wisdom in decision making
- Opportunities to serve the Lord
- Your prayer list, the concerns of your heart, and today's activities

5. Closing Prayer: Finally, offer this closing prayer to the Lord:

Now to You, the King eternal, immortal, invisible, to God who alone is wise, be honor and glory forever and ever. Amen. (1 Timothy 1:17)

Memory Verse: This Book of the Law shall not depart from your mouth, but you shall meditate in it day and night, that you may observe to do according to all that is written in it. For then you will make your way prosperous, and then you will have good success.

Joshua 1:8
Bible Study Theme

JUNE 18

READING

The passage for today centers on the Shunammite widow's miracles. Elisha saves the widow from economic disaster and revives her son from death.

Read 2 Kings 4.

REFLECTING

Elisha's ministry is not startling. It is redemptive and constructive. Elijah was a prophet of fire and judgment; Elisha is a prophet of mercy and compassion. Elijah was a man on the move; Elisha enjoyed a tranquil life at home. Elijah's miracles were destructive; Elisha's were constructive. It must have been tempting for Elisha to want to be like Elijah. But he resists it. That is not what the Lord has for Elisha. He is his own man before the Lord. It is often tempting for us to want to be like someone else, to be dissatisfied with who we are and what we can do. Yet God made us to be what He wanted us to be. We must be content with who we are. It is so liberating. Accept yourself. God does.

RESPONDING

1. Praise: Because the Lord made us and cares for us as we are, we offer Him the praise of our lips:

O Lord, our Lord, How excellent is Your name in all the earth, You who set Your glory above the heavens! . . . When I consider Your heavens, the work of Your fingers, . . . what is man that You are mindful of him, and the son of man that You visit him? O Lord, our Lord, How majestic is Your name in all the earth! (Psalm 8:1, 3-4, 9)

Pause for personal praise and thanksgiving.

2. Confession: Pray this confession to the Lord as you seek to keep your life free from sin and in fellowship with Him:

I acknowledged my sin to You, and my iniquity I have not hidden. I said, "I will confess my transgressions to the Lord," and You forgave the iniquity of my sin. (Psalm 32:3, 5)

Confess any personal sins which the Holy Spirit brings to your mind.

3. Affirmation: Now pause to pray this affirmation to the Lord:

You, O Lord, will keep me in perfect peace, when my mind is stayed on You, because I trust in You. (Isaiah 26:3)

4. Requests: As you make your requests known to the Lord, include:

- Victory over temptation
- The work of missions in North and South America
- Your prayer list, the concerns of your heart, and today's activities

5. Closing Prayer: Finally, offer this closing prayer to the Lord:

You who are the blessed and only Potentate, the King of kings and Lord of lords, who alone have immortality, dwelling in unapproachable light, whom no man has seen or can see, to You be honor and everlasting power. Amen. (1 Timothy 6:15-16)

Memory Verse: Be diligent to present yourself approved to God, a worker who does not need to be ashamed, rightly dividing the word of truth.

2 Timothy 2:15
Bible Study Theme

READING

The passage for today centers on the healing of Naaman. The captain of the army of the king of Aram is healed of leprosy when he obeys Elisha's directives.

Read 2 Kings 5.

REFLECTING

Faith is central to the Christian life because it is the only thing you can do and still not do anything. It is God who has the power to move in the realm of the spiritual and miraculous, not man. So whether that which God asks of us is difficult or simple, it doesn't matter. He will do the work behind our faith. Naaman learns this the hard way. His heart is open to God, for he goes to Elisha in hopes that God will heal him of leprosy. Elisha tells him to go wash in the Jordan seven times. In a fit of anger, Naaman roars, "Is there not cleaner water in Damascus?" He misses the point. The point is not clean water or unclean. The point is, does he believe God? The Jordan is merely a test of his faith in God. When he realizes that, he washes and is made clean.

RESPONDING

1. **Praise:** By faith, we offer our praise to the Lord and thank Him for the power that makes us clean:

Blessed be Your glorious name, which is exalted above all blessing and praise! You alone are the Lord; You have made heaven, the heaven of heavens, with all their host, the earth and all things on it, the seas and all that is in them, and You preserve them all. The host of heaven worships You. (Nehemiah 9:5-6)

Pause for personal praise and thanksgiving.

2. **Confession:** Pray this confession to the Lord as you seek to keep your life free from sin and in fellowship with Him:

The righteous cry out and the Lord hears, and delivers them out of all their troubles. The Lord is near to those who have a broken heart, and saves such as have a contrite spirit. (Psalm 34:17-18)

Confess any personal sins which the Holy Spirit brings to your mind.

3. **Affirmation:** Now pause to pray this affirmation to the Lord:

I know whom I have believed and I am persuaded that You, O Lord, are able to keep what I have entrusted to You until that day. (2 Timothy 1:12)

4. **Requests:** As you make your requests known to the Lord, include:

- Love for your family
- Revival among Christians in America
- Your prayer list, the concerns of your heart, and today's activities

5. **Closing Prayer:** Finally, offer this closing prayer to the Lord:

Make me complete in every good work to do Your will, working in me what is well pleasing in Your sight, through Jesus Christ, to whom be glory forever and ever. Amen. (Hebrews 13:20-21)

Memory Verse: Be diligent to present yourself approved to God, a worker who does not need to be ashamed, rightly dividing the word of truth.

2 Timothy 2:15
Bible Study Theme

READING

The passage for today centers on the opening of the heavens. When the Syrians threatened Elisha, the heavens were filled with angels, and the Syrians were struck blind.

Read 2 Kings 6.

REFLECTING

We often have no idea what is going on around us in the spiritual realm, although that realm is just as real as the physical realm in which we live. Spiritual battles roar before our very eyes, but we neither see them nor hear them (Daniel 10:13). Guardian angels minister to our needs (Hebrews 1:14), and we entertain angels without knowing it (Hebrews 13:2). How real and alive is the spiritual realm, yet without the Scripture, we would know little about it, and we would not learn how to rely on spiritual truths that go beyond this physical reality. The Syrian army is camped around Dothan, but Elisha is not concerned because an army of the angels of the Lord encircles the horizon. We walk by faith and not by sight.

RESPONDING

1. **Praise:** Offer your praise to the Lord in these passages as you fellowship with Him:

Oh, sing to the Lord a new song! Sing to the Lord, all the earth. Sing to the Lord, bless His name; proclaim the good news of His salvation from day to day. Declare His glory among the nations, His wonders among all peoples. For the Lord is great and greatly to be praised. (Psalm 96:1-4)

2. **Confession:** Pray this confession to the Lord as you seek to keep your life free from sin and in fellowship with Him:

Now no chastening seems to be joyful for the present, but grievous; nevertheless, afterward it yields the peaceable fruit of righteousness when I have been trained by it. (Hebrews 12:11)

Confess any personal sins which the Holy Spirit may bring to your mind.

3. **Affirmation:** As you agree with the will of God, voice your affirmation of His word:

If I drink of the water that You, Lord Jesus, give me, I will never thirst. The water that You shall give me will become in me a fountain of water springing up into everlasting life. (John 4:14)

4. **Requests:** As you make your requests known to the Lord, include:

- Faithfulness with your treasures
- The Great Commission
- Your prayer list, the concerns of your heart, and today's activities

5. **Closing Prayer:** Finally, offer this closing prayer to the Lord:

May You, the God of grace, who called me to Your eternal glory by Christ Jesus, after I have suffered a while, perfect, establish, strengthen, and settle me. To You be the glory and the dominion forever and ever. Amen. (1 Peter 5:10-11)

Memory Verse: Be diligent to present yourself approved to God, a worker who does not need to be ashamed, rightly dividing the word of truth.

2 Timothy 2:15
Bible Study Theme

READING

The passage for today centers on the divine deliverance from Syria. As the Syrians are camped against the Israelites, the Lord causes them to hear the sound of a great army, and they flee in terror.

Read 2 Kings 7.

REFLECTING

While we must be careful about "spiritualizing" information in the Old Testament and making it say something it doesn't, there is at least an excellent illustration in the defeat of the Syrian army relating to the message of the Gospel today. The lepers are lost and starving and come upon abundance adequate for their own welfare, as well as the welfare of all others. They realize it is wrong to keep it to themselves, and they go out to tell others. The same is true of the Gospel of Christ. Those of us who have had our needs met by Him cannot be satisfied keeping it to ourselves—we must tell others. Someone has described our condition as beggars who have found food telling other beggars where to find it too—the Bread of Life.

RESPONDING

1. Praise: As you continue your time with the Lord, offer Him your praise through His word.

The Lord made the heavens. Honor and majesty are before Him; strength and beauty are in His sanctuary. Give to the Lord, O kindreds of the peoples, give to the Lord glory and strength. Give to the Lord the glory due His name; bring an offering, and come into His courts. . . . Let the heavens rejoice, and let the earth be glad. (Psalm 96:5-8, 11)

Take a moment to offer the Lord you personal praise and thanksgiving.

2. Confession: Pray this confession to the Lord as you seek to keep your life free from sin and in fellowship with Him:

If I sin, I have an Advocate with You, Father, Jesus Christ the righteous. And He Himself is the propitiation for my sins, and not for mine only, but also for the whole world. (1 John 2:1-2)

Confess any personal sins which the Holy Spirit may bring to your mind.

3. Affirmation: As you agree with the will of God, voice your affirmation of His word:

For to me, to live is Christ, and to die is gain. (Philippians 2:21)

4. Requests: As you make your requests known to the Lord, include:

* Spiritual insight
* Campus ministries
* Your prayer list, the concerns of your heart, and today's activities

5. Closing Prayer: Finally, offer this closing prayer to the Lord:

May I grow in the grace and knowledge of our Lord and Savior Jesus Christ. To Him be the glory both now and forever. Amen. (2 Peter 3:18)

Memory Verse: Be diligent to present yourself approved to God, a worker who does not need to be ashamed, rightly dividing the word of truth.

2 Timothy 2:15
Bible Study Theme

JUNE 22

READING

The passage for today centers on the restoration of the widow's land. The Shunammite widow vacated her land for seven years at Elisha's suggestion, and afterward her land and wealth were restored by Jehoram.

Read 2 Kings 8.

REFLECTING

Nothing happens in our life or in the world apart from divine appointment or permission. Behind every event and incident there is divine providence. The Shunammite widow who has done so much for Elisha is remembered and cared for years afterward. The Lord has a wonderful memory for those who feed Him when He is hungry and minister to Him when He is in need (see Matthew 25:37). The conversation between Gehazi, Elisha's servant, and the king might seem an accident, but it is providence. When we abide in the will of God, life is sown with divine coincidences. The Lord promises to care for His own.

RESPONDING

1. Praise: For the Lord's sovereignty and goodness to us, offer this passage of praise:

You are the Rock, Your work is perfect; for all Your ways are justice, a God of truth and without injustice, righteous and upright are You. (Deuteronomy 32:4)

The Lord lives! Blessed be my Rock! Let God be exalted, the Rock of my salvation! (2 Samuel 22:47)

Pause for personal praise and thanksgiving.

2. Confession: Pray this confession to the Lord as you seek to keep your life free from sin and in fellowship with Him:

Lord, be merciful to me; heal my soul, for I have sinned against You. . . . O Lord, be merciful to me, and raise me up. . . . Blessed be the Lord God . . . from everlasting to everlasting! Amen and Amen. (Psalm 41:4, 10, 13)

Confess any personal sins which the Holy Spirit brings to mind.

3. Affirmation: Now pause to pray this affirmation to the Lord:

Have I known? Have I heard? O Lord, the everlasting God, the Creator of the ends of the earth, is neither faint nor is weary. There is no searching of Your understanding. You give power to the weak, and when I have no might, You increase my strength. (Isaiah 40:27-29)

4. Requests: As you make your requests known to the Lord, include:

- Desire to be like Christ
- Needs in inner cities
- Your prayer list, the concerns of your heart, and today's activities

5. Closing Prayer: Finally, offer this closing prayer to the Lord:

Blessing and honor and glory and power be to You who sit on the throne, and to You, Lord, forever and ever! (Revelation 5:13)

Memory Verse: Be diligent to present yourself approved to God, a worker who does not need to be ashamed, rightly dividing the word of truth.

2 Timothy 2:15
Bible Study Theme

READING

The passage for today centers on Hezekiah's reign over Judah. Hezekiah institutes a reign of righteousness and faces the wrath of the king of Assyria.

Read 2 Kings 18.

REFLECTING

It is wonderful that such a wicked man as Ahaz had such a righteous son as Hezekiah. Hezekiah was a great man. It is difficult to stand against moral disintegration, especially when it is all around you and generally accepted. It is likely that Hezekiah had a godly mother. It is also likely that the fall of the Northern kingdom was a great incentive to root out idolatry. God richly rewards Hezekiah for his moral courage and leadership. It demonstrates the validity of 2 Chronicles 16:9 which says, "The eyes of the Lord run to and fro throughout the whole earth, to show Himself strong on behalf of those whose heart is perfect toward Him."

RESPONDING

1. Praise: Offer your praise to the Lord that He is eager to bless our righteous acts.

Give to the Lord, O kindreds of the peoples. . . . Give to the Lord the glory due His name; bring an offering, and come before Him. Oh, worship the Lord in the beauty of holiness! (1 Chronicles 16:28-29)

I will praise the Lord according to His righteousness, and will sing praise to the name of the Lord Most High. (Psalm 7:17)

Pause for personal praise and thanksgiving.

2. Confession: Pray this confession to the Lord as you seek to keep your life free from sin and in fellowship with Him:

Have mercy upon me, O God, according to Your lovingkindness; according to the multitude of Your tender mercies, blot out my transgressions. Wash me thoroughly from my iniquity and cleanse me from my sin. For I acknowledge my transgressions and my sin is ever before me. (Psalm 51:1-3)

Confess any personal sins which the Holy Spirit brings to your mind.

3. Affirmation: Now pause to pray this affirmation to the Lord:

Behold, You, O God, are my salvation, I will trust and not be afraid; "For YAH, the Lord, is my strength and my song; He also has become my salvation." (Isaiah 12:2)

4. Requests: As you make your requests known to the Lord, include:

● Personal witness for Christ

● Local churches around the nation

● Your prayer list, the concerns of your heart, and today's activities

5. Closing Prayer: Finally, offer this closing prayer to the Lord:

Amen! Blessing and glory and wisdom, thanksgiving and honor and power and might, be to You, God, forever and ever. Amen. (Revelation 7:12)

Memory Verse: Be diligent to present yourself approved to God, a worker who does not need to be ashamed, rightly dividing the word of truth.

2 Timothy 2:15
Bible Study Theme

JUNE 24

READING

The passage for today centers on Judah's deliverance from Assyria. When Sennacherib attacks Jerusalem, Hezekiah calls upon the Lord for deliverance and is answered.

Read 2 Kings 19.

REFLECTING

In spite of all the trouble which comes upon Israel and Judah, God wants to bless them. He is eager to bless them. It is only as He is blessing them that His desire for the world is advanced. All that is needed for blessing is obedience. With just that simple matter of faithfulness to the Law, everything can turn around, and the Israelites can bask in the glory of unbridled blessing. Hezekiah demonstrates just how quickly everything can turn around. He is looking into the jaws of an Assyrian military machine one minute, and the machine is routed the next. God is not reluctant to bless us. But we must be sure we are eligible by being faithful to Him.

RESPONDING

1. Praise: Bless the Lord and praise Him for His blessings in our lives:

Blessed are You, Lord God . . . our Father, forever and ever. Yours, O Lord, is the greatness, the power and the glory, the victory and the majesty; for all that is in heaven and in earth is Yours; Yours is the kingdom, O Lord, and You are exalted as head over all. Both riches and honor come from You, and You reign over all. In Your hand is power and might; in Your hand it is to make great and to give strength to all. Now therefore, our God, we thank You and praise Your glorious name. (1 Chronicles 29:10-13)

Pause for personal praise and thanksgiving.

2. Confession: Pray this confession to the Lord as you seek to keep your life free from sin:

Against You, You only, have I sinned, and done this evil in Your sight—that You may be found just when You speak, and blameless when You judge. (Psalm 51:4)

Confess any personal sins which the Holy Spirit brings to mind.

3. Affirmation: Now pause to pray this affirmation to the Lord:

If I wait on the Lord, my strength shall be renewed; I shall mount up with wings like eagles, I shall run and not be weary, I shall walk and not faint. (Isaiah 40:31)

4. Requests: As you make your requests known to the Lord, include:

* An eternal perspective
* Needs of work or school mates
* Your prayer list, the concerns of your heart, and today's activities

5. Closing Prayer: Finally, offer this closing prayer to the Lord:

I will wait on You, the Lord; I will be of good courage, and You shall strengthen my heart; I will wait on You! (Psalm 27:14)

Memory Verse: Be diligent to present yourself approved to God, a worker who does not need to be ashamed, rightly dividing the word of truth.

2 Timothy 2:15
Bible Study Theme

READING

The passage for today centers on Hezekiah's illness and recovery. Hezekiah is on the verge of death, but in answer to his prayer, the Lord extends his life.

Read 2 Kings 20.

REFLECTING

Hezekiah's contribution to our lives is probably a very great one. We read of his zeal for the house of Jehovah (2 Chronicles 29:3-19), and for the worship of Jehovah (verses 20-26), and his strict adherence to the Davidic traditions (verses 25, 27, 30). His delight was in the word of Jehovah. In 2 Chronicles 31:21 we read of the "work" which he began "in the Law and in the commandments." In addition, he formed a guild of men for this devout literary work. Proverbs 25:1 tells us that these men had a good hand in shaping the book of Proverbs into its present form. We read that these "men of Hezekiah" evidently included Isaiah (2 Kings 18:18). What a contribution this ancient has made to our lives today!

RESPONDING

1. Praise: The Lord's dominion is forever, and we can praise Him that He never changes:

Sing to Him a new song; play skillfully with a shout of joy. For the word of the Lord is right. And all His work is done in truth. He loves righteousness and justice; The earth is full of the goodness of the Lord. (Psalm 33:3-5)

Pause for personal praise and thanksgiving.

2. Confession: Pray this confession to the Lord as you seek to keep your life free from sin and in fellowship with Him:

Purge me with hyssop, and I shall be clean. Wash me, and I shall be whiter than snow. Make me to hear joy and gladness, that the bones which You have broken may rejoice. Hide Your face from my sins, and blot out all my iniquities. (Psalm 51:7-9)

Confess any personal sins which the Holy Spirit brings to your mind.

3. Affirmation: Now pause to pray this affirmation to the Lord:

I will not lay up for myself treasures on earth, where moth and rust destroy, and where thieves break in and steal. But I shall lay up for myself treasures in heaven, where neither moth nor rust destroys and where thieves do not break in and steal. (Matthew 6:19-20)

4. Requests: As you make your requests known to the Lord, include:

- Personal discipline
- Christians worldwide who are persecuted for their faith
- Your prayer list, the concerns of your heart, and today's activities

5. Closing Prayer: Finally, offer this closing prayer to the Lord:

Show me the path of life; in Your presence is fullness of joy; at Your right hand are pleasures forevermore. (Psalm 16:11)

Memory Verse: Your word I have hidden in my heart, that I might not sin against You.

Psalm 119:11
Bible Study Theme

JUNE 26

READING

The passage for today centers on the destruction of Jerusalem. In culmination of a succession of unrighteous kings, God judges Judah by allowing Nebuchadnezzar to capture Jerusalem.

Read 2 Kings 25.

REFLECTING

Judah had a total of twenty kings after Solomon. Only eight of them were righteous, giving moral and spiritual leadership. And, as the king went, so went the nation. As a result, it is inevitable that God has to bring final judgment on them. The ghastly succession of horrors promised for chronic disobedience in Deuteronomy 28 and reiterated to Solomon in 2 Kings 9 begins to unfold. "I will cast them out of My sight. So Israel will become a proverb and a byword among all peoples." Nebuchadnezzar besieges Jerusalem, captures it, transports her main people to captivity in Babylonia, robs her treasury, and violates worship in the temple. Sin has a terrible price.

RESPONDING

1. Praise: Offer your praise to the Lord that we can be spared from His judgment on sin:

O God, You are my God; early will I seek You; My soul thirsts for You, my flesh longs for You in a dry and weary land where there is no water. So I have looked for You in the sanctuary, to see Your power and Your glory. (Psalm 63:1-2)

Pause for personal praise and thanksgiving.

2. Confession: Pray this confession to the Lord as you seek to keep your life free from sin and in fellowship with Him:

Bless the Lord, O my soul; and all that is within me, bless His holy name! Bless the Lord, O my soul, and forget not all His benefits, who forgives all your iniquities. (Psalm 103:1-3)

Confess any personal sins which the Holy Spirit brings to mind.

3. Affirmation: Now pause to pray this affirmation to the Lord:

I may come to You, O Lord, weary and heavy laden, and You will give me rest. I may take Your yoke upon me, and learn from You, for You are gentle and lowly in heart, and I shall find rest for my soul. For Your yoke is easy, and Your burden is light. (Matthew 11:28:30)

4. Requests: As you make your requests known to the Lord, include:

* Love for the Lord

* The work of missions in the Middle East, Australia, and the Islands

* Your prayer list, the concerns of your heart, and today's activities

5. Closing Prayer: Finally, offer this closing prayer to the Lord:

Save Your people, and bless Your inheritance; shepherd us also, and bear us up forever. (Psalm 28:9)

Memory Verse: Your word I have hidden in my heart, that I might not sin against You.

Psalm 119:11
Bible Study Theme

READING

The passage for today centers on God's covenant with David. God promises David that He will propagate David's lineage forever.

Read 1 Chronicles 17.

REFLECTING

David is described as being a "man after God's own heart" (1 Samuel 13:14). For all of David's strengths, it is difficult for us to accept that description when he is guilty of lying, adultery, murder, and other indiscretions. However, to be a man after God's own heart means that David acknowledges that what God calls sin is sin and that he wants the same things God wants. His noble desires and intentions are overruled several times by his passions, but when his senses are restored, and he has repented of his sin, again his heart beats after the same things God wants. We may not be as bad as David was in his bad moments, but are we as good as David was in his good moments? Are we quick to repent of sin? Do our hearts return to beating after God?

RESPONDING

1. Praise: Realizing it is never too late to repent, praise God with these words:

You who love the Lord, hate evil! He preserves the souls of His saints; He delivers them out of the hand of the wicked. Light is sown for the righteous, and gladness for the upright in heart. Rejoice in the Lord, you righteous, and give thanks at the remembrance of His holy name. (Psalm 97:10-12)

Take a moment to offer the Lord your personal praise and thanksgiving.

2. Confession: Pray this confession to the Lord as you seek to keep your life free from sin and in fellowship with Him:

If I say that I have no sin, I deceive myself, and the truth is not in me. If I confess my sins, You, O Lord, are faithful and just to forgive me my sins and to cleanse me from all unrighteousness. (1 John 1:8-9)

Confess any personal sins which the Holy Spirit may bring to your mind.

3. Affirmation: As you agree with the will of God, voice your affirmation of His word:

And this is Your commandment: that I should believe on the name of Your Son Jesus Christ and love others, as He commanded me. (1 John 3:23)

4. Requests: As you make your requests known to the Lord, include:

- Faithfulness in sharing Christ
- The Lord's work in national and world affairs
- Your prayer list, the concerns of your heart, and today's activities

5. Closing Prayer: Finally, offer this closing prayer to the Lord:

You, the Lord, will command Your lovingkindness in the daytime, and in the night Your song shall be with me—a prayer to You, the God of my life. (Psalm 42:8)

Memory Verse: Your word I have hidden in my heart, that I might not sin against You.

Psalm 119:11
Bible Study Theme

READING

The passage for today centers on David's death. Just before David dies, he blesses the assembly of Israel and gives his blessing to Solomon.

Read 1 Chronicles 29.

REFLECTING

How we spend our money is a powerful reflection of our value system. If we have strong spiritual values, we give our money generously to spiritual things. If we have primarily temporal values, we resist—and perhaps even resent—giving to spiritual things. After completing the temple, the Israelites "rejoiced because they had offered so willingly, for they made their offering to the Lord with a whole heart" (1 Chronicles 29:9). Where are your values?

RESPONDING

1. Praise: Worship the Lord by offering Him your praise in spirit and in truth.

Make a joyful shout to the Lord, all you lands! Serve the Lord with gladness; come before His presence with singing. Know that the Lord, He is God; it is He who has made us, and not we ourselves; we are His people and the sheep of His pasture. Enter into His gates with thanksgiving, and into His courts with praise . . . for the Lord is good. (Psalm 100:1-5)

Take a moment to offer the Lord your personal praise and thanksgiving.

2. Confession: Pray this confession to the Lord as you seek to keep your life free from sin and in fellowship with Him:

Forgive me, Lord, when I am unmindful of You, the Rock who begot me, and when I have forgotten you, the God who fathered me. (Deuteronomy 32:18)

Confess any personal sins which the Holy Spirit may bring to your mind.

3. Affirmation: As you agree with the will of God, voice your affirmation of His word:

Most assuredly, You say to me, O Lord, if I hear Your word and believe in Him who sent You, I have everlasting life, and shall not come into judgment, but have passed from death into life. (John 5:24)

4. Requests: As you make your requests known to the Lord, include:

- Compassion for others
- Missions in America
- Your prayer list, the concerns of your heart, and today's activities

5. Closing Prayer: Finally, offer this closing prayer to the Lord:

Now to You who are able to keep me from stumbling, and to present me faultless before the presence of Your glory with exceeding joy, to You, my God and Savior, who alone are wise, be glory and majesty, dominion and power, both now and forever. Amen. (Jude 24-25)

Memory Verse: Your word I have hidden in my heart, that I might not sin against You.

Psalm 119:11
Bible Study Theme

READING

The passage for today centers on revival under Josiah. Josiah leads Judah in righteousness, and the Law is reinstated after having been lost and rediscovered.

Read 2 Chronicles 34.

REFLECTING

It is incredible to imagine that the Law could have gotten lost in Jerusalem. How could that have happened? The whole nation was to worship the Lord. The dominant building in Jerusalem was the temple. Their entire history revolved around the giving and preservation of the Law. How could that have happened? Neglect has a poor memory. How quickly we can drift from the Lord in just a short time of spiritual staleness. Consider our nation today. Just twenty years ago, there was a moral fiber that is nonexistent today. People are people. Israel drifted the same way, but for longer. It ought to serve as a warning to us. The same can happen to us as individuals.

RESPONDING

1. Praise: The Lord will guard and care for the heart that follows Him and is a heart of praise:

Be merciful to me, O God, be merciful to me! For my soul trusts in You; and in the shadow of Your wings I make my refuge . . . until these calamities have passed by. . . . I will praise You, O Lord, among the peoples; I will sing to You among the nations. For Your mercy reaches unto the heavens, and Your truth unto the clouds. Be exalted, O God, above the heavens; let Your glory be above all the earth. (Psalm 57:1, 9-11)

Pause for personal praise and thanksgiving.

2. Confession: Pray this confession to the Lord as you seek to keep your life free from sin and in fellowship with Him:

Deliver me from bloodguiltiness, O God, the God of my salvation. And my tongue shall sing aloud of Your righteousness. O Lord, open my lips, and my mouth shall show forth Your praise. (Psalm 51:14-15)

Confess any personal sins which the Holy Spirit brings to your mind.

3. Affirmation: Now pause to pray this affirmation to the Lord:

You, Lord Jesus, are the Way, the Truth, and the Life. I come to the Father only through You. (John 14:6)

4. Requests: As you make your requests known to the Lord, include:

- Personal spiritual growth
- Military ministries
- Your prayer list, the concerns of your heart, and today's activities

5. Closing Prayer: Finally, offer this closing prayer to the Lord:

Glory to You in the highest, and on earth peace, good will toward men! (Luke 2:14)

Memory Verse: Your word I have hidden in my heart, that I might not sin against You.

Psalm 119:11
Bible Study Theme

JUNE 30

READING

The passage for today centers on the reinstatement of Passover. In the culmination of the revival of Judaism under Josiah, the Passover, which had not been observed for years, is reinstated.

Read 2 Chronicles 35.

REFLECTING

Abraham Lincoln once said, "A man's about as happy as he makes up his mind to be." That is perhaps an oversimplified statement, yet it presents a basic truth that often we must consciously decide what we want to become. Those who grow spiritually are those who have made a conscious decision to pursue spiritual things. Josiah was one of the great kings of Judah. He was a strong reformer and tried to lead the nation in righteousness. In verse 31, we read, "the king stood in his place and made a covenant before the Lord to walk after the Lord, and to keep His commandments and His testimonies with all his heart and with all his soul." Have you ever made the decision to follow the Lord with your whole heart?

RESPONDING

1. Praise: Praise the Lord for the privilege of following Him fully:

Make a joyful shout to God, all the earth! Sing out the honor of His name; make His praise glorious. Say to God, "How awesome are Your works! Through the greatness of Your power Your enemies shall submit themselves to You. All the earth shall worship You and sing praises to You; they shall sing praises to Your name." (Psalm 66:1-4)

Pause for personal praise and thanksgiving.

2. Confession: Pray this confession to the Lord as you seek to keep your life free from sin and in fellowship with Him:

O Lord, You are merciful and gracious, slow to anger, and abounding in mercy. . . . As a father pities his children, so You, Lord, pity those who fear You. For You know our frame; You remember that we are dust. (Psalm 103:8, 13-14)

Confess any personal sins which the Holy Spirit brings to your mind.

3. Affirmation: Now pause to pray this affirmation to the Lord:

Yes, if I cry out for discernment, and lift up my voice for understanding, if I seek her as silver, and search for her as for hidden treasures; then I will understand the fear of You, O Lord, and find the knowledge of You, O God. For You, O Lord, give wisdom; from Your mouth come knowledge and understanding; You store up sound wisdom for me and are a shield to me when I walk uprightly. (Proverbs 2:3-7)

4. Requests: As you make your requests to the Lord, include:

- Fruit of the Spirit in your life
- The ministry of Christian literature
- Your prayer list, the concerns of your heart, and today's activities

5. Closing Prayer: Finally, offer this closing prayer to the Lord:

Grace, mercy, and peace from You, the Father, and the Lord Jesus Christ our Savior. (Titus 1:4)

Memory Verse: Your word I have hidden in my heart, that I might not sin against You.

Psalm 119:11
Bible Study Theme

READING

The passage for today centers on the proclamation of Cyrus. The Lord prompts Cyrus, king of Persia, to rebuild the temple in Jerusalem and restore worship of Him among returning Jews.

Read Ezra 1.

REFLECTING

The Bible says that God "removes kings and establishes kings" (Daniel 2:21) and that "the king's heart is like channels of water in the hand of the Lord; He turns it wherever He wishes" (Proverbs 21:1). We see a classic example of these truths in Ezra. The Israelites have been taken into captivity at the hands of the Babylonians and remain there for seventy years. During that time, the Babylonians are conquered by Persia. Then the Lord moves the king of Persia to orchestrate the return of the Jews to Jerusalem. God is in control. Today, we are concerned about the fragile condition of life on Earth. Nuclear war, environmental pollution, world hunger, overpopulation, terrorism, and hostile governments threaten our security. The world seems out of control. We know differently, however. Bad things will still happen. We live in a fallen world. But God is in control, and history is moving toward His end. We must cling to the fact that we are pilgrims, sojourners going to another world. We should do all within our power to make this a better place to live, while putting our hopes and affections in heaven, where our true citizenship lies.

RESPONDING

1. Praise: As you rest in God's sovereign care, offer Him this praise:

I will hope continually, and will praise You yet more and more. My mouth shall tell of Your righteousness and Your salvation all the day, for I do not know their limits. (Psalm 71:14-15)

Now express any additional thoughts of praise or thanksgiving.

2. Confession: Pray this confession to the Lord to keep your life free from sin and in fellowship with Him:

"Now, therefore," says the Lord, "turn to Me with all your heart. . . ." Return to the Lord your God, for He is gracious and merciful, slow to anger, and of great kindness; and He relents from doing harm. (Joel 2:12-13)

Confess any personal sins which the Holy Spirit brings to your mind.

3. Affirmation: Now pray this affirmation to the Lord as you agree with and submit yourself to the will of God:

I have sinned and fall short of Your glory, O God, being justified as a gift by Your grace through the redemption which is in Christ Jesus. (Romans 3:23-24)

4. Requests: As you make your requests known to the Lord, include:

- Health and strength to serve God
- God's will to be done on earth
- Your prayer list, the concerns of your heart, and today's activities

5. Closing Prayer: Finally, offer this closing prayer to the Lord:

Blessed are You, the Lord, forevermore! Amen and amen. (Psalm 89:52).

Memory Verse: Your word I have hidden in my heart, that I might not sin against You.

Psalm 119:11
Bible Study Theme

JULY 2

READING

The passage for today centers on the restoration of sacrificial worship. The priests restore the altar and worship of the Lord, and restoration of the temple begins.

Read Ezra 3.

REFLECTING

The basis of most discontent is comparison. We could be happy with our car if the neighbor didn't have a better one. We would be satisfied with our house if it were as nice as everyone else's. We would be proud of our job if our former classmates didn't have better ones. Yet, were we to have our present possessions in Africa, we would be considered rich. Once our basic needs are met, the issue isn't "how are we," but rather "how are we compared to how everyone else is." When the foundation of the new temple was laid, the new generation rejoiced at the work of God, but the older generation lamented that the new temple was not as impressive as the old. We should content ourselves with what God has chosen to give us and not compare. He is rich who rejoices in his portion.

RESPONDING

1. Praise: Offer your praise to the Lord for what He has given you, and rejoice in your portion:

Lord, You have been our dwelling place in all generations. Before the mountains were brought forth, or ever You had formed the earth and the world, even from everlasting to everlasting, You are God. O satisfy us early with Your mercy, that we may rejoice and be glad all our days! (Psalm 90:1-2, 14)

Take a moment to offer the Lord your personal praise and thanksgiving.

2. Confession: Pray this confession to the Lord as you seek to keep your life free from sin and in fellowship with Him:

Cleanse me from all my iniquity by which I have sinned against You, and pardon all my iniquities by which I have sinned and by which I have transgressed against You. (Jeremiah 33:8)

Confess any personal sins which the Holy Spirit may bring to your mind.

3. Affirmation: As you agree with the will of God, voice your affirmation of His word:

I am not ashamed, for I know You, in whom I have believed, and am persuaded that You are able to keep what I have committed to You until that Day. (2 Timothy 1:12)

4. Requests: As you make your requests known to the Lord, include:

- Sensitivity to sin
- The ministry of your local church
- Your prayer list, the concerns of your heart, and today's activities

5. Closing Prayer: Finally, offer this closing prayer to the Lord:

Let the words of my mouth and the meditation of my heart be acceptable in Your sight, O Lord, my strength and my redeemer. (Psalm 19:14)

Memory Verse: Trust in the Lord with all your heart, and lean not on your own understanding; in all your ways acknowledge Him, and He shall direct your paths.

Proverbs 3:5-6
God's Will Theme

READING

The passage for today centers on progress hindered by adversaries. Gentiles in the area write to the king suggesting insurrection on the part of the Jews, after which the king orders a halt to the restoration.

Read Ezra 4.

REFLECTING

There is a common perception in the Christian world that if you are doing the Lord's will you will not suffer hardships for it. The example of the Jews rebuilding the temple certainly does not support that supposition. The Lord clearly intends for them to rebuild the temple, yet throughout the entire time, they suffer opposition. It is not necessarily a sign of God's displeasure when work begun for Him fails. There may be other reasons for the failure which are hidden in His sovereignty. That is why it is so important to be in fellowship with Him. If something we are doing fails, we have confidence that it was not because of our sin, but because of His sovereignty.

RESPONDING

1. Praise: Because He faithfully loves us, faithfully praise Him in the words of this psalm:

It is good to give thanks to the Lord, and to sing praises to Your name, O Most High; to declare Your lovingkindness in the morning, and Your faithfulness every night . . . to declare that the Lord is upright; He is my rock, and there is no unrighteousness in Him. (Psalm 92:1-2, 15)

Take a moment to offer the Lord your personal praise and thanksgiving.

2. Confession: Pray this confession to the Lord as you seek to keep your life free from sin and in fellowship with Him:

I return to You, O Lord my God, for I have stumbled because of my iniquity; I take words with me, and return to You, Lord. I say to You, "Take away all iniquity; receive me graciously, for I will offer the sacrifices of my lips." (Hosea 14:1-2)

Confess any personal sins which the Holy Spirit may bring to your mind.

3. Affirmation: As you agree with the will of God, voice your affirmation of His word:

And this is eternal life, that I may know You, the only true God, and Jesus Christ whom You have sent. (John 17:3)

4. Requests: As you make your requests known to the Lord, include:

- Wisdom for living life
- Needs of your immediate family
- Your prayer list, the concerns of your heart, and today's activities

5. Closing Prayer: Finally, offer this closing prayer to the Lord:

Surely goodness and mercy shall follow me all the days of my life, and I will dwell in the house of the Lord forever. (Psalm 23:6)

Memory Verse: Trust in the Lord with all your heart, and lean not on your own understanding; in all your ways acknowledge Him, and He shall direct your paths.

Proverbs 3:5-6
God's Will Theme

JULY 4

READING

The passage for today centers on the continued restoration. In the confusion resulting in a change in the monarchy, work is resumed on the temple, and another challenge is made to the restoration work.

Read Ezra 5 .

REFLECTING

In the early days of World War II, England is being crushed by the powerful German military machine. A young man is elected Prime Minister in England, Winston Churchill, whose speeches electrify Parliament and galvanize the nation to his vision and resolve. One man is almost single-handedly responsible for England's victory over Germany. In like manner, the prophets Haggai and Zechariah encourage the Jews to continue rebuilding the temple: "Be strong! Take courage!" What force there is in encouragement. Be an encourager.

RESPONDING

1. Praise: Continue your time with the Lord by offering to the God of creation and the new creation your praise through the words of this psalm:

I will bless the Lord at all times; His praise shall continually be in my mouth. My soul shall make its boast in the Lord; the humble shall hear of it and be glad. Oh, magnify the Lord with me, and let us exalt His name together. . . . Oh, taste and see that the Lord is good; blessed is the man who trusts in Him! (Psalm 34:1-3, 8)

Now express any additional thoughts of praise or thanksgiving.

2. Confession: Pray this confession to the Lord as you seek to keep your life free from sin:

Create in me a clean heart, O God, and renew a steadfast spirit within me. . . . Restore to me the joy of Your salvation, and uphold me with Your generous Spirit; then I will teach transgressors Your ways, and sinners shall be converted to You. (Psalm 51:10, 12-13)

Confess any personal sins which the Holy Spirit brings to your mind.

3. Affirmation: Now pray this affirmation to the Lord as you agree with and submit yourself to the will of God:

If I am wise, I will not glory in my wisdom; if I am mighty, I will not glory in my might; nor if I am rich, in my riches. But if I glory, I will only glory in the fact that I understand and know You; that You are the Lord, exercising lovingkindness, judgment, and righteousness in the earth. For in these You delight. (Jeremiah 9:23-24)

4. Requests: The Lord encourages us to come to Him with our concerns and desires. As you make your requests known to the Lord, include:

- Insight into Scripture
- The hungry around the world
- Your prayer list, the concerns of your heart, and today's activities.

5. Closing Prayer: Finally, offer this closing prayer to the Lord:

We will be of good courage, and You shall strengthen our hearts, all we who hope in the Lord. (Psalm 31:24)

Memory Verse: Trust in the Lord with all your heart, and lean not on your own understanding; in all your ways acknowledge Him, and He shall direct your paths.

Proverbs 3:5-6
God's Will Theme

READING

The passage for today centers on the completion of the temple. The original decree is found, and permission is given to complete the temple restoration.

Read Ezra 6.

REFLECTING

It is often darkest before the dawn. Impatience comes when we forget who is in control. Just as it looks as if the work on the temple is going to be stopped, the Lord turns the situation around in an almost humorous fashion. Not only is permission given to complete the temple, but the provokers are also required to finance the remainder of the restoration. Stewing and worrying do little to further the work of God; He is quite capable of accomplishing His work. God even uses enemies of His work at times to help complete His task. Are there those who oppose the work of God in your life? God will not be thwarted. Our work is trust, obedience, and faithfulness.

RESPONDING

1. Praise: In full confidence in the character of God, offer your praise to Him through this psalm:

The Lord reigns, He is clothed with majesty; the Lord is clothed, He has girded Himself with strength. Surely the world is established, so that it cannot be moved. (Psalm 93:1-2)

Take a moment to offer the Lord your personal praise and thanksgiving.

2. Confession: Pray this confession to the Lord as you seek to keep your life free from sin and in fellowship with Him:

O Lord, You ask me to return to You with all my heart. I will return to You, O Lord, for You are gracious and merciful, slow to anger, and of great kindness; and You relent from doing harm. (Joel 2:12-13)

Confess any personal sins which the Holy Spirit may bring to your mind.

3. Affirmation: As you agree with the will of God, voice your affirmation of His word:

Eye has not seen, nor ear heard, nor have entered into the heart of man the things which You, O God, have prepared for those who love You. (1 Corinthians 2:9)

4. Requests: As you make your requests known to the Lord, include:

- Love for fellow Christians
- The work of missions in Europe and Asia
- Your prayer list, the concerns of your heart, and today's activities.

5. Closing Prayer: Finally, offer this closing prayer to the Lord:

This is the day which You have made; I will rejoice and be glad in it. (Psalm 118:24)

Memory Verse: Trust in the Lord with all your heart, and lean not on your own understanding; in all your ways acknowledge Him, and He shall direct your paths.

Proverbs 3:5-6
God's Will Theme

JULY 6

READING

The passage for today centers on Nehemiah's grief for Jerusalem. Nehemiah learns of the deterioration of the people and city of Jerusalem and weeps for them.

Read Nehemiah 1.

REFLECTING

One of the essential characteristics of leadership is that the leader feels the full weight of the plight of certain people and assumes responsibility for their condition. Many people knew of the condition of Jerusalem, but few felt the impact and had the vision for response. Jeremiah did, and God used him in a mighty way. What in life "hits" you? What situations cause you to feel the impact of the plight of others, and for what situations do you have a vision for response? It might be as large as a nation or as small as a church nursery. But if you feel it and have a vision for it, chances are God would like to use you there, and nothing is small if God has called you to it.

RESPONDING

1. Praise: Being used by the Lord is a joyful experience. Praise Him as you consider how He might use you:

Let us come before His presence with thanksgiving; let us shout joyfully to Him with psalms. For the Lord is the great God, and the great King above all gods. . . . Oh come, let us worship and bow down; let us kneel before the Lord our Maker. For He is our God, and we are the people of his pasture, and the sheep of His hand. (Psalm 95:2-3, 6-7)

Take a moment to offer the Lord your personal praise and thanksgiving.

2. Confession: Pray this confession to the Lord as you seek to keep your life free from sin and in fellowship with Him:

No temptation has overtaken me except such as is common to man; but You are faithful, O God, who will not allow me to be tempted beyond what I am able, but with the temptation will also make the way of escape, that I may be able to bear it. (1 Corinthians 10:13)

Confess any personal sins which the Holy Spirit may bring to your mind.

3. Affirmation: As you agree with the will of God, voice your affirmation of His word:

But You, O God, demonstrate Your own love toward me, in that while I was still a sinner, Christ died for me. (Romans 5:8)

4. Requests: As you make your requests known to the Lord, include:

- Faithfulness with your time
- The president and national leaders and affairs
- Your prayer list, the concerns of your heart, and today's activities

5. Closing Prayer: Finally, offer this closing prayer to the Lord:

Oh, satisfy me early with Your mercy, that I may rejoice and be glad all my days! (Psalm 90:14)

Memory Verse: Trust in the Lord with all your heart, and lean not on your own understanding; in all your ways acknowledge Him, and He shall direct your paths.

Proverbs 3:5-6
God's Will Theme

JULY 7

READING

The passage for today centers on Nehemiah's visit to Jerusalem. Nehemiah prays that the king will give him permission to visit Jerusalem, which he does. Read Nehemiah 2.

REFLECTING

It has been said that luck is the residue of preparation. As Christians, we don't believe in mere "luck," but the principle has merit anyway. Good fortune flows out of being prepared. Nehemiah comes before the king unable to conceal his agitation over the situation in Jerusalem. The king asks him what his request is. Then Nehemiah gives a thorough answer, revealing that he has already given the situation a great deal of thought. When we are faced with situations which need change, preparation is vital. We may not be able to do anything about it at the moment. But we can ask ourselves a question: if it lay within our power to do anything we wanted to, what would we do? If we can answer that, then we will recognize opportunity when it knocks and can capitalize on it as Nehemiah did.

RESPONDING

1. Praise: God is a God of wisdom and order, who blesses our wisdom and order. For this we praise Him:

Oh, sing to the Lord a new song! Sing to the Lord, all the earth. Sing to the Lord, bless His name; proclaim the good news of His salvation from day to day. Declare His glory among the nations, His wonders among all peoples. For the Lord is great and greatly to be praised. (Psalm 96:1-4)

2. Confession: Pray this confession to the Lord as you seek to keep your life free from sin and in fellowship with Him:

Now no chastening seems to be joyful for the present, but grievous; nevertheless, afterward it yields the peaceable fruit of righteousness when I have been trained by it. (Hebrews 12:11)

Confess any personal sins which the Holy Spirit may bring to your mind.

3. Affirmation: As you agree with the will of God, voice your affirmation of His word:

If I drink of the water that You, Lord Jesus, give me, I will never thirst. The water that You shall give me will become in me a fountain of water springing up into everlasting life. (John 4:14)

4. Requests: As you make your requests known to the Lord, include:

* Your financial needs
* The needs of the poor
* Your prayer list, the concerns of your heart, and today's activities

5. Closing Prayer: Finally, offer this closing prayer to the Lord:

Let the beauty of You, Lord, be upon me, and establish the work of my hands for me; yes, establish the work of my hands. (Psalm 90:17)

Memory Verse: Trust in the Lord with all your heart, and lean not on your own understanding; in all your ways acknowledge Him, and He shall direct your paths.

Proverbs 3:5-6
God's Will Theme

JULY 8

READING

The passage for today centers on the work being discouraged by adversaries. After Nehemiah surveys the wall and organizes the work on it, construction begins but is ridiculed by those opposing it.

Read Nehemiah 4.

REFLECTING

It is difficult to do any work when we are strongly opposed. We begin to doubt the validity of the task or our ability to perform it. When we are assailed for doing God's work, we must evaluate the source of opposition. We cannot assume that opposition means that God is against us. While it is of little value to blame the devil for everything that goes wrong, the Bible makes it clear that spiritual opposition is a reality in the work of God. If we suspect spiritual opposition, we must oppose the warfare. When we have done everything we are supposed to, we are then to stand firm and pray. Nehemiah did.

RESPONDING

1. Praise: Because the Lord preserves us through spiritual battles, offer your praise as you read this psalm:

The Lord made the heavens. Honor and majesty are before Him; strength and beauty are in His sanctuary. Give to the Lord, O kindreds of the peoples, give to the Lord glory and strength. Give to the Lord the glory due His name; bring an offering, and come into His courts. . . . Let the heavens rejoice, and let the earth be glad. (Psalm 96:5-8, 11)

Take a moment to offer the Lord your personal praise and thanksgiving.

2. Confession: Pray this confession to the Lord as you seek to keep your life free from sin and in fellowship with Him:

If I sin, I have an Advocate with You, Father, Jesus Christ the righteous. And He Himself is the propitiation for my sins, and not for mine only, but also for the whole world. (1 John 2:1-2)

Confess any personal sins which the Holy Spirit may bring to your mind.

3. Affirmation: As you agree with the will of God, voice your affirmation of His word:

For to me, to live is Christ, and to die is gain. (Philippians 2:21)

4. Requests: As you make your requests known to the Lord, include:

- Protection from the "evil one"
- Laborers for the "harvest"
- Your prayer list, the concerns of your heart, and today's activities

5. Closing Prayer: Finally, offer this closing prayer to the Lord:

Bless the Lord, all you His hosts, you ministers of His, who do His pleasure. Bless the Lord, all His works, in all places of His dominion. (Psalm 103:21-22)

Memory Verse: Trust in the Lord with all your heart, and lean not on your own understanding; in all your ways acknowledge Him, and He shall direct your paths.

Proverbs 3:5-6
God's Will Theme

READING

The passage for today centers on the internal mistreatment among Jews. Some Jews are taking financial advantage of others, a practice which Nehemiah stopped by decree and by force of example.

Read Nehemiah 5.

REFLECTING

The prospects for some of the returned exiles is bleak. They have to mortgage their lands to their wealthier brethren and in extreme cases sell their children into slavery to pay the king's taxes. The rich Jews, rather than helping out, are capitalizing on the situation to line their own pockets. This is inexcusable! Few things bring on more reproach to the cause of the Lord than worldliness and hard-heartedness of those who claim to follow Him. Such hypocrisy reaps the justified scorn of all who witness it. Unselfish dedication to the common welfare of our brothers and sisters in Christ is our spiritual obligation.

RESPONDING

1. Praise: Because the Lord loves each of us equally, and accepts our welfare as His obligation, we praise Him:

You who love the Lord, hate evil! He preserves the souls of His saints; He delivers them out of the hand of the wicked. Light is sown for the righteous, and gladness for the upright in heart. Rejoice in the Lord, you righteous, and give thanks at the remembrance of His holy name. (Psalm 97:10-12)

Take a moment to offer the Lord your personal praise and thanksgiving.

2. Confession: Pray this confession to the Lord as you seek to keep your life free from sin and in fellowship with Him:

If I say that I have no sin, I deceive myself, and the truth is not in me. If I confess my sins, You, O Lord, are faithful and just to forgive me my sins and to cleanse me from all unrighteousness. (1 John 1:8-9)

Confess any personal sins which the Holy Spirit may bring to your mind.

3. Affirmation: As you agree with the will of God, voice your affirmation of His word:

And this is Your commandment: that I should believe on the name of Your Son Jesus Christ and love others, as He commanded me. (1 John 3:23)

4. Requests: As you make your requests known to the Lord, include:

- Commitment to the Lord
- Parachurch ministries
- Your prayer list, the concerns of your heart, and today's activities

5. Closing Prayer: Finally, offer this closing prayer to the Lord:

Lord, preserve me from all evil; preserve my soul. Lord, preserve my going out and my coming in from this time forth, and even forevermore. (Psalm 121:7-8)

Memory Verse: For we are His workmanship, created in Christ Jesus for good works, which God prepared beforehand that we should walk in them.

Ephesians 2:10
God's Will Theme

JULY 10

READING

The passage for today centers on the completion of the wall. After a treacherous plot to interfere with work on the wall is revealed, work is completed.

Read Nehemiah 6.

REFLECTING

Nehemiah resists the efforts of the adversaries to discourage him or distract from working on the wall. He is convinced that he is doing the right thing ("I am doing a great work"), and he steadfastly resists attempts to interfere ("why should the work stop . . .?"). The Old Testament is often a literal illustration of a spiritual truth in the New Testament. In Ephesians 6:10ff, we read that we are to put on the armor of God: the belt of truth, the breastplate of righteousness, the shoes of the gospel of peace, the shield of faith, the helmet of salvation, and the sword of the spirit. Once these are in place, and they must all be in place, we "resist," and "stand firm!" And pray!

RESPONDING

1. Praise: We have victory in the spiritual warfare as we use God's armor, and we can praise Him for His power:

Make a joyful shout to the Lord, all you lands! Serve the Lord with gladness; come before His presence with singing. Know that the Lord, He is God; it is He who has made us, and not we ourselves; we are His people and the sheep of His pasture. Enter into His gates with thanksgiving, and into His courts with praise. . . . For the Lord is good. (Psalm 100:1-5)

Take a moment to offer the Lord your personal praise and thanksgiving.

2. Confession: Pray this confession to the Lord as you seek to keep your life free from sin and in fellowship with Him:

Forgive me, Lord, when I am unmindful of You, the Rock who begot me, and when I have forgotten You, the God who fathered me. (Deuteronomy 32:18)

Confess any personal sins which the Holy Spirit may bring to your mind.

3. Affirmation: As you agree with the will of God, voice your affirmation of His word:

Most assuredly, You say to me, O Lord; if I hear Your word and believe in Him who sent You, I have everlasting life, and shall not come into judgment, but have passed from death into life. (John 5:24)

4. Requests: As you make your requests known to the Lord, include:

- Renewing of your mind
- Needs of your extended family
- Your prayer list, the concerns of your heart, and today's activities

5. Closing Prayer: Finally, offer this closing prayer to the Lord:

May we with one mind and one mouth glorify the God and Father of our Lord Jesus Christ. (Romans 15:6)

Memory Verse: For we are His workmanship, created in Christ Jesus for good works, which God prepared beforehand that we should walk in them.

Ephesians 2:10
God's Will Theme

JULY 11

READING

The passage for today centers on the reading of the Law. After the completion of the wall, the people gather at the square to hear Ezra, who reads the Law publicly for the first time.

Read Nehemiah 8.

REFLECTING

No one appreciates a glass of water like a man who is truly thirsty. It takes deprivation to appreciate the significance of our blessings. That is why the Christian life is not always easy, with blessing flowing unabated. We get dull and stale to it—just as we do when we have too much food and too little exercise. We are indeed blessed to have the Word of God in such abundance. The returning Jews have never heard the Word, and they are truly thirsty. They stand—from dawn till dusk—and drink it in. Has the ready availability of the Scriptures dulled your appetite for it? To appreciate the Word in your life, imagine not having it at all.

RESPONDING

1. Praise: With gratitude for His revelation, praise the Lord from His word:

You are worthy, O Lord, to receive glory and honor and power; for You created all things, and by Your will they exist and were created. (Revelation 4:11)

I will praise the Lord according to His righteousness, and will sing praise to the name of the Lord Most High. (Psalm 7:17)

Take a moment to offer the Lord your personal praise and thanksgiving.

2. Confession: Pray this confession to the Lord as you seek to keep your life free from sin and in fellowship with Him:

You do not desire sacrifice, or else I would give it; You do not delight in burnt offering. The sacrifices of God are a broken spirit, a broken and a contrite heart—these, O God, You will not despise. (Psalm 51:16-17)

Confess any personal sins which the Holy Spirit may bring to your mind.

3. Affirmation: As you agree with the will of God, voice your affirmation of His word:

By this I know love, because You, Lord Jesus, laid down Your life for me. And I also ought to lay down my life for others. (1 John 3:16)

4. Requests: As you make your requests known to the Lord, include:

- The Lord's leading in your life
- Opportunities for personal evangelism
- Your prayer list, the concerns of your heart, and today's activities.

5. Closing Prayer: Finally, offer this closing prayer to the Lord:

Now may the God of hope fill me with all joy and peace in believing, that I may abound in hope by the power of the Holy Spirit. (Romans 15:13)

Memory Verse: For we are His workmanship, created in Christ Jesus for good works, which God prepared beforehand that we should walk in them.

Ephesians 2:10
God's Will Theme

JULY 12

READING

The passage for today centers on the confession of sin. Upon hearing the Law, the people realize they have transgressed the Law, and they publicly confess their sin.

Read Nehemiah 9.

REFLECTING

Paul says in the New Testament that it was not until he heard the Law that he was conscious of sin. How true! It is not until you know the truth that the truth can set you free (John 8:32). The returning Jews experience this in a dramatic way. Upon hearing the Law, Israel repents of her sins and rededicates herself to serving the Lord. This clears her conscience, results in rich worship, and makes her eligible for the blessings of the Lord. It sets her free! The Scripture always has this as one of its purposes, to bring to light our need for forgiveness and to direct us toward the path of restoration. Israel experienced its purifying work. Repentance will do the same for you.

RESPONDING

1. Praise: What a joy to have a clear conscience and be free to praise God:

Oh, the depth of the riches both of the wisdom and knowledge of God! How unsearchable are His judgments and His ways past finding out! (Romans 11:33)

Blessed are You, the God and Father of our Lord Jesus Christ, who has blessed us with every spiritual blessing in the heavenly places in Christ. (Ephesians 1:3)

Take a moment to offer the Lord your personal praise and thanksgiving.

2. Confession: Pray this confession to the Lord as you seek to keep your life free from sin and in fellowship with Him:

Deliver me from blood guiltiness, O God, the God of my salvation, and my tongue shall sing aloud of Your righteousness. O Lord, open my lips, and my mouth shall show forth Your praise. (Psalm 51:14-15)

Confess any personal sins which the Holy Spirit may bring to your mind.

3. Affirmation: As you agree with the will of God, voice your affirmation of His word:

Unless You, O Lord, build my house, I labor in vain to build it; unless You, O Lord, guard my city, I stay awake watching in vain. (Psalm 127:1)

4. Requests: As you make your requests known to the Lord, include:

- Love for the lost
- The work of missions in Africa
- Your prayer list, the concerns of your heart, and today's activities

5. Closing Prayer: Finally, offer this closing prayer to the Lord:

Now to You who are able to establish us according to the gospel and preaching of Jesus Christ—to You, alone wise, be glory through Jesus Christ forever. Amen. (Romans 16:25-27)

Memory Verse: For we are His workmanship, created in Christ Jesus for good works, which God prepared beforehand that we should walk in them.

Ephesians 2:10
God's Will Theme

READING

The passage for today centers on the deposal of Queen Vashti. Because Vashti refuses to dance for King Ahasuerus, he removes her as his queen.

Read Esther 1.

REFLECTING

The sovereignty of God is a dominant theme in the book of Esther. In Ezra and Nehemiah we learn how God watches over the Jews who return from captivity. Esther tells us how those who remain in exile, scattered through the East, were marvelously preserved. Though the name of God does not occur in the book, His hand is clearly manifest throughout. The significance of the "narrow escapes" cannot be dismissed as coincidental. The stage is set for drama as the king, Ahasuerus, perpetrates a tasteless debacle, getting drunk and then demanding that his queen appear before the party. Why she refuses is uncertain, but it costs her the crown. The stage is now set for God's miraculous plan of deliverance for His people.

RESPONDING

1. Praise: We can take comfort in the sovereignty of God and His goodness and praise Him for His faithfulness:

Bless the Lord, O my soul! O Lord my God, You are very great: You are clothed with honor and majesty, who cover Yourself with light as with a garment, who stretch out the heavens like a curtain. . . . May the glory of the Lord endure forever; may the Lord rejoice in His works. . . . Bless the Lord, O my soul! Praise the Lord! (Psalm 104:1-2, 31, 35)

Take a moment to offer the Lord your personal praise and thanksgiving.

2. Confession: Pray this confession to the Lord as you seek to keep your life free from sin and in fellowship with Him:

I have sinned greatly in what I have done; but now, I pray, O Lord, take away the iniquity of Your servant, for I have done very foolishly. (2 Samuel 24:10)

Confess any personal sins which the Holy Spirit may bring to your mind.

3. Affirmation: As you agree with the will of God, voice your affirmation of His word:

Your eyes, O Lord, run to and fro throughout the whole earth, to show Yourself strong on my behalf if my heart is loyal to You. (2 Chronicles 16:9)

4. Requests: As you make your requests known to the Lord, include:

- Faithfulness with your talents
- Your state and local leaders and affairs
- Your prayer list, the concerns of your heart, and today's activities

5. Closing Prayer: Finally, offer this closing prayer to the Lord:

The grace of the Lord Jesus Christ, and the love of God, and the communion of the Holy Spirit be with us all. Amen. (2 Corinthians 13:14)

Memory Verse: For we are His workmanship, created in Christ Jesus for good works, which God prepared beforehand that we should walk in them.

Ephesians 2:10
God's Will Theme

JULY 14

READING

The passage for today centers on the selection of Esther. After a nationwide search for the most beautiful woman, Esther is chosen to become the new queen.

Read Esther 2.

REFLECTING

No one is hidden from the eyes of God. No one escapes His notice. Isaiah 40:27 says, "Why do you say . . . my way is hidden from the Lord, and the justice due me escapes the notice of my God?" God is a specialist at taking ordinary people and doing extraordinary things through them. Abraham, Moses, David, Gideon, and Esther were all living lives of obscurity when God chose them and used them for great things because they were faithful to him in the little things. While not all of us can be destined to do great things in the eyes of man, greatness in the eyes of God is simply being faithful to Him the best way we know how. God has not forgotten about us. His eye is on us. And He will use us, even if only in small ways.

RESPONDING

1. Praise: Give the Lord your praise because He knows us and loves us and will never leave or forsake us:

O Lord, how manifold are Your works! In wisdom You have made them all. The earth is full of Your possessions. . . . I will sing praise to my God while I have my being. May my meditation be sweet to Him; I will be glad in the Lord. (Psalm 104:24, 33, 34)

Take a moment to offer the Lord your personal praise and thanksgiving.

2. Confession: Pray this confession to the Lord as you seek to keep your life free from sin and in fellowship with Him:

O my God: I am too ashamed and humiliated to lift up my face to You, my God; for my iniquities have risen higher than my head, and my guilt has grown up to the heavens. (Ezra 9:6)

Confess any personal sins which the Holy Spirit may bring to your mind.

3. Affirmation: As you agree with the will of God, voice your affirmation of His word:

Before I was afflicted I went astray, but now I keep Your word. . . . It is good for me that I have been afflicted, that I may learn Your statutes. . . . I know, O Lord, that Your judgments are right, and that in faithfulness You have afflicted me. (Psalm 119:67, 71, 75)

4. Requests: As you make your requests known to the Lord, include:

- Strength for obedience
- International students in America
- Your prayer list, the concerns of your heart, and today's activities

5. Closing Prayer: Finally, offer this closing prayer to the Lord:

Now to You who are able to do exceedingly abundantly above all that I ask or think, according to the power that works in me, to You be glory in the church by Christ Jesus throughout all ages, world without end. Amen. (Ephesians 3:20-21)

Memory Verse: For we are His workmanship, created in Christ Jesus for good works, which God prepared beforehand that we should walk in them.

Ephesians 2:10
God's Will Theme

READING

The passage for today centers on Haman's plot against the Jews. Haman deceives the king into signing an edict that all Jews be killed because of political threat.

Read Esther 3.

REFLECTING

Man's inhumanity to man over the ages has been astounding. Some of the acts of violence and degradation have defied comprehension. In this vein, Haman hatches a savage and inhumane plot against the Jews to have them annihilated—men, women, and children. On a specific day the Jews are given a death-row sentence that they must sit and wait for, as their neighbors plot to slaughter them as they would an infestation of rats. The dark heart of Haman is an evil and sinister place. The king, Ahasuerus, is also a monstrous mind, willing to sanction such savagery without question. When sin progresses to such extremes, we see just how repulsive it is. It should help us walk toward the light and long for goodness.

RESPONDING

1. Praise: God is good and, through Jesus, allows us to partake of that goodness, for which we praise Him:

Oh, give thanks to the Lord! Call upon His name; make known His deeds among the peoples. Sing to Him, sing psalms to Him; talk of all His wondrous works. Glory in His holy name; let the hearts of those rejoice who seek the Lord. Seek the Lord and His strength; seek His face evermore. (Psalm 105:1-4)

Take a moment to offer the Lord your personal praise and thanksgiving.

2. Confession: Pray this confession to the Lord as you seek to keep your life free from sin and in fellowship with Him:

O Lord, do not rebuke me in Your anger, nor chasten me in Your hot displeasure. Have mercy on me, O Lord, for I am weak; O Lord, heal me, for . . . my soul also is greatly troubled. (Psalm 6:1-3)

Confess any personal sins which the Holy Spirit may bring to your mind.

3. Affirmation: As you agree with the will of God, voice your affirmation of His word:

For You, O Lord, will bless me when I am righteous; with favor You will surround me as with a shield. (Psalm 5:12)

4. Requests: As you make your requests known to the Lord, include:

- Your "daily bread"
- Christian education institutions
- Your prayer list, the concerns of your heart, and today's activities

5. Closing Prayer: Finally, offer this closing prayer to the Lord:

Now may You, the God of peace, sanctify me completely, and may my whole spirit, soul, and body be preserved blameless at the coming of my Lord Jesus Christ. (1 Thessalonians 5:23)

Memory Verse: For we are His workmanship, created in Christ Jesus for good works, which God prepared beforehand that we should walk in them.

Ephesians 2:10
God's Will Theme

JULY 16

READING

The passage for today centers on the discovery of the plot. Esther learns of the plot to kill the Jews, which would include her, and she plans to intercede.

Read Esther 4.

REFLECTING

"I will go into the king, which is not according to the law; and if I perish, I perish." Those are not the words of someone being melodramatic. They are the words of a realist who accurately assesses the situation. By law, no one could go into the presence of the king unless invited. To do so meant execution. If the king chose to extend grace to the person, he offered his scepter, whereupon the subject was to kneel and touch the top of the scepter. Esther had no idea what Ahasuerus would do. He deposed Vashti with a clap of his hands. He signed the edict to kill the Jews without asking a question. Though she had no other choice, it still took courage. Are there things which you ought to do, but are afraid? Take courage, and do them.

RESPONDING

1. Praise: Our courage comes from confidence in the God who loves us, and for this we give Him our praise:

Unto You I lift up my eyes, O You who dwell in the heavens. Behold, as the eyes of servants look to the hand of their masters, as the eyes of a maid to the hand of her mistress, so our eyes look to the Lord our God, until He has mercy on us. (Psalm 123:1-2)

Take a moment to offer the Lord your personal praise and thanksgiving.

2. Confession: Pray this confession to the Lord as you seek to keep your life free from sin and in fellowship with Him:

Can I understand my errors? Cleanse me, O Lord, from my secret faults. Keep back Your servant also from presumptuous sins; let them not have dominion over me. Then I shall be blameless, and I shall be innocent of great transgression. (Psalm 19:12-13)

Confess any personal sins which the Holy Spirit may bring to your mind.

3. Affirmation: As you agree with the will of God, voice your affirmation of His word:

Jesus Christ, You are the same yesterday, today, and forever. (Hebrews 13:8)

4. Requests: As you make your requests known to the Lord, include:

- Passion for moral excellence
- Needs of personal friends
- Your prayer list, the concerns of your heart, and today's activities

5. Closing Prayer: Finally, offer this closing prayer to the Lord:

Now may the Lord Jesus Christ Himself, and You, my God and Father, who have loved me and given me everlasting consolation and good hope by grace, comfort my heart and establish me in every good word and work. (2 Thessalonians 2:16-17)

Memory Verse: He who says he abides in Him ought himself also to walk just as He walked.

1 John 2:6
God's Will Theme

READING

The passage for today centers on the planning of the banquet. To set the stage for the revelation of the death plot, Esther plans a banquet. Read Esther 5.

REFLECTING

"Pride goeth before a fall." One of the supreme examples of this in all the Bible is Haman. His ego is on a feeding frenzy. He has power, wealth, position, family, friends, and honor. Yet all of this fails to satisfy his ego. Mordecai's unwillingness to bow down to him sticks like a bone in his throat. And, as sharks only travel with sharks, Haman's wife reveals her character by suggesting a flamboyant display of vengeance. "Build a gallows fifty cubits high [75 feet, the height of a seven story building] and hang him on it," she counsels. The same shadow is darkening both hearts. When pride is taken to this extreme, we see how exceedingly ugly it is. It is the mother hen under which all other sins are hatched. Beware of pride!

RESPONDING

1. Praise: Our pride is mellowed when we see how Jesus humbled Himself for us. Praise Him for His love:

Praise the Lord! Praise the name of the Lord; praise Him, O you servants of the Lord! . . . Praise the Lord, for the Lord is good; sing praises to His name, for it is pleasant. . . . For I know that the Lord is great, and our Lord is above all gods. . . . Blessed be the Lord! . . . Praise the Lord! (Psalm 135:1, 3, 5, 21)

Take a moment to offer the Lord your personal praise and thanksgiving.

2. Confession: Pray this confession to the Lord as you seek to keep your life free from sin and in fellowship with Him:

Show me Your ways, O Lord; teach me Your paths. Lead me in Your truth and teach me, for You are the God of my salvation; on You I wait all the day. (Psalm 25:4-5)

Confess any personal sins which the Holy Spirit may bring to your mind.

3. Affirmation: As you agree with the will of God, voice your affirmation of His word:

You, Lord Jesus, are the living bread which came down from heaven. If I eat of this bread, I will live forever; and the bread that You have given is Your flesh, which You gave for the life of the world. (John 6:51)

4. Requests: As you make your requests known to the Lord, include:

- Wisdom in decision making
- Opportunities to serve the Lord
- Your prayer list, the concerns of your heart, and today's activities

5. Closing Prayer: Finally, offer this closing prayer to the Lord:

Now to You, the King eternal, immortal, invisible, to God who alone is wise, be honor and glory forever and ever. Amen. (1 Timothy 1:17)

Memory Verse: He who says he abides in Him ought himself also to walk just as He walked.

1 John 2:6
God's Will Theme

READING

The passage for today centers on Mordecai's exaltation. In an ironic turn of events, Haman must honor Mordecai with acts which Haman himself suggested.

Read Esther 6.

REFLECTING

Very few things in the Bible are actually funny. However, taken in isolation, chapter 6 of Esther is probably the funniest event in the Bible. The king asks Haman what he thinks is a good way to honor someone. His intent is to honor someone who has done a secret good in protection of the king. Haman thinks to himself, "Whom would the king want to honor more than I?" (6:6). Then he tells the king what he, Haman, would like to have done for himself, including a royal robe and official parade through the city. The king replies, "Fine. Go do that for Mordecai." The irony is overwhelming—the humor irrepressible. The wrath of man is made to praise God.

RESPONDING

1. Praise: As you praise the Lord in these words, focus on His sovereignty and goodness:

Great and marvelous are Your works, Lord God Almighty! Just and true are Your ways, O King of the saints! Who shall not fear You, O Lord, and glorify Your name? For You alone are holy. For all nations shall come and worship before You, for Your judgments have been manifested. (Revelation 15:3-4)

Take a moment to offer the Lord your personal praise and thanksgiving.

2. Confession: Pray this confession to the Lord as you seek to keep your life free from sin and in fellowship with Him:

I give You thanks, O Lord, that I may reason with You. Though my sins are like scarlet, they shall be as white as snow; though they are red like crimson, they shall be as wool. (Isaiah 1:18)

Confess any personal sins which the Holy Spirit may bring to your mind.

3. Affirmation: As you agree with the will of God, voice your affirmation of His word:

You who did not spare Your own Son, Jesus Christ, but delivered Him up for me, how shall You not with Him also freely give me all things? (Romans 8:32)

4. Requests: As you make your requests known to the Lord, include:

• Victory over temptation

• The work of missions in North and South America and Asia.

• Your prayer list, the concerns of your heart, and today's activities

5. Closing Prayer: Finally, offer this closing prayer to the Lord:

You who are the blessed and only Potentate, the King of kings and Lord of lords, who alone have immortality, dwelling in unapproachable light, whom no man has seen or can see, to You be honor and everlasting power. Amen. (1 Timothy 6:15-16)

Memory Verse: He who says he abides in Him ought himself also to walk just as He walked.

1 John 2:6
God's Will Theme

READING

The passage for today centers on Esther's plea. At the banquet, Esther reveals to the king the sinister nature of Haman's plot, and Haman is hanged.

Read Esther 7.

REFLECTING

The final irony falls. Haman is hanged on the gallows which he has constructed for Mordecai. Pride has come full circle; sin has self-destructed. "Pride goes before destruction, a haughty spirit before a fall" (Proverbs 16:18). Haman personally experiences this truth. Satan is called the Deceiver and the Destroyer; he deceives in order to destroy. He gets us to commit ourselves to a course of action that we think will achieve our aims and, in the end, destroys us. If you are on any course of action which you feel will achieve your aims, but the course of action is wrong (ambition, greed, manipulation), give it up. Unchecked, you will eventually be destroyed by it.

RESPONDING

1. Praise: Offer the Lord your praise for His goodness through these words:

O Lord, our Lord, how excellent is Your name in all the earth. You who set Your glory above the heavens! When I consider Your heavens, the work of Your fingers, what is man that You are mindful of him, and the son of man that You visit him? O Lord, our Lord, how excellent is Your name in all the earth! (Psalm 8:1, 3-4, 9)

Take a moment to offer the Lord your personal praise and thanksgiving.

2. Confession: Pray this confession to the Lord as you seek to keep your life free from sin and in fellowship with Him:

Out of the depths I have cried to You, O Lord; Lord, hear my voice! If You, Lord, should mark iniquities, O Lord, who could stand? But there is forgiveness with You, that You may be feared. (Psalm 130:1-4)

Confess any personal sins which the Holy Spirit may bring to your mind.

3. Affirmation: As you agree with the will of God, voice your affirmation of His word:

I have believed on the Lord Jesus Christ and I am saved . . . . (Acts 16:31)

4. Requests: As you make your requests known to the Lord, include:

- Love for your family
- Revival among Christians in America
- Your prayer list, the concerns of your heart, and today's activities

5. Closing Prayer: Finally, offer this closing prayer to the Lord:

Make me complete in every good work to do Your will, working in me what is well pleasing in Your sight, through Jesus Christ, to whom be glory forever and ever. Amen. (Hebrews 13:20-21)

Memory Verse: He who says he abides in Him ought himself also to walk just as He walked.

1 John 2:6
God's Will Theme

READING

The passage for today centers on Mordecai's promotion. In return for a previous act of devotion to the king, Mordecai is honored and promoted to power.

Read Esther 8.

REFLECTING

The law of the Medes and Persians cannot be revoked. Once written, no one, not even the king, can rescind it. The law to annihilate the Jews is carved in stone. Since the original plan cannot be revoked, a clever counter-plan is conceived to neutralize it. Permission is given to the Jews to arm themselves and to assemble and to defend themselves. In addition, Mordecai is raised to power, taking the position Haman had previously occupied. God's sovereign protection of His people in exile is beginning to finalize. The integrity of Esther and Mordecai is rewarded. Righteousness triumphs. Good does not always win over evil in this life, but when it does, it is a heartwarming and gratifying thing.

RESPONDING

1. Praise: Praise the Lord for His watchfulness over the circumstances of our lives:

Not unto us, O Lord, not unto us, but to Your name give glory, because of Your mercy, and because of Your truth. . . . We who fear You, O Lord, trust in You; You are our help and our shield. . . . We will bless the Lord from this time forth and forevermore. Praise the Lord! (Psalm 115:1, 11, 18)

Take a moment to offer the Lord your personal praise and thanksgiving.

2. Confession: Pray this confession to the Lord as you seek to keep your life free from sin and in fellowship with Him:

Remember, O Lord, Your tender mercies and Your lovingkindnesses, for they have been from of old. Do not remember the sins of my youth, nor my transgressions; according to Your mercy remember me, for Your goodness' sake, O Lord. (Psalm 25:6-7)

Confess any personal sins which the Holy Spirit may bring to your mind.

3. Affirmation: As you agree with the will of God, voice your affirmation of His word:

I must reckon myself to be dead indeed to sin, but alive to You, O God, in Christ Jesus my Lord. (Romans 6:11)

4. Requests: As you make your requests known to the Lord, include:

- Faithfulness with your treasures
- The Great Commission
- Your prayer list, the concerns of your heart, and today's activities

5. Closing Prayer: Finally, offer this closing prayer to the Lord:

May You, the God of grace, who called me to Your eternal glory by Christ Jesus, after I have suffered a while, perfect, establish, strengthen, and settle me. To You be the glory and the dominion forever and ever. Amen. (1 Peter 5:10-11)

Memory Verse: He who says he abides in Him ought himself also to walk just as He walked.

1 John 2:6
God's Will Theme

READING

The passage for today centers on the deliverance of the Jews. With the king's permission, the Jews are allowed to protect themselves from the original plot.

Read Esther 9.

REFLECTING

National salvation is culminated for the Jews. When the fateful day arrives, the Jews throughout the empire stand on the defense. 75,000 of their assailants fall in the provinces and 500 in the capital of Susa alone. Among these are the ten sons of Haman. No attempt at plunder is made by the victors, demonstrating their lack of malice. They simply want peace and safety. The providence of God is clearly discernible in all the incidents recorded here. Through all human governments and events a divine purpose runs; and as God exalted Mordecai to honor and glory, so will He work for those who love Him. And so, ultimately, will He put all enemies under His feet.

RESPONDING

1. Praise: God is a God of power and glory, yet loves to call us His own. Praise Him for His love for us:

Men shall speak of the might of Your awesome acts; and I will declare Your greatness. They shall utter the memory of Your great goodness, and shall sing of Your righteousness. The Lord is gracious and full of compassion, slow to anger and great in mercy. The Lord is good to all, and His tender mercies are over all His works. (Psalm 145:6-9)

Take a moment to offer the Lord your personal praise and thanksgiving.

2. Confession: Pray this confession to the Lord as you seek to keep your life free from sin and in fellowship with Him:

Good and upright are You, Lord; therefore You teach me, though a sinner, in Your way. If I am humble, You will guide me in justice and teach me Your way. All Your paths for me are mercy and truth, if I keep Your covenant and Your testimonies. For Your name's sake, O Lord, pardon my iniquity, for it is great. (Psalm 25:8-11)

Confess any personal sins which the Holy Spirit may bring to your mind.

3. Affirmation: As you agree with the will of God, voice your affirmation of His word:

You, O Lord, are my light and my salvation; whom shall I fear? You are the strength of my life; of whom shall I be afraid? (Psalm 27:1)

4. Requests: As you make your requests known to the Lord, include:

• Spiritual insight

• Campus ministries

• Your prayer list, the concerns of your heart, and today's activities

5. Closing Prayer: Finally, offer this closing prayer to the Lord:

May I grow in the grace and knowledge of our Lord and Savior Jesus Christ. To Him be the glory both now and forever. Amen. (2 Peter 3:18)

Memory Verse: He who says he abides in Him ought himself also to walk just as He walked.

1 John 2:6
God's Will Theme

JULY 22

READING

The passage for today centers on Satan's permission to test Job. After meeting with God, Satan receives permission to test Job, within prescribed limits.

Read Job 1.

REFLECTING

If God is all good and all powerful, then why do the righteous suffer? Throughout the book of Job, questions of the ages rise. Job is a righteous man, and while he does not curse God, he does put some hard questions to Him. Why must he, a righteous man, suffer? What sins have brought on this pain? Why is God so inconsistent in His punishment of the wicked? Why must bad things happen to good people? These questions form in the minds of all thinking people who observe or experience suffering. It is a comfort at such a time to know that it is not wicked to form the questions. All people struggle with these questions sooner or later. We can learn from Job that we can struggle without sinning.

RESPONDING

1. Praise: Offer your praise to the Lord that though He does not always spare us from pain, He is always with us through the pain:

The Lord is righteous in all His ways, gracious in all His works. The Lord is near to all who call upon Him, to all who call upon Him in truth. He will fulfill the desire of those who fear Him; He also will hear their cry and save them. . . . My mouth shall speak the praise of the Lord, and all flesh shall bless His holy name forever and ever. (Psalm 145:17-19, 21)

Take a moment to offer the Lord your personal praise and thanksgiving.

2. Confession: Pray this confession to the Lord as you seek to keep your life free from sin and in fellowship with Him:

Turn Yourself to me, and have mercy on me, for I am desolate and afflicted. The troubles of my heart have enlarged; oh, bring me out of my distresses! Look on my affliction and my pain, and forgive all my sins. (Psalm 25:16-18)

Confess any personal sins which the Holy Spirit may bring to your mind.

3. Affirmation: As you agree with the will of God, voice your affirmation of His word:

For the wages of sin is death, but Your gift, O God, is eternal life in Christ Jesus my Lord. (Romans 6:23)

4. Requests: As you make your requests known to the Lord, include:

- Desire to be like Christ
- Needs in inner cities
- Your prayer list, the concerns of your heart, and today's activities

5. Closing Prayer: Finally, offer this closing prayer to the Lord:

Blessing and honor and glory and power be to You who sit on the throne, and to You, Lord, forever and ever! (Revelation 5:13)

Memory Verse: He who says he abides in Him ought himself also to walk just as He walked.

1 John 2:6
God's Will Theme

READING

The passage for today centers on Job's final response to testing. After severe and extended trial, Job is fully submissive to the will of God, and God blesses him, restoring his good fortunes.

Read Job 42.

REFLECTING

Throughout life, we come up against things we do not understand. The two-year-old child does not understand why he cannot live on ice cream. The ten-year-old does not understand why he must make his bed. The teenager does not understand why he cannot stay out all night long. Yet when they mature, they come to understand. Likewise, we do not understand why the righteous must suffer. But some day, in heaven, we will understand. It will make sense. Our struggle will end. In the midst of Job's struggle, he makes some incisive observations which help us cope until we receive full understanding: "I know that I have eternal life" (19:16). "I know that when He has tried me I shall come forth as gold" (23:10). "So even if He were to slay me, yet would I trust Him" (13:15).

RESPONDING

1. Praise: Though we do not always understand the Lord, we can always trust Him and give Him our praise:

All Your works shall praise You, O Lord, and Your saints shall bless You. They shall speak of the glory of Your kingdom, and talk of Your power, to make known to the sons of men His mighty acts. . . . Your kingdom is an everlasting kingdom, and Your dominion endures throughout all generations. (Psalm 145:10-13)

Take a moment to offer the Lord your personal praise and thanksgiving.

2. Confession: Pray this confession to the Lord as you seek to keep your life free from sin and in fellowship with Him:

Blessed am I, my transgression is forgiven, my sin is covered. Blessed am I, the Lord does not impute iniquity to me, and in my spirit there is no guile. (Psalm 32:1-2)

Confess any personal sins which the Holy Spirit may bring to your mind.

3. Affirmation: As you agree with the will of God, voice your affirmation of His word:

For You, O God, have not given me a spirit of fear, but of power and of love and of a sound mind. (2 Timothy 1:7)

4. Requests: As you make your requests known to the Lord, include:

- Personal witness for Christ
- Local churches around the nation
- Your prayer list, the concerns of your heart, and today's activities

5. Closing Prayer: Finally, offer this closing prayer to the Lord:

Amen! Blessing and glory and wisdom, thanksgiving and honor and power and might, be to You, God, forever and ever. Amen. (Revelation 7:12)

Memory Verse: And we know that all things work together for good to those who love God, to those who are the called according to His purpose.
Romans 8:28
God's Will Theme

JULY 24

READING

The passage for today centers on the contrast between the wicked and the righteous. The righteous prosper as they delight in the Lord, while the wicked perish.

Read Psalm 1.

REFLECTING

In Jerusalem, there are many gates leading out of the city, and each gate is named for the destination of the road leading away from it. There is the Joppa Gate, leading to Joppa. There is the Damascus Gate, leading to Damascus. Some of these gates are very close together, but their destinations are very far apart. Life is like that. The Psalmist says there are basically two gates in life: the "wicked gate" and the "righteous gate." Your destination in life depends upon which gate you choose. The "righteous gate" begins at the Word of God and leads to trees, water, and fruit. The "wicked gate" starts with man's counsel and leads to wind and chaff. Which gate have you chosen?

RESPONDING

1. Praise: Thank and praise the Lord that He always leads us in paths of righteousness for His name's sake.

I will extol You, my God, O King; and I will bless Your name forever and ever. Every day I will bless You, and I will praise Your name forever and ever. Great is the Lord, and greatly to be praised; and His greatness is unsearchable. One generation shall praise Your works to another, and shall declare Your mighty acts. I will meditate on the glorious splendor of Your majesty, and on Your wondrous works. (Psalm 145:1-5)

Take a moment to offer the Lord your personal praise and thanksgiving.

2. Confession: Pray this confession to the Lord as you seek to keep your life free from sin and in fellowship with Him:

I acknowledged my sin to You, and my iniquity I have not hidden. I said, "I will confess my transgressions to the Lord," and You forgave the iniquity of my sin. (Psalm 32:5)

Confess any personal sins which the Holy Spirit may bring to your mind.

3. Affirmation: As you agree with the will of God, voice your affirmation of His word:

I have Your commandments and when I keep them, it shows I love You. And if I love You, Lord Jesus, I will be loved by Your Father, and You will love me and manifest Yourself to me. (John 14:21)

4. Requests: As you make your requests known to the Lord, include:

- An eternal perspective
- Needs of work or school mates
- Your prayer list, the concerns of your heart, and today's activities

5. Closing Prayer: Finally, offer this closing prayer to the Lord:

I will wait on You, the Lord; I will be of good courage, and You shall strengthen my heart; I will wait on You! (Psalm 27:14)

Memory Verse: And we know that all things work together for good to those who love God, to those who are the called according to His purpose.
Romans 8:28
God's Will Theme

READING

The passage for today centers on the works and word of God. The works of God are declared in the heavens, and the words of God lead to righteousness.

Read Psalm 19.

REFLECTING

A creator is known by his creation. An artist is known by his art; a musician by his music, and a sculptor by his sculpture. Each product reflects the ability and perspective of the personal source. God can be known by the universe which He has created. The earth and the heavens both reflect upon the nature of the Creator. Psalm 19:1 says, "The heavens are telling of the glory of God, and their expanse is declaring the work of His hands." Romans 1:20 says, "Since the creation of the world His invisible attributes, His eternal power and divine nature, have been clearly seen. . . ." Judging from nature, God exists and has power, intelligence, and a flair for beauty!

RESPONDING

1. Praise: Praise your Creator in these words:

You who love the Lord, hate evil! He preserves the souls of His saints; He delivers them out of the hand of the wicked. Light is sown for the righteous, and gladness for the upright in heart. Rejoice in the Lord, you righteous, and give thanks at the remembrance of His holy name. (Psalm 97:10-12)

Take a moment to offer the Lord your personal praise and thanksgiving.

2. Confession: Pray this confession to the Lord as you seek to keep your life free from sin and in fellowship with Him:

Forgive me Lord when I am unmindful of the Rock who begot me, and forget the God who fathered me. (Deuteronomy 32:18)

Confess any personal sins which the Holy Spirit may bring to your mind.

3. Affirmation: As you agree with the will of God, voice your affirmation of His word:

Do I not know that my body is the temple of the Holy Spirit who is in me, whom I have from You, O God, and I am not my own? For I was bought at a price; therefore I should glorify You in my body and in my spirit, which are Yours. (1 Corinthians 6:19-20)

4. Requests: As you make your requests known to the Lord, include:

- Personal discipline
- Christians worldwide who are persecuted for their faith
- Your prayer list, the concerns of your heart, and today's activities

5. Closing Prayer: Finally, offer this closing prayer to the Lord:

Show me the path of life; in Your presence is fullness of joy; at Your right hand are pleasures forevermore. (Psalm 16:11)

Memory Verse: And we know that all things work together for good to those who love God, to those who are the called according to His purpose.
Romans 8:28
God's Will Theme

READING

The passage for today centers on the divine shepherd. The Lord is pictured as David's shepherd, leading him in righteousness and giving eternal life.

Read Psalm 23.

REFLECTING

Perhaps the most outstanding characteristic of sheep is that they cannot take care of themselves. Left to themselves, they follow each other in confusion and fall prey to the enemies of this world. The demands of life exceed their intelligence and their abilities. Therefore, they must have a shepherd. Man is the same. While there is a vast and gratifying difference between men and sheep, the demands of life for men exceed their intelligence and abilities. Our end would be equally devastating. We also need a shepherd. The Lord. He is the Great Shepherd, who guards, provides, and comforts. He will lead us through the perils of this life. The question is: Will we follow?

RESPONDING

1. Praise: The Lord is worthy to receive my praise because of all that He has done for me:

You are the Rock, Your work is perfect; for all Your ways are justice, a God of truth and without injustice; righteous and upright are You. (Deuteronomy 32:4)

The Lord lives! Blessed be my Rock! Let God be exalted, the Rock of my salvation! (2 Samuel 22:47)

Take a moment to offer the Lord your personal praise and thanksgiving.

2. Confession: Pray this confession to the Lord as you seek to keep your life free from sin and in fellowship with Him:

You, O Lord, are merciful and gracious, slow to anger, and abounding in mercy. . . . As a father pities his children, so You, Lord, pity me who fears You. For You know my frame; You remember that I am dust. (Psalm 103:8, 13-14)

Confess any personal sins which the Holy Spirit may bring to your mind.

3. Affirmation: As you agree with the will of God, voice your affirmation of His word:

If I am in Christ, I am a new creation; old things have passed away; behold, all things have become new. (2 Corinthians 5:17)

4. Requests: As you make your requests known to the Lord, include:

- Love for the Lord
- The work of missions in the Middle East, Australia, and the Islands
- Your prayer list, the concerns of your heart, and today's activities

5. Closing Prayer: Finally, offer this closing prayer to the Lord:

Save Your people, and bless Your inheritance; shepherd us also, and bear us up forever. (Psalm 28:9)

Memory Verse: And we know that all things work together for good to those who love God, to those who are the called according to His purpose.
Romans 8:28
God's Will Theme

READING

The passage for today centers on the contrast of the righteous and wicked. The righteous will receive eternal life, while the wicked will ultimately be destroyed.

Read Psalm 37.

REFLECTING

It doesn't pay to serve the Lord. Well, of course it does in one way. We receive eternal life, freedom from the bondage of sin, the blessings of righteousness. But in a temporal and material sense, it doesn't pay. The righteous still experience misfortune. Financial reversals, physical illnesses, natural disasters, persecution. At the same time, the unrighteous often prosper, enjoying wealth, fame, honor, and health. It doesn't seem right. Yet that is the way it must be. Rain falling on the righteous and unrighteous alike. Otherwise, people would serve the Lord for selfish motives. When it doesn't pay to serve the Lord, it tends to weed out the insincere. Persevere! Your reward is coming. In the next world.

RESPONDING

1. Praise: Praise the Lord that while serving Him might cost us in "time," it will reward us in "eternity":

Praise the Lord! Praise the Lord, O my soul! While I live I will praise the Lord; I will sing praises to my God while I have my being. . . . Happy is he who has the God of Jacob for his help, whose hope is in the Lord his God. . . . The Lord shall reign forever—Your God, O Zion, to all generations. Praise the Lord! (Psalm 145:1-2, 5, 10)

Take a moment to offer the Lord your personal praise and thanksgiving.

2. Confession: Pray this confession to the Lord as you seek to keep your life free from sin and in fellowship with Him:

I am righteous before You, O Lord; You hear when I cry out, and You deliver me out of all my troubles. You, O Lord, are near to me when I have a broken heart, and You save me when I have a contrite spirit. (Psalm 34:17-18)

Confess any personal sins which the Holy Spirit may bring to your mind.

3. Affirmation: As you agree with the will of God, voice your affirmation of His word:

Now faith is the substance of things hoped for, the evidence of things not seen. (Hebrews 11:1)

4. Requests: As you make your requests known to the Lord, include:

- Faithfulness in sharing Christ
- The Lord's work in national and world affairs
- Your prayer list, the concerns of your heart, and today's activities

5. Closing Prayer: Finally, offer this closing prayer to the Lord:

You, the Lord, will command Your lovingkindness in the daytime, and in the night Your song shall be with me—a prayer to You, the God of my life. (Psalm 42:8)

Memory Verse: And we know that all things work together for good to those who love God, to those who are the called according to His purpose.
Romans 8:28
God's Will Theme

JULY 28

READING

The passage for today centers on the thirsting soul. Spiritual thirst is satisfied only by spiritual intimacy with God, through worship and meditation.

Read Psalm 63.

REFLECTING

There is a God-shaped vacuum in every human heart. Man was made for God, and his soul will be restless until it finds its rest in Him. The deepest longings of the human heart are only and can only be found in God. Our longings for love, relationships, belonging, security, meaning, purpose, identity, are all only met, ultimately, in Him. We find temporary fulfillment in the pursuit of people, possessions, and circumstances outside of the Lord, but eventually, these will pass away, or change, or we change, and they no longer satisfy. We have been made for God and will find our deepest longings met only in Him. Make David's prayer your own prayer for spiritual fulfillment.

RESPONDING

1. Praise: The Lord is equal to our deep longings, and we praise Him that He satisfies our hearts:

Praise the Lord! Praise God in His sanctuary; praise Him in His mighty firmament! Praise Him for His mighty acts; praise Him according to His excellent greatness! Praise Him with the sound of the trumpet; praise Him with the lute and harp! . . . Let everything that has breath praise the Lord. Praise the Lord! (Psalm 150:1-3, 6)

Take a moment to offer the Lord your personal praise and thanksgiving.

2. Confession: Pray this confession to the Lord as you seek to keep your life free from sin and in fellowship with Him:

O Lord, be merciful to me; heal my soul, for I have sinned against You. . . . O Lord, be merciful to me, and raise me up, . . . Blessed be You, O Lord God of Israel, from everlasting to everlasting! Amen and Amen. (Psalm 41:4, 10, 13)

Confess any personal sins which the Holy Spirit may bring to your mind.

3. Affirmation: As you agree with the will of God, voice your affirmation of His word:

You, O Lord, will instruct me and teach me in the way I should go; You will guide me with Your eye. (Psalm 32:8)

4. Requests: As you make your requests known to the Lord, include:

- Compassion for others
- Missions in America
- Your prayer list, the concerns of your heart, and today's activities

5. Closing Prayer: Finally, offer this closing prayer to the Lord:

Blessed are You, the Lord, forevermore! Amen and amen. (Psalm 89:52)

Memory Verse: And we know that all things work together for good to those who love God, to those who are the called according to His purpose.
Romans 8:28
God's Will Theme

READING

The passage for today centers on God's eternality and man's frailty. God is eternal in time past and future, while man is temporal and weak, needing the blessing of the Lord.

Read Psalm 90.

REFLECTING

In this Psalm, Moses declares the eternalilty of God: "Thou has been our dwelling place in all generations. From everlasting to everlasting, Thou art God." Then, he contrasts the frailty of man: "Thou dost turn man back into dust." God's displeasure with sin next occupies his attention: "Thou hast placed our iniquities before Thee. We have been consumed by Thine anger." Finally, based on these three realities, Moses calls upon God in a series of petitions: "teach us to number our days, O satisfy us in the morning with Thy lovingkindness; make us glad; let Your favor be upon us, and confirm the work of our hands." You can make these petitions your own.

RESPONDING

1. Praise: Thank the Lord that He hears and answers our prayers, and praise Him that His answers are good:

Ah, Lord God! Behold, You have made the heavens and the earth by Your great power and outstretched arm. There is nothing too hard for You. You show lovingkindness to thousands . . . O Great and Mighty God, whose name is the Lord of hosts. You are great in counsel and mighty in work. (Jeremiah 32:17-19)

Take a moment to offer the Lord your personal praise and thanksgiving.

2. Confession: Pray this confession to the Lord as you seek to keep your life free from sin and in fellowship with Him:

Have mercy upon me, O God, according to Your lovingkindness; according to the multitude of Your tender mercies, blot out my transgressions. Wash me thoroughly from my iniquity, and cleanse me from my sin. For I acknowledge my transgressions, and my sin is ever before me. (Psalm 51:1)

Confess any personal sins which the Holy Spirit may bring to your mind.

3. Affirmation: As you agree with the will of God, voice your affirmation of His word:

These things You have spoken to me, Lord Jesus, that in You I may have peace. In the world I will have tribulation; but I will be of good cheer, You have overcome the world. (John 16:33)

4. Requests: As you make your requests known to the Lord, include:

- Personal spiritual growth
- Military ministries
- Your prayer list, the concerns of your heart, and today's activities

5. Closing Prayer: Finally, offer this closing prayer to the Lord:

Glory to You in the highest, and on earth peace, good will toward men! (Luke 2:14)

Memory Verse: And we know that all things work together for good to those who love God, to those who are the called according to His purpose.
Romans 8:28
God's Will Theme

JULY 30

READING

The passage for today centers on praise to the Lord. All men are exhorted to praise the Lord because He made us, we are His, and He is eternally kind to us.

Read Psalm 100.

REFLECTING

David writes in Psalm 33:1 that praise is becoming to the upright. God delights in the praise of His children. Psalm 100 is perhaps the finest example of a praise psalm in the Bible. The righteous heart pours forth a spontaneous stream of undefiled praise. First, he calls upon all men everywhere to praise the Lord. Then he identifies the relationship which God has with His children. We are not our own. He has made us. We are His people and the sheep of His pasture. Next, he calls for us to praise Him again. Enter His gates with thanksgiving and His courts with praise. Give thanks. Bless Him. Then he finishes with attributes of God. He is good. He loves forever. Make this your personal psalm of praise.

RESPONDING

1. Praise: Offer the Lord your praise that He is good and loves us forever:

Lord, You have been our dwelling place in all generations. Before the mountains were brought forth, or ever You had formed the earth and the world, even from everlasting to everlasting, You are God. . . . Oh, satisfy us early with Your mercy, that we may rejoice and be glad all our days! (Psalm 90:1-2,14)

Take a moment to offer the Lord your personal praise and thanksgiving.

2. Confession: Pray this confession to the Lord as you seek to keep your life free from sin and in fellowship with Him:

I return to You, O Lord my God, for I have stumbled because of my iniquity; I take words with me, and return to You, Lord. I say to You, "Take away all iniquity; receive me graciously, for I will offer the sacrifices of my lips." (Hosea 14:1-2)

Confess any personal sins which the Holy Spirit may bring to your mind.

3. Affirmation: As you agree with the will of God, voice your affirmation of His word:

If I love You, Lord Jesus, I will keep Your commandments. (John 14:15)

4. Requests: As you make your requests known to the Lord, include:

- Fruit of the Spirit in your life
- The ministry of Christian literature
- Your prayer list, the concerns of your heart, and today's activities

5. Closing Prayer: Finally, offer this closing prayer to the Lord:

Grace, mercy, and peace from You, the Father, and the Lord Jesus Christ our Savior. (Titus 1:4)

Memory Verse: And the world is passing away, and the lust of it; but he who does the will of God abides forever.

1 John 2:17
God's Will Theme

READING

The passage for today centers on the goodness of the Lord. The Lord is extolled for the goodness of who He is and what He has done for us. Read Psalm 145.

REFLECTING

From Adam to today, there has never been a generation that did not praise God. Since the beginning of time, salvation and praise have been passed down in unbroken succession. David writes, "One generation shall praise Thy works to another, and shall declare Thy mighty acts." That praise is directed to God for who He is (His character) and what He has done (His works). Of His character, David writes that He is gracious, merciful, slow to anger, and great in lovingkindness. The Lord is good.

Writing of His work, he says that the Lord sustains all who fall, raises up those bowed down, is near to all who call upon Him, and will fulfill the desire of those who fear Him. He keeps all who love Him. For these reasons, we praise Him along with David.

RESPONDING

1. Praise: All the earth will one day praise the Lord. We can begin now, in the words of this psalm:

It is good to give thanks to the Lord, and to sing praises to Your name, O Most High; to declare Your lovingkindness in the morning, and Your faithfulness every night. . . . You are my rock, and there is no unrighteousness in You. (Psalm 92:1-2, 15)

Now offer to the Lord your personal praise and thanksgiving.

2. Confession: Pray this confession to the Lord as you seek to keep your life free from sin and in fellowship with Him:

The heart is deceitful above all things, and desperately wicked; who can know it? You, the Lord, search the heart, You test the mind, even to give every man according to his ways, and according to the fruit of his doings. . . . Heal me, O Lord, and I shall be healed; save me, and I shall be saved, for You are my praise. (Jeremiah 17:9,10,14)

Confess any personal sins which the Holy Spirit brings to your mind.

3. Affirmation: As you agree with the will of God, voice your affirmation of His word:

All that the Father gives You, O Lord Jesus, will come to You, and if I come to You, I will not be cast out by any means. (John 6:37)

4. Requests: As you make your requests known to the Lord, include:

- Boldness in living for Christ
- God's blessing on America
- Your prayer list, the concerns of your heart and today's activities.

5. Closing Prayer: Finally, offer this closing prayer to the Lord:

Be glad in the Lord and rejoice, you righteous; and shout for joy, all you upright in heart!. (Psalm 32:11)

Memory Verse: And the world is passing away, and the lust of it; but he who does the will of God abides forever.

1 John 2:17
God's Will Theme

AUGUST 1

READING

The passage for today centers on Wisdom's warning. After an introductory statement on the usefulness of proverbs, Solomon writes a metaphorical warning from "Wisdom."

Read Proverbs 1.

REFLECTING

Every freedom we want has a corresponding slavery. We can be free from the toothbrush and a slave to cavities, or a slave to the toothbrush and free from cavities. For everything we want to get, we must give up something else. Wisdom calls us to slavery. If we become a slave to Wisdom, we must heed the Word of God, heed our parents' instruction, shun the enticement to sin. If we neglect these, calamity will strike our lives. Distress and anguish will come. We will experience the natural consequences of our actions. We will self-destruct. There is no escape from this cause/effect law. Christians have no monopoly on wisdom. There are many non-Christians who are wise and many Christians who are very foolish. We have all done foolish things. We must receive instruction from ourselves and others and realize that we cannot ignore wisdom and expect to suffer no penalty. Rededicate yourself to becoming a "wise" person. Wisdom begins with "fearing" (respecting) the Lord. So we must rededicate ourselves to Him. It is to His glory, but it is also in our best interest.

RESPONDING

1. Praise: As you continue your time with the Lord, offer to Him this psalm of praise as you ponder the need for wisdom in your life:

Who is like You, O Lord, among the gods? Who is like You, glorious in holiness, fearful in praises, doing wonders? (Exodus 15:11)

You are great, O Lord God. For there is none like You, nor is there any God besides You, according to all that we have heard with our ears. (2 Samuel 7:22)

Pause for personal praise and thanksgiving.

2. Confession: Pray this confession to the Lord as you seek to keep your life free from sin and in fellowship with Him:

O my God: I am too ashamed and humiliated to lift up my face to You, my God; for my iniquity has risen higher than my head, and my guilt has grown even to the heavens. (Ezra 9:6)

Confess any personal sins which the Holy Spirit brings to your mind.

3. Affirmation: Now pause to pray this affirmation to the Lord:

The fear of You, O Lord, is the beginning of wisdom, and the knowledge of You is understanding. (Proverbs 9:10).

4. Requests: As you make your requests known to the Lord, include:

- Health and strength to serve God
- God's will to be done on earth
- Your prayer list, the concerns of your heart, and today's activities

5. Closing Prayer: Finally, offer this closing prayer to the Lord:

This is the day which You have made; I will rejoice and be glad in it. (Psalm 118:24)

Memory Verse: And the world is passing away, and the lust of it; but he who does the will of God abides forever.

1 John 2:17
God's Will Theme

AUGUST 2

READING

The passage for today centers on the security of wisdom. If you seek wisdom with your whole being, it will save you from the natural consequences of indiscretion.

Read Proverbs 2.

REFLECTING

Nothing valuable is easily obtained. If it were easily obtained, it would no longer be valuable. Inherent within the concept of "value" is the feature of scarcity. If all gravel were made of pure gold, then gold would not be valuable. The same is true with intangibles, like wisdom. It is an exceedingly valuable life commodity. But it is not easy to come by. If we want wisdom, we must "make our ears attentive," "incline our hearts," "cry" for it, "lift our voices for it," "seek it" as we would silver, and "search" for it as for hidden treasures. Then, and only then, will we discern the fear of the Lord and discover the knowledge of God. How much effort do you put into becoming wiser? How great is your commitment to it? Wisdom does not come easily.

RESPONDING

1. Praise: Offer the Lord this psalm of praise as you consider the goodness that comes with His wisdom:

Praise the Lord! Praise the Lord, O my soul! While I live I will praise the Lord; I will sing praises to my God while I have my being. . . . Happy is he who has the God of Jacob for his help, whose hope is in the Lord his God, . . . The Lord shall reign forever—your God, O Zion, to all generations. Praise the Lord! (Psalm 146:1-2, 5, 10)

Take a moment to offer the Lord Your personal praise and thanksgiving.

2. Confession: Pray this confession to the Lord as you seek to keep your life free from sin and in fellowship with Him:

Against You, You only, have I sinned, and done this evil in Your sight—that You may be found just when You speak and blameless when You judge. (Psalm 51:4)

Confess any personal sins which the Holy Spirit may bring to your mind.

3. Affirmation: As you agree with the will of God, voice your affirmation of His word:

You, Lord Jesus, are the resurrection and the life. If I believe in You, though I may die, I shall live. (John 11:25)

4. Requests: As you make your requests known to the Lord, include:

- Sensitivity to sin
- The ministry of your local church
- Your prayer list, the concerns of your heart, and today's activities

5. Closing Prayer: Finally, offer this closing prayer to the Lord:

Let the words of my mouth and the meditation of my heart be acceptable in Your sight, O Lord, my strength and my redeemer. (Psalm 19:14)

Memory Verse: And the world is passing away, and the lust of it; but he who does the will of God abides forever.

1 John 2:17
God's Will Theme

READING

The passage for today centers on the rewards of wisdom. The profit of wisdom is better than gold, giving peace, quality of life, and good relationships with God and man.

Read Proverbs 3.

REFLECTING

Inherent within the human heart is a longing for peace, love, and joy. Among Christians and non-Christians alike, the desire is the same. Yet peace, love, and joy do not answer just any "beck and call." They will only come by certain means. They are fruit on the tree of wisdom. Wisdom will bring length of days, peace, favor with God and man, healing to your body, honor, pleasant ways, paths of peace, confidence in life, freedom from the snares of life. Foolishness brings harm, violence, and dishonor. We all long for the benefits of wisdom. We must remember that it comes with a price: submission to the will of God and the truth of Scripture. If you are willing to pay the price, you may have wisdom and all its benefits.

If you aren't, you can't.

RESPONDING

1. Praise: As you consider the benefits of wisdom, praise the Lord that we may share in His character.

Oh come, let us sing to the Lord! Let us shout joyfully to the Rock of our salvation. Let us come before His presence with thanksgiving; let us shout joyfully to Him with psalms. For the Lord is the great God, and the great King above all gods. . . . Oh come, let us worship and bow down; let us kneel before the Lord our Maker. For He is our God, and we are the people of His pasture, and the sheep of His hand. (Psalm 95:1-3,6-7)

Now express any additional thoughts you may have of thanks or praise.

2. Confession: Pray this confession to the Lord as you seek to keep your life free from sin and in fellowship with Him:

Purge me with hyssop, and I shall be clean; wash me, and I shall be whiter than snow. Make me to hear joy and gladness, that the bones which You have broken may rejoice. Hide Your face from my sins, and blot out all my iniquities. (Psalm 51:7-9)

Confess any personal sins which the Holy Spirit brings to your mind.

3. Affirmation: Now pray this affirmation to the Lord as you agree with and submit yourself to the will of God:

I consider that the sufferings of this present time are not worthy to be compared with the glory which shall be revealed in me. (Romans 8:18).

4. Requests: As you make your requests known to the Lord, include:

- Wisdom for living life
- Needs of your immediate family
- Your prayer list, the concerns of your heart, and today's activities

5. Closing Prayer: Finally, offer this closing prayer to the Lord:

Surely goodness and mercy shall follow me all the days of my life, and I will dwell in the house of the Lord forever. (Psalm 23:6)

Memory Verse: And the world is passing away, and the lust of it; but he who does the will of God abides forever.

1 John 2:17
God's Will Theme

AUGUST 4

READING

The passage for today centers on the description of an excellent wife. An excellent wife cares for her home, is kind to the needy, and is an example of good character.

Read Proverbs 31.

REFLECTING

We live in an age that views women in extremes. One views women as merely caretakers of the house, who have no role other than changing diapers, cooking food, and cleaning house. Another seeks to free women from the responsibilities at home. Both are wrong. Women are to care for their homes, and maintain certain responsibilities, just as men should. But their role carries with it great flexibility and variety. The woman in Proverbs 31 is a skillful buyer of household goods, deals in real estate, oversees agricultural operations, engages in philanthropic activities, operates a retail outlet. Yet she does it all for the welfare of her home, to enrich her relationships within the home, not to escape the home. Her heart is with her family.

RESPONDING

1. **Praise:** Since the earthly family pictures the heavenly family, offer your praise to the Lord that He is your heavenly Father:

Praise the Lord! Praise God in His sanctuary; praise Him in His mighty firmament! Praise Him for His mighty acts; praise Him according to His excellent greatness! Praise Him with the sound of the trumpet; praise Him with the lute and harp! . . . Let everything that has breath praise the Lord. Praise the Lord. (Psalm 150:1-3, 6)

Now offer to the Lord your personal praise and thanksgiving.

2. **Confession:** Pray this confession to the Lord as you keep your life free from sin and in fellowship with Him:

Cleanse me from all my iniquity by which I have sinned against You, and pardon all my iniquities by which I have sinned and by which I have transgressed against You. (Jeremiah 33:8)

Confess any personal sins which the Holy Spirit brings to your mind.

3. **Affirmation:** As you agree with God's will, voice your affirmation of His word:

My body is the temple of the Holy Spirit who is in me, whom I have from You, O Lord, and I am not my own. I was bought at a price; therefore I will glorify You in my body and in my spirit, which are Yours. (1 Corinthians 6:19-20)

4. **Requests:** As you make your requests known to the Lord, include:

- Insight into Scripture
- The hungry around the world
- Your prayer list, the concerns of your heart, and today's activities

5. **Closing Prayer:** Finally, offer this closing prayer to the Lord:

We will be of good courage, and You shall strengthen our hearts, all we who hope in the Lord. (Psalm 31:24)

Memory Verse: And the world is passing away, and the lust of it; but he who does the will of God abides forever.

1 John 2:17
God's Will Theme

AUGUST 5

READING

The passage for today centers on the vanity of life. The pursuit of temporal things is futile; rather, we must fear God and keep His commandments.

Read Ecclesiastes 12.

REFLECTING

A wise man makes learning enjoyable. And sweetness of speech increases persuasiveness. After all, more flies are caught with honey than with vinegar. The Preacher in Ecclesiastes amplifies this theme. A good teacher is well prepared: "he pondered, searched out, arranged." A good teacher is interesting and accurate: "he found delightful words and wrote them truthfully." A good teacher is practical: his words are like "goads and well-driven nails." Not all of us can be master teachers, but all of us can be better teachers by focusing on those three principles: being well-prepared, being interesting, and being practical. Being interesting and practical depends on being well prepared. Being a better teacher is *hard* work, but well worth the effort.

RESPONDING

1. Praise: Thank the Lord and praise Him that He is so skillful and patient in teaching us His way:

Inasmuch as there is none like You, O Lord (You are great, and Your name is great in might), who would not fear You, O King of the nations? For this is Your rightful due, for among all the wise men of the nations, and in all their kingdoms, there is none like You. (Jeremiah 10:6-7)

Now offer to the Lord your personal praise and thanksgiving.

2. Confession: Pray this confession to the Lord as you seek to keep your life free from sin and in fellowship with Him:

Deliver me from bloodguiltiness, O God, the God of my salvation. And my tongue shall sing aloud of Your righteousness. O Lord, open my lips, and my mouth shall show forth Your praise. (Psalm 51:14-15)

Confess any personal sins which the Holy Spirit brings to your mind.

3. Affirmation: As you agree with God's will, voice your affirmation of His word:

If I confess with my mouth the Lord Jesus, and believe in my heart that You, O God, raised Him from the dead, I shall be saved. For with the heart I believe, resulting in righteousness, and with the mouth I confess, resulting in salvation. For the Scripture says, "Whoever believes in Him will not be disappointed." (Romans 10:9-11)

4. Requests: As you make your requests known to the Lord, include:

- Love for fellow Christians
- The work of missions in Europe and Asia
- Your prayer list, the concerns of your heart, and today's activities

5. Closing Prayer: Finally, offer this closing prayer to the Lord:

Now to You who are able to keep me from stumbling, and to present me faultless before the presence of Your glory with exceeding joy, to You, my God and Savior, who alone are wise, be glory and majesty, dominion and power, both now and forever. Amen. (Jude 24-25)

Memory Verse: And the world is passing away, and the lust of it; but he who does the will of God abides forever.

1 John 2:17
God's Will Theme

AUGUST 6

READING

The passage for today centers on the beauty of married love. Solomon and his bride exchange expressions of love and admiration for each other.

Read Song of Solomon 1.

REFLECTING

In Hebrews 13:4 we read, "Let the marriage bed be undefiled." In his commentary on the Song of Solomon, *A Song for Lovers,* Craig Glickman writes: "No artist could have fashioned two people better suited for one another. He was the king of their great nation; she, his chosen bride. Spring had seen their love blossom like the flowers in the palace gardens. Their love had been the talk of the court. It was destined to be a song for the world. For their romance was a romance for all seasons. And, in fact, so ideal was their love that the song about them was chosen as one of the books of sacred Scripture. It became the only one of the entire collection devoted exclusively to courtship and marriage." It gives us God's perspective on marriage and love.

RESPONDING

1. Praise: Offer the Lord your praise for the unconditional love He gives you as a member of the Church, the "Bride of Christ":

Blessed be the name of God forever and ever, for wisdom and might are His. . . . He gives wisdom to the wise and knowledge to those who have understanding. He reveals deep and secret things; He knows what is in the darkness, and light dwells with Him. (Daniel 2:20-22)

Now offer to the Lord your personal praise and thanksgiving.

2. Confession: Pray this confession to the Lord as you seek to keep your life free from sin and in fellowship with Him:

The sacrifices of God are a broken spirit, a broken and contrite heart—these, O God, You will not despise. (Psalm 51:16-17)

Confess any personal sins which the Holy Spirit brings to your mind.

3. Affirmation: As you agree with God's will, voice your affirmation of His word:

By this I know love, because You, Lord Jesus, laid down Your life for me. And I also ought to lay down my life for my brother. (1 John 3:16)

4. Requests: As you make your requests known to the Lord, include:

- Faithfulness with your time
- The president and national leaders and affairs
- Your prayer list, the concerns of your heart, and today's activities

5. Closing Prayer: Finally, offer this closing prayer to the Lord:

Oh, satisfy me early with Your mercy, that I may rejoice and be glad all my days! (Psalm 90:14)

Memory Verse: Go therefore and make disciples of all the nations, baptizing them in the name of the Father and of the Son and of the Holy Spirit.
Matthew 28:19
Evangelism Theme

READING

The passage for today centers on Isaiah's vision. Isaiah sees the Lord on His throne with His holy angels and is commissioned to become a prophet to Israel.

Read Isaiah 6.

REFLECTING

Isaiah sees the Lord in a terrifying vision which makes him acutely aware of his personal sin. The Lord takes away his sin, seeing the repentance of his heart and then commissions Isaiah to serve Him as a prophet to the Jews. This event illustrates how the Lord calls His servants. First, He reveals Himself through His Word. When the Scriptures are received by the hearer, he becomes aware of his sin, and asks God for forgiveness and salvation. God then sends him into the world to take the message of salvation to others. Our ministry is always based on our lifestyle, and our lifestyle is based on our knowledge of God. Our lifestyle will not go beyond our knowledge of God, and our ministry will never go beyond our lifestyle.

RESPONDING

1. Praise: God is holy, and we praise Him because He makes us holy, cleansing us spiritually with the blood of Christ, His Son:

My soul magnifies the Lord, and my spirit has rejoiced in God my Savior. . . . You who are mighty have done great things for me, and holy is Your name, And Your mercy is on those who fear You from generation to generation. (Luke 1:46-50)

Now offer to the Lord your personal praise and thanksgiving.

2. Confession: Pray this confession to the Lord as you seek to keep your life free from sin and in fellowship with Him:

Bless the Lord, O my soul; and all that is within me, bless His holy name! Bless the Lord, O my soul, and forget not all His benefits: who forgives all your iniquities. Bless the Lord, O my soul! (Psalm 103:1-4)

Confess any personal sins which the Holy Spirit brings to your mind.

3. Affirmation: As you agree with God's will, voice your affirmation of His word:

You, O Lord, are the Bread of Life. If I come to You I shall never hunger, and If I believe in You, I shall never thirst. (John 6:35)

4. Requests: As you make your requests known to the Lord, include:

- Your financial needs
- The needs of the poor
- Your prayer list, the concerns of your heart, and today's activities

5. Closing Prayer: Finally, offer this closing prayer to the Lord:

Let the beauty of You, Lord, be upon me, and establish the work of my hands for me; yes, establish the work of my hands. (Psalm 90:17)

Memory Verse: Go therefore and make disciples of all the nations, baptizing them in the name of the Father and of the Son and of the Holy Spirit.
Matthew 28:19
Evangelism Theme

AUGUST 8

READING

The passage for today centers on the greatness of God. Behold the Lord your God, who sits over creation and who gives strength to those who wait on Him.

Read Isaiah 40.

REFLECTING

God has given us the Christian family to picture the relationship between Him and His children. We are given earthly fathers that we might more fully understand our Heavenly Father. Just as an earthly father takes no delight in disciplining his children—yet does so, knowing it is necessary for growth—so our Heavenly Father takes no delight in disciplining His children, yet is committed to our growth. Hear the tenderness in these words: "Comfort, O comfort My people. Speak kindly to Jerusalem; and call out to her, that her warfare has ended, that her iniquity has been removed" (40:1-2). God tenderly loves us and takes no pleasure in our pain.

RESPONDING

1. Praise: Offer your praise to the Lord in these passages as you fellowship with Him:

Because Your lovingkindness is better than life, My lips shall praise You. Thus I will bless You while I live; I will lift up my hands in Your name. . . . When I remember You on my bed, I meditate on You in the night watches. Because You have been my help, Therefore in the shadow of Your wings I will rejoice. (Psalm 63:3-5, 7)

Pause for personal praise and thanksgiving.

2. Confession: Pray this confession to the Lord as you seek to keep your life free from sin and in fellowship with Him:

Indeed I have sinned against You, O Lord God. (Joshua 7:20)

Show me Your ways, O Lord; teach me Your paths. Lead me in Your truth and teach me, for You are the God of my salvation; On You I wait all the day. (Psalm 25:4-5)

Confess any personal sins which the Holy Spirit brings to your mind.

3. Affirmation: Now pause to pray this affirmation to the Lord:

The wages of sin is death, but my free gift from You, O Lord, is eternal life in Christ Jesus my Lord. (Romans 6:23)

4. Requests: As you make your requests known to the Lord, pray for:

- Protection from the "evil one"
- Laborers for the "harvest"
- Your prayer list, the concerns of your heart, and today's activities

5. Closing Prayer: Finally, offer this closing prayer to the Lord:

Bless the Lord, all you His hosts, you ministers of His, who do His pleasure. Bless the Lord, all His works, in all places of His dominion. (Psalm 103:21-22)

Memory Verse: Go therefore and make disciples of all the nations, baptizing them in the name of the Father and of the Son and of the Holy Spirit.
Matthew 28:19
Evangelism Theme

READING

The passage for today centers on the suffering Servant. Our Savior bore the chastisement for our iniquity and so will intercede for our transgressions.

Read Isaiah 53.

REFLECTING

When Christians suffer, they are tempted to resent God, to wonder, "Why me?" If God is all good and all powerful, why must His children suffer? The answer to that question is difficult—and not totally satisfying to the finite mind. Jesus maintains His credibility, however, in that He readily suffered for us all—suffering more than He will ever ask of us. Why must God's children suffer? We don't know all the answers or presume to know all of God's purposes. What we do know is that God was willing to suffer for us. Our part is to follow Him. "To this you were called, because Christ suffered for you, leaving you an example, that you should follow in His steps" (1 Peter 2:21). He asks nothing *of* us that He was not willing to do *for* us.

RESPONDING

1. Praise: As you respond to God's willingness to suffer for you, offer Him your praise through His word:

I will love You, O Lord, my strength. The Lord is my Rock and my fortress and my deliverer; my God, my strength, in whom I will trust; my shield and the horn of my salvation, my stronghold. I call upon the Lord, who is worthy to be praised; so shall I be saved from my enemies. . . . The Lord lives! Blessed be my Rock! Let the God of my salvation be exalted. (Psalm 18:1-3, 46)

Pause for personal praise and thanksgiving.

2. Confession: Pray this confession to the Lord as you seek to keep your life free from sin and in fellowship with Him:

Good and upright is the Lord; therefore He teaches sinners in the way. The humble He guides in justice, and the humble He teaches His way. . . . For Your name's sake, O Lord, pardon my iniquity, for it is great. (Psalm 25:8-9, 11)

Confess any personal sins which the Holy Spirit brings to your mind.

3. Affirmation: Now pause to pray this affirmation to the Lord:

You are the living bread which came down from heaven. If I eat of this bread, I will live forever; and the bread that You shall give is Your flesh, which You shall give for the life of the world. (John 6:51)

4. Requests: As you make your requests known to the Lord, include:

- Commitment to the Lord
- Parachurch ministries
- Your prayer list, the concerns of your heart, and today's activities

5. Closing Prayer: Finally, offer this closing prayer to the Lord:

Lord, preserve me from all evil; preserve my soul. Lord, preserve my going out and my coming in from this time forth, and even forevermore. (Psalm 121:7-8)

Memory Verse: Go therefore and make disciples of all the nations, baptizing them in the name of the Father and of the Son and of the Holy Spirit.
Matthew 28:19
Evangelism Theme

AUGUST 10

READING

The passage for today centers on the free offer of mercy. Seek the Lord while He may be found; let the wicked forsake his way, and God will have compassion on him.

Read Isaiah 55.

REFLECTING

Coming to the Lord costs a man nothing and at the same time costs him everything. The offer is free in that a man need not give anything in exchange for his salvation. "Ho, everyone who thirsts, come to the waters; and you who have no money come, buy and eat. Come, buy wine and milk without money and without cost." Yet it costs him his life. He no longer has the freedom of self-determination. "Seek the Lord while He may be found. Let the wicked forsake his way, and the unrighteous man his thoughts; and let him return to the Lord, and He will have compassion on him." All that it costs, everyone can give: oneself. For salvation costs a man nothing, yet it costs him everything.

RESPONDING

1. Praise: Nothing can exceed the importance of the salvation which the Lord offers us in Christ, and for it give Him your praise:

Oh, the depth of the riches both of the wisdom and knowledge of God! How unsearchable are Your judgments and Your ways past finding out! . . . Blessed are You, the God and Father of our Lord Jesus Christ, who has blessed us with every spiritual blessing in the heavenly places in Christ. (Romans 11:33, Ephesians 1:3)

Now offer to the Lord your personal praise and thanksgiving.

2. Confession: Pray this confession to the Lord as you seek to keep your life free from sin and in fellowship with Him:

O God, You know my foolishness; and my sins are not hidden from You. Let not those who wait for You, O Lord God of hosts, be ashamed because of me. (Psalm 69:5-6)

Confess any personal sins which the Holy Spirit brings to your mind.

3. Affirmation: As you agree with God's will, voice your affirmation of His word:

You, O Lord, are the light of the world. If I follow You I shall not walk in darkness, but have the light of life. (John 8:12)

4. Requests: As you make your requests known to the Lord, include:

- Renewing of your mind
- Needs of your extended family
- Your prayer list, the concerns of your heart, and today's activities

5. Closing Prayer: Finally, offer this closing prayer to the Lord:

May we with one mind and one mouth glorify the God and Father of our Lord Jesus Christ. (Romans 15:6)

Memory Verse: Go therefore and make disciples of all the nations, baptizing them in the name of the Father and of the Son and of the Holy Spirit.
Matthew 28:19
Evangelism Theme

READING

The passage for today centers on God's new covenant with Israel. Israel's mourning is turned to joy, and God establishes a new covenant with them, to forgive their iniquity and write the Law in their heart.

Read Jeremiah 31.

REFLECTING

The primary theme of nearly all the prophetic books is warning of judgment for sin. The prophets proclaim the Word of God as their basic ministry, but from time to time the Lord reveals to them a specific message for the children of Israel. Usually, this specific message involves a warning concerning a sin that the nation is committing, that if it does not turn from the sin, a specific judgment will follow. It is comforting to see, however, that in nearly all instances, the judgment is to be followed with restoration. God's judgment for His children is not retaliation, but is intended to get His children to turn from their sin to Him. In Jeremiah 31, we see a heartening message of hope and restoration for Israel.

RESPONDING

1. Praise: Thank the Lord that He has warned us of the consequences of our sin, and praise Him that, in Christ, we can escape them:

You are worthy, O Lord, to receive glory and honor and power; for You created all things, and by Your will they exist and were created. . . . I will praise You, O Lord, according to Your righteousness, and will sing praise to Your name, O Lord Most High. (Revelation 4:11, Psalm 7:17)

Now offer to the Lord your personal praise and thanksgiving.

2. Confession: Pray this confession to the Lord as you seek to keep your life free from sin and in fellowship with Him:

You have not dealt with me according to my sins, nor punished me according to my iniquities. For as the heavens are high above the earth, so great is Your mercy toward those who fear You; as far as the east is from the west, so far have You removed our transgressions from us. (Psalm 103:10-12)

Confess any personal sins which the Holy Spirit brings to your mind.

3. Affirmation: As you agree with God's will, voice your affirmation of His word:

You, O Lord, have shown me what is good; and what do You require of me, but to do justly, to love mercy, and to walk humbly with You. (Mica 6:8)

4. Requests: As you make your requests known to the Lord, include:

- The Lord's leading in your life
- Opportunities for personal evangelism
- Your prayer list, the concerns of your heart, and today's activities

5. Closing Prayer: Finally, offer this closing prayer to the Lord:

Now may the God of hope fill me with all joy and peace in believing, that I may abound in hope by the power of the Holy Spirit. (Romans 15:13)

Memory Verse: Go therefore and make disciples of all the nations, baptizing them in the name of the Father and of the Son and of the Holy Spirit.
Matthew 28:19
Evangelism Theme

AUGUST 12

READING

The passage for today centers on the hope of relief in God's mercy. In the midst of Israel's judgment, hope is given that God will restore them to favor.

Read Lamentations 3.

REFLECTING

A lament is a sorrowful song, a song of grief or mourning. In the Book of Lamentations, the prophet Jeremiah weeps over the impending destruction of his beloved city Jerusalem. Through the prophets, God has been warning Judah for many years to turn from idolatry to serve Him only. Through a succession of 20 kings that Judah had, only eight of them were righteous and led the nation in righteousness. Finally, their sin has compounded to the point that judgment is no longer avoidable if God is to be true to His word. Jerusalem will fall. There is hope on the horizon, however. Jeremiah writes, "The Lord's lovingkindnesses indeed never cease, for His compassions never fail. . . . They are new every morning. The Lord is my portion. Therefore I have hope in Him" (Lamentations 3:22-24). With the warning for judgment always comes the hope of restoration.

RESPONDING

1. Praise: Praise the Lord that though all of us sin, yet God's compassions are new every morning:

Great and marvelous are Your works, Lord God Almighty! Just and true are Your ways, O King of the saints! Who shall not fear You, O Lord, and glorify Your name? For You alone are holy. For all nations shall come and worship before You, for Your judgments have been manifested. (Revelation 15:3-4)

Now offer to the Lord your personal praise and thanksgiving.

2. Confession: Pray this confession to the Lord as you seek to keep your life free from sin and in fellowship with Him:

O Lord, You are merciful and gracious, slow to anger, and abounding in mercy. . . . As a father pities his children, so You, Lord, pity those who fear You. For You know our frame; You remember that we are dust. (Psalm 103:8, 13-14)

Confess any personal sins which the Holy Spirit brings to your mind.

3. Affirmation: As you agree with God's will, voice your affirmation of His word:

There is therefore now no condemnation for me if I am in You, Christ Jesus. For the law of the Spirit of life in You has set me free from the law of sin and death. (Romans 8:1-2)

4. Requests: As you make your requests known to the Lord, include:

- Love for the lost
- The work of missions in Africa
- Your prayer list, the concerns of your heart, and today's activities.

5. Closing Prayer: Finally, offer this closing prayer to the Lord:

Now to You who are able to establish us according to the gospel and preaching of Jesus Christ—to You, alone wise, be glory through Jesus Christ forever. Amen. (Romans 16:25-27)

Memory Verse: Go therefore and make disciples of all the nations, baptizing them in the name of the Father and of the Son and of the Holy Spirit.
Matthew 28:19
Evangelism Theme

AUGUST 13

READING

The passage for today centers on the vision of the valley of dry bones. Ezekiel's vision is explained as being the restoration of the nations of Israel and Judah.

Read Ezekiel 37.

REFLECTING

The Apostle John writes: "In the beginning was the Word, and the Word was with God, and the Word was God. In Him was life, and the life is the light of men." God is life. And not just life for today, but forever. Timothy writes that God alone "possesses immortality." God is life, and He is the giver of life. He can take dead things and make them live. In Ezekiel's vision, a huge valley is filled with dead men's bones. Then God begins to move. The bones form skeletons, upon which form flesh and clothes. Then God breathes into that valley of bodies the breath of life, and the bodies come alive. That is a picture of what God will do with Israel. He will give her life again. That is what He will do with anyone who believes in Him and asks Him for life. Have you asked Him for eternal life?

RESPONDING

1. Praise: The Lord gives us His immortality, and we praise Him for His wonderful gift of life to us:

Who is like You, O Lord, among the gods? Who is like You, glorious in holiness, fearful in praises, doing wonders? . . . You are great, O Lord God. For there is none like You, nor is there any God besides You, according to all that we have heard with our ears. (Exodus 15:11, 2 Samuel 7:22)

Now offer to the Lord your personal praise and thanksgiving.

2. Confession: Pray this confession to the Lord as you seek to keep your life free from sin and in fellowship with Him:

Out of the depths I have cried to You, O Lord; . . . If You, Lord, should mark iniquities, O Lord, who could stand? But there is forgiveness with You, that You may be feared. (Psalm 130:1, 3-4)

Confess any personal sins which the Holy Spirit brings to your mind.

3. Affirmation: As you agree with God's will, voice your affirmation of His word:

Your grace, O Lord, is sufficient for me, for Your strength is made perfect in weakness. (2 Corinthians 12:9)

4. Requests: As you make your requests known to the Lord, include:

- Faithfulness with your talents
- Your state and local leaders and affairs
- Your prayer list, the concerns of your heart, and today's activities

5. Closing Prayer: Finally, offer this closing prayer to the Lord:

The grace of the Lord Jesus Christ, and the love of God, and the communion of the Holy Spirit be with us all. Amen. (2 Corinthians 13:14)

Memory Verse: Go into all the world and preach the gospel to every creature.

Mark 16:15
Evangelism Theme

AUGUST 14

READING

The passage for today centers on Daniel's resolve. Nebuchadnezzar, king of Babylon, chooses young men from the Israelite captives to be trained to serve him.

Read Daniel 1.

REFLECTING

Moral courage. It is the resolve to do what is right, even if no one knows. It is the resolve to do what is right regardless of the consequences. It is the resolve to keep on doing what is right, even when you are weary. It is the resolve to do what is right even when there are extenuating circumstances and everyone would understand if you "caved in." Daniel is a man of moral courage. The food he is offered probably violates the dietary restrictions in the Law of Moses. Note the words: "Daniel made up his mind." Then God brings him into favor. He gives him skill. He causes his face to exude health. When faced with moral challenges, we must do our part: be obedient from the heart; and then, trust God to do His part.

RESPONDING

1. Praise: Because God honors our commitment to moral excellence, praise Him in the words of this psalm:

You are the Rock, Your work is perfect; for all Your ways are just, a God of truth and without injustice, righteous and upright are You. (Deuteronomy 32:4)

The Lord lives! Blessed be my Rock! Let God be exalted, the Rock of my salvation! (2 Samuel 22:47)

Now offer to the Lord your personal praise and thanksgiving.

2. Confession: Pray this confession to the Lord as you seek to keep your life free from sin and in fellowship with Him:

We give You thanks, O Lord, that we may reason with You. Though our sins are like scarlet, they shall be as white as snow; though they are red like crimson, They shall be as wool. (Isaiah 1:18)

Confess any personal sins which the Holy Spirit brings to your mind.

3. Affirmation: As you agree with God's will, voice your affirmation of His word:

You will keep me in perfect peace, my mind is stayed on You, because I trust in You. (Isaiah 26:3)

4. Requests: As you make your requests known to the Lord, include:

- Strength for obedience
- International students in America
- Your prayer list, the concerns of your heart, and today's activities

5. Closing Prayer: Finally, offer this closing prayer to the Lord:

Now to You who are able to do exceedingly abundantly above all that I ask or think, according to the power that works in me, to You be glory in the church by Christ Jesus throughout all ages, world without end. Amen. (Ephesians 3:20-21)

Memory Verse: Go into all the world and preach the gospel to every creature.

Mark 16:15
Evangelism Theme

AUGUST 15

READING

The passage for today centers on the king's troublesome dream. Nebuchadnezzar has a dream which bothers him, and he requires that the wise men of the land tell him not only the dream but also the interpretation.

Read Daniel 2.

REFLECTING

One of our responsibilities as children of God is to give God credit for who He is and what He does. "Always giving thanks to God the Father for everything. . . " (Ephesians 5:20). It is the careless Christian who stands under the showers of God's blessing without recognizing them. It is the irresponsible Christian who recognizes God's blessing and does not give God the credit. Daniel recognizes God's work and tells the king, "It is He who reveals the profound and hidden things" (2:2). And through this, God is glorified. We must always be alert to the blessings of God in our lives, express our gratitude to Him, and give Him public credit. Have you named your blessings recently? Does anyone else know?

RESPONDING

1. Praise: In the eyes of God, it is wisdom to praise Him for who He is and what He has done for us:

Give to the Lord, O kindreds of the peoples. . . . Give to the Lord the glory due His name; bring an offering, and come before Him. Oh, worship the Lord in the beauty of holiness! (1 Chronicles 16:28-29)

Pause for personal praise and thanksgiving.

2. Confession: Pray this confession to the Lord as you seek to keep your life free from sin and in fellowship with Him:

Lord, be merciful to me; heal my soul, for I have sinned against You. . . . O Lord, be merciful to me, and raise me up. . . . Blessed be the Lord God . . . from everlasting to everlasting! Amen and amen. (Psalm 41:4, 10, 13)

Confess any personal sins which the Holy Spirit brings to mind.

3. Affirmation: Now pause to pray this affirmation to the Lord:

You, O Lord, the everlasting God, the Creator of the ends of the earth, neither faint nor are weary. There is no searching of Your understanding. You give power to the weak, and when I have no might, You increase my strength. (Isaiah 40:27-29)

4. Requests: As you make your requests known to the Lord, include:

- Your "daily bread"

- Christian education institutions

- Your prayer list, the concerns of your heart, and today's activities

5. Closing Prayer: Finally, offer this closing prayer to the Lord:

Now may You, the God of peace, sanctify me completely, and may my whole spirit, soul, and body be preserved blameless at the coming of my Lord Jesus Christ. (1 Thessalonians 5:23)

Memory Verse: Go into all the world and preach the gospel to every creature.

Mark 16:15
Evangelism Theme

AUGUST 16

READING

The passage for today centers on the king's golden image. The king makes a golden image, and when Shadrach, Meshach, and Abed-nego do not worship the image, they are thrown into a furnace, where God supernaturally protects them. Read Daniel 3.

REFLECTING

What courage it took to live in the days of martyrs! Nebuchadnezzar sets up a golden image and orders everyone to bow down to it. Daniel's three friends refuse to participate in such idolatry. When the Jews are brought to him in violation of the order, they say, "God may protect us from the fire, but even if He doesn't, let it be known that we are not going to serve your gods!" They are willing to suffer the apparent consequences of their obeying God rather than man. Surely God gives His grace in times such as those. For us, who are living in easier times, our total dedication to the Lord must be seen in our selfless commitment to serving Him and furthering the Great Commission, willing to follow God no matter what the earthly consequences.

RESPONDING

1. Praise: Show your dedication to the Lord by offering Him your praise:

Blessed are You, Lord God . . . our Father, forever and ever. Yours, O Lord, is the greatness, the power and the glory, the victory and the majesty; for all that is in heaven and in earth is Yours; Yours is the kingdom, O Lord, and You are exalted as head over all. Both riches and honor come from You, and You reign over all. In Your hand is power and

might; in Your hand it is to make great and to give strength to all. Now therefore, our God, we thank You and praise Your glorious name. (1 Chronicles 29:10-13)

Pause for personal praise and thanksgiving.

2. Confession: Pray this confession to the Lord as you seek to keep your life free from sin and in fellowship with Him:

Against You, You only, have I sinned, and done this evil in Your sight—that You may be found just when You speak, and blameless when You judge. (Psalm 51:4)

Confess any personal sins which the Holy Spirit brings to mind.

3. Affirmation: Now pause to pray this affirmation to the Lord:

If I wait on the Lord, my strength shall be renewed; I shall mount up with wings like eagles, I shall run and not be weary, I shall walk and not faint. (Isaiah 40:31)

4. Requests: As you make your requests known to the Lord, include:

- Passion for moral excellence
- Needs of personal friends
- Your prayer list, the concerns of your heart, and today's activities

5. Closing Prayer: Finally, offer this closing prayer to the Lord:

Now may the Lord Jesus Christ Himself, and You, my God and Father, who have loved me and given me everlasting consolation and good hope by grace, comfort my heart and establish me in every good word and work. (2 Thessalonians 2:16-17)

Memory Verse: Go into all the world and preach the gospel to every creature.

Mark 16:15
Evangelism Theme

READING

The passage for today centers on Nebuchadnezzar's dream. The king has a dream which Daniel interprets, indicating that the king will live like an animal until he acknowledges God, after which his throne will be restored.

Read Daniel 4.

REFLECTING

What a towering figure is Nebuchadnezzar! Sovereign over the greatest nation on earth at the time, wealthy beyond description, subject to fits of rage, and yet somehow vulnerable and teachable. He rages in fury at the three Jews who refuse to worship his image, yet proclaims their God the only God when He saves them from the furnace. Then, warned by Daniel that unless he repents he will be stripped of his kingdom, he lapses into convenient forgetfulness and self-adulation. True to "the decree of the Most High" spoken through Daniel, the king becomes like an animal and roams the forest. Yet, when his senses are restored, he again worships God and proclaims His praise to the ends of the earth.

RESPONDING

1. Praise: The Lord is the sovereign ruler of the universe, and we praise Him for ruling in love and wisdom:

O Lord God of Israel, the One who dwells between the cherubim, You are God, You alone, of all the kingdoms of the earth. You have made heaven and earth. (2 Kings 19:15)

Lord God of Israel, there is no God in heaven above or on earth below like You, who keep Your covenant and mercy with Your ser-vants who walk before You with all their heart. (1 Kings 8:23)

Now offer to the Lord your personal praise and thanksgiving.

2. Confession: Pray this confession to the Lord as you seek to keep your life free from sin and in fellowship with Him:

I will praise You, for I am fearfully and wonderfully made; marvelous are Your works, and that my soul knows very well. . . . Search me, O God, and know my heart; try me, and know my anxieties; and see if there is any wicked way in me, and lead me in the way everlasting. (Psalm 139:14, 23-24)

Confess any personal sins which the Holy Spirit brings to your mind.

3. Affirmation: As you agree with God's will, voice your affirmation of His word:

If I love You, O Lord, I will keep Your word; and the Father will love me, and You and the Father will come to me and make Your home with me. (John 14:23)

4. Requests: As you make your requests known to the Lord, include:

- Wisdom in decision making
- Opportunities to serve the Lord
- Your prayer list, the concerns of your heart and today's activities

5. Closing Prayer: Finally, offer this closing prayer to the Lord:

Now to You, the King eternal, immortal, invisible, to God who alone is wise, be honor and glory forever and ever. Amen. (1 Timothy 1:17)

Memory Verse: Go into all the world and preach the gospel to every creature.

Mark 16:15
Evangelism Theme

AUGUST 18

READING

The passage for today centers on Belshazzar's death. At a banquet at which the king desecrates the gold vessels from the temple, handwriting from God is seen on the wall, prophesying the king's death.

Read Daniel 5.

REFLECTING

It is always a terrible thing to go into the presence of God on our own merit. In and of ourselves, we are inherently deficient, and unworthy of the presence of God. All have sinned and fall short of His glory. Belshazzar discovers this in a terrible and frightening way. While he revels, desecrating the holy implements from the temple, the hand of God writes on the wall against him, "You have been weighed and found wanting." That same inscription can be written of all who come before God on their own merit. We have all been weighed and found wanting. In the providence and grace of God, we can come before Him in the merit of Christ. Jesus, having paid the penalty for our sin, clothes us in His righteousness, and in Him, we can stand in the presence of God, holy and undefiled.

RESPONDING

1. Praise: Thank the Lord and give Him your praise for saving you by faith and clothing you in Christ's righteousness:

I will praise the Lord according to His righteousness, and will sing praise to the name of the Lord Most High. (Psalm 7:17)

Now offer to the Lord your personal praise and thanksgiving.

2. Confession: Pray this confession to the Lord as you seek to keep your life free from sin and in fellowship with Him:

O Lord, You blot out my transgressions for Your own sake; and You will not remember my sins. (Isaiah 43:25)

Confess any personal sins which the Holy Spirit brings to your mind.

3. Affirmation: As you agree with God's will, voice your affirmation of His word:

I have sinned and fall short of Your glory, O God, being justified as a gift by Your grace through the redemption which is in Christ Jesus. (Romans 3:23-24)

4. Requests: As you make your requests known to the Lord, include:

- Victory over temptation
- The work of missions in North and South America
- Your prayer list, the concerns of your heart, and today's activities

5. Closing Prayer: Finally, offer this closing prayer to the Lord:

You who are the blessed and only Potentate, the King of kings and Lord of lords, who alone have immortality, dwelling in unapproachable light, whom no man has seen or can see, to You be honor and everlasting power. Amen. (1 Timothy 6:15-16)

Memory Verse: Go into all the world and preach the gospel to every creature.

Mark 16:15
Evangelism Theme

READING

The passage for today centers on Daniel in the lion's den. Darius, the king, is tricked into putting Daniel in the lion's den, but God miraculously delivers him.

Read Daniel 6.

REFLECTING

All men of God are men of prayer. Though we wrestle with prayer, things we don't understand, things we don't know, nevertheless, when all is said and done, in the Scripture, all men of God are men of prayer. From Daniel we learn a number of instructive things. Daniel prays three times a day (6:13). Certainly he must have prayed at other times, but he sets aside three times a day for prayer, even though he is exceedingly busy, one of the primary rulers of the land. His prayer includes giving thanks (6:10) and petition and supplication (6:11); that is, he asks God for things for himself and others. If our prayer reflects the commitment and balance of Daniel's, our relationship with the Lord will be a growing one.

RESPONDING

1. Praise: Offer your praise to the Lord, who encourages your prayer, hears, and answers according to His will:

Tremble before Him, all the earth. The world also is firmly established, it shall not be moved. Let the heavens rejoice, and let the earth be glad. . . . Oh, give thanks to the Lord, for He is good! For His mercy endures forever. . . . Blessed be the Lord God of Israel from everlasting to everlasting! (1 Chronicles 16:30-31, 34, 36)

Now offer to the Lord your personal praise and thanksgiving.

2. Confession: Pray this confession to the Lord as you seek to keep your life free from sin and in fellowship with Him:

You have blotted out, like a thick cloud, my transgressions, and like a cloud, my sins. I will return to You, for You have redeemed me. (Isaiah 44:22)

Confess any personal sins which the Holy Spirit brings to your mind.

3. Affirmation: As you agree with God's will, voice your affirmation of His word:

The Spirit also helps me in weaknesses. For I do not know what I should pray for as I ought, but the Spirit Himself makes intercession for me with groanings which cannot be uttered. (Romans 8:26)

4. Requests: As you make your requests known to the Lord, include:

● Love for your family

● Revival among Christians in America

● Your prayer list, the concerns of your heart, and today's activities

5. Closing Prayer: Finally, offer this closing prayer to the Lord:

Make me complete in every good work to do Your will, working in me what is well pleasing in Your sight, through Jesus Christ, to whom be glory forever and ever. Amen. (Hebrews 13:20-21)

Memory Verse: Go into all the world and preach the gospel to every creature.

Mark 16:15
Evangelism Theme

AUGUST 20

READING

The passage for today centers on Israel's future blessing. After pronouncing judgment on Israel for sin, Hosea prophesies future restoration and blessing.

Read Hosea 14.

REFLECTING

Hosea is instructed by the Lord to take a wife whose name is Gomer (not one of your more popular names today), who later becomes unfaithful to him. Though he loves her steadfastly, her infidelity compounds, and she finally leaves him. Some time later as Hosea is walking down the street, he sees his wife being sold as a slave on an auction block. In a profound gesture of unconditional love, Hosea redeems (buys back) his wife and restores her to her former position of honor and comfort as his wife. In doing so, Hosea sounds a warning to Israel and plays out a moving example of the unconditional love of God for His people. If they sin, He will judge them, but after judgment, He will restore them to His grace.

RESPONDING

1. Praise: God loves His children unconditionally. Praise Him that He does not leave us to our own abilities in following Him:

Blessed be Your glorious name, which is exalted above all blessing and praise! You alone are the Lord; You have made heaven, the heaven of heavens, with all their host, the earth and all things on it, the seas and all that is in them, and You preserve them all. The host of heaven worships You. (Nehemiah 9:5-6)

Now offer to the Lord your personal praise and thanksgiving.

2. Confession: Pray this confession to the Lord as you seek to keep your life free from sin and in fellowship with Him:

Surely You, Lord Jesus, have borne our griefs and carried our sorrows. . . . You were wounded for our transgressions, You were bruised for our iniquities; the chastisement for our peace was upon You, and by Your stripes we are healed. (Isaiah 53:4-5)

Confess any personal sins which the Holy Spirit brings to your mind.

3. Affirmation: As you agree with God's will, voice your affirmation of His word:

You demonstrated Your own love toward me, in that while I was still a sinner, Christ died for me. (Romans 5:8)

4. Requests: As you make your requests known to the Lord, include:

- Faithfulness with your treasures
- The Great Commission
- Your prayer list, the concerns of your heart, and today's activities

5. Closing Prayer: Finally, offer this closing prayer to the Lord:

May You, the God of grace, who called me to Your eternal glory by Christ Jesus, after I have suffered a while, perfect, establish, strengthen, and settle me. To You be the glory and the dominion forever and ever. Amen. (1 Peter 5:10-11)

Memory Verse: Therefore we are ambassadors for Christ, as though God were pleading through us: we implore you on Christ's behalf, be reconciled to God.

2 Corinthians 5:20
Evangelism Theme

READING

The passage for today centers on the day of the Lord. A day of judgment is coming for the sins of the people, but after repentance, they will be restored.

Read Joel 2.

REFLECTING

Joel predicts a locust plague to come upon the land of Judah, which is both primary and secondary as a prophetic warning. The primary meaning is a literal locust plague. But the things he says about the locusts gradually transcend what could be true of mere bugs and could only be true of an invading army. In this way the locust plague becomes symbolic of an invading army swarming over the land of Judah like locusts, stripping it of everything that has life. The warning of the plague comes because of the sin of Judah in failing to serve the Lord. Joel holds out an escape. "Return to Me with all your heart. Rend your hearts and not your garments." History tells us that Judah ignores the warning, and the judgment eventually falls. Sin always has its consequences.

RESPONDING

1. Praise: Give your praise to the Lord that He always warns us of the consequences of sin and gives us a means of escape:

O Lord, our Lord, How excellent is Your name in all the earth, You who set Your glory above the heavens! . . . When I consider Your heavens, the work of Your fingers . . . what is man that You are mindful of him, and the son of man that You visit him? O Lord, our Lord, How majestic is Your name in all the earth! (Psalm 8:1, 3-4, 9)

Now offer to the Lord your personal praise and thanksgiving.

2. Confession: Pray this confession to the Lord as you seek to keep your life free from sin and in fellowship with Him:

All we like sheep have gone astray; we have turned, every one, to his own way; and You, O Lord, have laid on Him the iniquity of us all. (Isaiah 53:6)

Confess any personal sins which the Holy Spirit brings to your mind.

3. Affirmation: As you agree with God's will, voice your affirmation of His word:

You, O Lord, have delivered me from the power of darkness and translated me into the kingdom of the Son of Your love, in whom I have redemption through His blood, the forgiveness of sins. (Colossians 1:13-14)

4. Requests: As you make your requests known to the Lord, include:

- Spiritual insight
- Campus ministries
- Your prayer list, the concerns of your heart, and today's activities

5. Closing Prayer: Finally, offer this closing prayer to the Lord:

May I grow in the grace and knowledge of our Lord and Savior Jesus Christ. To Him be the glory both now and forever. Amen. (2 Peter 3:18)

Memory Verse: Therefore we are ambassadors for Christ, as though God were pleading through us: we implore you on Christ's behalf, be reconciled to God.

2 Corinthians 5:20
Evangelism Theme

AUGUST 22

READING

The passage for today centers on God's unavoidable judgment. Israel's sin has compounded to the point that she must be judged, but God offers hope of future restoration.

Read Amos 9.

REFLECTING

God reveals a warning of judgment on Israel through visions to Amos. One vision is a plumb line which God says he will hold up against the "wall" of Jerusalem, and it will be demonstrated that the wall is leaning and will fall (7:7-9). Another vision is of summer fruit in a basket which, left unattended, will rot and be good only for throwing out (chapter 8). These two illustrate the internal deterioration of the nation as well as the external outcome. Famine, military conquest, and pestilence are among the consequences of judgment brought on by Israel's disobedience. Israel does not repent, and judgment comes, yet the book of Amos holds out the promise of eventual restoration.

RESPONDING

1. Praise: Responding to the Lord's offer for restoration give Him your praise.

Oh, sing to the Lord a new song! Sing to the Lord, all the earth. Sing to the Lord, bless His name; proclaim the good news of His salvation from day to day. Declare His glory among the nations, His wonders among all peoples. For the Lord is great and greatly to be praised. (Psalm 96:1-4)

2. Confession: Pray this confession to the Lord as you seek to keep your life free from sin and in fellowship with Him:

Now no chastening seems to be joyful for the present, but grievous; nevertheless, afterward it yields the peaceable fruit of righteousness when I have been trained by it. (Hebrews 12:11)

Confess any personal sins which the Holy Spirit may bring to your mind.

3. Affirmation: As you agree with the will of God, voice your affirmation of His word:

If I drink of the water that You, Lord Jesus, give me, I will never thirst. The water that You shall give me will become in me a fountain of water springing up into everlasting life. (John 4:14)

4. Requests: As you make your requests known to the Lord, include:

- Desire to be like Christ
- Needs in inner cities
- Your prayer list, the concerns of your heart, and today's activities

5. Closing Prayer: Finally, offer this closing prayer to the Lord:

Blessing and honor and glory and power be to You who sit on the throne, and to You, Lord, forever and ever! (Revelation 5:13)

Memory Verse: Therefore we are ambassadors for Christ, as though God were pleading through us: we implore you on Christ's behalf, be reconciled to God.

2 Corinthians 5:20
Evangelism Theme

READING

The passage for today centers on the judgment on Edom. Edom is judged because she acted with violence toward Israel.

Read Obadiah.

REFLECTING

Esau and Jacob were brothers. Esau was the father of the nation of Edom, and Jacob was the father of the nation of Israel. Therefore, in a sense, the nations of Edom and Israel were brothers. A day comes when Assyria wages war against Jerusalem. Instead of joining Israel, their brothers, in the fight against Assyria, Edom joins Assyria and fights against its brothers in Jerusalem. Because of this breach of loyalty, God pronounces judgment on Edom through the prophet Obadiah. Edom is destroyed as a nation. God calls believers in Him to love one another and to get rid of bitterness, anger, and slander(Ephesians 4:31). Instead, we are to love, be kind, and forgive one another, by "the love of God (which) has been poured out within our hearts through the Holy Spirit who was given to us." (Romans 5:5)

RESPONDING

1. Praise: In full confidence in the love of God, offer your praise to Him.

You who love the Lord, hate evil! He preserves the souls of His saints; He delivers them out of the hand of the wicked. Light is sown for the righteous, and gladness for the upright in heart. Rejoice in the Lord, you righteous, and give thanks at the remembrance of His holy name. (Psalm 97:10-12)

Take a moment to offer the Lord your personal praise and thanksgiving.

2. Confession: Pray this confession to the Lord as you seek to keep your life free from sin and in fellowship with Him:

If I say that I have no sin, I deceive myself, and the truth is not in me. If I confess my sins, You, O Lord, are faithful and just to forgive me my sins and to cleanse me from all unrighteousness. (1 John 1:8-9)

Confess any personal sins which the Holy Spirit may bring to your mind.

3. Affirmation: As you agree with the will of God, voice your affirmation of His word:

And this is Your commandment: that I should believe on the name of Your Son Jesus Christ and love others, as He commanded me. (1 John 3:23)

4. Requests: As you make your requests known to the Lord, include:

- Personal witness for Christ
- Local churches around the nation
- Your prayer list, the concerns of your heart, and today's activities

5. Closing Prayer: Finally, offer this closing prayer to the Lord:

Amen! Blessing and glory and wisdom, thanksgiving and honor and power and might, be to You, God, forever and ever. Amen. (Revelation 7:12)

Memory Verse: Therefore we are ambassadors for Christ, as though God were pleading through us: we implore you on Christ's behalf, be reconciled to God.

2 Corinthians 5:20
Evangelism Theme

AUGUST 24

READING

The passage for today centers on Jonah's disobedience. For refusing to do God's will, Jonah is thrown into the sea and swallowed by a great fish.

Read Jonah 1.

REFLECTING

Jonah is mentioned in 2 Kings 14:25 and is very likely a strong patriot of the nation of Israel. As a result, he finds it an odious task to preach repentance to the city of Nineveh. Nineveh is the capital city of Assyria, the country which is one day to come and conquer Israel. Rather than go on this errand of mercy, Jonah chooses to hurry to the sea port at Joppa for the fastest transit in the opposite direction. This is a commission that will not be denied, however, and God causes him to be swallowed by a great fish in which, wisely, Jonah repents and from which he is released to carry the message of warning to Nineveh. Nineveh repents, as Jonah feared, and the nation is preserved as an instrument of judgment for Israel almost a hundred years later.

RESPONDING

1. Praise: God's ways are above our ways, and we praise Him for His wisdom:

O God, You are my God; early will I seek You; My soul thirsts for You, my flesh longs for You in a dry and weary land where there is no water. So I have looked for You in the sanctuary, to see Your power and Your glory. (Psalm 63:1-2)

Now offer to the Lord your personal praise and thanksgiving.

2. Confession: Pray this confession to the Lord as you seek to keep your life free from sin and in fellowship with Him:

You will again have compassion on us, and will subdue our iniquities. You will cast all our sins into the depths of the sea. (Micah 7:19)

Confess any personal sins which the Holy Spirit brings to your mind.

3. Affirmation: As you agree with God's will, voice your affirmation of His word:

For I did not receive the spirit of bondage again to fear, but I received the Spirit of adoption by whom I cry out, "Abba, Father." (Romans 8:15)

4. Requests: As you make your requests known to the Lord, include:

- An eternal perspective
- Needs of work or school mates
- Your prayer list, the concerns of your heart, and today's activities

5. Closing Prayer: Finally, offer this closing prayer to the Lord:

I will wait on You, the Lord; I will be of good courage, and You shall strengthen my heart; I will wait on You! (Psalm 27:14)

Memory Verse: Therefore we are ambassadors for Christ, as though God were pleading through us: we implore you on Christ's behalf, be reconciled to God.

2 Corinthians 5:20
Evangelism Theme

READING

The passage for today centers on the contrast of men and God. Micah laments the degradation of his fellow men, but hopes in the Lord.

Read Micah 7.

REFLECTING

Micah sets his narrative in an imaginary courtroom where he pours out scathing rebuke on the injustice he sees in his fellowmen around him. The evidence is brought forth, and the children of Israel are found guilty. Sins swarm from his pen, filling the first third of his book. False prophets preach for money. Princes rule with cruelty, violence, and corruption. Priests abandon their love for God; judges accept bribes; businessmen use false scales. The second third pictures the result of these sins. Jerusalem will be destroyed, the temple will be leveled, and the people will be banished to captivity in Babylon. But, as is typical of the prophets of God, in the final third, hope is held out on the horizon. A divine Deliverer will appear, and once again justice and righteousness will reign. Justice is now trampled, but it will eventually triumph.

RESPONDING

1. Praise: Offer to the Lord this psalm of praise as you express your gratitude for His justice:

I will praise You, O Lord, with my whole heart; I will tell of all Your marvelous works. I will be glad and rejoice in You; I will sing praise to Your name, O Most High. . . . The Lord also will be a refuge for the oppressed, a refuge in times of trouble. And those who know Your name will put their trust in You;

for You, Lord have not forsaken those who seek You. (Psalm 9:1-2, 9-10)

Now offer to the Lord your personal praise and thanksgiving.

2. Confession: Pray this confession to the Lord as you seek to keep your life free from sin and in fellowship with Him:

For a mere moment You have forsaken me, but with great mercies You will gather me. With a little wrath You hid Your face from me for a moment; but with everlasting kindness You will have mercy on me. (Isaiah 54:7-8)

Confess any personal sins which the Holy Spirit brings to your mind.

3. Affirmation: As you agree with God's will, voice your affirmation of His word:

You, O Lord, are Spirit, and I must worship You in spirit and truth. (John 4:24)

4. Requests: As you make your requests known to the Lord, include:

- Personal discipline
- Christians worldwide who are persecuted for their faith
- Your prayer list, the concerns of your heart, and today's activities

5. Closing Prayer: Finally, offer this closing prayer to the Lord:

Show me the path of life; in Your presence is fullness of joy; at Your right hand are pleasures forevermore. (Psalm 16:11)

Memory Verse: Therefore we are ambassadors for Christ, as though God were pleading through us: we implore you on Christ's behalf, be reconciled to God.

2 Corinthians 5:20
Evangelism Theme

AUGUST 26

READING

The passage for today centers on the awesomeness of God. Nahum exalts the character and power of God and warns Nineveh to turn from idolatry and be true to vows.

Read Nahum 1.

REFLECTING

Over 100 years ago, Jonah preached repentance to the city of Nineveh, and she repented in sackcloth and ashes. Now, their second prophet, Nahum, is sent from God to urge them to repent. This message must seem absurd. In the ensuing years, Nineveh has grown to become the most powerful city in the known world. Her walls seem impregnable. Rising one hundred feet into the air and dotted by fifteen hundred huge towers, they are wide enough to enable three chariots to race side by side on top of them. Water totally surrounds the city, and inside there is a self-sufficient agricultural system. Feeling self-sufficient, they do not repent. God sends a flood to wash away part of that great wall. The Babylonian army marches through the breach in the wall, and Nineveh falls. The word of God is sure!

RESPONDING

1. Praise: Praise the Lord that His word can be trusted:

I will love You, O Lord, my strength. The Lord is my rock and my fortress and my deliverer; my God, my strength, in whom I will trust; my shield and the horn of my salvation, my stronghold. I call upon the Lord, who is worthy to be praised; so shall I be saved from my enemies. . . . The Lord lives! Blessed be my Rock! Let the God of my salvation be exalted. (Psalm 18:1-3, 46)

Now offer to the Lord your personal praise and thanksgiving.

2. Confession: Pray this confession to the Lord as you seek to keep your life free from sin and in fellowship with Him:

Let the wicked forsake his way, and the unrighteous man his thoughts; let him return to You, the Lord, and You will have mercy on him; and You, our God, for You will abundantly pardon. (Isaiah 55:7)

Confess any personal sins which the Holy Spirit brings to your mind.

3. Affirmation: As you agree with God's will, voice your affirmation of His word:

And now, Lord, what do I wait for? My hope is in You. (Psalm 39:7)

4. Requests: As you make your requests known to the Lord, include:

- Love for the Lord
- The work of missions in the Middle East, Australia, and the Islands
- Your prayer list, the concerns of your heart, and today's activities.

5. Closing Prayer: Finally, offer this closing prayer to the Lord:

Save Your people, and bless Your inheritance; shepherd us also, and bear us up forever. (Psalm 28:9)

Memory Verse: Therefore we are ambassadors for Christ, as though God were pleading through us: we implore you on Christ's behalf, be reconciled to God.

2 Corinthians 5:20
Evangelism Theme

READING

The passage for today centers on God's deliverance of His people. Contrasted with the judgment of God, Habakkuk exults in the God of his salvation.

Read Habakkuk 3.

REFLECTING

Habakkuk wrestles with God concerning the sinfulness of his fellow Jews. Why does God not do something? Why does God not judge His people? As Habakkuk puts this question to the Lord, He responds that He *is* doing something: He is raising up the Chaldeans to come and conquer Judah. Astounded by this revelation, Habakkuk cries out, "How can you use a nation that is more sinful than Judah to conquer Judah?" God's answer? God's people are deserving of judgment. The righteousness of the instrument of judgment is inconsequential. And as far as Habakkuk is concerned personally, "The righteous shall live by faith!" Habakkuk responds in faith: "Even if disaster strikes, I will rejoice, because You are my strength."

RESPONDING

1. Praise: Because the Lord can be trusted, no matter what the appearance of the circumstances, offer Him your praise:

Because Your lovingkindness is better than life, My lips shall praise You. Thus I will bless You while I live; I will lift up my hands in Your name. My soul shall be satisfied as with marrow and fatness, and my mouth shall praise You with joyful lips. . . . Because You have been my help, therefore in the shadow of Your wings I will rejoice. (Psalm 63:3-5, 7)

Now offer to the Lord your personal praise and thanksgiving.

2. Confession: Pray this confession to the Lord as you seek to keep your life free from sin and in fellowship with Him:

Lord, be merciful to me; heal my soul, for I have sinned against You. . . . O Lord, be merciful to me, and raise me up, . . . Blessed be the Lord God of Israel from everlasting to everlasting! Amen and Amen. (Psalm 41:4, 10, 13)

Confess any personal sins which the Holy Spirit brings to your mind.

3. Affirmation: As you agree with God's will, voice your affirmation of His word:

I delight to do Your will, O my God, and Your law is within my heart. (Psalm 40:8)

4. Requests: As you make your requests known to the Lord, include:

- Faithfulness in sharing Christ
- The Lord's work in national and world affairs
- Your prayer list, the concerns of your heart, and today's activities.

5. Closing Prayer: Finally, offer this closing prayer to the Lord:

You, the Lord, will command Your lovingkindness in the daytime, and in the night Your song shall be with me—a prayer to You, the God of my life. (Psalm 42:8)

Memory Verse: And for me, that utterance may be given to me, that I may open my mouth boldly to make known the mystery of the gospel.
Ephesians 6:19
Evangelism Theme

AUGUST 28

READING

The passage for today centers on judgment on Jerusalem and the nations. Woes are pronounced for sin, but restoration is promised for repentance.

Read Zephaniah 3.

REFLECTING

Blue blood flows in Zephaniah's veins. He is the great-great-grandson of Hezekiah, the thirteenth king of Judah, and one of the most righteous of all kings. The flame for revival and religious reform burns as hot in Zephaniah's heart as it had in his forefather's. His book has been called one of the "hottest" books in the Old Testament. He portrays "the final crash of the universe." The impending Day of the Lord is his all-encompassing message. Twenty-three times in the short book he refers specifically to that day which signifies the final judgment of God on the earth. Following the time of terrible judgment is the time of restoration and peace. Beyond judgment there is joy.

RESPONDING

1. Praise: Give thanks to the Lord, and praise Him that all events are in control and that eventually His children will know only joy.

Let my mouth be filled with Your praise and with Your glory all the day. . . . But I will hope continually, and will praise You yet more and more. My mouth shall tell of Your righteousness and Your salvation all the day, for I do not know their limits. I will go in the strength of the Lord God; I will make mention of Your righteousness, of Yours only. O God, You have taught me from my youth and to this day declare Your wondrous works. (Psalm 71:8, 14-17)

Now offer to the Lord your personal praise and thanksgiving.

2. Confession: Pray this confession to the Lord as you seek to keep your life free from sin and in fellowship with Him:

Cleanse me from all my iniquity which I have sinned against You, and pardon all my iniquities by which I have sinned and by which I have transgressed against You. (Jeremiah 33:8)

Confess any personal sins which the Holy Spirit brings to your mind.

3. Affirmation: As you agree with God's will, voice your affirmation of His word:

I consider that the sufferings of this present time are not worthy to be compared with the glory which shall be revealed in me. (Romans 8:18)

4. Requests: As you make your requests known to the Lord, include:

- Compassion for others
- Missions in America
- Your prayer list, the concerns of your heart, and today's activities

5. Closing Prayer: Finally, offer this closing prayer to the Lord:

Blessed are You, the Lord, forevermore! Amen and amen. (Psalm 89:52)

Memory Verse: And for me, that utterance may be given to me, that I may open my mouth boldly to make known the mystery of the gospel.
Ephesians 6:19
Evangelism Theme

READING

The passage for today centers on the building of the temple. Haggai explains that God's people are suffering for neglecting the building of the temple.

Read Haggai 1.

REFLECTING

As the children of Israel return from the Babylonian captivity, the first order of business is to rebuild the temple in order to restore worship. Haggai is a prophet of God who is ministering at the time, encouraging the people to complete the work. The foundation is laid quickly and with great enthusiasm. Discouragement sets in quickly, however, and work on the temple is soon forgotten in favor of their own houses. Finally, after fifteen years, Haggai tells them that the afflictions which they are suffering are because of their neglect of the temple. They must finish the temple first and then build their houses. First things first. God demands proper priorities.

RESPONDING

1. Praise: To God, who helps us order our priorities, offer these words of praise:

Be glad in the Lord and rejoice, you righteous; and shout for joy, all you upright in heart! (Psalm 32:11)

Rejoice in the Lord, O you righteous! For praise from the upright is beautiful. Praise the Lord with the harp; make melody to Him with an instrument of ten strings. (Psalm 33:1-2)

Pause for personal praise and thanksgiving.

2. Confession: Pray this confession to the Lord as you seek to keep your life free from sin and in fellowship with Him:

Sing praise to the Lord, you saints of His, and give thanks at the remembrance of His holy name. For His anger is but for a moment, His favor is for a life; weeping may endure for a night but joy comes in the morning. (Psalm 30:4-5)

Confess any personal sins which the Holy Spirit brings to your mind.

3. Affirmation: Now pause to pray this affirmation to the Lord:

O God, You are Spirit, and I must worship in spirit and truth. (John 4:24)

4. Requests: As you make your requests known to the Lord, include:

- Personal spiritual growth
- Military ministries
- Your prayer list, the concerns of your heart, and today's activities

5. Closing Prayer: Finally, offer this closing prayer to the Lord:

Glory to You in the highest, and on earth peace, good will toward men! (Luke 2:14)

Memory Verse: And for me, that utterance may be given to me, that I may open my mouth boldly to make known the mystery of the gospel.
Ephesians 6:19
Evangelism Theme

AUGUST 30

READING

The passage for today centers on the King of the earth. The day is coming when God will battle all Jerusalem's enemies and be a righteous King over all the earth. Read Zechariah 14.

REFLECTING

Haggai and Zechariah minister to the same people at the same time. Their goal is the same: to motivate the people to rebuild the temple. Haggai utters rebuke; Zechariah breathes encouragement. Both exercise gifts needed to spur the nation to complete the task. Haggai makes them feel that they *ought* to rebuild the temple. Zechariah makes them *want* to rebuild the temple. He reinforces God's love and care for Israel and the certainty of the ultimate defeat of her enemies. Whether through exhortation or encouragement, God uses many individuals to prompt us to obedience. He wants our obedience motivated out of love for Him, yet He uses a variety of means to remind us of our goal.

RESPONDING

1. Praise: What a joy to know the Lord is always working in our lives. Praise Him for His goodness:

The Lord made the heavens. Honor and majesty are before Him; strength and beauty are in His sanctuary. Give to the Lord, O kindreds of the peoples, give to the Lord glory and strength. Give to the Lord the glory due His name; bring an offering, and come into His courts. . . . Let the heavens rejoice, and let the earth be glad. (Psalm 96:5-8, 11)

Take a moment to offer the Lord your personal praise and thanksgiving.

2. Confession: Pray this confession to the Lord as you seek to keep your life free from sin and in fellowship with Him:

If I sin, I have an Advocate with You, Father, Jesus Christ the righteous. And He Himself is the propitiation for my sins, and not for mine only, but also for the whole world. (1 John 2:1-2)

Confess any personal sins which the Holy Spirit may bring to your mind.

3. Affirmation: As you agree with the will of God, voice your affirmation of His word:

For to me, to live is Christ, and to die is gain. (Philippians 2:21)

4. Requests: As you make your requests known to the Lord, include:

- Fruit of the Spirit in your life
- The ministry of Christian literature
- Your prayer list, the concerns of your heart, and today's activities

5. Closing Prayer: Finally, offer this closing prayer to the Lord:

Grace, mercy, and peace from You, the Father, and the Lord Jesus Christ our Savior. (Titus 1:4)

Memory Verse: And for me, that utterance may be given to me, that I may open my mouth boldly to make known the mystery of the gospel.
Ephesians 6:19
Evangelism Theme

AUGUST 31

READING

The passage for today centers on robbing God. Malachi challenges the Israelites that they are robbing God but are refusing to acknowledge it. Read Malachi 3.

REFLECTING

The Israelites who have returned to Jerusalem have grown comfortable and complacent through the years. They have grown arrogantly insensitive. Through His messenger, Malachi, God confronts them with their complacency. He charges that the priests are despising His name and defiling His altar. They ask how. God says He will no longer accept their offerings. They ask why. God states that they have been wearisome with their words. They ask how. God asks them to return to Him. They ask how. God reproaches them for robbing Him. They ask how. They have hardened their hearts, and they no longer feel the pull of God in their lives. The result is a barren period of 400 years with no word from God. Be certain you respond to the work of God in your heart, lest you experience spiritual barrenness as a result.

RESPONDING

1. Praise: Praise the Lord that He calls us to Himself and enriches our lives when we follow Him:

Lord, You have been our dwelling place in all generations. Before the mountains were brought forth, or ever You had formed the earth and the world, even from everlasting to everlasting, You are God. . . . Oh, satisfy us with Your mercy, that we may rejoice and be glad all our days! (Psalm 90:1-2, 14)

Now offer to the Lord your personal praise and thanksgiving.

2. Confession: Pray this confession to the Lord as you seek to keep your life free from sin and in fellowship with Him:

O Lord, I know the way of man is not in himself; it is not in man who walks to direct his own steps. O Lord, correct me, but with justice; not in Your anger, lest You bring me to nothing. (Jeremiah 10:23-24)

Confess any personal sins which the Holy Spirit brings to your mind.

3. Affirmation: As you agree with God's will, voice your affirmation of His word:

All Scripture is given by Your inspiration, O God, and is profitable for doctrine, for reproof, for correction, for instruction in righteousness, that the man of God may be complete, thoroughly equipped for every good work. (2 Timothy 3:16-17)

4. Requests: As you make your requests known to the Lord, include:

- Boldness in living for Christ
- God's blessing on America
- Your prayer list, the concerns of your heart, and today's activities

5. Closing Prayer: Finally, offer this closing prayer to the Lord:

Now to You who are able to keep me from stumbling, and to present me faultless before the presence of Your glory with exceeding joy, to You, my God and Savior, who alone are wise, be glory and majesty, dominion and power, both now and forever. Amen. (Jude 24-25)

Memory Verse: And for me, that utterance may be given to me, that I may open my mouth boldly to make known the mystery of the gospel.
Ephesians 6:19
Evangelism Theme

READING

The passage for today centers on Luke's introduction to the Acts of the Apostles. After the Ascension of Christ, the Apostles meet in an upper room to choose a replacement for Judas.

Read Acts 1.

REFLECTING

God is moving. He is putting in place the essential element for a cataclysmic change in things. For thousands of years, He has worked in the world through the nation of Israel and the Law of Moses. Now He will work through the Church and the Gospel of Christ. Men are His methods, but the power is His own. Like a grand master setting up chess pieces on a board, God instructs the Apostles to wait in Jerusalem until they receive power from on high. Then, when they are baptized with the power necessary to begin the task at hand, the power of the Holy Spirit, they are to be His witnesses to Him in their city, the surrounding country, and the entire world.

The greatest work of man is prayer, for God moves in response to the prayers of man. As the holy Apostles of old heeded God's instructions and moved, not in their own power but by faithful obedience to the revealed will of God, so must we, by the strength which God supplies. (1 Peter 4:11)

RESPONDING

1. Praise: Offer to God this praise as you think about His power and the significance of serving Him:

The Lord lives! Blessed be my Rock! Let God be exalted, the Rock of my salvation! (2 Samuel 22:47)

Now express any additional thoughts you may have of thanks or praise.

2. Confession: Pray this confession to the Lord as you seek to keep your life free from sin and in fellowship with Him:

If I say that I have no sin, I deceive myself, and the truth is not in me. If I confess my sins, You, O Lord, are faithful and just to forgive me of my sins and to cleanse me from all unrighteousness. (1 John 1:8-9)

Confess any personal sins which the Holy Spirit brings to your mind.

3. Affirmation: Now pray this affirmation to the Lord as you agree with and submit yourself to the will of God:

Your word is a lamp to my feet and a light to my path. (Psalm 119:105)

4. Requests: The Lord encourages us to come to Him with our concerns and desires. As you make your requests known to the Lord, include:

- Health and strength to serve God

- God's will to be done on earth

- Your prayer list, the concerns of your heart, and today's activities

5. Closing Prayer: Finally, offer this closing prayer to the Lord:

Be glad in the Lord and rejoice, you righteous; and shout for joy, all you upright in heart! (Psalm 32:11)

Memory Verse: And for me, that utterance may be given to me, that I may open my mouth boldly to make known the mystery of the gospel.
Ephesians 6:19
Evangelism Theme

SEPTEMBER 2

READING

The passage for today centers on the Day of Pentecost. After the ascension, on the Jewish Feast Day of Pentecost, the Holy Spirit comes upon the believing Jews gathered at the temple.

Read Acts 2.

REFLECTING

Who would have expected the coming of the Holy Spirit in the New Testament to be like this? A rushing of wind, flames of fire, many languages present, yet all understand. Unbelieving hearts find a "natural" explanation: "These men are drunk." A simple, tidy, uncomplicated explanation which requires no response on their part. They can walk away unscathed. But the believing hearts drop to their knees and cry out to God! "Brothers, what shall we do?" Revelation always demands a response. The unbelieving heart can always find a way to slink out from under the authority of Scripture. But the believing heart will cry out, "O God, what shall I do?" Search your mind. Is there some response you should be making to God right now?

RESPONDING

1. Praise: Offer your praise to the Lord as your proper response to the revelation you have received of Him:

You are the Rock, Your work is perfect; for all Your ways are justice, a God of truth and without injustice, righteous and upright are You. (Deuteronomy 32:4)

Take a moment to offer the Lord your personal praise and thanksgiving.

2. Confession: Pray this confession to the Lord as you seek to keep your life free from sin and in fellowship with Him:

Forgive me, Lord, when I am unmindful of You, the Rock who begot me, and when I forget you, the God who fathered me. (Deuteronomy 32:18)

Confess any personal sins which the Holy Spirit may bring to your mind.

3. Affirmation: As you agree with the will of God, voice your affirmation of His word:

You, O Lord, will instruct me and teach me in the way I should go; You will guide me with Your eye. (Psalm 32:8)

4. Requests: As you make your requests known to the Lord, include:

- Sensitivity to sin
- The ministry of your local church
- Your prayer list, the concerns of your heart, and today's activities

5. Closing Prayer: Finally, offer this closing prayer to the Lord:

Let the words of my mouth and the meditation of my heart be acceptable in Your sight, O Lord, my strength and my redeemer. (Psalm 19:14)

Memory Verse: And for me, that utterance may be given to me, that I may open my mouth boldly to make known the mystery of the gospel.
Ephesians 6:19
Evangelism Theme

READING

The passage for today centers on the martyrdom of Stephen. Stephen is arrested for preaching the gospel, and after he brilliantly defends his message, he is killed for his faith. Read Acts 7.

REFLECTING

The unbeliever must either accept the message of God or find a way to kill the message. He must either drop to his knees or strike out with his sword. The New Testament was written in times that, in some ways, seem barbaric to us. That respectable people would pick up stones and kill another man with their own hands is difficult for us to imagine. Yet culture was different then. We do not kill men to get rid of unwanted messages today. We must use other tactics. We can kill his message by making it look foolish or discredit the man by destroying his reputation. Or we can attack God Himself, declaring that He is dead. But unless we accept the message of salvation which Stephen preached, we are as guilty before God as the ones who threw the stones.

RESPONDING

1. Praise: Thank the Lord, and give Him your praise for offering you salvation through Christ:

It is good to give thanks to the Lord, and to sing praises to Your name, O Most High; to declare Your lovingkindness in the morning, and Your faithfulness every night. . . . For You, Lord, have made me glad through Your work; I will triumph in the works of Your hands. . . . To declare that the Lord is upright; He is my rock, and there is no unrighteousness in Him. (Psalm 92:1-2, 4, 15)

Take a moment to offer the Lord your personal praise and thanksgiving.

2. Confession: Pray this confession to the Lord as you seek to keep your life free from sin and in fellowship with Him:

I have stumbled because of my iniquity. Take away all iniquity, receive me graciously, for I will offer the sacrifices of my lips. (Hosea 14:1-2)

Confess any personal sins which the Holy Spirit may bring to your mind.

3. Affirmation: As you agree with the will of God, voice your affirmation of His word:

If I overcome, You, Lord Jesus, will grant to me to sit with You on Your throne, as You overcame and sat down with Your Father on His throne. (Revelation 3:21)

4. Requests: As you make your requests known to the Lord, include:

- Wisdom for living life
- Needs of your immediate family
- Your prayer list, the concerns of your heart, and today's activities

5. Closing Prayer: Finally, offer this closing prayer to the Lord:

Surely goodness and mercy shall follow me all the days of my life, and I will dwell in the house of the Lord forever. (Psalm 23:6)

Memory Verse: Let your speech always be with grace, seasoned with salt, that you may know how you ought to answer each one.

Colossians 4:6
Evangelism Theme

SEPTEMBER 4

READING

The passage for today centers on the persecution of the Church. The stoning of Stephen initiates a wave of persecution, led by Saul and others, which drives the Jewish believers from Jerusalem.

Read Acts 8.

REFLECTING

As the Jewish believers flee Jerusalem for their very lives, taking the gospel with them, Philip comes upon an Ethiopian dignitary who is struggling to understand the Scripture. "Do you understand what you are reading?" Philip asks. "How can I, unless someone guides me?" the eunuch replies. (8:30-31)

Men are God's method. He has chosen to reach the world for Christ through men. The Lord could have resorted to skywriting or personal visions en masse to all people or had angels visit everyone. But He chose men to reach other men.

Our responsibility, in principle, is simple: to manifest the character and proclaim the name of Christ wherever we go. The work is God's but He will use you, if you will let Him.

RESPONDING

1. Praise: Because the Lord led someone to give His message of salvation to us, praise Him with this psalm:

The Lord reigns, He is clothed with majesty; the Lord is clothed, He has girded Himself with strength. Surely the world is established, so that it cannot be moved. Your throne is established from of old; You are from everlasting. (Psalm 93:1-2)

Take a moment to offer the Lord your personal praise and thanksgiving.

2. Confession: Pray this confession to the Lord as you seek to keep your life free from sin and in fellowship with Him:

You, O Lord, say to me, "Now, therefore, turn to Me with all your heart, with fasting, with weeping, and with mourning." You ask me to rend my heart, and not my garments; to return to You, my God; for You are gracious and merciful, slow to anger, and of great kindness; and You relent from doing harm. (Joel 2:12-13)

Confess any personal sins which the Holy Spirit may bring to your mind.

3. Affirmation: As you agree with the will of God, voice your affirmation of His word:

For You, O God, have not given me a spirit of fear, but of power and of love and of a sound mind. (2 Timothy 1:7)

4. Requests: As you make your requests known to the Lord, include:

- Insight into Scripture
- The hungry around the world
- Your prayer list, the concerns of your heart, and today's activities

5. Closing Prayer: Finally, offer this closing prayer to the Lord:

We will be of good courage, and You shall strengthen our hearts, all we who hope in the Lord. (Psalm 31:24)

Memory Verse: Let your speech always be with grace, seasoned with salt, that you may know how you ought to answer each one.

Colossians 4:6
Evangelism Theme

READING

The passage for today centers on the conversion of Saul. Saul, on his way to Damascus to persecute Christians, has a divine revelation of Jesus and is converted to Christianity.

Read Acts 9.

REFLECTING

From God's perspective, the relationship between Christ and the Church is a very close and dear one. Jesus is the Son of God and bridegroom; the Church is His bride. The connection is so close that to harm the Church is to harm Christ, just as harming a wife hurts her husband. Though Paul never lays a hand on Him, Jesus speaks from heaven, "Saul, Saul, why are you persecuting Me?" (9:4) Saul's actions against the Church hurt the Son. We must strive to gain God's perspective on who we are. We are His bride, His chosen one, the delight of His life. God longs for us to act as His beloved. When we see ourselves as He sees us, we can be more successful at living as we should, like who we really are.

RESPONDING

1. Praise: In response to the love and care of the Bridegroom, offer Him this praise:

Unto You I lift up my eyes, O You who dwell in the heavens. Behold, as the eyes of servants look to the hand of their masters, as the eyes of a maid to the hand of her mistress, so our eyes look to the Lord our God, until He has mercy on us. (Psalm 123:1-2)

I will praise the Lord according to His righteousness, and will sing praise to the name of the Lord Most High. (Psalm 7:17)

Pause for personal praise and thanksgiving.

2. Confession: Pray this confession to the Lord as you seek to keep your life free from sin and in fellowship with Him:

Have mercy upon me, O God, according to Your lovingkindness; according to the multitude of Your tender mercies, blot out my transgressions. Wash me thoroughly from my iniquity and cleanse me from my sin. For I acknowledge my transgressions and my sin is ever before me. (Psalm 51:1-3)

Confess any personal sins which the Holy spirit brings to your mind.

3. Affirmation: Now pause to pray this affirmation to the Lord:

Behold, You, O God, are my salvation, I will trust and not be afraid; "For YAH, the Lord, is my strength and my song; He also has become my salvation." (Isaiah 12:2)

4. Requests: As you make your requests known to the Lord, include:

- Love for fellow Christians
- The work of missions in Europe and Asia
- Your prayer list, the concerns of your heart, and today's activities

5. Closing Prayer: Finally, offer this closing prayer to the Lord:

This is the day which You have made; I will rejoice and be glad in it. (Psalm 118:24)

Memory Verse: Let your speech always be with grace, seasoned with salt, that you may know how you ought to answer each one.

Colossians 4:6
Evangelism Theme

SEPTEMBER 6

READING

The passage for today centers on Paul's first missionary journey. Saul, adopting a Christian name, Paul, travels to Galatia with the message of the Gospel.

Read Acts 13.

REFLECTING

Chapter 13 records a remarkable fulfillment of prophecy which is easily missed. In chapter 1, Jesus commissions the disciples to be witnesses for Him and proclaims that they will personally take the gospel to the ends of the earth. Now, the Holy Spirit sets apart Paul and Barnabas to begin traveling to the ends of the earth, taking the message with them. In their lifetimes the then-known world was indeed reached with the message. You and I are extensions of this commission and can be extensions of its prophetic fulfillment—as we accept the commission as our personal commission—and help take the message to the ends of the world in which we live. This requires personal commitment and involvement through prayer, support, giving, and participation.

RESPONDING

1. Praise: Offer the Lord your praise for His goodness through the words of this psalm:

O God, You are my God; early will I seek You; My soul thirsts for You, my flesh longs for You in a dry and weary land where there is no water. So I have looked for You in the sanctuary, to see Your power and Your glory. (Psalm 63:1-2)

Pause for personal praise and thanksgiving.

2. Confession: Pray this confession to the Lord as you seek to keep your life free from sin and in fellowship with Him:

Bless the Lord, O my soul; and all that is within me, bless His holy name! Bless the Lord, O my soul, and forget not all His benefits: who forgives all your iniquities. (Psalm 103:1-3)

Confess any personal sins which the Holy Spirit brings to mind.

3. Affirmation: Now pause to pray this affirmation to the Lord:

I may come to You, O Lord, weary and heavy laden, and You will give me rest. I may take Your yoke upon me, and learn from You, for You are gentle and lowly in heart, and I shall find rest for my soul. For Your yoke is easy, and Your burden is light. (Matthew 11:28:30)

4. Requests: As you make your requests known to the Lord, include:

- Faithfulness with your time
- The president and national leaders and affairs
- Your prayer list, the concerns of your heart, and today's activities

5. Closing Prayer: Finally, offer this closing prayer to the Lord:

Oh, satisfy me early with Your mercy, that I may rejoice and be glad all my days! (Psalm 90:14)

Memory Verse: Let your speech always be with grace, seasoned with salt, that you may know how you ought to answer each one.

Colossians 4:6
Evangelism Theme

READING

The passage for today centers on Paul's second missionary journey. After a council at Jerusalem to clarify doctrinal issues, Paul begins his second missionary journey.

Read Acts 15.

REFLECTING

Inherent within man is a tendency to want to work his way to heaven. It does not seem to be enough to accept a gift with gratitude. He wants to do something to earn it. He does not quite dare to believe that he does not have to do something to "hold up his end of the bargain." While Paul and Barnabas are at Antioch, some men came down from Judea and were teaching that "unless you are circumcised and obey the Law of Moses, you cannot be saved." This question grows into a major debate in Jerusalem, but in the final analysis, Peter's argument wins out: "Why put on the necks of the disciples a yoke that neither we nor our fathers have been able to bear?" "Works" will follow our salvation, but will never cause it.

RESPONDING

1. Praise: Since none of us could earn it, praise the Lord who gives us our salvation:

Blessed be Your glorious name, which is exalted above all blessing and praise! You alone are the Lord; You have made heaven, the heaven of heavens, with all their host, the earth and all things on it, the seas and all that is in them, and You preserve them all. The host of heaven worships You. (Nehemiah 9:5-6)

Now offer to the Lord your personal praise and thanksgiving.

2. Confession: Pray this confession to the Lord as you seek to keep your life free from sin and in fellowship with Him:

Surely You, Lord Jesus, have borne our griefs and carried our sorrows; . . . You were wounded for our transgressions, You were bruised for our iniquities; the chastisement for our peace was upon You, and by Your stripes we are healed. (Isaiah 53:4-5)

Confess any personal sins which the Holy Spirit brings to your mind.

3. Affirmation: As you agree with God's will, voice your affirmation of His word:

If I love You, O Lord, I will keep Your word; and the Father will love me, and You and the Father will come to me and make Your home with me. (John 14:23)

4. Requests: As you make your requests known to the Lord, include:

- Your financial needs
- The needs of the poor
- Your prayer list, the concerns of your heart, and today's activities

5. Closing Prayer: Finally, offer this closing prayer to the Lord:

Let the beauty of You, Lord, be upon me, and establish the work of my hands for me; yes, establish the work of my hands. (Psalm 90:17)

Memory Verse: Let your speech always be with grace, seasoned with salt, that you may know how you ought to answer each one.

Colossians 4:6
Evangelism Theme

SEPTEMBER 8

READING

The passage for today centers on Paul's Macedonian vision. As a result of seeing a man of Macedonia in a vision, Paul travels to Macedonia, Achaia, and Greece, carrying the gospel.

Read Acts 16.

REFLECTING

Sometimes in the crises of life, we think more clearly than at any other time. The superfluous evaporates. The essentials rise up. Things swing into perspective. Often, it is only in the face of danger or loss that we perceive what is important and what is unimportant in life. In World War 2, many soldiers "got religion" while in their fox holes under enemy fire. Because many of these fox hole conversions were not genuine, people have become skeptical of anyone who becomes a Christian under stress. Yet there are many, including the Philippian jailer, who will testify that some "fox hole conversions" are genuine. Be sensitive to the Lord when you are under stress. It may be the Lord trying to help you get your life into perspective.

RESPONDING

1. **Praise:** Offer your praise to the Lord because he turns even the difficult things in our lives into good:

Give to the Lord, O kindreds of the peoples. . . . Give to the Lord the glory due His name; bring an offering, and come before Him. Oh, worship the Lord in the beauty of holiness! (1 Chronicles 16:28-29)

I will praise the Lord according to His righteousness, and will sing praise to the name of the Lord Most High. (Psalm 7:17)

Now offer to the Lord your personal praise and thanksgiving.

2. **Confession:** Pray this confession to the Lord as you seek to keep your life free from sin and in fellowship with Him:

O Lord, You blot out my transgressions for Your own sake; and You will not remember my sins. (Isaiah 43:25)

Confess any personal sins which the Holy Spirit brings to your mind.

3. **Affirmation:** As you agree with God's will, voice your affirmation of His word:

The Spirit also helps me in weaknesses. For I do not know what I should pray for as I ought, but the Spirit Himself makes intercession for me with groanings which cannot be uttered. (Romans 8:26)

4. **Requests:** As you make your requests known to the Lord, include:

- Protection from the "evil one"
- Laborers for the "harvest"
- Your prayer list, the concerns of your heart, and today's activities

5. **Closing Prayer:** Finally, offer this closing prayer to the Lord:

Bless the Lord, all you His hosts, you ministers of His, who do His pleasure. Bless the Lord, all His works, in all places of His dominion. (Psalm 103:21-22)

Memory Verse: Let your speech always be with grace, seasoned with salt, that you may know how you ought to answer each one.

Colossians 4:6
Evangelism Theme

READING

The passage for today centers on the founding of new churches. As Paul continues his journeys, he establishes churches at Thessalonica and Athens.

Read Acts 17.

REFLECTING

It is often necessary to establish common ground with others in order to win a hearing for the gospel. This common ground may be a point of mutual interest or the development of a relationship or a common experience. Paul used a point of common ground when he began with the idol "To The Unknown God." Catching their ears with this starting point, he developed his argument to present to them the living Christ. His message to them was simple and unadorned. "God is now declaring to men that all everywhere should repent, because He has fixed a day in which He will judge the world in righteousness through a Man whom He has appointed, having furnished proof to all men by raising Him from the dead." That is the message which the Holy Spirit uses to bring people to Christ.

RESPONDING

1. Praise: Offer the following praise to the Lord for allowing you to hear the message of salvation:

Tremble before Him, all the earth. The world also is firmly established, it shall not be moved. Let the heavens rejoice, and let the earth be glad. . . . Oh, give thanks to the Lord, for He is good! For His mercy endures forever. . . . Blessed be the Lord God of Israel from everlasting to everlasting! (1 Chronicles 16:30-31, 34, 36)

Now offer to the Lord your personal praise and thanksgiving.

2. Confession: Pray this confession to the Lord as you seek to keep your life free from sin and in fellowship with Him:

You have blotted out, like a thick cloud, my transgressions, and like a cloud, my sins. I will return to You, for You have redeemed me. (Isaiah 44:22)

Confess any personal sins which the Holy Spirit brings to your mind.

3. Affirmation: As you agree with God's will, voice your affirmation of His word:

If I keep Your commandments, O Lord, I will abide in Your love, just as You have kept Your Father's commandments and abide in His love. (John 15:10)

4. Requests: As you make your requests known to the Lord, include:

- Commitment to the Lord
- Parachurch ministries
- Your prayer list, the concerns of your heart, and today's activities

5. Closing Prayer: Finally, offer this closing prayer to the Lord:

Lord, preserve me from all evil; preserve my soul. Lord, preserve my going out and my coming in from this time forth, and even forevermore. (Psalm 121:7-8)

Memory Verse: Let your speech always be with grace, seasoned with salt, that you may know how you ought to answer each one.

Colossians 4:6
Evangelism Theme

SEPTEMBER 10

READING

The passage for today centers on Paul's third missionary journey. Shortly after Paul returns from his second missionary journey, he embarks on his third journey, which takes him first to Ephesus.

Read Acts 18.

REFLECTING

Apollos combined the eloquence of the Greek with the religious instinct of the Jew. Most likely a student from the great university at Alexandria, a convert to the gospel, deeply conversant with the Old Testament, gifted with marvelous eloquence, he was a strong ally of the Christian forces of his age. But he needed to know of the death, resurrection, and ascended power of Christ. Into all these he was led by Aquila and Priscilla. How wonderful is that holy wisdom which the Spirit of God gives to humble believers so that they can become teachers of men who are intellectually their superiors. When teaching children or new believers, encourage them and have hope that some may become "mighty in the Scriptures."

RESPONDING

1. Praise: Offer your praise to the Lord for the ministry which He provides in your life through other believers.

O Lord God of Israel, the One who dwells between the cherubim, You are God, You alone, of all the kingdoms of the earth. You have made heaven and earth. (2 Kings 19:15)

Lord God of Israel, there is no God in heaven above or on earth below like You, who keep Your covenant and mercy with Your servants who walk before You with all their heart. (1 Kings 8:23)

Now offer to the Lord your personal praise and thanksgiving.

2. Confession: Pray this confession to the Lord as you seek to keep your life free from sin and in fellowship with Him:

I will praise You, for I am fearfully and wonderfully made; marvelous are Your works, and that my soul knows very well. . . . Search me, O God, and know my heart; try me, and know my anxieties; and see if there is any wicked way in me, and lead me in the way everlasting. (Psalm 139:14, 23-24)

Confess any personal sins which the Holy Spirit brings to your mind.

3. Affirmation: As you agree with God's will, voice your affirmation of His word:

I have sinned and fall short of Your glory, O God, being justified as a gift by His grace through the redemption which is in Christ Jesus. (Romans 3:23-24)

4. Requests: As you make your requests known to the Lord, include:

- Renewing of your mind
- Needs of your extended family
- Your prayer list, the concerns of your heart, and today's activities

5. Closing Prayer: Finally, offer this closing prayer to the Lord:

May we with one mind and one mouth glorify the God and Father of our Lord Jesus Christ. (Romans 15:6)

Memory Verse: But sanctify the Lord God in your hearts, and always be ready to give a defense to everyone who asks you a reason for the hope that is in you, with meekness and fear.

1 Peter 3:15
Evangelism Theme

READING

The passage for today centers on Paul's arrest in Jerusalem. After Paul's travels, he preaches in Jerusalem and is arrested for violating the law.

Read Acts 21.

REFLECTING

When Paul preaches, a riot or a revival usually breaks out. When he goes to Jerusalem for the last time, a riot breaks out. Having been told by the Holy Spirit, he is aware that he will be imprisoned and handed over to the Gentiles. Even though his friends beg him to avoid Jerusalem, Paul "would not be persuaded," remarking, "The will of the Lord be done!" Paul views himself as a sojourner on this earth. His true citizenship is in heaven. He is simply to be a steward, an ambassador of Christ while his time lasts. What power and vision that gives him to avoid the entanglements of this world. How much more completely would we realize our calling if we saw ourselves as the same.

RESPONDING

1. Praise: Give praise and thanks to the Lord for giving us citizenship in heaven:

O Lord, our Lord, How excellent is Your name in all the earth, You who set Your glory above the heavens! . . . When I consider Your heavens, the work of Your fingers . . . what is man that You are mindful of him, and the son of man that You visit him? O Lord, our Lord, How majestic is Your name in all the earth! (Psalm 8:1, 3-4, 9)

Now offer to the Lord your personal praise and thanksgiving.

2. Confession: Pray this confession to the Lord as you seek to keep your life free from sin and in fellowship with Him:

All we like sheep have gone astray; we have turned, every one, to his own way; and You, O Lord, have laid on Him the iniquity of us all. (Isaiah 53:6)

Confess any personal sins which the Holy Spirit brings to your mind.

3. Affirmation: As you agree with God's will, voice your affirmation of His word:

You, O Lord, have delivered me from the power of darkness and translated me into the kingdom of the Son of Your love, in whom I have redemption through His blood, the forgiveness of sins. (Colossians 1:13-14)

4. Requests: As you make your requests known to the Lord, include:

- The Lord's leading in your life
- Opportunities for personal evangelism
- Your prayer list, the concerns of your heart, and today's activities

5. Closing Prayer: Finally, offer this closing prayer to the Lord:

Now may the God of hope fill me with all joy and peace in believing, that I may abound in hope by the power of the Holy Spirit. (Romans 15:13)

Memory Verse: But sanctify the Lord God in your hearts, and always be ready to give a defense to everyone who asks you a reason for the hope that is in you, with meekness and fear.

1 Peter 3:15
Evangelism Theme

SEPTEMBER 12

READING

The passage for today centers on Paul's defense before the Jews. Upon his arrest at the temple, Paul attempts, in vain, to justify his message to the Jews.

Read Acts 22.

REFLECTING

Even though Paul lives in complete recognition of the will of the Lord and acceptance of the sovereignty of God, still he is not passive regarding his personal welfare or the welfare of his mission. Paul knows it is illegal to scourge a Roman citizen without his having been found guilty. When he is about to be beaten, Paul brings up this issue and saves himself. He exercises his legal right to protection. Acceptance of the sovereignty of God does not mean passiveness in the things of this world. Paul does what he can with what he has, and *then* leaves the results to the Lord. God will be faithful to do His part, but He will not step in and do what we can and must do.

RESPONDING

1. Praise: Let us praise our God in the words of this psalm:

O Lord, how manifold are Your works! In wisdom You have made them all. The earth is full of Your possessions. . . . I will sing praise to my God while I have my being. May my meditation be sweet to Him; I will be glad in the Lord. (Psalm 104:24, 33, 34)

Take a moment to offer the Lord your personal praise and thanksgiving.

2. Confession: Pray this confession to the Lord as you seek to keep your life free from sin and in fellowship with Him:

O my God: I am too ashamed and humiliated to lift up my face to You, my God; for my iniquities have risen higher than my head, and my guilt has grown up to the heavens. (Ezra 9:6)

Confess any personal sins which the Holy Spirit may bring to your mind.

3. Affirmation: As you agree with the will of God, voice your affirmation of His word:

Before I was afflicted I went astray, but now I keep Your word. . . . It is good for me that I have been afflicted, that I may learn Your statutes. . . . I know, O Lord, that Your judgments are right, and that in faithfulness You have afflicted me. (Psalm 119:67, 71, 75)

4. Requests: As you make your requests known to the Lord, include:

- Love for the lost
- The work of missions in Africa
- Your prayer list, the concerns of your heart, and today's activities

5. Closing Prayer: Finally, offer this closing prayer to the Lord:

Now to You who are able to establish us according to the gospel and preaching of Jesus Christ—to You, alone wise, be glory through Jesus Christ forever. Amen. (Romans 16:25-27)

Memory Verse: But sanctify the Lord God in your hearts, and always be ready to give a defense to everyone who asks you a reason for the hope that is in you, with meekness and fear.

1 Peter 3:15
Evangelism Theme

READING

The passage for today centers on the trials of Paul. Because of attempts to kill Paul, he is taken to Caesarea to await trial.

Read Acts 23.

REFLECTING

Jesus said, "I send you out as sheep in the midst of wolves; therefore, be wise as serpents and harmless as doves" (Matthew 10:16). This certainly describes Paul. As he stands before the Jewish Council, Paul knows that his life is in peril. He also knows that the Council is divided between Pharisees, who believe in a resurrection of the dead, and Sadducees, who do not. When Paul deliberately brings up that issue, the ensuing dissension is so great that the soldiers take him away, thwarting the immediate plot against him. This fulfills Luke 12:11-12, " . . . do not worry about how you will defend yourselves or what you will say, for the Holy Spirit will teach you at that time what you should say."

RESPONDING

1. Praise: The Lord is worthy to receive our praise because of all that He has done for us:

Inasmuch as there is none like You, O Lord (You are great, and Your name is great in might), who would not fear You, O King of the nations? For this is Your rightful due, for among all the wise men of the nations, and in all their kingdoms, there is none like You. (Jeremiah 10:6-7)

Take a moment to offer the Lord your personal praise and thanksgiving.

2. Confession: Pray this confession to the Lord as you seek to keep your life free from sin and in fellowship with Him:

O Lord, do not rebuke me in Your anger, nor chasten me in Your hot displeasure. Have mercy on me, O Lord, for I am weak; O Lord, heal me, for . . . my soul also is greatly troubled. (Psalm 6:1-3)

Confess any personal sins which the Holy Spirit may bring to your mind.

3. Affirmation: As you agree with the will of God, voice your affirmation of His word:

For You, O Lord, will bless me when I am righteous; with favor You will surround me as with a shield. (Psalm 5:12)

4. Requests: As you make your requests known to the Lord, include:

- Faithfulness with your talents
- Your state and local leaders and affairs
- Your prayer list, the concerns of your heart, and today's activities

5. Closing Prayer: Finally, offer this closing prayer to the Lord:

The grace of the Lord Jesus Christ, and the love of God, and the communion of the Holy Spirit be with us all. Amen. (2 Corinthians 13:14)

Memory Verse: But sanctify the Lord God in your hearts, and always be ready to give a defense to everyone who asks you a reason for the hope that is in you, with meekness and fear.

1 Peter 3:15
Evangelism Theme

SEPTEMBER 14

READING

The passage for today centers on Paul's defense before Felix. Paul's first trial before Felix, the governor of the region, is not decisive.

Read Acts 24.

REFLECTING

In World War II there was a popular song that had in it the phrase, "Praise the Lord and pass the ammunition." This snatch of poetic verse captures a theme which runs throughout the Bible: assume human responsibility while relying on the sovereignty of God. Throughout the Bible, men pray and then act . . . pray and then act. Paul's arguments are as clever, his logic as deft as though he were relying on himself for his freedom. And yet, under it all is a peace, a trust, a confidence that can only be explained by his resting in the Lord whom he served. Whether his circumstances are good or bad, Paul regards wherever he is as the "world" into which the Lord wants him to go to preach the gospel (Mark 16:15).

RESPONDING

1. Praise: Praise the Lord that we do not act alone in the world, but that we serve Him who acts in our behalf:

Praise the Lord! Praise the Lord, O my soul! While I live I will praise the Lord; I will sing praises to my God while I have my being. . . . Happy is he who has the God of Jacob for his help, whose hope is in the Lord his God. . . . The Lord shall reign forever—Your God, O Zion, to all generations. Praise the Lord! (Psalm 142:1-2, 5, 10)

Take a moment to offer the Lord your personal praise and thanksgiving.

2. Confession: Pray this confession to the Lord as you seek to keep your life free from sin and in fellowship with Him:

Against You, You only, have I sinned, and done this evil in Your sight—that You may be found just when You speak, and blameless when You judge. (Psalm 51:4)

Confess any personal sins which the Holy Spirit may bring to your mind.

3. Affirmation: As you agree with the will of God, voice your affirmation of His word:

Blessed am I when I make You, O Lord, my trust, and when I do not respect the proud, nor such as turn aside to lies. (Psalm 40:4)

4. Requests: As you make your requests known to the Lord, include:

- Strength for obedience
- International students in America
- Your prayer list, the concerns of your heart, and today's activities

5. Closing Prayer: Finally, offer this closing prayer to the Lord:

Now to You who are able to do exceedingly abundantly above all that I ask or think, according to the power that works in me, to You be glory in the Church by Christ Jesus throughout all ages, world without end. Amen. (Ephesians 3:20-21)

Memory Verse: But sanctify the Lord God in your hearts, and always be ready to give a defense to everyone who asks you a reason for the hope that is in you, with meekness and fear.

1 Peter 3:15
Evangelism Theme

SEPTEMBER 15

READING

The passage for today centers on Paul's defense before Festus. Felix vacates his office without resolving Paul's status and leaves him for Festus's administration.

Read Acts 25.

REFLECTING

With what seething venom the Jews must have hated Paul, that after two years they still thirsted for his blood! Had Paul been transferred to Jerusalem, his life would have been imperiled. The reason for transferring him to Caesarea in the first place was a plot against his life. The danger is augmented if Festus is as susceptible to a bribe as his predecessor. Festus is prepared to humor the Jews by arranging the transfer, and there is no way of averting it other than Paul's availing himself of his right as a Roman citizen to be tried by the Emperor himself. How strangely is God fulfilling His own word: "So must you bear witness also at Rome!" Paul had known he would have to go to Rome. He didn't expect to go under Roman guard and at Roman expense.

RESPONDING

1. Praise: Because the Lord is sovereign, we praise Him, and trust in His goodness on our behalf:

Praise the Lord! For it is good to sing praises to our God; for it is pleasant, and praise is beautiful. . . . Great is our Lord, and mighty in power. . . . The Lord takes pleasure in those who fear Him, in those who hope in His mercy. . . . He has not dealt thus with any nation; and as for His judgments, they have not known them. Praise the Lord! (Psalm 147:1, 5a, 11, 20)

Take a moment to offer the Lord your personal praise and thanksgiving.

2. Confession: Pray this confession to the Lord as you seek to keep your life free from sin and in fellowship with Him:

Purge me with hyssop, and I shall be clean; wash me, and I shall be whiter than snow. . . . Hide Your face from my sins, and blot out all my iniquities. (Psalm 51:7, 9)

Confess any personal sins which the Holy Spirit may bring to your mind.

3. Affirmation: As you agree with the will of God, voice your affirmation of His word:

Behold, God is my salvation, I will trust and not be afraid; "For YAH, the Lord is my strength and my song; He also has become my salvation." (Isaiah 12:2)

4. Requests: As you make your requests known to the Lord, include:

- Your "daily bread"
- Christian education institutions
- Your prayer list, the concerns of your heart, and today's activities

5. Closing Prayer: Finally, offer this closing prayer to the Lord:

Now may You, the God of peace, sanctify me completely, and may my whole spirit, soul, and body be preserved blameless at the coming of my Lord Jesus Christ. (1 Thessalonians 5:23)

Memory Verse: But sanctify the Lord God in your hearts, and always be ready to give a defense to everyone who asks you a reason for the hope that is in you, with meekness and fear.

1 Peter 3:15
Evangelism Theme

SEPTEMBER 16

READING

The passage for today centers on Paul's defense before Agrippa. Festus is uncertain what to do with Paul and gives him an audience with King Agrippa.

Read Acts 26.

REFLECTING

To repent means to turn around, to go the opposite direction, or to think opposite thoughts. Someone could be walking north and repent, turn around, and begin walking south. In the abstract sense, it means to change your mind about something. If you did not believe in God, it means that you begin believing. If you have not received Christ, it means that you receive him. In Paul's defense before King Agrippa and Festus, Paul says that he preached to everyone "that they should repent and turn to God, performing deeds appropriate to repentance." One cannot repent without changing. Yet the repentance toward Christ brings the new birth and the Holy Spirit who then gives us the power to change. Have you repented and turned to God?

RESPONDING

1. Praise: It is by grace through faith that we can repent and turn to God and give Him our praise:

Praise the Lord! Praise God in His sanctuary; praise Him in His mighty firmament! Praise Him for His mighty acts; praise Him according to His excellent greatness! Praise Him with the sound of the trumpet; praise Him with the lute and harp! . . . Let everything that has breath praise the Lord. Praise the Lord! (Psalm 150:1-3, 6)

Take a moment to offer the Lord your personal praise and thanksgiving.

2. Confession: Pray this confession to the Lord as you seek to keep your life free from sin and in fellowship with Him:

O God, You know my foolishness; and my sins are not hidden from You. Let not those who wait for You, O Lord God of hosts, be ashamed because of me. (Psalm 69:5-6)

Confess any personal sins which the Holy Spirit may bring to your mind.

3. Affirmation: As you agree with the will of God, voice your affirmation of His word:

I cast my burden on You, O Lord, and You shall sustain me; when I am righteous, You shall never permit me to be moved. (Psalm 55:22)

4. Requests: As you make your requests known to the Lord, include:

- Passion for moral excellence
- Needs of personal friends
- Your prayer list, the concerns of your heart, and today's activities

5. Closing Prayer: Finally, offer this closing prayer to the Lord:

Now may the Lord Jesus Christ Himself, and You, my God and Father, who have loved me and given me everlasting consolation and good hope by grace, comfort my heart and establish me in every good word and work. (2 Thessalonians 2:16-17)

Memory Verse: But sanctify the Lord God in your hearts, and always be ready to give a defense to everyone who asks you a reason for the hope that is in you, with meekness and fear.

1 Peter 3:15
Evangelism Theme

SEPTEMBER 17

READING

The passage for today centers on Paul's journey to Rome. Paul exercises his right as a Roman citizen to take his case before Caesar.

Read Acts 27.

REFLECTING

One of the secrets of peace is believing the promises of God. There are many things which we think we believe, but our anxiety level demonstrates that we do not. The Lord promises to meet all our needs, but our labor and worry demonstrate that we are not so sure. Paul received a word from God that he would not perish. In relating this to the sailors, he said, "Therefore, keep up your courage, men, *for I believe God*." If we believe, we can be at peace. If we do not believe, we cannot. Review the promises of Scripture when you are troubled. What among them are you not believing? If you are trying to believe, but still struggle, you may pray the prayer of the Centurion to Christ, "Lord, I believe. Help my unbelief!"

RESPONDING

1. Praise: Praise the Lord that He rewards our faith, even if it is as small as a mustard seed:

Ah, Lord God! Behold, You have made the heavens and the earth by Your great power and outstretched arm. There is nothing too hard for You. You show lovingkindness to thousands. . . . The Great, the Mighty God, whose name is the Lord of hosts. You are great in counsel and mighty in work. (Jeremiah 32:17-19)

Take a moment to offer the Lord your personal praise and thanksgiving.

2. Confession: Pray this confession to the Lord as you seek to keep your life free from sin and in fellowship with Him:

Deliver me from bloodguiltiness, O God, the God of my salvation, and my tongue shall sing aloud of Your righteousness. O Lord, open my lips, and my mouth shall show forth Your praise. (Psalm 51:14-15)

Confess any personal sins which the Holy Spirit may bring to your mind.

3. Affirmation: As you agree with the will of God, voice your affirmation of His word:

Therefore, having been justified by faith, I have peace with You, O God, through my Lord Jesus Christ, through whom also I have access by faith into this grace in which I stand, and rejoice in the hope of the glory of You, O God. (Romans 5:1-2)

4. Requests: As you make your requests known to the Lord, include:

- Wisdom in decision making
- Opportunities to serve the Lord
- Your prayer list, the concerns of your heart, and today's activities

5. Closing Prayer: Finally, offer this closing prayer to the Lord:

Now to You, the King eternal, immortal, invisible, to God who alone is wise, be honor and glory forever and ever. Amen. (1 Timothy 1:17)

Memory Verse: But the manifestation of the Spirit is given to each one for the profit of all.
1 Corinthians 12:7
Spiritual Gifts Theme

SEPTEMBER 18

READING

The passage for today centers on Paul's arrival at Rome. After a harrowing journey by sea, Paul finally arrives at Rome and settles into a pattern of evangelism and encouragement.

Read Acts 28.

REFLECTING

Our lives are a constant struggle between our own will and the will of God. The circumstances of God's will are often strange and enigmatic. They do not always make sense. However, His will is being worked out, even in ways we cannot see or understand. Peace, love, and joy can only be continuously enjoyed in our lives, however, when we relinquish control of our own lives and go with the flow of God's will. Paul must have wondered from time to time how shipwreck and imprisonment were working into God's will, yet with historical perspective, we can see. In the words of the old hymn, we must "trust and obey, for there's no other way to be happy in Jesus, but to trust and obey."

RESPONDING

1. Praise: Thank the Lord, and praise Him because He is good and can be trusted:

Who is like You, O Lord, among the gods? Who is like You, glorious in holiness, fearful in praises, doing wonders? . . . You are great, O Lord God. For there is none like You, nor is there any God besides You, according to all that we have heard with our ears. (Exodus 15:11, 2 Samuel 7:22)

Take a moment to offer the Lord your personal praise and thanksgiving.

2. Confession: Pray this confession to the Lord as you seek to keep your life free from sin and in fellowship with Him:

For You do not desire sacrifice, or else I would give it; You do not delight in burnt offering. The sacrifices of God are a broken spirit, a broken and a contrite heart—these, O God, You will not despise. (Psalm 51:16-17)

Confess any personal sins which the Holy Spirit may bring to your mind.

3. Affirmation: As you agree with the will of God, voice your affirmation of His word:

For I consider that the sufferings of this present time are not worthy to be compared with the glory which shall be revealed in us. (Romans 8:18)

4. Requests: As you make your requests known to the Lord, include:

- Victory over temptation
- The work of missions in North and South America
- Your prayer list, the concerns of your heart, and today's activities

5. Closing Prayer: Finally, offer this closing prayer to the Lord:

You who are the blessed and only Potentate, the King of kings and Lord of lords, who alone has immortality, dwelling in unapproachable light, whom no man has seen or can see, to You be honor and everlasting power. Amen. (1 Timothy 6:15-16)

Memory Verse: But the manifestation of the Spirit is given to each one for the profit of all.

1 Corinthians 12:7
Spiritual Gifts Theme

SEPTEMBER 19

READING

The passage for today centers on the importance of the gospel message. Paul emphasizes the centrality of the Gospel to his life, and the consequences of unbelief.

Read Romans 1.

REFLECTING

According to Romans 1:18-20, all men have two avenues for beginning to learn about God. First, men have an inner awareness of God, or conscience (verse 19). God places a void within all men that only He can fill. Second, they can look at nature and learn several truths about God: 1) His invisible attributes (beauty, intelligence, etc.); 2) His eternal power (what awesome power it takes to put the stars in place!); 3) His divine nature (that there is a God who is higher than man and nature). God places creation before men as His greatest object lesson. Whenever anyone looks at nature and searches his own heart, he can know that there is a God. The evidence is present for all people to believe.

RESPONDING

1. Praise: With thankfulness to God for making Himself known, offer Him this praise:

Not unto us, O Lord, not unto us, but to Your name give glory, because of Your mercy, and because of Your truth. . . . We who fear You, O Lord, trust in You; You are our help and our shield. . . . We will bless the Lord from this time forth and forevermore. Praise the Lord! (Psalm 115:1, 11, 18)

Take a moment to offer the Lord your personal praise and thanksgiving.

2. Confession: Pray this confession to the Lord as you seek to keep your life free from sin and in fellowship with Him:

Remember, O Lord, Your tender mercies and Your lovingkindnesses, for they have been from of old. Do not remember the sins of my youth, nor my transgressions; according to Your mercy remember me, for Your goodness' sake, O Lord. (Psalm 25:6-7)

Confess any personal sins which the Holy Spirit may bring to your mind.

3. Affirmation: As you agree with the will of God, voice your affirmation of His word:

I must reckon myself to be dead indeed to sin, but alive to You, O God, in Christ Jesus my Lord. (Romans 6:11)

4. Requests: As you make your requests known to the Lord, include:

- Love for your family
- Revival among Christians in America
- Your prayer list, the concerns of your heart, and today's activities

5. Closing Prayer: Finally, offer this closing prayer to the Lord:

Make me complete in every good work to do Your will, working in me what is well pleasing in Your sight, through Jesus Christ, to whom be glory forever and ever. Amen. (Hebrews 13:20-21)

Memory Verse: But the manifestation of the Spirit is given to each one for the profit of all.
1 Corinthians 12:7
Spiritual Gifts Theme

SEPTEMBER 20

READING

The passage for today centers on the impartiality of God. Jews have no advantage with God because they have the Law, for God is offering salvation to whoever will believe.

Read Romans 2.

REFLECTING

Without God, there is no right and wrong. There is only preference. We can say that we prefer something to be or not to be, but unless we appeal to God as the standard, we cannot use the words "right and wrong." The words have no meaning. If one man says something is right, and another says it is wrong, their opinions as equals in the human race cancel each other out unless they can appeal to an authority source higher than man. We need God, not only for our salvation, but also for the normal functioning of society. Without Him men wrestle for the power to decide whose preferences will prevail. It is instructive to ask, "If everyone were exactly like me, what kind of society would we have?" Thank God that He is the standard!

RESPONDING

1. Praise: As you continue your time with the Lord, offer Him your praise through His word:

Bless the Lord, O my soul! O Lord my God, You are very great: You are clothed with honor and majesty, who cover Yourself with light as with a garment, who stretch out the heavens like a curtain. . . . May the glory of the Lord endure forever; may the Lord rejoice in His works. . . . Bless the Lord, O my soul! Praise the Lord! (Psalm 104:1-2, 31, 35)

Take a moment to offer the Lord your personal praise and thanksgiving.

2. Confession: Pray this confession to the Lord as you seek to keep your life free from sin and in fellowship with Him:

I have sinned greatly in what I have done; but now, I pray, O Lord, take away the iniquity of Your servant, for I have done very foolishly. (2 Samuel 24:10)

Confess any personal sins which the Holy Spirit may bring to your mind.

3. Affirmation: As you agree with the will of God, voice your affirmation of His word:

Your eyes, O Lord, run to and fro throughout the whole earth, to show Yourself strong on my behalf if my heart is loyal to You. (2 Chronicles 16:9)

4. Requests: As you make your requests known to the Lord, include:

- Faithfulness with your treasures
- The Great Commission
- Your prayer list, the concerns of your heart, and today's activities

5. Closing Prayer: Finally, offer this closing prayer to the Lord:

May You, the God of grace, who called me to Your eternal glory by Christ Jesus, after I have suffered a while, perfect, establish, strengthen, and settle me. To You be the glory and the dominion forever and ever. Amen. (1 Peter 5:10-11)

Memory Verse: But the manifestation of the Spirit is given to each one for the profit of all.

1 Corinthians 12:7
Spiritual Gifts Theme

READING

Justification by faith. All the world stands guilty before God and can only be forgiven through faith in Christ.

Read Romans 3.

REFLECTING

There are several commonly held concepts about how God evaluates the goodness of men. One concept is that as long as we do nothing "terrible," God will overlook our little sins. Another is that God weighs all our good works on one side of a scale and all our bad on the other, and if our good works outweigh our bad, we're okay. The truth which the Bible teaches is that God demands sinlessness. And since all have sinned and fall short of the glory of God, all men are condemned. There is one way out. Receive Jesus as your personal savior. Through Him, all your sins can be forgiven.

RESPONDING

1. Praise: Offer your praise to the Lord that you can depend on His mercy, rather than your own goodness, for your salvation:

The Lord made the heavens. Honor and majesty are before Him; strength and beauty are in His sanctuary. Give to the Lord, O kindreds of the peoples . . . Give to the Lord the glory due His name; bring an offering, and come into His courts. Let the heavens rejoice, and let the earth be glad. (Psalm 96:5a-8,11)

Now express any additional thoughts you may have of thanks or praise.

2. Confession: Pray this confession to the Lord as you seek to keep your life free from sin and in fellowship with Him:

The heart is deceitful above all things, and desperately wicked; who can know it? You, the Lord, search the heart, You test the mind, even to give every man according to his ways, and according to the fruit of his doings. . . . Heal me, O Lord, and I shall be healed; save me, and I shall be saved, for You are my praise. (Jeremiah 17:9, 10, 14)

Confess any personal sins which the Holy Spirit brings to your mind.

3. Affirmation: Now pray this affirmation to the Lord as you agree with and submit yourself to the will of God:

The Spirit Himself bears witness with my spirit that I am a child of Yours, O God, and if a child, then an heir—heir of Yours and joint heirs with Christ, if indeed I suffer with Him, that I may also be glorified. (Romans 8:16-17)

4. Requests: As you make your requests known to the Lord, include:

- Spiritual insight
- Campus ministries
- Your prayer list, the concerns of your heart, and today's activities

5. Closing Prayer: Finally, offer this closing prayer to the Lord:

May I grow in the grace and knowledge of our Lord and Savior Jesus Christ. To Him be the glory both now and forever. Amen. (2 Peter 3:18)

Memory Verse: But the manifestation of the Spirit is given to each one for the profit of all.

1 Corinthians 12:7
Spiritual Gifts Theme

SEPTEMBER 22

READING

The passage for today centers on Old Testament faith. Justification by faith is illustrated in the Old Testament by the lives of Abraham and David.

Read Romans 4.

REFLECTING

To impute something means to "apply something to your account." If someone imputes money to your bank account, it means he gives it to you, he applies it to your account. If someone imputes righteousness to you, it means he gives it to you, he applies it to your account before God. The Bible teaches that no one can earn salvation. However, God will give it to us if we have faith in Him. God honors the attitude of our heart and imputes righteousness to our account. In the Old Testament, God looked forward to the work of Christ on the cross to be able to impute righteousness, and now He looks back. But in both cases, God's people have been saved by grace through faith.

RESPONDING

1. Praise: The righteousness of God has been imputed to you if you are a child of God, and you can praise Him in holiness and truth:

Blessed be the name of God forever and ever, for wisdom and might are His. . . . He gives wisdom to the wise and knowledge to those who have understanding. He reveals deep and secret things; He knows what is in the darkness, and light dwells with Him. (Daniel 2:20-22)

Pause for personal praise and thanksgiving.

2. Confession: Pray this confession to the Lord as you seek to keep your life free from sin and in fellowship with Him:

If we say we have no sin, we are deceiving ourselves, and the truth is not in us. If we confess our sins, He is faithful and just to forgive us our sins and to cleanse us from all unrighteousness. (1 John 1:8-9)

Confess any personal sins which the Holy Spirit brings to mind.

3. Affirmation: Now pause to pray this affirmation to the Lord:

I am not ashamed of the gospel of Christ, for it is Your power to salvation for everyone who believes, for the Jew first and also for the Greek. For in it Your righteousness is revealed from faith to faith; as it is written, "the just shall live by faith." (Romans 1:16-17)

4. Requests: As you make your requests known to the Lord, pray for:

- Desire to be like Christ
- Needs in inner cities
- Your prayer list, the concerns of your heart, and today's activities

5. Closing Prayer: Finally, offer this closing prayer to the Lord:

Blessing and honor and glory and power be to You who sit on the throne, and to You, Lord, forever and ever! (Revelation 5:13)

Memory Verse: But the manifestation of the Spirit is given to each one for the profit of all.
1 Corinthians 12:7
Spiritual Gifts Theme

READING

The passage for today centers on the results of justification. "Therefore, having been justified by faith, we have peace with God through our Lord Jesus Christ."

Read Romans 5.

REFLECTING

In the greatest salvation chapter in the Bible, Paul spells out in specific terms how our salvation is accomplished. In chapter 3, we learn that all have sinned and fall short of the glory of God. Now, we learn that God demonstrates His love toward us, in that while we were yet sinners, Christ died for us. Sin entered the world through Adam, and death through sin, for all sinned. Now, salvation is offered to the world through one man, Christ. We can escape death by believing in Christ as our personal savior. Then, the gift of God, eternal life, is given to us. We are declared righteous. We now have peace with God. We now have the hope of eternal life with God and abundant life now on earth. It is the work of Christ, and only the work of Christ, that makes it possible.

RESPONDING

1. Praise: Give praise and thanks to the Lord for the matchless gift of eternal life through Christ:

My soul magnifies You, Lord, and my spirit has rejoiced in You, O God my Savior. . . . You who are mighty have done great things for me; and holy is Your name. And Your mercy is on those who fear You from generation to generation. (Luke 1:46-50)

Pause for personal praise and thanksgiving.

2. Confession: Pray this confession to the Lord as you seek to keep your life free from sin and in fellowship with Him:

Remember, O Lord, Your tender mercies and Your lovingkindnesses, for they have been from of old. Do not remember the sins of my youth, nor my transgressions; according to Your mercy remember me, for Your goodness' sake, O Lord. (Psalm 25:6-7)

Confess any personal sins which the Holy Spirit brings to your mind.

3. Affirmation: Now pause to pray this affirmation to the Lord:

You are the door. If anyone enters by You he will be saved, and will go in and out and find pasture. The thief does not come except to steal, and to kill, and to destroy. You have come that we may have life, and that we may have it more abundantly. You are the Good Shepherd. The Good Shepherd gives his life for the sheep. (John 10:9-11)

4. Requests: As you make your requests known to the Lord, pray for:

- Personal witness for Christ
- Local churches around the nation
- Your prayer list, the concerns of your heart, and today's activities
- Whatever else is on your heart

5. Closing Prayer: Finally, offer this closing prayer to the Lord:

Amen! Blessing and glory and wisdom, thanksgiving and honor and power and might, be to You, God, forever and ever. Amen. (Revelation 7:12)

Memory Verse: But the manifestation of the Spirit is given to each one for the profit of all.

1 Corinthians 12:7
Spiritual Gifts Theme

SEPTEMBER 24

READING

The passage for today centers on our relationship to sin. Rather than to continue to serve sin, we are to present our bodies to God as instruments of righteousness.

Read Romans 6.

REFLECTING

Micky Cohen, a noted gangster of a past generation, felt betrayed when he claimed Christianity because no one told him of the changes required of him. "There are Christian athletes and Christian businessmen. Why not Christian gangsters?" When we claim Christ, we are no longer free to continue living as we were in the world. Our affections, our activities must change to reflect the God whom we serve. There can be no Christian gangsters because the activities of a gangster are an inherent contradiction to the character of Christ. While few of us would want to go so far as to be a Christian gangster, many of us do try to hang on to things from our past. But those things, too, must go, in favor of serving God without inconsistency.

RESPONDING

1. Praise: Praise the Lord that by His power we can be conformed to the character of Christ:

Oh, the depth of the riches both of the wisdom and knowledge of God! How unsearchable are Your judgments and Your ways past finding out! Blessed are You, the God and Father of our Lord Jesus Christ, who has blessed us with every spiritual blessing in the heavenly places in Christ. (Ephesians 1:3)

Pause for personal praise and thanksgiving.

2. Confession: Pray this confession to the Lord as you seek to keep your life free from sin and in fellowship with Him:

Blessed is he whose transgression is forgiven, whose sin is covered. How blessed is the man to whom the Lord does not impute iniquity, and in whose spirit there is no guile. (Psalm 32:1-2)

Confess any personal sins which the Holy Spirit brings to mind.

3. Affirmation: Now pause to pray this affirmation to the Lord:

Let me not glory in my own wisdom, let me not glory in my own might, nor let me glory in my own riches; but let me glory in this, that I understand and know You. That You are the Lord, for in this You delight. (Jeremiah 9:23-24)

4. Requests: As you make your requests known to the Lord, pray for:

- An eternal perspective
- Needs of work or school mates
- Your prayer list, the concerns of your heart, and today's activities

5. Closing Prayer: Finally, offer this closing prayer to the Lord:

I will wait on You, the Lord; I will be of good courage, and You shall strengthen my heart; I will wait on You! (Psalm 27:14)

Memory Verse: Now you are the body of Christ, and members individually.

1 Corinthians 12:27
Spiritual Gifts Theme

READING

The passage for today centers on the conflict of the Christian. The inner man and outer man wage war in the Christian, who can only be delivered by Christ.

Read Romans 7.

REFLECTING

A civil war rages in the heart of every Christian. The inner man is created in holiness and righteousness (Ephesians 4:24), wishes to do good (verse 21), joyfully concurs with the law of God (verse 22), and serves the law of God (verse 25). The outer man practices the thing the inner man hates (verse 15), nothing good dwells in the outer man (verse 18), it wages war against the law of the mind (verse 23), and serves the law of sin (verse 25). As a result of this civil war, our life does not run smoothly. We do things we don't want to do, and we fail to do things we want to do. Who can deliver us from the body of this death? It is only Jesus. When we receive Him as our personal savior, the spiritual forces are put into place to free us from the bondage of sin.

RESPONDING

1. Praise: Offer your praise to the Lord because He frees you from the bondage to sin:

Ah, Lord God! Behold, You have made the heavens and the earth by Your great power and outstretched arm. There is nothing too hard for You. You show lovingkindness to thousands. . . . the Great, the Mighty God, whose name is the Lord of hosts. You are great in counsel and mighty in work. (Jeremiah 32:17-19)

Pause for personal praise and thanksgiving.

2. Confession: Pray this confession to the Lord as you seek to keep your life free from sin and in fellowship with Him:

Who can understand his errors? Cleanse me from secret faults. Keep back Your servant from presumptuous sins; Let them not have dominion over me. Then I shall be blameless, and I shall be innocent of great transgression. (Psalm 19:12-13)

Confess any personal sins which the Holy Spirit brings to mind.

3. Affirmation: Now pause to pray this affirmation to the Lord:

O God, Your thoughts are not my thoughts, nor are my ways Your ways, for as the heavens are higher than the earth, so are Your ways higher than my ways, and Your thoughts than my thoughts. (Isaiah 55:8-9)

4. Requests: As you make your requests known to the Lord, pray for:

- Personal discipline
- Christians worldwide who are persecuted for their faith
- Your prayer list, the concerns of your heart, and today's activities

5. Closing Prayer: Finally, offer this closing prayer to the Lord:

Show me the path of life; in Your presence is fullness of joy; at Your right hand are pleasures forevermore. (Psalm 16:11)

Memory Verse: Now you are the body of Christ, and members individually.

1 Corinthians 12:27
Spiritual Gifts Theme

SEPTEMBER 26

READING

The passage for today centers on deliverance from bondage. What the Law could not do in delivering us from sin, God did through Christ.

Read Romans 8.

REFLECTING

In Greece, a little boy might run into the kitchen and cry, "Mama, Mama!" when he wants to greet his mother. "Mama" is a term of close family endearment. Sometime later he may hear familiar masculine footsteps approaching the house, and he may run out of the house toward his father who is coming home and cry, "Abba, Abba!"—the close family term of endearment for his father. God loves the whole world, but He loves His spiritual children even more closely. With respect, but with tender love, we can cry out to God, "Abba, Abba"—a term of endearment in the spiritual family.

RESPONDING

1. Praise: To our tender Heavenly Father, offer these words of praise:

Men shall speak of the might of Your awesome acts; and I will declare Your greatness. They shall utter the memory of Your great goodness, and shall sing of Your righteousness. The Lord is gracious and full of compassion, slow to anger and great in mercy. The Lord is good to all, and His tender mercies are over all His works. (Psalm 145:6-9)

Take a moment to offer the Lord your personal praise and thanksgiving.

2. Confession: Pray this confession to the Lord as you seek to keep your life free from sin and in fellowship with Him:

Good and upright are You Lord, therefore You teach me, though a sinner, in Your way. If I am humble, You will guide me in justice and teach me Your way. All Your paths for me are mercy and truth, if I keep Your covenant and Your testimonies. For Your name's sake, O Lord, pardon my iniquity, for it is great. (Psalm 25:8-11)

Confess any personal sins which the Holy Spirit may bring to your mind.

3. Affirmation: As you agree with the will of God, voice your affirmation of His word:

You, O Lord, are my light and my salvation; whom shall I fear? You are the strength of my life; of whom shall I be afraid? (Psalm 27:1)

4. Requests: As you make your requests known to the Lord, include:

- Love for the Lord
- The work of missions in the Middle East, Australia, and the Islands
- Your prayer list, the concerns of your heart, and today's activities

5. Closing Prayer: Finally, offer this closing prayer to the Lord:

Save Your people, and bless Your inheritance; shepherd us also, and bear us up forever. (Psalm 28:9)

Memory Verse: Now you are the body of Christ, and members individually.

1 Corinthians 12:27
Spiritual Gifts Theme

READING

The passage for today centers on service through dedication. The Christian life is a life of total dedication and service to others.

Read Romans 12.

REFLECTING

To better understand the implications of the first two verses of chapter 12, it is helpful to read them backwards. We all want to be a living demonstration of the fact that the will of God is "good and acceptable and perfect." In order to do that, we must have our minds transformed and renewed. In order to have our minds transformed and renewed, we must make our bodies "a living sacrifice" to God. Someone has said that the problem with living sacrifices is that they keep crawling off the altar! We all want the product of the will of God in our lives. We can experience it if we follow the process of continually presenting ourselves as living sacrifices.

RESPONDING

1. Praise: Worship the Lord by offering Him the sacrifice of your praise with these words:

All Your works shall praise You, O Lord, and Your saints shall bless You. They shall speak of the glory of Your kingdom, and talk of Your power, to make known to the sons of men His mighty acts. . . . Your kingdom is an everlasting kingdom, and Your dominion endures throughout all generations. (Psalm 145:10-13)

Take a moment to offer the Lord your personal praise and thanksgiving.

2. Confession: Pray this confession to the Lord as you seek to keep your life free from sin and in fellowship with Him:

Create in me a clean heart, O God, and renew a steadfast spirit within me. Restore to me the joy of Your salvation, and uphold me with Your generous Spirit, then I will teach transgressors Your ways, and sinners shall be converted to You. (Psalm 51:10,12-13)

Confess any personal sins which the Holy Spirit may bring to your mind.

3. Affirmation: As you agree with the will of God, voice your affirmation of His word:

For You, O God, have not given me a spirit of fear, but of power and of love and of a sound mind. (2 Timothy 1:7)

4. Requests: As you make your requests known to the Lord, include:

- Faithfulness in sharing Christ
- The Lord's work in national and world affairs
- Your prayer list, the concerns of your heart, and today's activities

5. Closing Prayer: Finally, offer this closing prayer to the Lord:

You, the Lord, will command Your lovingkindness in the daytime, and in the night Your song shall be with me—a prayer to You, the God of my life. (Psalm 42:8)

Memory Verse: Now you are the body of Christ, and members individually.

1 Corinthians 12:27
Spiritual Gifts Theme

SEPTEMBER 28

READING

The passage for today centers on the Christian and others. The Christian is to obey government and love his fellowman.

Read Romans 13.

REFLECTING

Love is the central characteristic of the Christian. In Matthew 22:36-40 Jesus explained this when a lawyer asked Him what the greatest commandment was. Jesus said, "You shall love the Lord your God with all your heart and with all your soul, and with all your mind." Then He volunteered the second greatest commandment: "You shall love your neighbor as yourself. On these two commandments depend the whole Law and the Prophets." In chapter 13 of 1 Corinthians, Paul writes that love is the greatest characteristic, greater than faith and hope. God is love, and if we are to be like Him, we must also love.

RESPONDING

1. Praise: Thank the Lord that He loves you, and praise Him that through Him, you can love others:

Let my mouth be filled with Your praise and with Your glory all the day. . . . I will hope continually, and will praise You yet more and more. My mouth shall tell of Your righteousness and Your salvation all the day, for I do not know their limits. I will go in the strength of the Lord God; I will make mention of Your righteousness, of Yours only. O God, You have taught me from my youth; and to this day I declare Your wondrous works. (Psalm 71:8, 14-17)

Now express any additional thoughts of praise or thanksgiving.

2. Confession: Pray this confession to the Lord as you seek to keep your life free from sin and in fellowship with Him:

"Now, therefore," says the Lord, "Turn to Me with all your heart. . . ." Return to the Lord your God, for He is gracious and merciful, slow to anger, and of great kindness; and He relents from doing harm. (Joel 2:12-13)

Confess any personal sins which the Holy Spirit brings to your mind.

3. Affirmation: Now pray this affirmation to the Lord as you agree with and submit yourself to the will of God:

Yes, if I cry out for discernment, and lift up my voice for understanding, if I seek her as silver, and search for her as for hidden treasures; then I will understand the fear of You, O Lord, and find the knowledge of You, O God. For You, O Lord, give wisdom; from Your mouth come knowledge and understanding; You store up sound wisdom for me and are a shield to me when I walk uprightly. (Proverbs 2:3-7)

4. Requests: The Lord encourages us to come to Him with our concerns and desires. As you make your requests known to the Lord, include:

- Compassion for others
- Missions in America
- Your prayer list, the concerns of your heart, and today's activities

5. Closing Prayer: Finally, offer this closing prayer to the Lord:

Blessed are You, the Lord, forevermore! Amen and amen. (Psalm 89:52)

Memory Verse: Now you are the body of Christ, and members individually.

1 Corinthians 12:27
Spiritual Gifts Theme

READING

The passage for today centers on principles of conscience. A Christian is not to exercise personal liberty if it destroys another Christian.

Read Romans 14.

REFLECTING

No man is a rock. No man is an island. No man lives unto himself entirely. We are part of others. What we say and what we do affect others. This is especially true of Christians. We are part of the body of Christ. We are part of one another. Not only does God not want us to live alone, He has made it so that we cannot make it alone. Therefore, we must always be on the lookout for how our actions affect others. If something we do harms another person, we must take that into account. If our freedom causes hurt to a brother or sister in Christ, then love dictates that we limit our freedom. The kingdom of God is not eating and drinking (temporal pleasures), but righteousness and peace and joy in the Holy Spirit.

RESPONDING

1. Praise: Because the Lord has made us a part of such a loving entity as the body of Christ, offer your praise to Him:

Lord, You have been our dwelling place in all generations. Before the mountains were brought forth, or ever You had formed the earth and the world, even from everlasting to everlasting, You are God. O satisfy us early with Your mercy, that we may rejoice and be glad all our days! (Psalm 90:1-2, 14)

Take a moment to offer the Lord your personal praise and thanksgiving.

2. Confession: Pray this confession to the Lord as you seek to keep your life free from sin and in fellowship with Him:

O God, cleanse me from all my iniquity by which I have sinned against You, and pardon all my iniquities by which I have sinned and by which I have transgressed against You. (Jeremiah 33:8)

Confess any personal sins which the Holy Spirit may bring to your mind.

3. Affirmation: As you agree with the will of God, voice your affirmation of His word:

I am not ashamed, for I know You, in whom I have believed, and am persuaded that You are able to keep what I have committed to You until that Day. (2 Timothy 1:12)

4. Requests: As you make your requests known to the Lord, include:

● Personal spiritual growth

● Military ministries

● Your prayer list, the concerns of your heart, and today's activities

5. Closing Prayer: Finally, offer this closing prayer to the Lord:

Glory to You in the highest, and on earth peace, good will toward men! (Luke 2:14)

Memory Verse: Now you are the body of Christ, and members individually.

1 Corinthians 12:27
Spiritual Gifts Theme

SEPTEMBER 30

READING

The passage for today centers on the principle of God's glory. We are to conduct our lives in such a way as to bring glory to God.

Read Romans 15.

REFLECTING

When we become a Christian we exchange our citizenship on earth for citizenship in heaven. Therefore, we live according to the value system in heaven, not the value system on earth. On earth, we look out for ourselves. We satisfy our own wants and desires. In heaven, we look out for the welfare of others. Paul writes, "Those who are strong ought to bear the weaknesses of those without strength, and not just to please ourselves. Let each of us please his neighbor for his good." This does not mean that we neglect ourselves and our families. Other passages in Scripture indicate that we are to love our spouse and children and parents and care for their needs and so bring this teaching into balance with other truth. But we are to consider the welfare of others and not act indiscriminately toward them.

RESPONDING

1. Praise: Praise God for the bond of love that binds us to Him and to other Christians:

It is good to give thanks to the Lord, and to sing praises to Your name, O Most High; to declare Your lovingkindness in the morning, and Your faithfulness every night . . . to declare that the Lord is upright; He is my rock, and there is no unrighteousness in Him. (Psalm 92:1-2, 15)

Take a moment to offer the Lord your personal praise and thanksgiving.

2. Confession: Pray this confession to the Lord as you seek to keep your life free from sin and in fellowship with Him:

I return to You, O Lord my God, for I have stumbled because of my iniquity; I take words with me, and return to You, Lord. I say to You, "Take away all iniquity; receive me graciously, for I will offer the sacrifices of my lips." (Hosea 14:1-2)

Confess any personal sins which the Holy Spirit may bring to your mind.

3. Affirmation: As you agree with the will of God, voice your affirmation of His word:

And this is eternal life, that I may know You, the only true God, and Jesus Christ whom You have sent. (John 17:3)

4. Requests: As you make your requests known to the Lord, include:

- Fruit of the Spirit in your life
- The ministry of Christian literature
- Your prayer list, the concerns of your heart, and today's activities

5. Closing Prayer: Finally, offer this closing prayer to the Lord:

Grace, mercy, and peace from You, the Father, and the Lord Jesus Christ our Savior. (Titus 1:4)

Memory Verse: Now you are the body of Christ, and members individually.

1 Corinthians 12:27
Spiritual Gifts Theme

OCTOBER 1

READING

The passage for today centers on Paul's appeal for unity. Paul urges the Corinthian believers not to splinter into factions following different men, but to follow Christ.

Read 1 Corinthians 1.

REFLECTING

The Corinthian church had split into factions. Some said, "I follow Paul." Others said, "I follow Apollos." The most pious among them disdained to follow mere men, and said, "I follow Christ." It is foolishness based on misunderstanding that causes such factions. Using the image of a husbandman, Paul says, "I planted (brought the message of salvation), Apollos watered (taught you more advanced things), but *God* gave the increase. So then neither the one who plants nor the one who waters is anything, but God who causes the growth."

God does the work of God. Man does the work of man. We have a genius for reversing the two. We want to do the work of God while neglecting the work of man. It will not work. We must be certain we have the two straight. Otherwise, we will be utterly frustrated in our Christian walk. Pursue the work of man with all diligence. Then wait, and rest in the work of God.

RESPONDING

1. Praise: As you continue your time with the Lord, offer Him your praise that He cares for the things which are out of our control:

All Your works shall praise You, O Lord, and Your saints shall bless You. They shall speak of the glory of Your kingdom, and talk of Your power, to make known to the sons of men Your mighty acts, and the glorious majesty of Your kingdom. (Psalm 145:10-12)

Take a moment to offer the Lord your personal praise and thanksgiving.

2. Confession: Pray this confession to the Lord as you seek to keep your life free from sin and in fellowship with Him:

I acknowledged my sin to You, and my iniquity I have not hidden. I said, "I will confess my transgressions to the Lord," and You forgave the iniquity of my sin. (Psalm 32:5)

Confess any personal sins which the Holy Spirit may bring to your mind.

3. Affirmation: As you agree with the will of God, voice your affirmation of His word:

For I did not receive the spirit of bondage again to fear, but the Spirit of adoption by whom I cry out to You, "Abba, Father." (Romans 8:15)

4. Requests: As you make your requests known to the Lord, include:

- Health and strength to serve God

- God's will to be done on earth

- Your prayer list, the concerns of your heart, and today's activities

5. Closing Prayer: Finally, offer this closing prayer to the Lord:

Let the words of my mouth and the meditation of my heart be acceptable in Your sight, O Lord, my strength and my redeemer. (Psalm 19:14)

Memory Verse: Therefore, as we have opportunity, let us do good to all, especially to those who are of the household of faith.

Galatians 6:10
Spiritual Gifts Theme

OCTOBER 2

READING

The passage for today centers on Paul's reliance upon the Holy Spirit. When Paul first ministers to the Corinthians, he does so, not in his own ability, but relying on the work of the Spirit.

Read 1 Corinthians 2.

REFLECTING

When we speak, teach, or preach to the unsaved, we are not speaking to those who are blindfolded. We are speaking to those who are blind. It is not as though we can appeal to them to remove their blindfolds. Rather, we must appeal to the Lord that He would remove their blindness. "The man without the Spirit does not accept the things that come from the Spirit of God, for they are foolishness to him, and he cannot understand them, because they are spiritually discerned" (verse 14). Therefore, it is foolishness on our part to attempt to minister to others without first bathing that ministry in prayer, asking the Lord to draw those hearts to Christ.

RESPONDING

1. Praise: Thank the Lord and praise Him that He broke through your blindness with the light of life:

Men shall speak of the might of Your awesome acts; and I will declare Your greatness. They shall utter the memory of Your great goodness, and shall sing of Your righteousness. The Lord is gracious and full of compassion, slow to anger and great in mercy. The Lord is good to all, and His tender mercies are over all His works. (Psalm 145:6-9)

Take a moment to offer the Lord your personal praise and thanksgiving.

2. Confession: Pray this confession to the Lord as you seek to keep your life free from sin and in fellowship with Him:

Have mercy upon me, O God, according to Your lovingkindness; according to the multitude of Your tender mercies, blot out my transgressions. (Psalm 51:1)

Confess any personal sins which the Holy Spirit may bring to your mind.

3. Affirmation: As you agree with the will of God, voice your affirmation of His word:

For You so loved me that You gave Your only begotten Son, that if I would believe in Him, I should not perish, but have everlasting life. For You did not send Your Son into the world to condemn me, but that through Him I might be saved. (John 3:16-17)

4. Requests: As you make your requests known to the Lord, include:

- Sensitivity to sin
- The ministry of your local church
- Your prayer list, the concerns of your heart, and today's activities

5. Closing Prayer: Finally, offer this closing prayer to the Lord:

Now to You who are able to keep me from stumbling, and to present me faultless before the presence of Your glory with exceeding joy, to You, my God and Savior, who alone are wise, be glory and majesty, dominion and power, both now and forever. Amen. (Jude 24-25)

Memory Verse: Therefore, as we have opportunity, let us do good to all, especially to those who are of the household of faith.

Galatians 6:10
Spiritual Gifts Theme

READING

The passage for today centers on the foundation for living. Paul says that no foundation can be laid other than Jesus and that anything else is worthless in eternity.

Read 1 Corinthians 3.

REFLECTING

When the events of life are viewed with an eternal perspective, things which initially seemed important become unimportant, and things which seemed unimportant suddenly take on a whole new importance. Spiritual activity which is not undertaken with the right spirit or motive is worthless in view of eternity regardless of how much weight it is given by men. And conversely, the smallest cup of water, although seemingly insignificant, given in the name of Christ receives eternal reward. It is all a matter of perspective and motive. Be careful how you build your life work. Keep eternity in mind at all times. John 6:27 says, "Do not work for food that spoils, but for food that endures to eternal life."

RESPONDING

1. Praise: Thankful that He helps us purify our motives, offer the Lord your praise:

Blessed be the name of God forever and ever, for wisdom and might are His. . . . He gives wisdom to the wise and knowledge to those who have understanding. He reveals deep and secret things; He knows what is in the darkness, and light dwells with Him. (Daniel 2:20-22)

Pause for personal praise and thanksgiving.

2. Confession: Pray this confession to the Lord as you seek to keep your life free from sin and in fellowship with Him:

If we say we have no sin, we are deceiving ourselves, and the truth is not in us. If we confess our sins, He is faithful and just to forgive us our sins and to cleanse us from all unrighteousness. (1 John 1:8-9)

Confess any personal sins which the Holy Spirit brings to mind.

3. Affirmation: Now pause to pray this affirmation to the Lord:

I am not ashamed of the gospel of Christ, for it is Your power to salvation for everyone who believes, for the Jew first and also for the Greek. For in it Your righteousness is revealed from faith to faith; as it is written, "the just shall live by faith." (Romans 1:16-17)

4. Requests: As you make your requests known to the Lord, pray for:

- Wisdom for living life
- Needs of your immediate family
- Your prayer list, the concerns of your heart, and today's activities

5. Closing Prayer: Finally, offer this closing prayer to the Lord:

Surely goodness and mercy shall follow me all the days of my life, and I will dwell in the house of the Lord forever. (Psalm 23:6)

Memory Verse: Therefore, as we have opportunity, let us do good to all, especially to those who are of the household of faith.

Galatians 6:10
Spiritual Gifts Theme

OCTOBER 4

READING

The passage for today centers on lawsuits and immorality. Christians should not go to court against other Christians and should keep their bodies, which are members of Christ, free from immorality.

Read 1 Corinthians 6.

REFLECTING

When we come to Christ, we give up title to all earthly possessions. The possessions we have are now considered His, of which we are to be stewards. In their place, we receive eternal possessions that are fabulous beyond imagination, the extent of which we will only realize in His presence. All of the riches of Christ are ours as co-inheritors with Him; all those things which we might have viewed as possessions must now be seen as "on loan." We are now merely administrators, stewards of these things which belong to the Lord. Misuse of these becomes embezzlement, taking the belongings of another and using them as if they were our own. We must hold them loosely with an open hand, not as possessions, and use them as we believe Christ would if He were in our shoes.

RESPONDING

1. Praise: Praise the Lord that He shares His inheritance with us:

Praise the Lord! Praise the Lord, O my soul! While I live I will praise the Lord; I will sing praises to my God while I have my being. . . . Happy is he who has the God of Jacob for his help, Whose hope is in the Lord his God. . . . The Lord shall reign forever—Your God, O Zion, to all generations. Praise the Lord! (Psalm 142:1-2, 5, 10)

Take a moment to offer the Lord your personal praise and thanksgiving.

2. Confession: Pray this confession to the Lord as you seek to keep your life free from sin and in fellowship with Him:

Against You, You only, have I sinned, and done this evil in Your sight—that You may be found just when You speak, and blameless when You judge. (Psalm 51:4)

Confess any personal sins which the Holy Spirit may bring to your mind.

3. Affirmation: As you agree with the will of God, voice your affirmation of His word:

Blessed am I when I make You, O Lord, my trust, and when I do not respect the proud, nor such as turn aside to lies. (Psalm 40:4)

4. Requests: As you make your requests known to the Lord, include:

- Insight into Scripture
- The hungry around the world
- Your prayer list, the concerns of your heart, and today's activities

5. Closing Prayer: Finally, offer this closing prayer to the Lord:

We will be of good courage, and You shall strengthen our hearts, all we who hope in the Lord. (Psalm 31:24)

Memory Verse: Therefore, as we have opportunity, let us do good to all, especially to those who are of the household of faith.

Galatians 6:10
Spiritual Gifts Theme

READING

The passage for today centers on advice on marriage. Paul instructs the Corinthians concerning marriage, divorce, and singleness.

Read 1 Corinthians 7.

REFLECTING

Within the bonds of marriage, there exist the spiritual dimension, the emotional, and the physical. The relationship should have a spiritual bond, out of which flows the emotional, out of which flows the physical. When this order is properly maintained, the relationship is balanced and satisfying. Most marriages proceed in the opposite direction. Out of physical attraction grow emotional bonds, and spiritual bonds may or may not follow. Strive to strengthen spiritual bonds as the basis for the balance of your relationship. Even with the unsaved, the relationship will be stronger and more satisfying if your spouse sees the reality of your spiritual life and if the love of Christ is the dominant characteristic in your relationship with him.

RESPONDING

1. Praise: Praise the Lord that our spiritual bond with Christ can strengthen the bonds of other relationships:

Bless the Lord, O my soul! O Lord my God, You are very great: You are clothed with honor and majesty, who cover Yourself with light as with a garment, who stretch out the heavens like a curtain. . . . May the glory of the Lord endure forever; may the Lord rejoice in His works. . . . Bless the Lord, O my soul! Praise the Lord! (Psalm 104:1-2, 31, 35)

Take a moment to offer the Lord your personal praise and thanksgiving.

2. Confession: Pray this confession to the Lord as you seek to keep your life free from sin and in fellowship with Him:

I have sinned greatly in what I have done; but now, I pray, O Lord, take away the iniquity of Your servant, for I have done very foolishly. (2 Samuel 24:10)

Confess any personal sins which the Holy Spirit may bring to your mind.

3. Affirmation: As you agree with the will of God, voice your affirmation of His word:

Your eyes, O Lord, run to and fro throughout the whole earth, to show Yourself strong on my behalf if my heart is loyal to You. (2 Chronicles 16:9)

4. Requests: As you make your requests known to the Lord, include:

- Love for fellow Christians
- The work of missions in Europe and Asia
- Your prayer list, the concerns of your heart, and today's activities

5. Closing Prayer: Finally, offer this closing prayer to the Lord:

This is the day which You have made; I will rejoice and be glad in it. (Psalm 118:24)

Memory Verse: Therefore, as we have opportunity, let us do good to all, especially to those who are of the household of faith.

Galatians 6:10
Spiritual Gifts Theme

OCTOBER 6

READING

The passage for today centers on caution with personal liberty. Take care that your actions do not wound another Christian.

Read 1 Corinthians 8.

REFLECTING

There is an inseparable link between Christ and the Church.

In Acts 9, Jesus appears to Saul on the road to Damascus and asks, "Saul, Saul, why do you persecute me?" Yet Saul had not persecuted Jesus. He had never even seen Jesus. Yet because he was persecuting the Church, Jesus considered Saul as persecuting Himself.

Again, in chapter 8 of 1 Corinthians, Paul teaches that if we sin against our brothers in Christ, wounding their consciences when they are weak, we sin against Christ. How cautious must be our words and actions. The kingdom of God is not temporal pleasures. Ought we not, therefore, to be willing to give up actions which might be an offense to a weaker brother?

RESPONDING

1. Praise: Praise the Lord that He loved us enough to sacrifice His pleasures in heaven for our welfare:

O Lord, how manifold are Your works! In wisdom You have made them all. The earth is full of Your possessions. . . . I will sing praise to my God while I have my being. May my meditation be sweet to Him; I will be glad in the Lord. (Psalm 104:24, 33, 34)

Take a moment to offer the Lord your personal praise and thanksgiving.

2. Confession: Pray this confession to the Lord as you seek to keep your life free from sin and in fellowship with Him:

O my God: I am too ashamed and humiliated to lift up my face to You, my God; for my iniquities have risen higher than my head, and my guilt has grown up to the heavens. (Ezra 9:6)

Confess any personal sins which the Holy Spirit may bring to your mind.

3. Affirmation: As you agree with the will of God, voice your affirmation of His word:

Before I was afflicted I went astray, but now I keep Your word. . . . It is good for me that I have been afflicted, that I may learn Your statutes. . . . I know, O Lord, that Your judgments are right, and that in faithfulness You have afflicted me. (Psalm 119:67, 71, 75)

4. Requests: As you make your requests known to the Lord, include:

- Faithfulness with your time
- The president and national leaders and affairs
- Your prayer list, the concerns of your heart, and today's activities

5. Closing Prayer: Finally, offer this closing prayer to the Lord:

Oh, satisfy me early with Your mercy, that I may rejoice and be glad all my days! (Psalm 90:14)

Memory Verse: Therefore, as we have opportunity, let us do good to all, especially to those who are of the household of faith.

Galatians 6:10
Spiritual Gifts Theme

OCTOBER 7

READING

The passage for today centers on Paul's personal liberty. Paul limits his freedom for the sake of other Christians.

Read 1 Corinthians 9.

REFLECTING

Spiritual maturity is not a product of human effort. The fruit of the Spirit is the fruit of the Spirit, not of self-effort. Yet God will not grant it to us unless we are striving for it. Paul says, "I run with aim, I box with purpose, I buffet my body . . ." in pursuit of spiritual goals. The reality is that most professional athletes, most corporate businessmen, and most renowned musicians are more dedicated to their pursuits than we Christians are to becoming more like Christ and spreading the Gospel. Few have spiritual passion to equal the temporal passion of the unsaved. It is a challenge to care about the same things God cares about—a challenge we must accept!

RESPONDING

1. Praise: Thank the Lord, and praise Him that Christ's passion for us went as far as the cross:

Oh, give thanks to the Lord! Call upon His name; make known His deeds among the peoples. Sing to Him, sing psalms to Him; talk of all His wondrous works. Glory in His holy name; let the hearts of those rejoice who seek the Lord. Seek the Lord and His strength; seek His face evermore. (Psalm 105:1-4)

Take a moment to offer the Lord your personal praise and thanksgiving.

2. Confession: Pray this confession to the Lord as you seek to keep your life free from sin and in fellowship with Him:

O Lord, do not rebuke me in Your anger, nor chasten me in Your hot displeasure. Have mercy on me, O Lord, for I am weak; O Lord, heal me, for . . . my soul also is greatly troubled. (Psalm 6:1-3)

Confess any personal sins which the Holy Spirit may bring to your mind.

3. Affirmation: As you agree with the will of God, voice your affirmation of His word:

For You, O Lord, will bless me when I am righteous; with favor You will surround me as with a shield. (Psalm 5:12)

4. Requests: As you make your requests known to the Lord, include:

- Your financial needs
- The needs of the poor
- Your prayer list, the concerns of your heart, and today's activities

5. Closing Prayer: Finally, offer this closing prayer to the Lord:

Let the beauty of You, Lord, be upon me, and establish the work of my hands for me; yes, establish the work of my hands. (Psalm 90:17)

Memory Verse: Therefore, as we have opportunity, let us do good to all, especially to those who are of the household of faith.

Galatians 6:10
Spiritual Gifts Theme

OCTOBER 8

READING

The passage for today centers on the excellence of love. Love is the greatest virtue, which all Christians should exhibit.

Read 1 Corinthians 13.

REFLECTING

Both Jesus and Paul taught that the greatest Christian virtue is love. Though love is clearly held throughout the Bible as the supreme virtue, it is not always easy to measure this love, because our society has such a distorted concept of what love is, often insisting that emotion be attached to it. We may think that if we don't "feel warm and fuzzy," we don't love. While emotions certainly may be attached to biblical love, love is primarily an act of the will. "Emotions" cannot be commanded, but the "will" can. And we are commanded to love. If you exhibit the qualities in today's chapter, you are loving, regardless of your emotions.

RESPONDING

1. Praise: Thank the Lord, and praise Him that He loves us with the same love He asks from us:

Unto You I lift up my eyes, O You who dwell in the heavens. Behold, as the eyes of servants look to the hand of their masters, as the eyes of a maid to the hand of her mistress, so our eyes look to the Lord our God, until He has mercy on us. (Psalm 123:1-2)

Take a moment to offer the Lord your personal praise and thanksgiving.

2. Confession: Pray this confession to the Lord as you seek to keep your life free from sin and in fellowship with Him:

Can I understand my errors? Cleanse me, O Lord, from my secret faults. Keep back Your servant also from presumptuous sins; let them not have dominion over me. Then I shall be blameless, and I shall be innocent of great transgression. (Psalm 19:12-13)

Confess any personal sins which the Holy Spirit may bring to your mind.

3. Affirmation: As you agree with the will of God, voice your affirmation of His word:

Jesus Christ, You are the same yesterday, today, and forever. (Hebrews 13:8)

4. Requests: As you make your requests known to the Lord, include:

- Protection from the "evil one"
- Laborers for the "harvest"
- Your prayer list, the concerns of your heart, and today's activities

5. Closing Prayer: Finally, offer this closing prayer to the Lord:

Bless the Lord, all you His hosts, you ministers of His, who do His pleasure. Bless the Lord, all His works, in all places of His dominion. (Psalm 103:21-22)

Memory Verse: And the things that you have heard from me among many witnesses, commit these to faithful men who will be able to teach others also.

2 Timothy 2:2
Spiritual Gifts Theme

READING

The passage for today centers on instructions on the resurrection. Christ's resurrection is the basis for our resurrection, which is the final victory over sin.

Read 1 Corinthians 15.

REFLECTING

It is difficult for us to imagine what our resurrected bodies will be like. Yet there are snatches of information in the Scripture which may give us some idea. In Matthew 17, for example, we see Jesus, Moses, and Elijah, having lost their earthly appearance, glowing in a dazzling light. From this one brief example we might conclude that our bodies will shine with dazzling light, that we will be free of gravity, that we may travel at fabulous speeds, that we may be able to appear and disappear. C.S. Lewis once wrote that if we were to see our glorified selves coming down the street, we would be tempted to fall at our own feet and worship ourselves. It is certainly something to look forward to.

RESPONDING

1. Praise: Offer the Lord your praise that we have such a body to look forward to:

Praise the Lord! Praise the name of the Lord; praise Him, O you servants of the Lord! . . . Praise the Lord, for the Lord is good; sing praises to His name, for it is pleasant. . . . For I know that the Lord is great, and our Lord is above all gods. . . . Blessed be the Lord! . . . Praise the Lord! (Psalm 135:1, 3, 5, 21)

Take a moment to offer the Lord your personal praise and thanksgiving.

2. Confession: Pray this confession to the Lord as you seek to keep your life free from sin and in fellowship with Him:

Show me Your ways, O Lord; teach me Your paths. Lead me in Your truth and teach me, for You are the God of my salvation; on You I wait all the day. (Psalm 25:4-5)

Confess any personal sins which the Holy Spirit may bring to your mind.

3. Affirmation: As you agree with the will of God, voice your affirmation of His word:

Your grace, O Lord, is sufficient for me, for Your strength is made perfect in weakness. (2 Corinthians 12:9)

4. Requests: As you make your requests known to the Lord, include:

• Commitment to the Lord

• Parachurch ministries

• Your prayer list, the concerns of your heart, and today's activities

5. Closing Prayer: Finally, offer this closing prayer to the Lord:

Lord, preserve me from all evil; preserve my soul. Lord, preserve my going out and my coming in from this time forth, and even forevermore. (Psalm 121:7-8)

Memory Verse: And the things that you have heard from me among many witnesses, commit these to faithful men who will be able to teach others also.

2 Timothy 2:2
Spiritual Gifts Theme

OCTOBER 10

READING

The passage for today centers on ministry through affliction. The Lord comforts us in our affliction so that we may comfort others.

Read 2 Corinthians 1.

REFLECTING

There is a fellowship of suffering. Someone who has suffered the same things we have suffered is better able to minister to us. And if we have been comforted in our suffering, we are better able to comfort someone else who experiences the same suffering. Relating to someone with a similar trouble becomes easier, yet 2 Corinthians 1:4 says the result is that we can comfort those in any trouble with the comfort we ourselves have received. As the sufferings of Christ overflow into our lives, so can the compassion of Christ overflow from our lives into the lives of others.

RESPONDING

1. Praise: To the God of all comfort, offer these words of praise:

Who is like You, O Lord, among the gods? Who is like You, glorious in holiness, fearful in praises, doing wonders? . . . You are great, O Lord God. For there is none like You, nor is there any God besides You, according to all that we have heard with our ears. (Exodus 15:11, 2 Samuel 7:22)

Now offer to the Lord your personal praise and thanksgiving.

2. Confession: Pray this confession to the Lord as you keep your life free from sin:

Out of the depths I have cried to You, O Lord. . . . If You, Lord, should mark iniquities, O Lord, who could stand? But there is forgiveness with You, that You may be feared. (Psalm 130:1, 3-4)

Confess any personal sins which the Holy Spirit brings to your mind.

3. Affirmation: As you agree with God's will, voice your affirmation of His word:

You, Lord Jesus, are the living bread which came down from heaven. If I eat of this bread, I will live forever; and the bread that You have given is Your flesh, which You gave for the life of the world. (John 6:51)

4. Requests: As you make your requests known to the Lord, include:

- Renewing of your mind
- Needs of your extended family
- Your prayer list, the concerns of your heart, and today's activities

5. Closing Prayer: Finally, offer this closing prayer to the Lord:

May we with one mind and one mouth glorify the God and Father of our Lord Jesus Christ. (Romans 15:6)

Memory Verse: And the things that you have heard from me among many witnesses, commit these to faithful men who will be able to teach others also.

2 Timothy 2:2
Spiritual Gifts Theme

READING

The passage for today centers on the weakness of men. The weakness of men gives an opportunity to manifest the power of God.

Read 2 Corinthians 4.

REFLECTING

Throughout history, God has worked through man to bring Himself glory. When we look at Israel and the Mosaic Law, we tend to think that the Jews performed poorly. All they had to do is be obedient to some basic laws, and God would bless them beyond containment. Blessing for them came through obedience. Yet, they might say the same about us. The Holy Spirit is living in us, we have only to live in love toward God and man, and God will bless us spiritually beyond containment. Blessing for us comes through dependence and trust. While human frailty is glaring in both systems, the work of God is being done nevertheless. The message is carried in jars of clay so that in eternity the glory of the redeemed will go to God and not to man.

RESPONDING

1. Praise: What a joy to relax in the sovereignty of God and praise Him for His goodness to us.

You are the Rock, Your work is perfect; for all Your ways are justice, a God of truth and without injustice, righteous and upright are You. (Deuteronomy 32:4)

The Lord lives! Blessed be my Rock! Let God be exalted, the Rock of my salvation! (2 Samuel 22:47)

Now offer to the Lord your personal praise and thanksgiving.

2. Confession: Pray this confession to the Lord as you keep your life free from sin:

We give You thanks, O Lord, that we may reason with You. Though our sins are like scarlet, they shall be as white as snow; though they are red like crimson, they shall be as wool. (Isaiah 1:18)

Confess any personal sins which the Holy Spirit brings to your mind.

3. Affirmation: As you agree with God's will, voice your affirmation of His word:

You will keep me in perfect peace; my mind is stayed on You, because I trust in You. (Isaiah 26:3)

4. Requests: As you make your requests known to the Lord, include:

- The Lord's leading in your life
- Opportunities for personal evangelism
- Your prayer list, the concerns of your heart, and today's activities

5. Closing Prayer: Finally, offer this closing prayer to the Lord:

Now may the God of hope fill me with all joy and peace in believing, that I may abound in hope by the power of the Holy Spirit. (Romans 15:13)

Memory Verse: And the things that you have heard from me among many witnesses, commit these to faithful men who will be able to teach others also.

2 Timothy 2:2
Spiritual Gifts Theme

OCTOBER 12

READING

The passage for today centers on the Christian's reward. The Christian is to live for the eternal rather than temporal and will be rewarded accordingly.

Read 2 Corinthians 5.

REFLECTING

One of the marks of maturity is the ability to put off immediate reward for the sake of a future goal. That is a good mark of Christian maturity: the willingness to put off temporal reward for the sake of eternal reward. Scripture teaches that we must all appear before the "bema" seat of Christ. The "bema" was the grandstand in ancient Greece where the judges gave out the honors to the winners of athletic competitions. It is before the divine "bema" that we will all appear. If we competed according to the eternal rules, we will gain the honor of reward from the Eternal Judge. First, we must, as Paul wrote, "set our minds on things above, not on things of earth."

RESPONDING

1. Praise: Offer your praise to the Lord as you "set your mind on things above":

I will love You, O Lord, my strength. The Lord is my rock and my fortress and my deliverer; my God, my strength, in whom I will trust; I will call upon the Lord, who is worthy to be praised; so shall I be saved from my enemies. . . . Blessed be my Rock! Let the God of my salvation be exalted. (Psalm 18:1-3, 46)

Take a moment to offer the Lord your personal praise and thanksgiving.

2. Confession: Pray this confession to the Lord as you seek to keep your life free from sin and in fellowship with Him:

All we like sheep have gone astray; we have turned, every one, to his own way; and You, O Lord, have laid on Him the iniquity of us all. (Isaiah 53:6)

Confess any personal sins which the Holy Spirit may bring to your mind.

3. Affirmation: As you agree with the will of God, voice your affirmation of His word:

You, Lord Jesus, are the Way, the Truth, and the Life. I cannot come to the Father except through You. (John 14:6)

4. Requests: As you make your requests known to the Lord, include:

- Love for the lost
- The work of missions in Africa
- Your prayer list, the concerns of your heart, and today's activities

5. Closing Prayer: Finally, offer this closing prayer to the Lord:

Now to You who are able to establish us according to the gospel and preaching of Jesus Christ—to You, alone wise, be glory through Jesus Christ forever. Amen. (Romans 16:25-27)

Memory Verse: And the things that you have heard from me among many witnesses, commit these to faithful men who will be able to teach others also.

2 Timothy 2:2
Spiritual Gifts Theme

READING

The passage for today centers on the mark of generosity. As Christ was rich, yet became poor for the sake of others, so should we be generous toward others.

Read 2 Corinthians 8.

REFLECTING

One of the most reliable indicators of whether a person is living for this world or for eternity is whether or not he is willing to give his money away for causes which do not benefit him in this world. If a person is living for eternity, he will be willing to give money to those things which reflect eternal values. If he isn't, he won't be. The Macedonian Christians beg Paul for the opportunity and privilege of sharing in the financial support of the poor Christians in Jerusalem. The secret was that they had first given themselves to the Lord and then they gave beyond their means. Do you support eternal causes with your temporal resources?

RESPONDING

1. Praise: Praise the Lord that Jesus was willing to lay down his immediate comfort for our sakes:

Be exalted, O God, above the heavens; let Your glory be above all the earth. . . . I will praise You, O Lord, among the peoples; I will sing to You among the nations. For Your mercy reaches unto the heavens, and Your truth unto the clouds. Be exalted, O God, above the heavens; let Your glory be above all the earth. (Psalm 57:5, 9-11)

Take a moment to offer the Lord your personal praise and thanksgiving.

2. Confession: Pray this confession to the Lord as you seek to keep your life free from sin and in fellowship with Him:

Let the wicked forsake his way, and the unrighteous man his thoughts; let him return to You, the Lord, and You will have mercy on him; and You, our God, for You will abundantly pardon. (Isaiah 55:7)

Confess any personal sins which the Holy Spirit may bring to your mind.

3. Affirmation: As you agree with the will of God, voice your affirmation of His word:

For I know the grace of You, O Lord Jesus Christ, that though You were rich, yet for my sake You became poor, that I through Your poverty might become rich. (2 Corinthians 8:9)

4. Requests: As you make your requests known to the Lord, include:

- Faithfulness with your talents
- Your state and local leaders and affairs
- Your prayer list, the concerns of your heart, and today's activities

5. Closing Prayer: Finally, offer this closing prayer to the Lord:

The grace of the Lord Jesus Christ, and the love of God, and the communion of the Holy Spirit be with us all. Amen. (2 Corinthians 13:14)

Memory Verse: And the things that you have heard from me among many witnesses, commit these to faithful men who will be able to teach others also.

2 Timothy 2:2
Spiritual Gifts Theme

OCTOBER 14

READING

The passage for today centers on Christian giving. As God has prospered them, Christians should generously give to others.

Read 2 Corinthians 9.

REFLECTING

God doesn't need your money. The One who created gold, silver, and diamonds will not go begging if you refuse to give your money to Him. He asks for your money, not for His sake, but for yours. What God wants is your heart, and the measure of how much of your heart He has is how willing you are to give your money back to Him. Closed wallet, closed heart. Open wallet, open heart. Remember, it is not the amount, but the willingness that counts. Give as He has prospered you. God's reason for asking Christians to give to other Christians is in order to foster mutual unity and concern among Christians and show the love of God to the unsaved. Be a cheerful giver.

RESPONDING

1. Praise: Offer your praise to the Lord as an expression of the cheerfulness of your heart:

O God, You are my God; early will I seek You; my soul thirsts for You; my flesh longs for You in a dry and thirsty land where there is no water. So I have looked for You in the sanctuary, to see Your power and Your glory. (Psalm 63:1-2)

Take a moment to offer the Lord your personal praise and thanksgiving.

2. Confession: Pray this confession to the Lord as you seek to keep your life free from sin and in fellowship with Him:

You will again have compassion on us, and will subdue our iniquities. You will cast all our sins into the depths of the sea. (Micah 7:19)

Confess any personal sins which the Holy Spirit may bring to your mind.

3. Affirmation: As you agree with the will of God, voice your affirmation of His word:

This is my commandment, that you love one another as I have loved you. (John 15:12)

4. Requests: As you make your requests known to the Lord, include:

- Strength for obedience
- International students in America
- Your prayer list, the concerns of your heart, and today's activities

5. Closing Prayer: Finally, offer this closing prayer to the Lord:

Now to You who are able to do exceedingly abundantly above all that I ask or think, according to the power that works in me, to You be glory in the church by Christ Jesus throughout all ages, world without end. Amen. (Ephesians 3:20-21)

Memory Verse: And the things that you have heard from me among many witnesses, commit these to faithful men who will be able to teach others also.

2 Timothy 2:2
Spiritual Gifts Theme

READING

The passage for today centers on Paul's heavenly vision. Paul was given a vision of heaven, after which he was given a "thorn in the flesh" to keep him humble.

Read 2 Corinthians 12.

REFLECTING

The Bible gives us a number of reasons why Christians suffer adversity. One reason is to strengthen and mature us. Another is to chasten us for wrongdoing. Another is the natural consequences of our own foolishness, which God does not necessarily protect us from. Another reason given us by Paul in today's chapter is to keep us humble. If things always went well for us, if life was always coming up roses, we would tend to become conceited, to think more highly of ourselves than we ought and, perhaps, less of others. Notice, Paul only prayed three times for the removal of the thorn in his flesh. When it was clear that God was not going to remove it, Paul accepted it.

RESPONDING

1. Praise: Because the Lord always has a reason for allowing adversity, we can praise Him for all things:

Because Your lovingkindness is better than life, my lips shall praise You. Thus I will bless You while I live; I will lift up my hands in Your name. My soul shall be satisfied as with marrow and fatness, and my mouth shall praise You with joyful lips. . . . Because You have been my help, therefore in the shadow of Your wings I will rejoice. (Psalm 63:3-5, 7)

Take a moment to offer the Lord your personal praise and thanksgiving.

2. Confession: Pray this confession to the Lord as you seek to keep your life free from sin and in fellowship with Him:

O Lord, I know the way of man is not in himself; it is not in man who walks to direct his own steps. O Lord, correct me, but with justice; not in Your anger, lest You bring me to nothing. (Jeremiah 10:23-24)

Confess any personal sins which the Holy Spirit may bring to your mind.

3. Affirmation: As you agree with the will of God, voice your affirmation of His word:

Your word is a lamp to my feet and a light to my path. (Psalm 119:105)

4. Requests: As you make your requests known to the Lord, include:

- Your "daily bread"
- Christian education institutions
- Your prayer list, the concerns of your heart, and today's activities

5. Closing Prayer: Finally, offer this closing prayer to the Lord:

Now may You, the God of peace, sanctify me completely, and may my whole spirit, soul, and body be preserved blameless at the coming of my Lord Jesus Christ. (1 Thessalonians 5:23)

Memory Verse: As each one has received a gift, minister it to one another, as good stewards of the manifold grace of God.

1 Peter 4:10
Spiritual Gifts Theme

OCTOBER 16

READING

The passage for today centers on the fruit of the Spirit. As Christians walk by the Spirit, they will manifest His characteristics.

Read Galatians 5.

REFLECTING

As Paul teaches in Romans 7, a civil war rages within the depths of every child of God. The opposing forces are the power of the flesh, in the "outer man," as Paul calls it, and the inner man, who is responsive to the Spirit of God and the Word of God. What is at stake is the control of the child of God. As we yield ourselves to the control of the Spirit, then love, joy, peace, patience, etc., begin to take root and bear fruit in our lives. As we yield ourselves to the control of our unrighteous promptings, then anger, jealousy, impurity, etc., begin to take root and bear fruit in our lives. We must yield our "members as instruments of righteousness" and begin to taste of the fruit of God.

RESPONDING

1. Praise: Because we can taste of the fruit of the Spirit in our lives, give thanks and praise to Him:

Tremble before Him, all the earth. The world also is firmly established, it shall not be moved. Let the heavens rejoice, and let the earth be glad. . . . Oh, give thanks to the Lord, for He is good! For His mercy endures forever. . . . Blessed be the Lord God of Israel from everlasting to everlasting! (1 Chronicles 16:30-31, 34, 36)

Take a moment to offer the Lord your personal praise and thanksgiving.

2. Confession: Pray this confession to the Lord as you seek to keep your life free from sin and in fellowship with Him:

We give You thanks, O Lord, that we may reason with You. Though our sins are like scarlet, they shall be as white as snow; though they are red like crimson, they shall be as wool. (Isaiah 1:18)

Confess any personal sins which the Holy Spirit may bring to your mind.

3. Affirmation: As you agree with the will of God, voice your affirmation of His word:

I will remember the works of the Lord; surely I will remember Your wonders of old. I will also meditate on all Your work, and talk of Your deeds. (Psalm 77:11-12)

4. Requests: As you make your requests known to the Lord, include:

- Passion for moral excellence
- Needs of personal friends
- Your prayer list, the concerns of your heart, and today's activities

5. Closing Prayer: Finally, offer this closing prayer to the Lord:

Now may the Lord Jesus Christ Himself, and You, my God and Father, who have loved me and given me everlasting consolation and good hope by grace, comfort my heart and establish me in every good word and work. (2 Thessalonians 2:16-17)

Memory Verse: As each one has received a gift, minister it to one another, as good stewards of the manifold grace of God.
1 Peter 4:10
Spiritual Gifts Theme

READING

The passage for today centers on mutual concern. Christians are to look out for one another and bear one another's burdens.

Read Galatians 6.

REFLECTING

John Donne once wrote: "No man is an island, entire of itself; every man is a piece of the continent, a part of the main; if a clod be washed away by the sea, Europe is the less. . . ." What Donne wrote generally and poetically, Paul wrote specifically hundreds of years earlier: "Restore" one another, and "bear one another's burdens" (verse 2); "do good to all, especially to those who are of the household of faith" (verse 10). Paul's reference to the church functioning as a body illustrates the equal importance of each part and necessity for each to function properly. We are part of one another, and we are to live for one another in harmony and mutual concern. We are all part of the "continent" of Christ.

RESPONDING

1. Praise: As we praise the Lord in the words of this psalm, focus on His sovereignty and goodness:

Blessed be Your glorious name, which is exalted above all blessing and praise! You alone are the Lord; You have made heaven, the heaven of heavens, with all their host, the earth and all things on it, the seas and all that is in them, and You preserve them all. The host of heaven worships You. (Nehemiah 9:5-6)

Now offer to the Lord your personal praise and thanksgiving.

2. Confession: Pray this confession to the Lord as you seek to keep your life free from sin and in fellowship with Him:

Surely You, Lord Jesus, have borne our griefs and carried our sorrows. . . . You were wounded for our transgressions, You were bruised for our iniquities; the chastisement for our peace was upon You, and by Your stripes we are healed. (Isaiah 53:4-5)

Confess any personal sins which the Holy Spirit brings to your mind.

3. Affirmation: As you agree with God's will, voice your affirmation of His word:

I have sinned and fall short of Your glory, O God, being justified as a gift by Your grace through the redemption which is in Christ Jesus. (Romans 3:23-24)

4. Requests: As you make your requests known to the Lord, include:

- Wisdom in decision making
- Opportunities to serve the Lord
- Your prayer list, the concerns of your heart, and today's activities

5. Closing Prayer: Finally, offer this closing prayer to the Lord:

Now to You, the King eternal, immortal, invisible, to God who alone is wise, be honor and glory forever and ever. Amen. (1 Timothy 1:17)

Memory Verse: As each one has received a gift, minister it to one another, as good stewards of the manifold grace of God.

1 Peter 4:10
Spiritual Gifts Theme

OCTOBER 18

READING

The passage for today centers on the blessings of redemption. Christians have forgiveness of sin, an eternal inheritance.

Read Ephesians 1.

REFLECTING

The past has a tendency to bind us up. Most Christians need to re-identify with who they are. We still see ourselves as mere human beings, children of the age—with the albatross of the world hung around our necks. That may be who we once were—but no longer. We have been adopted by God and are now His children. We are newly created in Him in holiness and righteousness. We have been given an inheritance in heaven that includes wealth and power. Our new position in Christ removes us from our old condition. We have been changed; we are no longer what we were. We are new creatures in Christ. When that truth sinks in, we begin to act like who we really are, rather than who we were.

RESPONDING

1. Praise: As a new child of God, offer the Lord your praise through the words of this psalm:

O Lord, our Lord, How excellent is Your name in all the earth, You who set Your glory above the heavens! . . . When I consider Your heavens, the work of Your fingers. . . . what is man that You are mindful of him, and the son of man that You visit him? O Lord, our Lord, How majestic is Your name in all the earth! (Psalm 8:1, 3-4, 9)

Now offer to the Lord your personal praise and thanksgiving.

2. Confession: Pray this confession to the Lord as you seek to keep your life free from sin and in fellowship with Him:

All we like sheep have gone astray; we have turned, every one, to his own way; and You, O Lord, have laid on Him the iniquity of us all. (Isaiah 53:6)

Confess any personal sins which the Holy Spirit brings to your mind.

3. Affirmation: As you agree with God's will, voice your affirmation of His word:

You, O Lord, have delivered me from the power of darkness and translated me into the kingdom of the Son of Your love, in whom I have redemption through His blood, the forgiveness of sins. (Colossians 1:13-14)

4. Requests: As you make your requests known to the Lord, include:

- Victory over temptation
- The work of missions in North and South America
- Your prayer list, the concerns of your heart, and today's activities.

5. Closing Prayer: Finally, offer this closing prayer to the Lord:

You who are the blessed and only Potentate, the King of kings and Lord of lords, who alone have immortality, dwelling in unapproachable light, whom no man has seen or can see, to You be honor and everlasting power. Amen. (1 Timothy 6:15-16)

Memory Verse: As each one has received a gift, minister it to one another, as good stewards of the manifold grace of God.

1 Peter 4:10
Spiritual Gifts Theme

READING

The passage for today centers on the means of salvation. All men are dead in sins, but by grace through faith in Christ, may be saved from sins.

Read Ephesians 2.

REFLECTING

Two of the most wonderful words in the Bible occur in this chapter: "But God. . . ." We were dead in our transgressions and sins, we followed the ways of this world and the ruler of the spirit of disobedience, we lived to gratify the cravings of our sinful nature, and we were by nature objects of wrath. *But God*, because of His great love for us, made us alive with Christ; we have been saved; God has raised us up with Christ and seated us with Him in the heavenly realms that in the coming ages He might show the incomparable riches of His grace, expressed in His kindness to us in Christ Jesus. And all this is by grace, that the glory should go to God.

RESPONDING

1. Praise: Praise the Lord that by grace the "but God" extends to you:

You are worthy, O Lord, to receive glory and honor and power; for You created all things, and by Your will they exist and were created. . . . I will praise You, O Lord, according to Your righteousness, and will sing praise to Your name, O Lord Most High. (Revelation 4:11, Psalm 7:17)

Pause for personal praise and thanksgiving.

2. Confession: Pray this confession to the Lord as you seek to keep your life free from sin and in fellowship with Him:

Forgive us, Lord, when we are unmindful of You, the Rock who begot us, and have forgotten You, the God who fathered us. (Deuteronomy 32:18)

Confess any personal sins which the Holy Spirit brings to mind.

3. Affirmation: Now pause to pray this affirmation to the Lord:

Behold what manner of love You, O Lord, have bestowed on me, that I should be called a child of God! Therefore the world does not know me, because it did not know my Lord Jesus. Now I am a child of God; and it has not yet been revealed what I shall be, but I know that when He is revealed, I shall be like Him, for I shall see Him as He is. (1 John 3:1-2)

4. Requests: As you make your requests known to the Lord, include:

- Love for your family
- Revival among Christians in America
- Your prayer list, the concerns of your heart, and today's activities

5. Closing Prayer: Finally, offer this closing prayer to the Lord:

Make me complete in every good work to do Your will, working in me what is well pleasing in Your sight, through Jesus Christ, to whom be glory forever and ever. Amen. (Hebrews 13:20-21)

Memory Verse: As each one has received a gift, minister it to one another, as good stewards of the manifold grace of God.

1 Peter 4:10
Spiritual Gifts Theme

OCTOBER 20

READING

The passage for today centers on Paul's ministry. Paul is called to be a minister, to take salvation to the Gentiles.

Read Ephesians 3.

REFLECTING

Paul calls his ministry the fulfillment of a "mystery." In the Bible a mystery is not mysterious, but something previously unknown. That Gentiles were to be saved was no mystery. That was made clear even in the Old Testament. The mystery is that Jew and Gentile were to make a wholly new thing, the Church, which is called Christ's body, formed by baptism with the Holy Spirit and in which the earthly distinction between Jew and Gentile disappears. This mystery was foretold by Jesus, but the details of the doctrine, walk, and destiny of the Church were committed to Paul and his fellow apostles. Now, as a new thing, the body of Christ, we are all to live as Christ would live if He were in our shoes.

RESPONDING

1. Praise: Offer your praise to the Lord because the message of the Church has come to you:

Blessed be the name of God forever and ever, for wisdom and might are His. . . . He gives wisdom to the wise and knowledge to those who have understanding. He reveals deep and secret things; He knows what is in the darkness, and light dwells with Him. (Daniel 2:20-22)

Pause for personal praise and thanksgiving.

2. Confession: Pray this confession to the Lord as you seek to keep your life free from sin and in fellowship with Him:

O Lord, You do not have as much delight in burnt offerings and sacrifices, as in our obeying Your voice. Behold, to obey is better than sacrifice, and to heed than the fat of rams. (1 Samuel 15:22)

Confess any personal sins which the Holy Spirit brings to your mind.

3. Affirmation: Now pause to pray this affirmation to the Lord:

There is therefore now no condemnation for me if I am in You, Christ Jesus. For the law of the Spirit of life in You has set me free from the law of sin and death. (Romans 8:1-2)

4. Requests: As you make your requests known to the Lord, include:

- Faithfulness with your treasures
- The Great Commission
- Your prayer list, the concerns of your heart, and today's activities

5. Closing Prayer: Finally, offer this closing prayer to the Lord:

May You, the God of grace, who called me to Your eternal glory by Christ Jesus, after I have suffered a while, perfect, establish, strengthen, and settle me. To You be the glory and the dominion forever and ever. Amen. (1 Peter 5:10-11)

Memory Verse: As each one has received a gift, minister it to one another, as good stewards of the manifold grace of God.

1 Peter 4:10
Spiritual Gifts Theme

READING

The passage for today centers on the Christian's walk. Christians are to walk in a manner worthy of their calling in Christ.

Read Ephesians 4.

REFLECTING

On the basis of who we are in Christ, redeemed, inheritors with Christ, adopted into God's family, destined to spend eternity with Him, on this basis, we are to live a lifestyle that reflects our identity. We are no longer to walk as we did before we knew the Lord or as those who do not know the Lord. We are to exhibit the likeness of God in our relationships. We are to be honest, not angry, generous, gracious with our speech, and kind to one another, tenderhearted, forgiving each other, just as God in Christ also has forgiven us. In this way, then, we will preserve the unity of the Spirit and manifest to the world that Christ is real and that He makes a difference in the life that is dedicated to Him.

RESPONDING

1. Praise: Because God has created in us the holiness of Christ by a work of regeneration, praise Him:

I will bless the Lord at all times; His praise shall continually be in my mouth. My soul shall make its boast in the Lord; the humble shall hear of it and be glad. Oh, magnify the Lord with me, and let us exalt His name together. . . . Oh, taste and see that the Lord is good; blessed is the man who trusts in Him! (Psalm 34:1-3, 8)

Pause for personal praise and thanksgiving.

2. Confession: Pray this confession to the Lord as you seek to keep your life free from sin and in fellowship with Him:

I have sinned greatly in what I have done; but now, I pray, O Lord, take away the iniquity of Your servant, for I have done very foolishly. (2 Samuel 24:10)

Confess any personal sins which the Holy Spirit brings to mind.

3. Affirmation: Now pause to pray this affirmation to the Lord:

My body is the temple of the Holy Spirit who is in me, whom I have from You, O God, and I am not my own. For I have been bought with a price; therefore I will glorify God in my body and in my spirit, which are Yours. (1 Corinthians 6:19-20)

4. Requests: As you make your requests known to the Lord, include:

- Spiritual insight
- Campus ministries
- Your prayer list, the concerns of your heart, and today's activities

5. Closing Prayer: Finally, offer this closing prayer to the Lord:

May I grow in the grace and knowledge of our Lord and Savior Jesus Christ. To Him be the glory both now and forever. Amen. (2 Peter 3:18)

Memory Verse: As each one has received a gift, minister it to one another, as good stewards of the manifold grace of God.

1 Peter 4:10
Spiritual Gifts Theme

OCTOBER 22

READING

The passage for today centers on the imitation of God. We are to walk in love and holiness, just as Christ did.

Read Ephesians 5.

REFLECTING

The wrath of God is coming on the sons of disobedience (the unsaved). Therefore, we are not to be partakers of their deeds. For we were formerly darkness, but now we are light in the Lord. Therefore, we are to walk as children of the light. We are not to participate in the unfruitful deeds of darkness, for it is disgraceful even to speak of the things which are done by them in secret. If this is so, do you as a Christian need to alter any of your present habits? What about your television viewing habits? If it is disgraceful even to speak of the things which are done by the children of darkness, how much more disgraceful is it to sit in our living rooms and watch it? What about movies, books, magazines, conversations with friends? Do your habits reflect the light of God?

RESPONDING

1. Praise: Praise the Lord that He has transferred us out of the kingdom of darkness into the kingdom of light:

Who is like You, O Lord, among the gods? Who is like You, glorious in holiness, fearful in praises, doing wonders? . . . You are great, O Lord God. For there is none like You, nor is there any God besides You, according to all that we have heard with our ears. (Exodus 15:11, 2 Samuel 7:22)

Pause for personal praise and thanksgiving.

2. Confession: Pray this confession to the Lord as you seek to keep your life free from sin and in fellowship with Him:

O my God: I am too ashamed and humiliated to lift up my face to You, my God; for my iniquity has risen higher than my head, and my guilt has grown even to the heavens. (Ezra 9:6)

Confess any personal sins which the Holy Spirit brings to your mind.

3. Affirmation: Now pause to pray this affirmation to the Lord:

If I confess with my mouth the Lord Jesus, and believe in my heart that You, O God, raised Him from the dead, I shall be saved. For with the heart I believe, resulting in righteousness, and with the mouth I confess, resulting in salvation. For the Scripture says, "Whoever believes in Him will not be disappointed." (Romans 10:9-11)

4. Requests: As you make your requests known to the Lord, include:

- Desire to be like Christ
- Needs in inner cities
- Your prayer list, the concerns of your heart, and today's activities

5. Closing Prayer: Finally, offer this closing prayer to the Lord:

Blessing and honor and glory and power be to You who sit on the throne, and to You, Lord, forever and ever! (Revelation 5:13)

Memory Verse: For the weapons of our warfare are not carnal but mighty in God for pulling down strongholds.
2 Corinthians 10:4
Spiritual Warfare Theme

READING

The passage for today centers on spiritual warfare. We are to put on the full armor of God, so that we may win the spiritual warfare in which we find ourselves.

Read Ephesians 6.

REFLECTING

Satan is a deceiver and a destroyer. He deceives in order to destroy. Part of his deception in our day is to have us believe that he is not at work opposing our pursuit of righteousness. But he is. To combat his efforts, we must do several things. First, recognize that we must be strong in the Lord and in the strength of His might (verse 10), not our own strength. Our struggle is not against flesh and blood. Therefore, the Lord must be our source of power. Second, we must put on the armor of God. Each piece described must be in place as we live our daily lives. Third, we must pray at all times in the Spirit (verse 18). And finally, having done all that, we may stand firm, without fear, knowing we are secure.

RESPONDING

1. Praise: Because the Lord will win our battles as we follow His instructions, we praise Him:

O Lord God, . . . the One who dwells between the cherubim, You are God, You alone, of all the kingdoms of the earth. You have made heaven and earth. (2 Kings 19:15)

Lord God, . . . there is no God in heaven above or on earth below like You, who keep Your covenant and mercy with Your servants who walk before You with all their heart. (1 Kings 8:23)

Pause for personal praise and thanksgiving.

2. Confession: Pray this confession to the Lord as you seek to keep your life free from sin and in fellowship with Him:

O Lord, do not rebuke me in Your anger, nor chasten me in Your hot displeasure. Have mercy on me, O Lord, for I am weak; O Lord, heal me, for . . . my soul also is greatly troubled. (Psalm 6:1-3)

Confess any personal sins which the Holy Spirit brings to your mind.

3. Affirmation: Now pause to pray this affirmation to the Lord:

Having been justified by faith, I have peace with You, O God, through the Lord Jesus Christ, through whom also I have obtained my introduction by faith into this grace in which I stand; and I rejoice in hope of the glory of God. (Romans 5:1-2)

4. Requests: As you make your requests known to the Lord, pray for:

- Personal witness for Christ
- Local churches around the nation
- Your prayer list, the concerns of your heart, and today's activities

5. Closing Prayer: Finally offer this closing prayer to the Lord:

Amen! Blessing and glory and wisdom, thanksgiving and honor and power and might, be to You, God, forever and ever. Amen. (Revelation 7:12)

Memory Verse: For the weapons of our warfare are not carnal but mighty in God for pulling down strongholds.
2 Corinthians 10:4
Spiritual Warfare Theme

OCTOBER 24

READING

The passage for today centers on Paul's life perspective. For Paul, to live is Christ, and to die is gain, which perspective he urges on us.

Read Philippians 1.

REFLECTING

With Paul's perspective in life, he couldn't lose. Wherever he is, Paul considers it "the world" into which the Lord wants him to go to preach the gospel. Even prison is a positive experience for Paul because he is able to spread the gospel there. And if he is to die, that is even better. To live is fruitful ministry, but to die is to be present with the Lord, a tremendous gain. Most of us have our affections too deeply implanted in the things given to us by the world system to identify with this perspective. Time spent studying our true position in Christ develops this proper perspective. We must learn to let go of this world and cling to the reality of our true citizenship in heaven.

RESPONDING

1. Praise: Let us praise our God in the words of this psalm:

My soul magnifies You, Lord, and my spirit has rejoiced in You, O God my Savior. . . . You who are mighty have done great things for me; and holy is Your name. And Your mercy is on those who fear You from generation to generation. (Luke 1:46-50)

Now offer to the Lord your personal praise and thanksgiving.

2. Confession: Pray this confession to the Lord as you seek to keep your life free from sin:

Let the wicked forsake his way, and the unrighteous man his thoughts; let him return to You, the Lord, and You will have mercy on him; and You, our God, for You will abundantly pardon. (Isaiah 55:7)

Confess any personal sins which the Holy Spirit brings to your mind.

3. Affirmation: As you agree with God's will, voice your affirmation of His word:

And now, Lord, what do I wait for? My hope is in You. (Psalm 39:7)

4. Requests: As you make your requests known to the Lord, include:

- An eternal perspective
- Needs of work or school mates
- Your prayer list, the concerns of your heart, and today's activities

5. Closing Prayer: Finally, offer this closing prayer to the Lord:

I will wait on You, the Lord; I will be of good courage, and You shall strengthen my heart; I will wait on You! (Psalm 27:14)

Memory Verse: For the weapons of our warfare are not carnal but mighty in God for pulling down strongholds.
2 Corinthians 10:4
Spiritual Warfare Theme

READING

The passage for today centers on an exhortation to Christlikeness. Be like Christ, who did nothing from selfish conceit, but looked out for the interests of others.

Read Philippians 2.

REFLECTING

Selfishness is the source of most interpersonal conflict. Someone is taking something from us (materially, emotionally, socially, etc.) what we don't want to give, and we fight to keep or gain our desires. Unselfishness is the source of most interpersonal harmony. Our experience tells us that many people don't really care about us, but rather about themselves. Think back over the people you really like in a personal way—even if you don't know them personally (they may be well-known persons). Usually the reason you like them is that they are nice, kind, and giving to others. If you want to be a harmonious person, well liked by others, you must be unselfish.

RESPONDING

1. Praise: The Lord is worthy to receive our praise because of all that He has done for us:

Because Your lovingkindness is better than life, My lips shall praise You. Thus I will bless You while I live; I will lift up my hands in Your name. My soul shall be satisfied as with marrow and fatness, and my mouth shall praise You with joyful lips. . . . Because You have been my help, therefore in the shadow of Your wings I will rejoice. (Psalm 63:3-5, 7)

Now offer to the Lord your personal praise and thanksgiving.

2. Confession: Pray this confession to the Lord as you seek to keep your life free from sin and in fellowship with Him:

Lord, be merciful to me; heal my soul, for I have sinned against You. . . . O Lord, be merciful to me, and raise me up. . . . Blessed be the Lord God of Israel from everlasting to everlasting! Amen and amen. (Psalm 41:4, 10, 13)

Confess any personal sins which the Holy Spirit brings to your mind.

3. Affirmation: As you agree with God's will, voice your affirmation of His word:

I delight to do Your will, O my God, and Your law is within my heart. (Psalm 40:8)

4. Requests: As you make your requests known to the Lord, include:

- Personal discipline

- Christians worldwide who are persecuted for their faith

- Your prayer list, the concerns of your heart, and today's activities

5. Closing Prayer: Finally, offer this closing prayer to the Lord:

Show me the path of life; in Your presence is fullness of joy; at Your right hand are pleasures forevermore. (Psalm 16:11)

Memory Verse: For the weapons of our warfare are not carnal but mighty in God for pulling down strongholds.
2 Corinthians 10:4
Spiritual Warfare Theme

OCTOBER 26

READING

The passage for today centers on the goal of life. Our goal in life should be to forsake temporal things for the sake of the eternal.

Read Philippians 3.

REFLECTING

Benjamin Franklin once decided to become morally perfect. He chose thirteen qualities which he felt embodied moral perfection and tried to perfect one a week so that at the end of thirteen weeks, he would be morally perfect. He failed, so he tried again and again for the rest of his life. He wrote that he had never become morally perfect but that he had become a much better man for trying and failing than if he had never tried at all. Our situation with the Lord is similar. We will never become morally perfect, as Paul writes. But we will gradually experience the maturation into the image of Christ and be more mature than if we did not commit ourselves to following Him.

RESPONDING

1. Praise: Because the Lord knows our weaknesses and loves us anyway, we can praise Him with enthusiasm:

O God, You are my God; early will I seek You; My soul thirsts for You, my flesh longs for You in a dry and weary land where there is no water. So I have looked for You in the sanctuary, to see Your power and Your glory. (Psalm 63:1-2)

Now offer to the Lord your personal praise and thanksgiving.

2. Confession: Pray this confession to the Lord as you seek to keep your life free from sin and in fellowship with Him:

You will again have compassion on us, and will subdue our iniquities. You will cast all our sins into the depths of the sea. (Micah 7:19)

Confess any personal sins which the Holy Spirit brings to your mind.

3. Affirmation: As you agree with God's will, voice your affirmation of His word:

For I did not receive the spirit of bondage again to fear, but I received the Spirit of adoption by whom I cry out, "Abba, Father." (Romans 8:15)

4. Requests: As you make your requests known to the Lord, include:

- Love for the Lord
- The work of missions in the Middle East, Australia, and the Islands
- Your prayer list, the concerns of your heart, and today's activities

5. Closing Prayer: Finally, offer this closing prayer to the Lord:

Save Your people, and bless Your inheritance; shepherd us also, and bear us up forever. (Psalm 28:9)

Memory Verse: For the weapons of our warfare are not carnal but mighty in God for pulling down strongholds.
2 Corinthians 10:4
Spiritual Warfare Theme

READING

The passage for today centers on the pursuit of excellence. We must think only of those things which are excellent and do the same.

Read Philippians 4.

REFLECTING

You are what you eat. That is, your body reflects what you feed it over time. If you eat lard, your body turns to lard. Eat well, and your body rewards you with health. The same is true spiritually, mentally, and emotionally. We become like what we put into our minds and like what we allow our minds to dwell on. Paul writes, "Whatever is true, honorable, right, pure, lovely, of good repute, if there is any excellence and if anything worthy of praise, *let your mind dwell on these things*" (verse 8). If you are unsatisfied with your spiritual, mental, emotional development, ask yourself, "What do I put into my mind, and what do I think about?" You may need some radical change in your spiritual diet.

RESPONDING

1. Praise: The Lord is excellent and worthy of our praise, and our minds may freely dwell on Him:

I will praise You, O Lord, with my whole heart; I will tell of all Your marvelous works. I will be glad and rejoice in You; I will sing praise to Your name, O Most High. . . . The Lord also will be a refuge for the oppressed, a refuge in times of trouble. And those who know Your name will put their trust in You; for You, Lord have not forsaken those who seek You. (Psalm 9:1-2, 9-10)

Now offer to the Lord your personal praise and thanksgiving.

2. Confession: Pray this confession to the Lord as you seek to keep your life free from sin and in fellowship with Him:

For a mere moment You have forsaken me, but with great mercies You will gather me. With a little wrath You hid Your face from me for a moment; but with everlasting kindness You will have mercy on me. (Isaiah 54:7-8)

Confess any personal sins which the Holy Spirit brings to your mind.

3. Affirmation: As you agree with God's will, voice your affirmation of His word:

You, O Lord, are Spirit, and I must worship You in spirit and truth. (John 4:24)

4. Requests: As you make your requests known to the Lord, include:

- Faithfulness in sharing Christ
- The Lord's work in national and world affairs
- Your prayer list, the concerns of your heart, and today's activities

5. Closing Prayer: Finally, offer this closing prayer to the Lord:

You, the Lord, will command Your lovingkindness in the daytime, and in the night Your song shall be with me—a prayer to You, the God of my life. (Psalm 42:8)

Memory Verse: For the weapons of our warfare are not carnal but mighty in God for pulling down strongholds.
2 Corinthians 10:4
Spiritual Warfare Theme

OCTOBER 28

READING

The passage for today centers on the Head of the Church. Christ is the image of the invisible God, the Head of the Church, which is the body of Christ.

Read Colossians 1.

REFLECTING

On the surface of things, it is pretty difficult to explain why you would believe in God. His existence cannot be proved. No one has seen Him, touched Him, felt Him, smelled Him, or heard Him. Therefore, you must get below the surface. You must enter the courtroom for evidence, rather than the laboratory for proof. And there you find illustrations of things not seen or not understood. God is invisible, but Jesus was not. Paul writes, Jesus is the "image of the invisible God" (verse 15). If you want to know about God, learn about Jesus. If you want to see God, look at Jesus. If you want to please God, follow Jesus. Jesus came that we might see and understand God. Jesus is God in the flesh.

RESPONDING

1. Praise: Thank the Lord that we see God in Christ, and praise Him for the privilege of knowing Him:

I will love You, O Lord, my strength. The Lord is my rock and my fortress and my deliverer; my God, my strength, in whom I will trust; my shield and the horn of my salvation, my stronghold. I call upon the Lord, who is worthy to be praised; so shall I be saved from my enemies. . . . The Lord lives! Blessed be my Rock! Let the God of my salvation be exalted. (Psalm 18:1-3, 46)

Now offer to the Lord your personal praise and thanksgiving.

2. Confession: Pray this confession to the Lord as you seek to keep your life free from sin and in fellowship with Him:

Let the wicked forsake his way, and the unrighteous man his thoughts; let him return to You, the Lord, and You will have mercy on him; and You, our God, for You will abundantly pardon. (Isaiah 55:7)

Confess any personal sins which the Holy Spirit brings to your mind.

3. Affirmation: As you agree with God's will, voice your affirmation of His word:

If I keep Your commandments, Lord Jesus, I will abide in Your love, just as You have kept Your Father's commandments and abide in His love. (John 15:10)

4. Requests: As you make your requests known to the Lord, include:

* Compassion for others
* Missions in America
* Your prayer list, the concerns of your heart, and today's activities

5. Closing Prayer: Finally, offer this closing prayer to the Lord:

Now to You who are able to keep me from stumbling, and to present me faultless before the presence of Your glory with exceeding joy, to You, my God and Savior, who alone are wise, be glory and majesty, dominion and power, both now and forever. Amen. (Jude 24-25)

Memory Verse: For the weapons of our warfare are not carnal but mighty in God for pulling down strongholds.
2 Corinthians 10:4
Spiritual Warfare Theme

READING

The passage for today centers on the centrality of Christ. Christ is the example and savior for the Christian, the center of life.

Read Colossians 2.

REFLECTING

Man can no more save himself than he could fly to the moon on feathered wings. Both are utterly impossible. Because of the laws of gravity and physics, man would stand a greater chance of drilling himself to China than flying to the moon. And because of man's spiritual condition and the spiritual laws of God, he stands a greater assurance of making his spiritual condition worse instead of better by trying to save himself. Paul says that we were dead and that we had decrees written against us which we were powerless to remove. God made us alive together with Christ and removed the decrees against us by nailing them to the cross. We must gain salvation by grace through faith in Christ or not have it at all.

RESPONDING

1. Praise: Praise the Lord that in our utter helplessness, He offered us salvation through Christ:

Lord, You have been our dwelling place in all generations. Before the mountains were brought forth, or ever You had formed the earth and the world, even from everlasting to everlasting, You are God. O satisfy us early with Your mercy, that we may rejoice and be glad all our days! (Psalm 90:1-2, 14)

Now offer to the Lord your personal praise and thanksgiving.

2. Confession: Pray this confession to the Lord as you seek to keep your life free from sin and in fellowship with Him:

"Turn to Me with all your heart. . . ." Return to the Lord your God, for He is gracious and merciful, slow to anger, and of great kindness; and He relents from doing harm. (Joel 2:12-13)

Confess any personal sins which the Holy Spirit brings to your mind.

3. Affirmation: As you agree with God's will, voice your affirmation of His word:

And this is Your commandment: that I should believe on the name of Your Son Jesus Christ and love others, as He commanded me. (1 John 3:23)

4. Requests: As you make your requests known to the Lord, include:

- Personal spiritual growth
- Military ministries
- Your prayer list, the concerns of your heart, and today's activities

5. Closing Prayer: Finally, offer this closing prayer to the Lord:

Glory to You in the highest, and on earth peace, good will toward men! (Luke 2:14)

> **Memory Verse:** Therefore take up the whole armor of God, that you may be able to withstand in the evil day, and having done all, to stand.
> Ephesians 6:13
> *Spiritual Warfare Theme*

OCTOBER 30

READING

The passage for today centers on the new self. We have been raised up with Christ and are to seek the things above.

Read Colossians 3.

REFLECTING

It is possible to be one place physically, and another place mentally. It happens every Sunday morning in church. Bodies warm the pews while minds roam the kitchens and golf courses of the nation. In a graver example, prisoners of war survive by taking themselves mentally into another world, away from the prison, and there find meaning and solace. We as Christians are to do the same. We are to take ourselves out of the physical world, into the spiritual world, and to operate according to its values, truths, and realities. "If then, you have been raised up with Christ, keep seeking the things above . . . set your mind on the things above, not on the things that are on earth" (verses 1-2).

RESPONDING

1. Praise: Place your mind on Christ, and give Him your praise as you seek the things above:

Let my mouth be filled with Your praise and with Your glory all the day. . . . But I will hope continually, and will praise You yet more and more. My mouth shall tell of Your righteousness and Your salvation all the day, for I do not know their limits. I will go in the strength of the Lord God; I will make mention of Your righteousness, of Yours only. O God, You have taught me from my youth and to this day declare Your wondrous works. (Psalm 71:8, 14-17)

Now offer to the Lord your personal praise and thanksgiving.

2. Confession: Pray this confession to the Lord as you seek to keep your life free from sin and in fellowship with Him:

I acknowledged my sin to You, and my iniquity I have not hidden. I said, "I will confess my transgressions to the Lord," and You forgave the iniquity of my sin. (Psalm 32:5)

Confess any personal sins which the Holy Spirit brings to your mind.

3. Affirmation: As you agree with God's will, voice your affirmation of His word:

I consider that the sufferings of this present time are not worthy to be compared with the glory which shall be revealed in me. (Romans 8:18)

4. Requests: As you make your requests known to the Lord, include:

- Fruit of the Spirit in your life
- The ministry of Christian literature
- Your prayer list, the concerns of your heart, and today's activities

5. Closing Prayer: Finally, offer this closing prayer to the Lord:

Grace, mercy, and peace from You, the Father, and the Lord Jesus Christ our Savior. (Titus 1:4)

Memory Verse: Therefore take up the whole armor of God, that you may be able to withstand in the evil day, and having done all, to stand.
Ephesians 6:13
Spiritual Warfare Theme

READING

The passage for today centers on personal conduct. Conduct yourself with wisdom, and let your speech be with grace.

Read Colossians 4.

REFLECTING

Out of the abundance of the heart, the mouth speaks. A man cannot claim his heart is kind if his words are unkind. He cannot claim his heart embraces heaven's values if his mouth speaks the values of the world. The heart is a reservoir, and the mouth a faucet. When the faucet is turned on, whatever is in the reservoir comes out. Paul writes, "Let your speech always be with grace, seasoned, as it were, with salt . . . ." (verse 6). Elsewhere, he writes, "Let no unwholesome word proceed out of your mouth, but only such a word as is good for edification, according to the need of the moment, that it may give grace to those who hear" (Ephesians 4:29). Listen to your speech! Analyze your heart!

RESPONDING

1. Praise: Out of the abundance of your heart, offer to the Lord the praise of your lips:

Blessed be the name of God forever and ever, for wisdom and might are His. . . . He gives wisdom to the wise and knowledge to those who have understanding. He reveals deep and secret things; He knows what is in the darkness, and light dwells with Him. (Daniel 2:20-22)

Now offer to the Lord your personal praise and thanksgiving.

2. Confession: Pray this confession to the Lord as you seek to keep your life free from sin and in fellowship with Him:

The sacrifices of God are a broken spirit, a broken and contrite heart—these, O God, You will not despise. (Psalm 51:16-17)

Confess any personal sins which the Holy Spirit brings to your mind.

3. Affirmation: As you agree with God's will, voice your affirmation of His word:

By this I know love, because You, Lord Jesus, laid down Your life for me. And I also ought to lay down my life for my brother. (1 John 3:16)

4. Requests: As you make your requests known to the Lord, include:

- Boldness in living for Christ
- God's blessing on America
- Your prayer list, the concerns of your heart, and today's activities

5. Closing Prayer: Finally, offer this closing prayer to the Lord:

Be glad in the Lord and rejoice, you righteous; and shout for joy, all you upright in heart!. (Psalm 32:11)

Memory Verse: Therefore take up the whole armor of God, that you may be able to withstand in the evil day, and having done all, to stand.
Ephesians 6:13
Spiritual Warfare Theme

NOVEMBER 1

READING

The passage for today centers on Paul's encouragement for spiritual growth. The Thessalonians follow Paul's life example, grow to spiritual maturity, and become an example themselves to the Macedonians and Achaians.

Read 1 Thessalonians 1.

REFLECTING

Because the Christian life is more easily caught than taught, personal godliness is the most powerful ministry tool, and imitation is the most powerful tool for spiritual growth. Paul imparted to the Thessalonians not just the words of the gospel, but also his very life ("you know what kind of men we were among you"[verse 5]). The Thessalonian believers witnessed Paul's life among them and imitated him, which resulted in spiritual growth for them ("you became followers [imitators] of us"[verse 6]). As a result of that spiritual growth, they became an example to the Macedonians and Achaians.

It is true that ministry from a mind reaches a mind. But ministry from a heart reaches a heart. Would you like to experience greater spiritual growth? Develop a relationship with someone who is more mature than you are, and become spiritually accountable to him.

RESPONDING

1. Praise: As you continue your time with the Lord, offer to Him your praise that He is our perfect example:

Praise the Lord! I will praise the Lord with my whole heart, in the assembly of the upright and in the congregation. . . . The fear of the

Lord is the beginning of wisdom; a good understanding have all those who do His commandments. His praise endures forever. (Psalm 111:1, 10)

Take a moment to offer the Lord your personal praise and thanksgiving.

2. Confession: Pray this confession to the Lord as you seek to keep your life free from sin and in fellowship with Him:

Show me Your ways, O Lord; teach me Your paths. Lead me in Your truth and teach me, for You are the God of my salvation; on You I wait all the day. (Psalm 25:4-5)

Confess any personal sins which the Holy Spirit may bring to your mind.

3. Affirmation: As you agree with the will of God, voice your affirmation of His word:

And now, Lord, what do I wait for? My hope is in You. (Psalm 39:7)

4. Requests: As you make your requests known to the Lord, include:

- Health and strength to serve God

- God's will to be done on earth

- Your prayer list, the concerns of your heart, and today's activities

5. Closing Prayer: Finally, offer this closing prayer to the Lord:

Blessed are You, the Lord, forevermore! Amen and amen. (Psalm 89:52)

Memory Verse: Therefore take up the whole armor of God, that you may be able to withstand in the evil day, and having done all, to stand.
Ephesians 6:13
Spiritual Warfare Theme

NOVEMBER 2

READING

Today's passage centers on Paul's method of ministry. Paul's words of the gospel are communicated in love and integrity.

Read 1 Thessalonians 2.

REFLECTING

Whenever the "message" of your words and the "message" of your actions conflict, the "message" of your actions will always win out. You may speak gruffly but act kindly, and you will be known as having a hard shell but being a "softie" on the inside. Or you may speak well but act selfishly, and you will be known as a hypocrite. There is no accusation leveled at Christians more consistently than that of hypocrisy. Our lives must support the reality of the gospel, or the gospel will not be taken seriously, and we will be resented. Paul writes, "We were pleased to impart to you not only the gospel of God, but also our own lives . . . ." (verse 8). Unless we are willing to impart our lives in ministry, our words will mean little.

RESPONDING

1. Praise: Thank the Lord, and praise Him that He was willing to impart to us His very life:

You who love the Lord, hate evil! He preserves the souls of His saints; He delivers them out of the hand of the wicked. Light is sown for the righteous, and gladness for the upright in heart. Rejoice in the Lord, you righteous, and give thanks at the remembrance of His holy name. (Psalm 97:10-12)

Take a moment to offer the Lord your personal praise and thanksgiving.

2. Confession: Pray this confession to the Lord as you seek to keep your life free from sin and in fellowship with Him:

If I say that I have no sin, I deceive myself, and the truth is not in me. If I confess my sins, You, O Lord, are faithful and just to forgive me my sins and to cleanse me from all unrighteousness. (1 John 1:8-9)

Confess any personal sins which the Holy Spirit may bring to your mind.

3. Affirmation: As you agree with the will of God, voice your affirmation of His word:

You, Lord Jesus, are the Living Bread which came down from heaven. If I eat of this bread, I will live forever; and the bread that You have given is Your flesh, which You gave for the life of the world. (John 6:51)

4. Requests: As you make your requests known to the Lord, include:

- Sensitivity to sin
- The ministry of your local church
- Your prayer list, the concerns of your heart, and today's activities

5. Closing Prayer: Finally, offer this closing prayer to the Lord:

Let the words of my mouth and the meditation of my heart be acceptable in Your sight, O Lord, my strength and my redeemer. (Psalm 19:14)

Memory Verse: Therefore take up the whole armor of God, that you may be able to withstand in the evil day, and having done all, to stand.
Ephesians 6:13
Spiritual Warfare Theme

READING

The passage for today centers on Timothy's ministry. Paul is not able to visit Thessalonica, and out of extreme concern for their welfare, he sends Timothy to them.

Read 1 Thessalonians 3.

REFLECTING

Affliction is part of life. Sometimes circumstances afflict us. Sometimes other people afflict us. Sometimes we afflict ourselves. In the midst of affliction, we need encouragement. Paul writes that he sent Timothy to visit the Thessalonians "to establish and encourage" them because of their afflictions. Paul feared for their spiritual well-being.

When we see others in the midst of affliction, we should be quick to encourage them. It might be true that in addition to encouragement they might need information or exhortation, but not without encouragement, too. Rebuke, exhortation, counsel, and instruction all have their time and place, but encouragement is one of the most powerful ministries on earth.

RESPONDING

1. Praise: Praise the Lord for the encouragement He gives us through the Word, the Holy Spirit, and through other believers:

Praise the Lord! Praise, O servants of the Lord, praise the name of the Lord! Blessed be the name of the Lord from this time forth and forevermore! From the rising of the sun to its going down, the Lord's name is to be praised. . . . Who is like the Lord our God, who dwells on high, who humbles Himself to behold the things that are in heavens and in earth? Praise the Lord! (Psalm 113:1-3, 5-6, 9)

Take a moment to offer the Lord your personal praise and thanksgiving.

2. Confession: Pray this confession to the Lord as you seek to keep your life free from sin and in fellowship with Him:

Remember, O Lord, Your tender mercies and Your lovingkindnesses, for they have been from of old. Do not remember the sins of my youth, nor my transgressions; according to Your mercy remember me, for Your goodness' sake, O Lord. (Psalm 25:6-7)

Confess any personal sins which the Holy Spirit may bring to your mind.

3. Affirmation: As you agree with the will of God, voice your affirmation of His word:

For I have sinned and fall short of Your glory, O God; being justified freely by Your grace through the redemption that is in Christ Jesus. (Romans 3:23-24)

4. Requests: As you make your requests known to the Lord, include:

- Wisdom for living life
- Needs of your immediate family
- Your prayer list, the concerns of your heart, and today's activities

5. Closing Prayer: Finally, offer this closing prayer to the Lord:

Surely goodness and mercy shall follow me all the days of my life, and I will dwell in the house of the Lord forever. (Psalm 23:6)

Memory Verse: Therefore take up the whole armor of God, that you may be able to withstand in the evil day, and having done all, to stand.
Ephesians 6:13
Spiritual Warfare Theme

NOVEMBER 4

READING

The passage for today centers on instructions in living and dying. After encouraging the Thessalonians to personal holiness, Paul informs them of the coming of the Lord.

Read 1 Thessalonians 4.

REFLECTING

Is it safe to die? Death is a yawning, gaping black hole swirling at the end of everyone's life. A foreboding and unknown experience, it is the common denominator that links all humanity. And the dominant question that passes through all generations is, "What happens when we die?"

Many of life's questions are not fully addressed in the Scripture. But death is, and the answer to what happens after we die is one of the most satisfying things in the Bible. The Thessalonians were concerned that their loved ones who had died might not be going to heaven. Paul assures them that they are. The dead in Christ shall rise first, and those who are alive and remain shall meet them in the air.

RESPONDING

1. Praise: Because the Lord has taken away the danger of death, because it is safe to die, offer Him your praise:

Not unto us, O Lord, not unto us, but to Your name give glory, because of Your mercy, and because of Your truth. . . . We who fear You, O Lord, trust in You; You are our help and our shield. . . . We will bless the Lord from this time forth and forevermore. Praise the Lord! (Psalm 115:1, 11, 18)

Take a moment to offer the Lord your personal praise and thanksgiving.

2. Confession: Pray this confession to the Lord as you seek to keep your life free from sin and in fellowship with Him:

Turn Yourself to me, O God, and have mercy on me, for I am desolate and afflicted. The troubles of my heart have enlarged; oh, bring me out of my distresses! Look on my affliction and my pain, and forgive all my sins. (Psalm 25:16-18)

Confess any personal sins which the Holy Spirit may bring to your mind.

3. Affirmation: As you agree with the will of God, voice your affirmation of His word:

Lord Jesus, You bid me come to You when I labor and am heavy laden, and You promise to give me rest. You ask that I take Your yoke upon me and learn from You; for You are gentle and lowly in heart, and I will find rest for my soul. (Matthew 11:28-30)

4. Requests: As you make your requests known to the Lord, include:

- Insight into Scripture
- The hungry around the world
- Your prayer list, the concerns of your heart, and today's activities

5. Closing Prayer: Finally, offer this closing prayer to the Lord:

We will be of good courage, and You shall strengthen our hearts, all we who hope in the Lord. (Psalm 31:24)

Memory Verse: Therefore take up the whole armor of God, that you may be able to withstand in the evil day, and having done all, to stand.
Ephesians 6:13
Spiritual Warfare Theme

READING

The passage for today centers on the Day of the Lord. The coming of the Lord will be instantaneous. Therefore, we ought always to be ready.

Read 1 Thessalonians 5.

REFLECTING

Many people who believe in God and Christ, but have never committed their lives to Them, say that at the end of their lives, they will accept the Lord. They don't want to accept Him now because they don't want His interference in their lives, but when they've lived life as they pleased, they will accept Him and get into heaven at the last minute. This is foolish and exceedingly dangerous. First, because such people rarely get more spiritually sensitive in their old age. Often, they get more resistant to the Lord. Second, because we never know when we will die. An accident might take us before we can repent. Or, the Lord could come at any minute, and it would be too late. The coming of the Lord is like a thief in the night. Are you prepared?

RESPONDING

1. Praise: In Christ, we can be ready for the coming of the Lord, so praise Him for this provision:

Unto You I lift up my eyes, O You who dwell in the heavens. Behold, as the eyes of servants look to the hand of their masters, as the eyes of a maid to the hand of her mistress, so our eyes look to the Lord our God, until He has mercy on us. (Psalm 123:1-2)

Take a moment to offer the Lord your personal praise and thanksgiving.

2. Confession: Pray this confession to the Lord as you seek to keep your life free from sin and in fellowship with Him:

Good and upright are You, Lord; therefore You teach me, though a sinner, in Your way. If I am humble, You will guide me in justice and teach me Your way. All Your paths for me are mercy and truth, if I keep Your covenant and Your testimonies. For Your name's sake, O Lord, pardon my iniquity, for it is great. (Psalm 25:8-11)

Confess any personal sins which the Holy Spirit may bring to your mind.

3. Affirmation: As you agree with the will of God, voice your affirmation of His word:

And now, Lord, what do I wait for? My hope is in You. (Psalm 39:7)

4. Requests: As you make your requests known to the Lord, include:

- Love for fellow Christians
- The work of missions in Europe and Asia
- Your prayer list, the concerns of your heart, and today's activities

5. Closing Prayer: Finally, offer this closing prayer to the Lord:

This is the day which You have made; I will rejoice and be glad in it. (Psalm 118:24)

Memory Verse: Praying always with all prayer and supplication in the Spirit, being watchful to this end with all perseverance and supplication for all the saints.

Ephesians 6:18
Spiritual Warfare Theme

NOVEMBER 6

READING

The passage for today centers on encouragement in persecution. Because God will avenge the righteous, we should be patient in persecution.

Read 2 Thessalonians 1.

REFLECTING

"This world is not my home, I'm just passing through. If heaven's not my home, O Lord, what would I do? The angels beckon me from heaven's open door, and I can't feel at home in this world any more." So go the words to an old song, and truer words were never sung. We are not of this world. We are sojourners, pilgrims. This world will deal with us unkindly. We cannot expect it to be otherwise.

If we insist on getting our meaning in life only from what comes to us in this world, most of us will be gravely disappointed. And, if we expect to receive complete justice in this world, we will be equally disappointed. Complete justice for us will come only "when the Lord Jesus is revealed from heaven with His mighty angels" (verse 7).

RESPONDING

1. Praise: The Lord gives us a home in heaven with Him, and so we praise Him for this wonderful gift to us:

Praise the Lord! Praise the name of the Lord; praise Him, O you servants of the Lord! . . . Praise the Lord, for the Lord is good; sing praises to His name, for it is pleasant. . . . For I know that the Lord is great, and our Lord is above all gods. . . . Blessed be the Lord . . . Praise the Lord! (Psalm 135:1, 3, 5, 21)

Take a moment to offer the Lord your personal praise and thanksgiving.

2. Confession: Pray this confession to the Lord as you seek to keep your life free from sin and in fellowship with Him:

I will sing praise to You, O Lord, as one of Your saints, and will give thanks at the remembrance of Your holy name. For Your anger is but for a moment, Your favor is for life; weeping may endure for a night, but joy comes in the morning. (Psalm 30:4-5)

Confess any personal sins which the Holy Spirit may bring to your mind.

3. Affirmation: As you agree with the will of God, voice your affirmation of His word:

I delight to do Your will, O my God, and Your law is within my heart. (Psalm 40:8)

4. Requests: As you make your requests known to the Lord, include:

- Faithfulness with your time
- The president and national leaders and affairs
- Your prayer list, the concerns of your heart, and today's activities

5. Closing Prayer: Finally, offer this closing prayer to the Lord:

Oh, satisfy me early with Your mercy, that I may rejoice and be glad all my days! (Psalm 90:14)

Memory Verse: Praying always with all prayer and supplication in the Spirit, being watchful to this end with all perseverance and supplication for all the saints.

Ephesians 6:18
Spiritual Warfare Theme

READING

The passage for today centers on signs of the Day of the Lord. The Day of the Lord will be preceded by a vast "falling away"; therefore, we must stand fast.

Read 2 Thessalonians 2.

REFLECTING

Unbelief is dangerous. It leads to deception, and deception leads to destruction. There are times when we must "know" in order to "believe." Jesus performed many convincing proofs of his identity so that people could have a basis for believing in Him. But there are other times when we must "believe" in order to "know," for there are times when whether or not we trust someone determines whether or not we will believe him. So it is with God. The more we trust, the more we can know. And unbelief allows deception.

RESPONDING

1. Praise: Because God is trustworthy and we can know Him, offer your praise from this psalm:

Let my mouth be filled with Your praise and with Your glory all the day. . . . But I will hope continually, and will praise You yet more and more. My mouth shall tell of Your righteousness and Your salvation all the day, for I do not know their limits. I will go in the strength of the Lord God; I will make mention of Your righteousness, of Yours only. O God, You have taught me from my youth and to this day declare Your wondrous works. (Psalm 71:8, 14-17)

Now offer to the Lord your personal praise and thanksgiving.

2. Confession: Pray this confession to the Lord as you seek to keep your life free from sin and in fellowship with Him:

O God, cleanse me from all my iniquity by which I have sinned against You, and pardon all my iniquities by which I have sinned and by which I have transgressed against You. (Jeremiah 33:8)

Confess any personal sins which the Holy Spirit brings to your mind.

3. Affirmation: As you agree with God's will, voice your affirmation of His word:

I consider that the sufferings of this present time are not worthy to be compared with the glory which shall be revealed in me. (Romans 8:18)

4. Requests: As you make your requests known to the Lord, include:

- Your financial needs
- The needs of the poor
- Your prayer list, the concerns of your heart, and today's activities

5. Closing Prayer: Finally, offer this closing prayer to the Lord:

Let the beauty of You, Lord, be upon me, and establish the work of my hands for me; yes, establish the work of my hands. (Psalm 90:17)

Memory Verse: Praying always with all prayer and supplication in the Spirit, being watchful to this end with all perseverance and supplication for all the saints.

Ephesians 6:18
Spiritual Warfare Theme

NOVEMBER 8

READING

The passage for today centers on lifestyle accountability. We are to hold other Christians accountable for the integrity of their lifestyle.

Read 2 Thessalonians 3.

REFLECTING

Past generations of Christians have been guilty of excess in judging other people. The Salem witch trials are the most glaring examples, but other examples abound throughout history. Today, we live in an age of greater understanding and acceptance, which is certainly preferable, unless it degenerates into careless acceptance of things which are clearly wrong, in which case, the pendulum swings too far the other way. We are to be tolerant of debatable things, but clear sin is to be dealt with. "Withdraw from every brother who walks disorderly" (verse 6).

RESPONDING

1. Praise: As you continue your time with the Lord, offer Him your praise through His word:

It is good to give thanks to the Lord, and to sing praises to Your name, O Most High; to declare Your lovingkindness in the morning, and Your faithfulness every night. . . . You are my Rock, and there is no unrighteousness in You. (Psalm 92:1-2,15)

Now offer to the Lord your personal praise and thanksgiving.

2. Confession: Pray this confession to the Lord as you seek to keep your life free from sin and in fellowship with Him:

The heart is deceitful above all things, and desperately wicked; who can know it? You, the Lord, search the heart, You test the mind, even to give every man according to his ways, and

according to the fruit of his doings. . . . Heal me, O Lord, and I shall be healed; save me, and I shall be saved, for You are my praise. (Jeremiah 17:9, 10, 14)

Confess any personal sins which the Holy Spirit brings to your mind.

3. Affirmation: As you agree with God's will, voice your affirmation of His word:

All that the Father gives You, O Lord Jesus, will come to You, and if I come to You, I will not be cast out by any means. (John 6:37)

4. Requests: As you make your requests known to the Lord, include:

- Protection from the "evil one"
- Laborers for the "harvest"
- Your prayer list, the concerns of your heart, and today's activities.

5. Closing Prayer: Finally, offer this closing prayer to the Lord:

Bless the Lord, all you His hosts, you ministers of His, who do His pleasure. Bless the Lord, all His works, in all places of His dominion. (Psalm 103:21-22)

Memory Verse: Praying always with all prayer and supplication in the Spirit, being watchful to this end with all perseverance and supplication for all the saints.

Ephesians 6:18
Spiritual Warfare Theme

READING

The passage for today centers on the dangers of false doctrine. False teachers lead others astray and are to be resisted.

Read 1 Timothy 1.

REFLECTING

Lack of integrity is fast becoming a sign of our age. Once highly respected, many professions are falling into disrepute: lawyers, doctors, journalists, and, most unfortunate of all, ministers. Whereas we once could invest considerable trust in these people, we must now exercise caution and discernment. With the proliferation of books, radio, television, and magazines, the opportunity for unscrupulous or inadequate ministers to foist themselves on the Christian public increases. Anything we hear being taught, we must carefully compare with the Bible and other Bible teachers whom we know to be credible. We must take care not to be led astray by false teaching.

RESPONDING

1. Praise: Offer your praise to the Lord for the Scripture, which leads us into truth:

You are the Rock, Your work is perfect; for all Your ways are justice, a God of truth and without injustice, righteous and upright are You. (Deuteronomy 32:4)

The Lord lives! Blessed be my Rock! Let God be exalted, the Rock of my salvation! (2 Samuel 22:47)

Pause for personal praise and thanksgiving.

2. Confession: Pray this confession to the Lord as you seek to keep your life free from sin and in fellowship with Him:

Lord, be merciful to me; heal my soul, for I have sinned against You. . . . O Lord, be merciful to me, and raise me up. . . . Blessed be the Lord God . . . from everlasting to everlasting! Amen and amen. (Psalm 41:4, 10, 13)

Confess any personal sins which the Holy Spirit brings to mind.

3. Affirmation: Now pause to pray this affirmation to the Lord:

Have I known? Have I heard? O Lord, the everlasting God, the Creator of the ends of the earth, You neither faint nor are weary. There is no searching of Your understanding. You give power to the weak, and when I have no might, You increase my strength. (Isaiah 40:27-29)

4. Requests: As you make your requests known to the Lord, include:

- Commitment to the Lord
- Parachurch ministries
- Your prayer list, the concerns of your heart, and today's activities

5. Closing Prayer: Finally, offer this closing prayer to the Lord:

Lord, preserve me from all evil; preserve my soul. Lord, preserve my going out and my coming in from this time forth, and even forevermore. (Psalm 121:7-8)

Memory Verse: Praying always with all prayer and supplication in the Spirit, being watchful to this end with all perseverance and supplication for all the saints.

Ephesians 6:18
Spiritual Warfare Theme

NOVEMBER 10

READING

The passage for today centers on directions for public worship. Prayers for others and proper appearance and actions are to characterize public worship.

Read 1 Timothy 2.

REFLECTING

Praying for our national and world leaders and our state and local leaders is not only a good idea; it is a biblical responsibility and should be a part of our regular public worship. The purpose, the ultimate focus, of our prayer is evangelism. Paul teaches that we are to pray first that we may lead a quiet and peaceable life in all godliness and reverence. That, then, is linked to evangelism, for he goes on to teach that God desires all men to be saved and come to a knowledge of the truth. In addition to instructing us about our prayer, the passage challenges us about our lifestyle. The quiet and peaceable life is to lead to godliness and reverence, which becomes the basis for our evangelism.

RESPONDING

1. Praise: Give the Lord your praise that we are free to worship Him, with our words and with our lives:

Give to the Lord, O kindreds of the peoples. . . . Give to the Lord the glory due His name; bring an offering, and come before Him. Oh, worship the Lord in the beauty of holiness! (1 Chronicles 16:28-29)

I will praise the Lord according to His righteousness, and will sing praise to the name of the Lord Most High. (Psalm 7:17)

Pause for personal praise and thanksgiving.

2. Confession: Pray this confession to the Lord as you seek to keep your life free from sin and in fellowship with Him:

Have mercy upon me, O God, according to Your lovingkindness; according to the multitude of Your tender mercies, blot out my transgressions. Wash me thoroughly from my iniquity and cleanse me from my sin. For I acknowledge my transgressions, and my sin is ever before me. (Psalm 51:1-3)

Confess any personal sins which the Holy Spirit brings to your mind.

3. Affirmation: Now pause to pray this affirmation to the Lord:

Behold, You, O God, are my salvation, I will trust and not be afraid; "For YAH, the Lord, is my strength and my song; He also has become my salvation." (Isaiah 12:2)

4. Requests: As you make your request known to the Lord, include:

- Renewing of your mind
- Needs of your extended family
- Your prayer list, the concerns of your heart, and today's activities

5. Closing Prayer: Finally, offer this closing prayer to the Lord:

May we with one mind and one mouth glorify the God and Father of our Lord Jesus Christ. (Romans 15:6)

Memory Verse: Praying always with all prayer and supplication in the Spirit, being watchful to this end with all perseverance and supplication for all the saints.

Ephesians 6:18
Spiritual Warfare Theme

READING

The passage for today centers on qualifications of bishops, or elders, and deacons. Spiritual leaders in the Church must meet spiritual qualifications.

Read 1 Timothy 3.

REFLECTING

The Church is inherently a spiritual entity and must have spiritual leadership. While it is valid to have leadership which has knowledge and experience in many of the practical matters facing a church, that practical leadership must be undergirded with spiritual maturity. A man is to be a Christian with a long enough track record that he is publicly known to be the husband of one wife, temperate, self-controlled, respectable, hospitable, able to teach, not given to drunkenness, not violent, but gentle, not quarrelsome, not a lover of money, managing his own family well, and having a good reputation with outsiders. These qualifications are to be taken at face value for all who would lead in the church.

RESPONDING

1. Praise: As you consider the love which the Lord has for us, praise Him that he guides our spiritual growth:

Blessed are You, Lord God. . . . our Father, forever and ever. Yours, O Lord, is the greatness, the power and the glory, the victory and the majesty; for all that is in heaven and in earth is Yours; Yours is the kingdom, O Lord, and You are exalted as head over all. Both riches and honor come from You, and You reign over all. In Your hand is power and might; in Your hand it is to make great and to give strength to all. Now therefore, our God,

we thank You and praise Your glorious name. (1 Chronicles 29:10-13)

Pause for personal praise and thanksgiving.

2. Confession: Pray this confession to the Lord as you seek to keep your life free from sin and in fellowship with Him:

Against You, You only, have I sinned, and done this evil in Your sight—that You may be found just when You speak, and blameless when You judge. (Psalm 51:4)

Confess any personal sins which the Holy Spirit brings to mind.

3. Affirmation: Now pause to pray this affirmation to the Lord:

If I wait on the Lord, my strength shall be renewed; I shall mount up with wings like eagles; I shall run and not be weary, I shall walk and not faint. (Isaiah 40:31)

4. Requests: As you make your requests known to the Lord, include:

- The Lord's leading in your life
- Opportunities for personal evangelism
- Your prayer list, the concerns of your heart, and today's activities

5. Closing Prayer: Finally, offer this closing prayer to the Lord:

Now may the God of hope fill me with all joy and peace in believing, that I may abound in hope by the power of the Holy Spirit. (Romans 15:13)

Memory Verse: Praying always with all prayer and supplication in the Spirit, being watchful to this end with all perseverance and supplication for all the saints.

Ephesians 6:18
Spiritual Warfare Theme

NOVEMBER 12

READING

The passage for today centers on proper teaching. Effective teaching of the truth of Scripture will benefit both the teacher and the hearers.

Read 1 Timothy 4.

REFLECTING

Anyone who has tasted of the maturity which the Lord has for those who serve Him over time will testify that it did not come quickly or easily. Paul writes that we should exercise ourselves to godliness . . . that bodily exercise profits a little, but godliness is profitable for all things. Like the athlete, the Christian should rejoice with a rigorous course of training, knowing that the more demanding the training, the greater will be the physical prowess at the end. The great discomfort of the present is fitting him all the more for victorious effort later. Present pain, later gain. This is a difficult message to communicate and even more difficult to learn. But "to this end, we must labor."

RESPONDING

1. Praise: Because the Lord uses them to make us spiritually strong, we can praise the Lord even in the trials:

Be exalted, O Lord, in Your own strength! We will sing and praise Your power. (Psalm 21:13)

Sing to Him a new song; play skillfully with a shout of joy. For the word of the Lord is right. And all His work is done in truth. He loves righteousness and justice; The earth is full of the goodness of the Lord. (Psalm 33:3-5)

Pause for personal praise and thanksgiving.

2. Confession: Pray this confession to the Lord as you seek to keep your life free from sin and in fellowship with Him:

Purge me with hyssop, and I shall be clean. Wash me, and I shall be whiter than snow. Make me to hear joy and gladness, that the bones which You have broken may rejoice. Hide Your face from my sins, and blot out all my iniquities. (Psalm 51:7-9)

Confess any personal sins which the Holy Spirit brings to your mind.

3. Affirmation: Now pause to pray this affirmation to the Lord:

I will not lay up for myself treasures on earth, where moth and rust destroy, and where thieves break in and steal. But I shall lay up for myself treasures in heaven, where neither moth nor rust destroys and where thieves do not break in and steal. (Matthew 6:19-20)

4. Requests: As you make your requests known to the Lord, include:

- Love for the lost
- The work of missions in Africa
- Your prayer list, the concerns of your heart, and today's activities

5. Closing Prayer: Finally, offer this closing prayer to the Lord:

Now to You who are able to establish us according to the gospel and preaching of Jesus Christ—to You, alone wise, be glory through Jesus Christ forever. Amen. (Romans 16:25-27)

Memory Verse: Therefore submit to God. Resist the devil and he will flee from you.

James 4:7
Spiritual Warfare Theme

READING

The passage for today centers on the treatment of widows and elders. Widows are to be guided and cared for, and elders are to be properly respected.

Read 1 Timothy 5.

REFLECTING

There are those in the Church who feel that they have the gift of discouragement. Others, the gift of confrontation. Still more, the gift of rebuke. And those within the Church will give ample testimony to the presence of these gifts. While we may smile at this, there indeed are those who have an acute sense of justice and gravitate toward exhortational ministries. While these people provide an important balance in the Church, they must be cautious to wield their words with truth and grace. Paul writes not to rebuke older men, younger men, older women, or younger women. The point is, such ministries are always to be done in a spirit of grace, in truth and love, doing unto others as we would have them do unto us.

RESPONDING

1. Praise: Because the truth of the Lord is intended to heal and strengthen us, we praise Him:

O God, You are my God; early will I seek You; My soul thirsts for You, my flesh longs for You in a dry and weary land where there is no water. So I have looked for You in the sanctuary, to see Your power and Your glory. (Psalm 63:1-2)

Pause for personal praise and thanksgiving.

2. Confession: Pray this confession to the Lord as you seek to keep your life free from sin and in fellowship with Him:

Forgive us, Lord, when we are unmindful of You, the Rock who begot us, and have forgotten You, the God who fathered us. (Deuteronomy 32:18)

Confess any personal sins which the Holy Spirit brings to mind.

3. Affirmation: Now pause to pray this affirmation to the Lord:

I may come to You, O Lord, weary and heavy laden, and You will give me rest. I may take Your yoke upon me, and learn from You, for You are gentle and lowly in heart, and I shall find rest for my soul. For Your yoke is easy, and Your burden is light. (Matthew 11:28-30)

4. Requests: As you make your requests known to the Lord, include:

- Faithfulness with your talents
- Your state and local leaders and affairs
- Your prayer list, the concerns of your heart, and today's activities

5. Closing Prayer: Finally, offer this closing prayer to the Lord:

The grace of the Lord Jesus Christ, and the love of God, and the communion of the Holy Spirit be with us all. Amen. (2 Corinthians 13:14)

Memory Verse: Therefore submit to God. Resist the devil and he will flee from you.

James 4:7
Spiritual Warfare Theme

NOVEMBER 14

READING

The passage for today centers on the quest for godliness. Because of the destructiveness of ungodliness, and the brevity of life, we are to "fight the good fight" of faith while we live on earth.

Read 1 Timothy 6.

REFLECTING

If any of us could have three wishes, most of us would include wealth as one of those wishes. Everything else being equal, we would rather be rich than poor. Yet that very desire is a snare, so much so that Paul urges Timothy to flee the love of money, and pursue righteousness, godliness, faith, love, patience, gentleness. And he adds, "I urge you that you keep this commandment without spot, blameless until our Lord Jesus Christ's appearing . . . " (verse 14). If we have wealth, we are to use it compassionately. If we do not have wealth, we are to be content.

RESPONDING

1. Praise: "According to the riches of His grace which He lavished upon us," offer God your praise:

I will bless the Lord at all times; His praise shall continually be in my mouth. My soul shall make its boast in the Lord; the humble shall hear of it and be glad. O magnify the Lord with me, and let us exalt His name together. (Psalm 34:1-3)

Now offer to the Lord your personal praise and thanksgiving.

2. Confession: Pray this confession to the Lord as you seek to keep your life free from sin and in fellowship with Him:

No temptation has overtaken me except such as is common to man; but God is faithful, who will not allow me to be tempted beyond what I am able, but with the temptation will also make the way of escape, that I may be able to bear it. (1 Corinthians 10:13)

Confess any personal sins which the Holy Spirit brings to your mind.

3. Affirmation: As you agree with God's will, voice your affirmation of His word:

You, O Lord, were manifested in the flesh, justified in the Spirit, seen by angels, preached among the Gentiles, believed on in the world, received up in glory. (1 Timothy 3:16)

4. Requests: As you make your requests known to the Lord, include:

- Strength for obedience
- International students in America
- Your prayer list, the concerns of your heart, and today's activities.

5. Closing Prayer: Finally, offer this closing prayer to the Lord:

Now to You who are able to do exceedingly abundantly above all that I ask or think, according to the power that works in me, to You be glory in the Church by Christ Jesus throughout all ages, world without end. Amen. (Ephesians 3:20-21)

Memory Verse: Therefore submit to God. Resist the devil and he will flee from you.

James 4:7
Spiritual Warfare Theme

NOVEMBER 15

READING

The passage for today centers on encouragement to Timothy. Timothy is to rekindle his zeal for the pursuit of his Christian life and ministry.

Read 2 Timothy 1.

REFLECTING

A number of years have passed between the writing of 1 Timothy and 2 Timothy. During that time, Timothy has faced great trial and opposition and is in danger of discontinuing his ministry. Paul writes a terse letter of exhortation, urging strength and constancy. A list of these exhortations include: stir up, do not be ashamed, hold fast, be strong, endure hardship, be diligent, flee youthful lusts, pursue righteousness, preach the Word! In the heat of battle, short and powerful commands are easy to understand.

RESPONDING

1. Praise: Through Him who strengthens us, offer God your praise:

The Lord reigns, He is clothed with majesty; the Lord is clothed, He has girded Himself with strength. Surely the world is established, so that it cannot be moved. (Psalm 93:1-2)

Now express any additional thoughts you may have of thanks or praise.

2. Confession: Pray this confession to the Lord as you seek to keep your life free from sin and in fellowship with Him:

Create in me a clean heart, O God, and renew a steadfast spirit within me. . . . Restore to me the joy of Your salvation, and uphold me with Your generous Spirit. Then I will teach transgressors Your ways, and sinners shall be converted to You. (Psalm 51:10,12-13)

Confess any personal sins which the Holy Spirit brings to your mind.

3. Affirmation: Now pray this affirmation to the Lord as you agree with and submit yourself to the will of God:

And I know that all things work together for good to those who love You, O God, to those who are the called according to Your purpose. For whom You foreknew, You also predestined to be conformed to the image of Your Son, that He might be the firstborn among many brethren. Moreover whom You predestined, these You also called; whom You called, these You also justified; and whom You justified, these You also glorified. (Romans 8:28-30)

4. Requests: As you make your requests known to the Lord, include:

- Your "daily bread"
- Christian education institutions
- Your prayer list, the concerns of your heart, and today's activities

5. Closing Prayer: Finally, offer this closing prayer to the Lord:

Now may You, the God of peace, sanctify me completely, and may my whole spirit, soul, and body be preserved blameless at the coming of my Lord Jesus Christ. (1 Thessalonians 5:23)

Memory Verse: Therefore submit to God. Resist the devil and he will flee from you.

James 4:7
Spiritual Warfare Theme

NOVEMBER 16

READING

The passage for today centers on pictures of the strong Christian. Paul uses the metaphors of a soldier, farmer, and workman to encourage Timothy to be strong.

Read 2 Timothy 2.

REFLECTING

In our hard-driving society, gentleness is almost a lost commodity. Not only is it rarely honored, it is often disdained as being undesirable. Yet Paul instructs Timothy that the servant of the Lord must be gentle and that our gentleness may help others repent from sin. Jesus said blessed are the gentle. It is not a word which suggests weakness or impotence. It is used of powerful war horses who have been skillfully trained to give instantaneous obedience to their master. It is a word which suggests power under complete control. It offers much. A quiet answer turns away wrath. It nurtures a marriage; it restores a brother; it encourages spiritual growth; it is a characteristic of Christ.

RESPONDING

1. Praise: The Lord is gentle with us, and for this we praise Him:

Oh come, let us sing to the Lord! Let us shout joyfully to the Rock of our salvation. Let us come before His presence with thanksgiving; let us shout joyfully to Him with psalms. For the Lord is the great God, and the great King above all gods. (Psalm 95:1-3)

Now express any additional thoughts you may have of thanks or praise.

2. Confession: Pray this confession to the Lord as you seek to keep your life free from sin and in fellowship with Him:

Purge me with hyssop, and I shall be clean; wash me, and I shall be whiter than snow. Make me to hear joy and gladness, that the bones which You have broken may rejoice. Hide Your face from my sins, and blot out all my iniquities. (Psalm 51:7-9)

Confess any personal sins which the Holy Spirit brings to your mind.

3. Affirmation: As you agree with God's will, voice your affirmation of His word:

You give power when I am weak, and when I have no might, You increase my strength. When I wait on You Lord, You shall renew my strength; I shall mount up with wings like an eagle, I shall run and not be weary, I shall walk and not faint. (Isaiah 40:29, 31)

4. Requests: As you make your requests known to the Lord, include:

- Passion for moral excellence
- Needs of personal friends
- Your prayer list, the concerns of your heart, and today's activities.

5. Closing Prayer: Finally, offer this closing prayer to the Lord:

Now may the Lord Jesus Christ Himself, and You, my God and Father, who have loved me and given me everlasting consolation and good hope by grace, comfort my heart and establish me in every good word and work. (2 Thessalonians 2:16-17)

Memory Verse: Therefore submit to God. Resist the devil and he will flee from you.

James 4:7
Spiritual Warfare Theme

READING

The passage for today centers on the coming apostasy. Because in the last days people will defect from the faith, we must be on our guard and continue following the truth.

Read 2 Timothy 3.

REFLECTING

The Scriptures are designed to be the truth base for leading a Christian to maturity in Christ. They are accurate and trustworthy ("inspired by God"). They afford an adequate knowledge base ("profitable for doctrine"). They lead to an adequate biblical lifestyle (profitable "for reproof, for correction, for instruction in righteousness"). And they yield a biblical ministry ("that the man of God may be complete, thoroughly equipped for every good work"). A mature Christian, then, is one who knows what he needs to know (knowledge), is what he needs to be (lifestyle), and does what he needs to do (ministry), and is guided by the Scriptures in all of these things.

RESPONDING

1. Praise: The Lord longs to mature us in Christ, the very thing for which we long, and so we praise Him:

Praise the Lord! Praise God in His sanctuary; praise Him in His mighty firmament! Praise Him for His mighty acts; praise Him according to His excellent greatness! Praise Him with the sound of the trumpet; praise Him with the lute and harp! . . . Let everything that has breath praise the Lord. Praise the Lord. (Psalm 150:1-3, 6)

Now offer to the Lord your personal praise and thanksgiving.

2. Confession: Pray this confession to the Lord as you seek to keep your life free from sin and in fellowship with Him:

Against You, You only, have I sinned, and done this evil in Your sight—that You may be found just when You speak and blameless when You judge. (Psalm 51:4)

Confess any personal sins which the Holy Spirit brings to your mind.

3. Affirmation: As you agree with God's will, voice your affirmation of His word:

My body is the temple of the Holy Spirit who is in me, whom I have from You, O Lord, and I am not my own. I was bought at a price; therefore I will glorify You in my body and in my spirit, which are Yours. (1 Corinthians 6:19-20)

4. Requests: As you make your requests known to the Lord, include:

- Wisdom in decision making
- Opportunities to serve the Lord
- Your prayer list, the concerns of your heart, and today's activities.

5. Closing Prayer: Finally, offer this closing prayer to the Lord:

Now to You, the King eternal, immortal, invisible, to God who alone is wise, be honor and glory forever and ever. Amen. (1 Timothy 1:17)

Memory Verse: Therefore submit to God. Resist the devil and he will flee from you.

James 4:7
Spiritual Warfare Theme

NOVEMBER 18

READING

The passage for today centers on Timothy's charge to preach. Paul charges Timothy to preach the Word of God and offset the ministry of the false teachers.

Read 2 Timothy 4.

REFLECTING

We all think of Paul as being one of the great spiritual giants of the ages. We don't pretend that we might receive the same reward in heaven that he will. Yet we must recognize that the Lord does not reward talent or results. He rewards motive and faithfulness. Toward the end of his life, Paul himself writes that "there is laid up for (him) the crown of righteousness which the Lord will give (him) on that Day, but not to (him) only, but to all who have loved His appearing" (verse 8). That is you and me. Furthermore, Jesus said, "He who receives a prophet in the name of a prophet shall receive a prophet's reward" (Matthew 10:41). What a joy it is to know that the ministry is the Lord's and that all He requires of us is proper motives, not results.

RESPONDING

1. Praise: Thank the Lord, and praise Him that what He requires of us is something we can give Him:

Inasmuch as there is none like You, O Lord (You are great, and Your name is great in might), who would not fear You, O King of the nations? For this is Your rightful due, for among all the wise men of the nations, and in all their kingdoms, there is none like You. (Jeremiah 10:6-7)

Now offer to the Lord your personal praise and thanksgiving.

2. Confession: Pray this confession to the Lord as you seek to keep your life free from sin and in fellowship with Him:

Deliver me from bloodguiltiness, O God, the God of my salvation. And my tongue shall sing aloud of Your righteousness. O Lord, open my lips, and my mouth shall show forth Your praise. (Psalm 51:14-15)

Confess any personal sins which the Holy Spirit brings to your mind.

3. Affirmation: As you agree with God's will, voice your affirmation of His word:

The fear of You, O Lord, is the beginning of wisdom, and the knowledge of You is understanding. (Proverbs 9:10)

4. Requests: As you make your requests known to the Lord, include:

- Victory over temptation
- The work of missions in North and South America
- Your prayer list, the concerns of your heart, and today's activities

5. Closing Prayer: Finally, offer this closing prayer to the Lord:

You who are the blessed and only Potentate, the King of kings and Lord of lords, who alone have immortality, dwelling in unapproachable light, whom no man has seen or can see, to You be honor and everlasting power. Amen. (1 Timothy 6:15-16)

Memory Verse: Therefore submit to God. Resist the devil and he will flee from you.

James 4:7
Spiritual Warfare Theme

READING

The passage for today centers on the ordination of elders. Paul instructs Titus to appoint spiritually qualified men to oversee the ministry of the church in Crete.

Read Titus 1.

REFLECTING

The Bible is an enormous book, difficult to master, with around 1,000 pages of information, none of which is insignificant. A little learning can be difficult or even dangerous because of the possibility of error. While it is true that a new Christian can go to the Scripture by himself and gain spiritual truth for his life, it is also true that it is highly unlikely that anyone can grow to a mature understanding of the Bible without relying on teachers who know more about the Bible than he does. Herein lies a danger. We may not know enough about the Bible to determine if what is being taught to us is accurate. That is the importance of aligning ourselves with a church which believes and teaches the Bible. The elders can help safeguard us from being led into error.

RESPONDING

1. Praise: Thank the Lord that He warns us of the danger of falling away from Him, and praise Him that He safeguards the faithful:

Blessed be the name of God forever and ever, for wisdom and might are His. . . . He gives wisdom to the wise and knowledge to those who have understanding. He reveals deep and secret things; He knows what is in the darkness, and light dwells with Him. (Daniel 2:20-22)

Now offer to the Lord your personal praise and thanksgiving.

2. Confession: Pray this confession to the Lord as you seek to keep your life free from sin and in fellowship with Him:

The sacrifices of God are a broken spirit, a broken and contrite heart—these, O God, You will not despise. (Psalm 51:16-17)

Confess any personal sins which the Holy Spirit brings to your mind.

3. Affirmation: As you agree with God's will, voice your affirmation of His word:

By this I know love, because You, Lord Jesus, laid down Your life for me. And I also ought to lay down my life for my brother. (1 John 3:16)

4. Requests: As you make your requests known to the Lord, include:

- Love for your family
- Revival among Christians in America
- Your prayer list, the concerns of your heart, and today's activities

5. Closing Prayer: Finally, offer this closing prayer to the Lord:

Make me complete in every good work to do Your will, working in me what is well pleasing in Your sight, through Jesus Christ, to whom be glory forever and ever. Amen. (Hebrews 13:20-21)

Memory Verse: Be sober, be vigilant; because your adversary the devil walks about like a roaring lion, seeking whom he may devour.

1 Peter 5:8
Spiritual Warfare Theme

NOVEMBER 20

READING

The passage for today centers on teaching sound doctrine. Titus is to encourage all age groups to live proper lives as Christians.

Read Titus 2.

REFLECTING

The knowledge of Christ must effect a transformation so that our life-example will "adorn the doctrine of God" (verse 10), so that the words we speak will have integrity and carry weight with others because our actions back up and support our words. God has redeemed us from slavery to sin, assuring us of the "blessed hope" of the coming of Christ. Seeing that we will one day be delivered from this world, as passengers might be delivered from a sinking ship, we are to live soberly, righteously, and godly in the present age, fixing our hope on the coming of the "blessed hope." This means that while we must try to be good stewards of the things of this world, we must transfer our affections to the next and live for the things Jesus would live for if He were in our place.

RESPONDING

1. Praise: Offer your praise to the Lord that we have another world to look forward to:

My soul magnifies the Lord, and my spirit has rejoiced in God my Savior. . . . You who are mighty have done great things for me, and holy is Your name, And Your mercy is on those who fear You from generation to generation. (Luke 1:46-50)

Now offer to the Lord your personal praise and thanksgiving.

2. Confession: Pray this confession to the Lord as you seek to keep your life free from sin and in fellowship with Him:

I acknowledged my sin to You, and my iniquity I have not hidden. I said, "I will confess my transgressions to the Lord," and You forgave the iniquity of my sin. (Psalm 32:5)

Confess any personal sins which the Holy Spirit brings to your mind.

3. Affirmation: As you agree with God's will, voice your affirmation of His word:

You, O Lord, are the Bread of Life. If I come to You I shall never hunger, and if I believe in You, I shall never thirst. (John 6:35)

4. Requests: As you make your requests known to the Lord, include:

- Faithfulness with your treasures
- The Great Commission
- Your prayer list, the concerns of your heart, and today's activities.

5. Closing Prayer: Finally, offer this closing prayer to the Lord:

May You, the God of grace, who called me to Your eternal glory by Christ Jesus, after I have suffered a while, perfect, establish, strengthen, and settle me. To You be the glory and the dominion forever and ever. Amen. (1 Peter 5:10-11)

Memory Verse: Be sober, be vigilant; because your adversary the devil walks about like a roaring lion, seeking whom he may devour.

1 Peter 5:8
Spiritual Warfare Theme

NOVEMBER 21

READING

The passage for today centers on maintaining good works. Those who believe in God should be careful to maintain good works.

Read Titus 3.

REFLECTING

It is difficult for us to separate our hope of heaven from our good works. We instinctively feel that we must be good to get to heaven. While God certainly wants us to live good lives, none of us can live a good enough life to get to heaven. One sin disqualifies us, and everyone has sinned at least once. "Not by works of righteousness which we have done, but according to His mercy He saved us . . . that having been justified by His grace we should become heirs according to the hope of eternal life" (verses 5,7). Salvation is a gift. In gratitude we are to "engage in good deeds" (verse 8).

RESPONDING

1. Praise: For God's great gift of mercy, offer Him your praise:

Tremble before Him, all the earth. The world also is firmly established, it shall not be moved. Let the heavens rejoice, and let the earth be glad. . . . Oh, give thanks to the Lord, for He is good! For His mercy endures forever. . . . Blessed be the Lord God . . . from everlasting to everlasting! (1 Chronicles 16:30-31, 34, 36)

Pause for personal praise and thanksgiving.

2. Confession: Pray this confession to the Lord as you seek to keep your life free from sin and in fellowship with Him:

O Lord, You do not have as much delight in burnt offerings and sacrifices, as in our obeying Your voice. Behold, to obey is better than sacrifice, and to heed than the fat of rams. (1 Samuel 15:22)

Confess any personal sins which the Holy Spirit brings to your mind.

3. Affirmation: Now pause to pray this affirmation to the Lord:

There is therefore now no condemnation for me if I am in You, Christ Jesus. For the law of the Spirit of life in You has set me free from the law of sin and death. (Romans 8:1-2)

4. Requests: As you make your requests known to the Lord, include:

- Spiritual insight
- Campus ministries
- Your prayer list, the concerns of your heart, and today's activities

5. Closing Prayer: Finally, offer this closing prayer to the Lord:

May I grow in the grace and knowledge of our Lord and Savior Jesus Christ. To Him be the glory both now and forever. Amen. (2 Peter 3:18)

Memory Verse: Be sober, be vigilant; because your adversary the devil walks about like a roaring lion, seeking whom he may devour.

1 Peter 5:8
Spiritual Warfare Theme

NOVEMBER 22

READING

The passage for today centers on an appeal for Onesimus. Paul appeals to Philemon to have mercy on his runaway slave Onesimus, who has become a Christian.

Read Philemon.

REFLECTING

If anyone is a servant to Christ, he cannot be a tyrant to men. Jesus taught forgiveness, compassion, and gentleness, not harshness, anger, and retribution. Paul urges Philemon to forgive, receive, and restore his runaway slave, Onesimus, as a brother in Christ, now that Onesimus has become a Christian. The fact that this letter has been preserved indicates Philemon's favorable response. Though we have no slaves, our employees, coworkers, associates, and neighbors deserve as much from us. Service to Christ requires a forgiving spirit.

RESPONDING

1. Praise: To Him who set us free from our slavery to sin, offer this praise:

I will love You, O Lord, my strength. The Lord is my Rock and my fortress and my deliverer; my God, my strength, in whom I will trust; my shield and the horn of my salvation, my stronghold. I call upon the Lord, who is worthy to be praised; so shall I be saved from my enemies. . . . The Lord lives! Blessed be my Rock! Let the God of my salvation be exalted. (Psalm 18:1-3, 46)

Pause for personal praise and thanksgiving.

2. Confession: Pray this confession to the Lord as you seek to keep your life free from sin and in fellowship with Him:

Remember, O Lord, Your tender mercies and Your lovingkindnesses, for they have been from of old. Do not remember the sins of my youth, nor my transgressions; according to Your mercy remember me, for Your goodness' sake, O Lord. (Psalm 25:6-7)

Confess any personal sins which the Holy Spirit brings to your mind.

3. Affirmation: Now pause to pray this affirmation to the Lord:

You are the door. If anyone enters by You he will be saved, and will go in and out and find pasture. The thief does not come except to steal, and to kill, and to destroy. You have come that we may have life, and that we may have it more abundantly. You are the Good Shepherd. The Good Shepherd gives his life for the sheep. (John 10:9-11)

4. Requests: As you make your requests known to the Lord, pray for:

- Desire to be like Christ
- Needs in inner cities
- Your prayer list, the concerns of your heart, and today's activities
- Whatever else is on your heart.

5. Closing Prayer: Finally, offer this closing prayer to the Lord:

Blessing and honor and glory and power be to You who sit on the throne, and to You, Lord, forever and ever! (Revelation 5:13)

Memory Verse: Be sober, be vigilant; because your adversary the devil walks about like a roaring lion, seeking whom he may devour.
1 Peter 5:8
Spiritual Warfare Theme

READING

The passage for today centers on Christ's superiority to angels. Because Christ is the Son of God, He is superior to angels in every way.

Read Hebrews 1.

REFLECTING

Angels don't seem real to us. They are found in fairy tales, and we tell children about them, but we tend not to take them seriously for our lives as adults. They are very real, however, and play a very important role to us as adults.

Throughout the Bible, we only get glimpses of the work of angels. They are sent forth to minister to those who will inherit salvation. This is perhaps the passage from which the idea of a guardian angel has come. Apparently angels appear in human form, for some have entertained angels without knowing it (13:2), and are very active in the affairs of men, even participating in world affairs (Daniel 10:29). They are much greater than man now, but one day, redeemed man will rule angels (1 Corinthians 6:3) as we reign with the preeminent Christ.

RESPONDING

1. Praise: Angels are ministers of love, and we praise the Lord who sends them:

Let us come before His presence with thanksgiving; let us shout joyfully to Him with psalms. For the Lord is the great God, and the great King above all gods. . . . Oh come, let us worship and bow down; let us kneel before the Lord our Maker. For He is our God, and we are the people of His pasture, and the sheep of His hand. (Psalm 95:2-3, 6-7)

Take a moment to offer the Lord your personal praise and thanksgiving.

2. Confession: Pray this confession to the Lord as you seek to keep your life free from sin and in fellowship with Him:

No temptation has overtaken me except such as is common to man; but You are faithful, O God, who will not allow me to be tempted beyond what I am able, but with the temptation will also make the way of escape, that I may be able to bear it. (1 Corinthians 10:13)

Confess any personal sins which the Holy Spirit may bring to your mind.

3. Affirmation: As you agree with the will of God, voice your affirmation of His word:

But You, O God, demonstrate Your own love toward me, in that while I was still a sinner, Christ died for me. (Romans 5:8)

4. Requests: As you make your requests known to the Lord, include:

- Personal witness for Christ
- Local churches around the nation
- Your prayer list, the concerns of your heart, and today's activities

5. Closing Prayer: Finally, offer this closing prayer to the Lord:

Amen! Blessing and glory and wisdom, thanksgiving and honor and power and might, be to You, God, forever and ever. Amen. (Revelation 7:12)

Memory Verse: Be sober, be vigilant; because your adversary the devil walks about like a roaring lion, seeking whom he may devour.

1 Peter 5:8
Spiritual Warfare Theme

NOVEMBER 24

READING

The passage for today centers on Christ's humanity. Because Christ was man as well as God, He is able to "give aid" to us, who are human alone.

Read Hebrews 2.

REFLECTING

Jesus was God, but He was also man. Jesus was man, but He was also God. It is essential that Christ was both God and man. If He were not man, He could not have died for our sins. If He were not God, His death would not have been sufficient to pay the price for the sin of mankind. He was the perfect sacrifice, in fact the only possible sacrifice to atone for the sins of man and appease the wrath of God. This theme runs throughout Hebrews. In the Old Testament, which pictures the work of Christ to come in the New Testament, there was an unblemished lamb to be sacrificed for sins and a high priest who offered the sacrifice. Both pictured Jesus who was the sacrifice and the sacrificer. He was both Lamb and High Priest.

RESPONDING

1. Praise: Praise the Lord that Jesus was sufficient to pay the price for our sins and that He was willing to pay the price:

Oh, sing to the Lord a new song! Sing to the Lord, all the earth. Sing to the Lord, bless His name; proclaim the good news of His salvation from day to day. Declare His glory among the nations, His wonders among all peoples. For the Lord is great and greatly to be praised. (Psalm 96:1-4)

Take a moment to offer the Lord your personal praise and thanksgiving.

2. Confession: Pray this confession to the Lord as you seek to keep your life free from sin and in fellowship with Him:

Now no chastening seems to be joyful for the present, but grievous; nevertheless, afterward it yields the peaceable fruit of righteousness when I have been trained by it. (Hebrews 12:11)

Confess any personal sins which the Holy Spirit may bring to your mind.

3. Affirmation: As you agree with the will of God, voice your affirmation of His word:

If I drink of the water that You, Lord Jesus, give me, I will never thirst. The water that You shall give me will become in me a fountain of water springing up into everlasting life. (John 4:14)

4. Requests: As you make your requests known to the Lord, include:

- An eternal perspective
- Needs of work or school mates
- Your prayer list, the concerns of your heart, and today's activities

5. Closing Prayer: Finally, offer this closing prayer to the Lord:

I will wait on You, the Lord; I will be of good courage, and You shall strengthen my heart; I will wait on You! (Psalm 27:14)

Memory Verse: Be sober, be vigilant; because your adversary the devil walks about like a roaring lion, seeking whom he may devour.

1 Peter 5:8
Spiritual Warfare Theme

READING

The passage for today centers on the grace of Christ. As we labor to enter into God's rest, we may call upon Christ for mercy and grace.

Read Hebrews 4.

REFLECTING

The Word of God is energized by the Spirit of God. Whenever the Word of God goes forth, it never returns without accomplishing the work for which it was intended. It is living and powerful, sharper than any two-edged sword. As we minister to others, the Word must be central to all that we say and do. It is the Word which is alive, not our own insights. It is the Word which is alive, not our clever arguments. It is the Word which is alive, not our interesting stories. When we try to help others along the road of life, it is the Word which they need to hear. They need to know what God says. Jesus said, "You shall know the truth, and the truth shall set you free" (John 8:32). If our ministries are to set people free, then they must be centered around the Word of God.

RESPONDING

1. Praise: The Word of God is alive, and we can use it to worship and praise the One who gave it:

The Lord made the heavens. Honor and majesty are before Him; strength and beauty are in His sanctuary. Give to the Lord, O kindreds of the peoples, give to the Lord glory and strength. Give to the Lord the glory due His name; bring an offering, and come into His courts. . . . Let the heavens rejoice, and let the earth be glad. (Psalm 96:5-8, 11)

Take a moment to offer the Lord your personal praise and thanksgiving.

2. Confession: Pray this confession to the Lord as you seek to keep your life free from sin and in fellowship with Him:

If I sin, I have an Advocate with You, Father, Jesus Christ the righteous. And He Himself is the propitiation for my sins, and not for mine only, but also for the whole world. (1 John 2:1-2)

Confess any personal sins which the Holy Spirit may bring to your mind.

3. Affirmation: As you agree with the will of God, voice your affirmation of His word:

I will remember the words of the Lord; surely I will remember Your wonders of old. I will also meditate on all Your work, and talk of Your deeds. (Psalm 77:11-12)

4. Requests: As you make your requests known to the Lord, include:

- Personal discipline
- Christians worldwide who are persecuted for their faith
- Your prayer list, the concerns of your heart, and today's activities

5. Closing Prayer: Finally, offer this closing prayer to the Lord:

Show me the path of life; in Your presence is fullness of joy; at Your right hand are pleasures forevermore. (Psalm 16:11)

Memory Verse: Be sober, be vigilant; because your adversary the devil walks about like a roaring lion, seeking whom he may devour.

1 Peter 5:8
Spiritual Warfare Theme

NOVEMBER 26

READING

The passage for today centers on the New Covenant. The first covenant, the Mosaic Law, is incomplete and is replaced by the New Covenant, based on the grace of Christ.

Read Hebrews 8.

REFLECTING

All the major features of the old covenant which existed on a literal, physical level are found in the New Covenant in a spiritual, heavenly level. The old covenant had a physical sanctuary, a human high priest, a real lamb as a sacrifice. "But if the first covenant had been faultless, then no place would have been sought for a second" (verse 7). This covenant was inadequate in that it could only deal with sins temporarily. It could not remove sins permanently. In the New Covenant, there is a spiritual sanctuary, a heavenly High Priest, and a celestial Lamb whose death could provide permanent forgiveness of sin for an infinite number of people. It is a "better covenant, which was established on better promises" (verse 6).

RESPONDING

1. Praise: Offer the Lord your praise that Jesus' sacrifice was sufficient for our sins:

You who love the Lord, hate evil! He preserves the souls of His saints; He delivers them out of the hand of the wicked. Light is sown for the righteous, and gladness for the upright in heart. Rejoice in the Lord, you righteous, and give thanks at the remembrance of His holy name. (Psalm 97:10-12)

Take a moment to offer the Lord your personal praise and thanksgiving.

2. Confession: Pray this confession to the Lord as you seek to keep your life free from sin and in fellowship with Him:

If I say that I have no sin, I deceive myself, and the truth is not in me. If I confess my sins, You, O Lord, are faithful and just to forgive me my sins and to cleanse me from all unrighteousness. (1 John 1:8-9)

Confess any personal sins which the Holy Spirit may bring to your mind.

3. Affirmation: As you agree with the will of God, voice your affirmation of His word:

And this is Your commandment: that I should believe on the name of Your Son Jesus Christ and love others, as He commanded me. (1 John 3:23)

4. Requests: As you make your requests known to the Lord, include:

- Love for the Lord
- The work of missions in the Middle East, Australia, and the Islands
- Your prayer list, the concerns of your heart, and today's activities

5. Closing Prayer: Finally, offer this closing prayer to the Lord:

Save Your people, and bless Your inheritance; shepherd us also, and bear us up forever. (Psalm 28:9)

Memory Verse: Honor the Lord with your possessions, and with the firstfruits of all your increase.
Proverbs 3:9
Stewardship Theme

READING

The passage for today centers on both old and new covenants. Both covenants are contrasted, the old covenant of law being a picture of the New Covenant of grace in Christ. Read Hebrews 9.

REFLECTING

Without the shedding of blood, there is no forgiveness of sin. We are not told why that is true . . . only that it is. "All have sinned and fall short of the glory of God" (Romans 3:23), and "the wages of sin is death" (Romans 6:23). Wherever there is sin, someone must die. We can pay the penalty for our own sin, which is our own eternal spiritual death. Or the death which Christ suffered can be placed on our account. His death can count for ours, and we do not have to die. Faith is the vehicle by which this transaction takes place. Whoever believes in Jesus will not perish, but have eternal life (John 3:16). Jesus, as the fulfillment of all that the Old Testament system pictured, has made this possible.

RESPONDING

1. Praise: Because the Lord has made it possible for Christ's death to count for ours, praise Him in the words of this psalm:

Make a joyful shout to the Lord, all you lands! Serve the Lord with gladness; come before His presence with singing. Know that the Lord, He is God; it is He who has made us, and not we ourselves; we are His people and the sheep of His pasture. Enter into His gates with thanksgiving, and into His courts with praise. . . . For the Lord is good. (Psalm 100:1-5)

Take a moment to offer the Lord your personal praise and thanksgiving.

2. Confession: Pray this confession to the Lord as you seek to keep your life free from sin and in fellowship with Him:

Forgive me, Lord, when I am unmindful of You, the Rock who begot me, and when I have forgotten You, the God who fathered me. (Deuteronomy 32:18)

Confess any personal sins which the Holy Spirit may bring to your mind.

3. Affirmation: As you agree with the will of God, voice your affirmation of His word:

Most assuredly, You say to me, O Lord, if I hear Your word and believe in Him who sent You, I have everlasting life, and shall not come into judgment, but have passed from death into life. (John 5:24)

4. Requests: As you make your requests known to the Lord, include:

- Faithfulness in sharing Christ
- The Lord's work in national and world affairs
- Your prayer list, the concerns of your heart, and today's activities

5. Closing Prayer: Finally, offer this closing prayer to the Lord:

You, the Lord, will command Your lovingkindness in the daytime, and in the night Your song shall be with me—a prayer to You, the God of my life. (Psalm 42:8)

Memory Verse: Honor the Lord with your possessions, and with the firstfruits of all your increase.

Proverbs 3:9
Stewardship Theme

NOVEMBER 28

READING

The passage for today centers on the Great Hall of Faith. A parade of great names from the Old Testament is given as examples of "living by faith."

Read Hebrews 11.

REFLECTING

Faith is the central operative ingredient in the Christian life. Without faith, it is impossible to please God. Faith is so important because it is the only thing you can do and still not do anything. All that is accomplished in the world of the work of God is accomplished by faith. Faith is believing God and acting accordingly. In the examples of the faithful, God spoke; His people listened, believed, and acted accordingly. In the words of the old hymn, "Trust and obey, for there's no other way to be happy in Jesus, but to trust and obey."

RESPONDING

1. Praise: Offer your personal praise to your personal Savior in these words:

Ah, Lord God! Behold, You have made the heavens and the earth by Your great power and outstretched arm. There is nothing too hard for You. You show lovingkindness to thousands, . . . the Great, the Mighty God, whose name is the Lord of hosts. You are great in counsel and mighty in work. (Jeremiah 32:17-19)

Pause for personal praise and thanksgiving.

2. Confession: Pray this confession to the Lord as you seek to keep your life free from sin:

Who can understand his errors? Cleanse me from secret faults. Keep back Your servant from presumptuous sins; Let them not have dominion over me. Then I shall be blameless, and I shall be innocent of great transgression. (Psalm 19:12-13)

Confess any personal sins which the Holy Spirit brings to mind.

3. Affirmation: Now pause to pray this affirmation to the Lord:

O God, Your thoughts are not my thoughts, nor are my ways Your ways. For as the heavens are higher than the earth, so are Your ways higher than my ways, and Your thoughts than my thoughts. (Isaiah 55:8-9)

4. Requests: As you make your requests known to the Lord, pray for:

- Compassion for others
- Missions in America
- Your prayer list, the concerns of your heart, and today's activities

5. Closing Prayer: Finally, offer this closing prayer to the Lord:

Now to You who are able to keep me from stumbling, and to present me faultless before the presence of Your glory with exceeding joy, to You, my God and Savior, who alone are wise, be glory and majesty, dominion and power, both now and forever. Amen. (Jude 24-25)

Memory Verse: Honor the Lord with your possessions, and with the firstfruits of all your increase.
Proverbs 3:9
Stewardship Theme

READING

The passage for today centers on encouragement for endurance. Following the example of Christ, we are to endure the chastening of God in our lives and to not fall into disobedience.

Read Hebrews 12.

REFLECTING

We don't mind suffering some things as long as someone else is suffering with us. We don't want to be the only one. Few things make us feel worse than for everything to be going well for everyone else and for us to be suffering. The writer to Hebrews encourages us to endure our present suffering as Christians in this world by reminding us that Christ suffered for us and we ought therefore to be willing to suffer for Him. One of the points of highest integrity for Jesus is that he never asks us to do anything for Him that He was not willing to do for us. "For consider Him who endured such hostility from sinners against Himself, lest you become weary and discouraged in your souls" (verse 3).

RESPONDING

1. Praise: As we consider what we have because Christ was willing to suffer for us, we praise God:

Who is like You, O Lord, among the gods? Who is like You, glorious in holiness, fearful in praises, doing wonders? . . . You are great, O Lord God. For there is none like You, nor is there any God besides You, according to all that we have heard with our ears. (Exodus 15:11, 2 Samuel 7:22)

Take a moment to offer the Lord your personal praise and thanksgiving.

2. Confession: Pray this confession to the Lord as you seek to keep your life free from sin and in fellowship with Him:

Bless the Lord, O my soul; and all that is within me, bless His holy name! Bless the Lord, O my soul, and forget not all His benefits, who forgives all my iniquities. (Psalm 103:1-3)

Confess any personal sins which the Holy Spirit may bring to your mind.

3. Affirmation: As you agree with the will of God, voice your affirmation of His word:

These things You have spoken to me, that in You I may have peace. In the world I will have tribulation; but I will be of good cheer, You have overcome the world. (John 16:33)

4. Requests: As you make your requests known to the Lord, include:

- Personal spiritual growth
- Military ministries
- Your prayer list, the concerns of your heart, and today's activities

5. Closing Prayer: Finally, offer this closing prayer to the Lord:

Glory to You in the highest, and on earth peace, good will toward men! (Luke 2:14)

Memory Verse: Honor the Lord with your possessions, and with the firstfruits of all your increase.

Proverbs 3:9
Stewardship Theme

NOVEMBER 30

READING

The passage for today centers on final instructions. We are to live righteously before our fellow man and to offer to God the sacrifice of praise.

Read Hebrews 13.

REFLECTING

Praise is good for the soul and pleasing to God. The writer of Hebrews says, " . . . let us continually offer the sacrifice of praise to God, that is, the fruit of our lips, giving thanks to His name" (verse 15). Again, in Psalm 33:1, we read, "Praise from the upright is beautiful." If you want to be certain that you can do something which pleases the Lord, praise Him. In addition, however, our actions must follow our praise. "But do not forget to do good and to share, for with such sacrifices God is well pleased" (verse 16). The praise of our lips must be followed with the pattern of our life. Note that both, praise and doing good, are sacrifices with which God is well pleased.

RESPONDING

1. Praise: Knowing that the Lord delights to hear it, offer Him your praise for who He is, and what He has done for you:

All Your works shall praise You, O Lord, and Your saints shall bless You. They shall speak of the glory of Your kingdom, and talk of Your power, to make known to the sons of men His mighty acts. . . . Your kingdom is an everlasting kingdom, and Your dominion endures throughout all generations. (Psalm 145:10-13)

Take a moment to offer the Lord your personal praise and thanksgiving.

2. Confession: Pray this confession to the Lord as you seek to keep your life free from sin and in fellowship with Him:

Against You, You only, have I sinned, and done this evil in Your sight—that You may be found just when You speak, and blameless when you judge. (Psalm 51:4)

Confess any personal sins which the Holy Spirit may bring to your mind.

3. Affirmation: As you agree with the will of God, voice your affirmation of His word:

You, the Father have given me to Jesus Christ, and I have come to Him and will by no means be cast out. (John 6:37)

4. Requests: As you make your requests known to the Lord, include:

- Fruit of the Spirit in your life
- The ministry of Christian literature
- Your prayer list, the concerns of your heart, and today's activities

5. Closing Prayer: Finally, offer this closing prayer to the Lord:

Grace, mercy, and peace from You, the Father, and the Lord Jesus Christ our Savior. (Titus 1:4)

Memory Verse: Honor the Lord with your possessions, and with the firstfruits of all your increase.
Proverbs 3:9
Stewardship Theme

DECEMBER 1

READING

The passage for today centers on the purpose of tests. Some trials come into the life of the Christian to strengthen him and bring him to spiritual maturity.

Read James 1.

REFLECTING

Trials are common to the experience of all Christians. And, trials aren't "trials" unless they bring you to the point at which you want to quit. When we read that "trials produce endurance," we can mentally ascend to the wisdom of that. But in real life, trials take us past the point at which we care anymore about the wisdom of anything! We just want relief! We have little trouble enduring trials as long as the duration and intensity seem reasonable. But let them go beyond reason, and suddenly we begin to question the wisdom and goodness of God. We question the rationality of the Christian life. Rather than feeling as though we are beginning to grow, we begin to feel abandoned by God.

By the grace of God, at this very point, we must accept that we are finally experiencing what James is talking about. Take courage! Endure it! God has not abandoned you. And as you endure, you will become spiritually mature, though you will probably only perceive the growth in retrospect—as you look back on the time of testing.

RESPONDING

1. Praise: Offer your praise to the God of love who brings growth out of the pain:

Unto You I lift up my eyes, O You who dwell in the heavens. Behold, as the eyes of servants look to the hand of their masters, as the eyes of a maid to the hand of her mistress, so our eyes look to the Lord our God, until He has mercy on us. (Psalm 123:1-2)

Take a moment to offer the Lord your personal praise and thanksgiving.

2. Confession: Pray this confession to the Lord as you seek to keep your life free from sin and in fellowship with Him:

We give You thanks, O Lord, that we may reason with You. Though our sins are like scarlet, they shall be as white as snow; though they are red like crimson, they shall be as wool. (Isaiah 1:18)

Confess any personal sins which the Holy Spirit may bring to your mind.

3. Affirmation: As you agree with the will of God, voice your affirmation of His word:

For to me, to live is Christ, and to die is gain. (Philippians 2:21)

4. Requests: As you make your requests known to the Lord, include:

- Health and strength to serve God
- God's will to be done on earth
- Your prayer list, the concerns of your heart, and today's activities

5. Closing Prayer: Finally, offer this closing prayer to the Lord:

Blessed are You, the Lord, forevermore! Amen and amen. (Psalm 89:52)

Memory Verse: Honor the Lord with your possessions, and with the firstfruits of all your increase.
Proverbs 3:9
Stewardship Theme

DECEMBER 2

READING

The passage for today centers on the test of brotherly love. True Christian love will not discriminate against the poor.

Read James 2.

REFLECTING

Birds of a feather flock together. Trite as that may sound, it is one of the fundamental laws of social interaction. We feel at home with those who are like us, and we tend to fraternize with them rather than with people who are unlike us. There is nothing wrong with this tendency. It is built in, and there is little value in denying it. If that tendency prompts us to act unlovingly toward anyone else, however, the action is wrong. The tendency cannot be avoided. Unloving actions can. James warns us about discriminating against the poor, though it is wrong to discriminate against anyone for any reason, whether wealth, creed, race, age, or national origin. Under the royal law we love our neighbor as ourselves, regardless of who the neighbor is.

RESPONDING

1. **Praise:** The Lord loves us just as we are, and we can praise Him that He does not discriminate against us:

Blessed be Your glorious name, which is exalted above all blessing and praise! You alone are the Lord; You have made heaven, the heaven of heavens, with all their host, the earth and all things on it, the seas and all that is in them, and You preserve them all. The host of heaven worships You. (Nehemiah 9:5-6)

Take a moment to offer the Lord your personal praise and thanksgiving.

2. **Confession:** Pray this confession to the Lord as you seek to keep your life free from sin and in fellowship with Him:

You have blotted out, like a thick cloud, my transgressions, and like a cloud, my sins. I will return to You, for You have redeemed me. (Isaiah 44:22)

Confess any personal sins which the Holy Spirit may bring to your mind.

3. **Affirmation:** As you agree with the will of God, voice your affirmation of His word:

I have been crucified with Christ; it is no longer I who live, but Christ lives in me; and the life which I now live in the flesh I live by faith in the Son of God, who loved me and gave Himself for me. (Galatians 2:20)

4. **Requests:** As you make your requests known to the Lord, include:

- Sensitivity to sin
- The ministry of your local church
- Your prayer list, the concerns of your heart, and today's activities

5. **Closing Prayer:** Finally, offer this closing prayer to the Lord:

Let the words of my mouth and the meditation of my heart be acceptable in Your sight, O Lord, my strength and my redeemer. (Psalm 19:14)

Memory Verse: Honor the Lord with your possessions, and with the firstfruits of all your increase.
Proverbs 3:9
Stewardship Theme

READING

The passage for today centers on control of the tongue. The exercise of genuine Christian faith results in controlling the tongue to speak good, not evil.

Read James 3.

REFLECTING

James warns us about the tongue, and yet he does so in a metaphorical sense. There is nothing good or bad, right or wrong about a tongue. It is a few ounces of muscle. But the tongue articulates the contents of the heart. If a flask full of acid is bumped, only acid will spill out. If a flask full of water is bumped, only water will spill out. Water will never spill out of a flask of acid, and acid will never spill out of a flask of water. In that sense, the tongue merely reveals the heart. Let the heart be bumped, and the tongue will reveal what is in the heart. In controlling the tongue, you must control the heart. If you want to change the words of the tongue, you must change the condition of the heart.

RESPONDING

1. Praise: Offer your praise to the Lord who can soften our hearts and sweeten our tongues:

Blessed are You, Lord God, . . . our Father, forever and ever. Yours, O Lord, is the greatness, the power and the glory, the victory and the majesty; for all that is in heaven and in earth is Yours; Yours is the kingdom, O Lord, and You are exalted as head over all. (1 Chronicles 29:10-11)

Take a moment to offer the Lord your personal praise and thanksgiving.

2. Confession: Pray this confession to the Lord as you seek to keep your life free from sin and in fellowship with Him:

For a mere moment You have forsaken me, but with great mercies You will gather me. With a little wrath You hid Your face from me for a moment; but with everlasting kindness You will have mercy on me. (Isaiah 54:7-8)

Confess any personal sins which the Holy Spirit may bring to your mind.

3. Affirmation: As you agree with the will of God, voice your affirmation of His word:

Unless the Lord builds my house, I labor in vain; unless the Lord guards my city, I stay awake watching in vain. (Psalm 127:1)

4. Requests: As you make your requests known to the Lord, include:

- Wisdom for living life
- Needs of your immediate family
- Your prayer list, the concerns of your heart, and today's activities

5. Closing Prayer: Finally, offer this closing prayer to the Lord:

Surely goodness and mercy shall follow me all the days of my life, and I will dwell in the house of the Lord forever. (Psalm 23:6)

Memory Verse: But seek first the kingdom of God and His righteousness, and all these things shall be added to you.

Matthew 6:33
Stewardship Theme

DECEMBER 4

READING

The passage for today centers on humility and submission. While selfishness produces conflict, humility produces submission to God and dependence on Him for the future.

Read James 4.

REFLECTING

Selfishness is the foundation for all conflict. When two hearts want two different things and neither is willing to sacrifice for the sake of the other, conflict arises. Selfishness is the cause of war, of crime, of interpersonal conflict. Selfishness is a prime motive of the human heart. By looking out for ourselves, we think we can get that which we want from life.

In contrast, the Lord teaches us that humility, not selfishness, results in satisfaction in life. Promote yourself, and wars and conflict result. Even God is against you (verse 6)!

But live in humility, and wars and conflict cease (assuming all parties participate). And the Lord will lift you up.

RESPONDING

1. Praise: Because the Lord resists the proud, but gives grace to the humble, offer Him your praise:

Praise the Lord! Praise the name of the Lord; praise Him, O you servants of the Lord! . . . Praise the Lord, for the Lord is good; sing praises to His name, for it is pleasant. . . . For I know that the Lord is great, and our Lord is above all gods. . . . Blessed be the Lord . . . Praise the Lord! (Psalm 135:1, 3, 5, 21)

Take a moment to offer the Lord your personal praise and thanksgiving.

2. Confession: Pray this confession to the Lord as you seek to keep your life free from sin and in fellowship with Him:

Lord, be merciful to me; heal my soul, for I have sinned against You. . . . O Lord, be merciful to me, and raise me up. . . . Blessed be the Lord God of Israel from everlasting to everlasting! Amen and amen. (Psalm 41:4, 10, 13)

Confess any personal sins which the Holy Spirit may bring to your mind.

3. Affirmation: As you agree with the will of God, voice your affirmation of His word:

For You, O Lord, made Him who knew no sin to be sin for me, that I might become the righteousness of You in Him. (2 Corinthians 5:21)

4. Requests: As you make your requests known to the Lord, include:

- Insight into Scripture
- The hungry around the world
- Your prayer list, the concerns of your heart, and today's activities

5. Closing Prayer: Finally, offer this closing prayer to the Lord:

We will be of good courage, and You shall strengthen our hearts, all we who hope in the Lord. (Psalm 31:24)

Memory Verse: But seek first the kingdom of God and His righteousness, and all these things shall be added to you.

Matthew 6:33
Stewardship Theme

DECEMBER 5

READING

The passage for today centers on the warning to the rich. The rich of this world are warned against an uncompassionate use of their wealth.

Read James 5.

REFLECTING

James does not condemn wealth; rather, he condemns the uncompassionate use of wealth. It is not wrong to have money, but it is very wrong to have money and not use it to further the gospel and the welfare of the needy of the world. Hoarding those resources or squandering them on ourselves is in direct violation of His commands. This is so because He designed those in need to be utterly dependent on those with wealth. The directive is then for the wealthy to give directly to the poor. In support, Paul writes in 1 Timothy 6:17-18, "Command those who are rich . . . that they be rich in good works . . . ." Neither Paul nor James says to let the rich give up their riches; rather, they say to let them use their riches compassionately and generously.

RESPONDING

1. Praise: Because of the Lord's compassionate generosity to us in Christ, offer Him your praise:

Great and marvelous are Your works, Lord God Almighty! Just and true are Your ways, O King of the saints! Who shall not fear You, O Lord and glorify Your name? For You alone are holy. For all nations shall come and worship before You, for Your judgments have been manifested. (Revelation 15:3-4)

Now offer to the Lord your personal praise and thanksgiving.

2. Confession: Pray this confession to the Lord as you seek to keep your life free from sin and in fellowship with Him:

O Lord, You are merciful and gracious, slow to anger, and abounding in mercy. . . . As a father pities his children, so You, Lord, pity those who fear You. For You know our frame; You remember that we are dust. (Psalm 103:8, 13-14)

Confess any personal sins which the Holy Spirit brings to your mind.

3. Affirmation: As you agree with God's will, voice your affirmation of His word:

There is therefore now no condemnation for me if I am in You, Christ Jesus. For the law of the Spirit of life in You has set me free from the law of sin and death. (Romans 8:1-2)

4. Requests: As you make your requests known to the Lord, include:

- Love for fellow Christians
- The work of missions in Europe and Asia
- Your prayer list, the concerns of your heart, and today's activities

5. Closing Prayer: Finally, offer this closing prayer to the Lord:

This is the day which You have made; I will rejoice and be glad in it. (Psalm 118:24)

Memory Verse: But seek first the kingdom of God and His righteousness, and all these things shall be added to you.

Matthew 6:33
Stewardship Theme

DECEMBER 6

READING

The passage for today centers on an eternal perspective. Because of our great hope for the future, we are to be steadfast in the face of present trials.

Read 1 Peter 1.

REFLECTING

One mark of maturity is the ability to put off present gratification for the sake of a future reward. A child of six is not willing to give up buying a piece of candy and save that money for college tuition. It is a matter of one's maturity of perspective. Though the stakes are much higher, the principle is the same. As a matter of growing as a disciple of Jesus Christ, Peter urges us to consider our future inheritance and endure present trials in expectation of our reward. Though the present cost may appear great, the goal far outweighs the costs.

RESPONDING

1. Praise: Offer the Lord your praise for His goodness through the words of this psalm:

O Lord God of Israel, the One who dwells between the cherubim, You are God, You alone, of all the kingdoms of the earth. You have made heaven and earth. (2 Kings 19:15)

Lord God of Israel, there is no God in heaven above or on earth below like You, who keep Your covenant and mercy with Your servants who walk before You with all their heart. (1 Kings 8:23)

Now offer to the Lord your personal praise and thanksgiving.

2. Confession: Pray this confession to the Lord as you seek to keep your life free from sin and in fellowship with Him:

I will praise You, for I am fearfully and wonderfully made; marvelous are Your works, and that my soul knows very well. . . . Search me, O God, and know my heart; try me, and know my anxieties; and see if there is any wicked way in me, and lead me in the way everlasting. (Psalm 139:14, 23-24)

Confess any personal sins which the Holy Spirit brings to your mind.

3. Affirmation: As you agree with God's will, voice your affirmation of His word:

If I love You, O Lord, I will keep Your word; and the Father will love me, and You and the Father will come to me and make Your home with me. (John 14:23)

4. Requests: As you make your requests known to the Lord, include:

- Faithfulness with your time
- The president and national leaders and affairs
- Your prayer list, the concerns of your heart, and today's activities

5. Closing Prayer: Finally, offer this closing prayer to the Lord:

Oh, satisfy me early with Your mercy, that I may rejoice and be glad all my days! (Psalm 90:14)

Memory Verse: But seek first the kingdom of God and His righteousness, and all these things shall be added to you.

Matthew 6:33
Stewardship Theme

READING

The passage for today centers on the Christian response to trials. Spiritual sacrifice and personal holiness should be the Christian response to trials.

Read 1 Peter 2.

REFLECTING

A pilgrim is a wanderer. A sojourner is one who lives somewhere temporarily, a visitor. Peter calls us pilgrims and sojourners in this world. We are no longer at home here. We are no longer a part of this world. Whatever we do should be evaluated in light of our true citizenship: heaven. As such, we live by the rules and values of heaven, not earth. Peter writes, "I beg you, as sojourners and pilgrims, abstain from fleshly lusts which war against the soul" (verse 11). When we violate the principles of heaven, it is not just God and His honor that suffer. We suffer. We are called to holiness, not only because God is holy, but also because sin is harmful and self-destructive. Be holy, for God is holy, for your own sake.

RESPONDING

1. Praise: The Lord has transferred us from the kingdom of darkness and made us citizens of the kingdom of light, for which we praise Him:

Not unto us, O Lord, not unto us, but to Your name give glory, because of Your mercy, and because of Your truth. . . . We who fear You, O Lord, trust in You; You are our help and our shield. . . . We will bless the Lord from this time forth and forevermore. Praise the Lord! (Psalm 115:1, 11, 18)

Take a moment to offer the Lord your personal praise and thanksgiving.

2. Confession: Pray this confession to the Lord as you seek to keep your life free from sin and in fellowship with Him:

Remember, O Lord, Your tender mercies and Your lovingkindnesses, for they have been from of old. Do not remember the sins of my youth, nor my transgressions; according to Your mercy remember me, for Your goodness' sake, O Lord. (Psalm 25:6-7)

Confess any personal sins which the Holy Spirit may bring to your mind.

3. Affirmation: As you agree with the will of God, voice your affirmation of His word:

I must reckon myself to be dead indeed to sin, but alive to You, O God, in Christ Jesus my Lord. (Romans 6:11)

4. Requests: As you make your requests known to the Lord, include:

- Your financial needs
- The needs of the poor
- Your prayer list, the concerns of your heart, and today's activities

5. Closing Prayer: Finally, offer this closing prayer to the Lord:

Let the beauty of You, Lord, be upon me, and establish the work of my hands for me; yes, establish the work of my hands. (Psalm 90:17)

Memory Verse: But seek first the kingdom of God and His righteousness, and all these things shall be added to you.

Matthew 6:33
Stewardship Theme

DECEMBER 8

READING

The passage for today centers on mutual submission in marriage. Both the husband and wife are to be sensitive to the role and needs of the other.

Read 1 Peter 3.

REFLECTING

In a Christian marriage, one of the dominant characteristics should be a mutual concern for the welfare of the spouse. The wife is to be submissive to the role of the husband, while living an exemplary life which validates her faith. The husband is to be sensitive, understanding, and giving honor to his wife. When both spouses assume a proper role before God and each other, a harmonious and satisfying relationship can be the result. If not, conflict or alienation can result. How important it is for the unmarried to insist not only on a Christian for a partner, but on a Christian who is spiritually mature and growing. Alienation can occur in a Christian marriage as well as a mixed marriage.

RESPONDING

1. Praise: Praise the Lord for the harmony which He can bring to relationships:

Men shall speak of the might of Your awesome acts; and I will declare Your greatness. They shall utter the memory of Your great goodness, and shall sing of Your righteousness. The Lord is gracious and full of compassion, slow to anger and great in mercy. The Lord is good to all, and His tender mercies are over all His works. (Psalm 145:6-9)

Take a moment to offer the Lord your personal praise and thanksgiving.

2. Confession: Pray this confession to the Lord as you seek to keep your life free from sin and in fellowship with Him:

Good and upright are You Lord, therefore You teach me, though a sinner, in Your way. If I am humble, You will guide me in justice and teach me Your way. All Your paths for me are mercy and truth, if I keep Your covenant and Your testimonies. For Your name's sake, O Lord, pardon my iniquity, for it is great. (Psalm 25:8-11)

Confess any personal sins which the Holy Spirit may bring to your mind.

3. Affirmation: As you agree with the will of God, voice your affirmation of His word:

You, O Lord, are my light and my salvation; whom shall I fear? You are the strength of my life; of whom shall I be afraid? (Psalm 27:1)

4. Requests: As you make your requests known to the Lord, include:

- Protection from the "evil one"
- Laborers for the "harvest"
- Your prayer list, the concerns of your heart, and today's activities

5. Closing Prayer: Finally, offer this closing prayer to the Lord:

Bless the Lord, all you His hosts, you ministers of His, who do His pleasure. Bless the Lord, all His works, in all places of His dominion. (Psalm 103:21-22)

Memory Verse: But seek first the kingdom of God and His righteousness, and all these things shall be added to you.

Matthew 6:33
Stewardship Theme

READING

The passage for today centers on a perspective on suffering. We are to follow the example of Christ in the face of suffering.

Read 1 Peter 4.

REFLECTING

Life is often difficult, whether you are a Christian or not. The rain—accidents, illnesses, difficult circumstances—falls on the righteous and unrighteous alike. The Christian life often adds to it. We may be discriminated against because of our faith, or we may not be able to take the easy way out of a problem because it is dishonest or immoral. Added together, life for the Christian is sometimes a formidable challenge. We usually wonder why God doesn't deliver us from it, why He doesn't love His children enough to spare us needless or senseless suffering. However, Christ does not ask us to suffer anything for Him that He was not willing to suffer for us. Someday, we will be redeemed and rewarded. Until then, "since Christ suffered for us . . . arm yourself also with the same mind" (verse 1).

RESPONDING

1. Praise: We can praise the Lord because He has promised to see us through the trials of life:

The Lord is righteous in all His ways, gracious in all His works. The Lord is near to all who call upon Him, to all who call upon Him in truth. He will fulfill the desire of those who fear Him; He also will hear their cry and save them. . . . My mouth shall speak the praise of the Lord, and all flesh shall bless His holy name forever and ever. (Psalm 145:17-19, 21)

Take a moment to offer the Lord your personal praise and thanksgiving.

2. Confession: Pray this confession to the Lord as you seek to keep your life free from sin and in fellowship with Him:

Turn Yourself to me, and have mercy on me, for I am desolate and afflicted. The troubles of my heart have enlarged; oh, bring me out of my distresses! Look on my affliction and my pain, and forgive all my sins. (Psalm 25:16-18)

Confess any personal sins which the Holy Spirit may bring to your mind.

3. Affirmation: As you agree with the will of God, voice your affirmation of His word:

For the wages of sin is death, but Your gift, O God, is eternal life in Christ Jesus my Lord. (Romans 6:23)

4. Requests: As you make your requests known to the Lord, include:

- Commitment to the Lord
- Parachurch ministries
- Your prayer list, the concerns of your heart, and today's activities

5. Closing Prayer: Finally, offer this closing prayer to the Lord:

Lord, preserve me from all evil; preserve my soul. Lord, preserve my going out and my coming in from this time forth, and even forevermore. (Psalm 121:7-8)

Memory Verse: But seek first the kingdom of God and His righteousness, and all these things shall be added to you.

Matthew 6:33
Stewardship Theme

DECEMBER 10

READING

The passage for today centers on relationships in the Church. Elders are to shepherd the Church, and the Church is to respect their leadership.

Read 1 Peter 5.

REFLECTING

True leaders are servants. Their task is to make those under them successful. As everyone is successful, the larger goal toward which they are all contributing is achieved. It is an example of a fundamental principle which runs throughout Scripture: the work of God is done through the people of God through mutual submission. It is not as we all look out for our own efforts. It is as we all submit to the needs and roles of others that His work is accomplished. Elders are to shepherd those in the Church, living the kind of a life that will be an example to others: showing them how to live, rather than merely telling them; living in submission to the needs and characteristics of those under them; humbling themselves under the mighty hand of God, that He may exalt them in due time.

RESPONDING

1. Praise: Because Jesus, our Shepherd, was submissive to the Father and cared for our needs on the cross, we praise Him:

Let us come before His presence with thanksgiving; let us shout joyfully to Him with psalms. For the Lord is the great God, and the Great King above all gods. . . . Oh come, let us worship and bow down; let us kneel before the Lord our Maker. For He is our God, and we are the people of His pasture, and the sheep of His hand. (Psalm 95:2-3, 6-7)

Take a moment to offer the Lord your personal praise and thanksgiving.

2. Confession: Pray this confession to the Lord as you seek to keep your life free from sin and in fellowship with Him:

Blessed am I, my transgression is forgiven, my sin is covered. Blessed am I, the Lord does not impute iniquity to me, and in my spirit there is no guile. (Psalm 32:1-2)

Confess any personal sins which the Holy Spirit may bring to your mind.

3. Affirmation: As you agree with the will of God, voice your affirmation of His word:

For You, O God, have not given me a spirit of fear, but of power and of love and of a sound mind. (2 Timothy 1:7)

4. Requests: As you make your requests known to the Lord, include:

- Renewing of your mind
- Needs of your extended family
- Your prayer list, the concerns of your heart, and today's activities

5. Closing Prayer: Finally, offer this closing prayer to the Lord:

May we with one mind and one mouth glorify the God and Father of our Lord Jesus Christ. (Romans 15:6)

Memory Verse: No servant can serve two masters; for either he will hate the one and love the other, or else he will be loyal to the one and despise the other. You cannot serve God and mammon.

Luke 16:13
Stewardship Theme

READING

The passage for today centers on cultivation of Christian character. God has given us the capacity to grow in Christian character and spiritual fruit.

Read 1 Peter 1.

REFLECTING

Throughout the Scripture, God calls us to act like who we are. Our self-image is flawed. We still see ourselves as beings of this world, enamored with the values and attitudes of this world. Yet we have died to this world, and have become citizens of another. We are children of God, subjects of the King of Creation. God calls us to act accordingly, but because we do not see ourselves accordingly, our actions follow our self-image. Peter writes in verse 4 that we have become "partakers of the divine nature, having escaped the corruption that is in the world . . . ." Then he adds, "for this very reason" pursue holiness. Those who don't have become short-sighted and have forgotten that they were purged from their old sin.

RESPONDING

1. Praise: We have become partakers of the divine nature through Christ and praise Him who made it possible:

I will extol You, my God, O King; and I will bless Your name forever and ever. Every day I will bless You, and I will praise Your name forever and ever. Great is the Lord, and greatly to be praised; and His greatness is unsearchable. One generation shall praise Your works to another, and shall declare Your mighty acts. I will meditate on the glorious splendor of Your majesty, and on Your wondrous works. (Psalm 145:1-5)

Take a moment to offer the Lord your personal praise and thanksgiving.

2. Confession: Pray this confession to the Lord as you seek to keep your life free from sin and in fellowship with Him:

I acknowledged my sin to You, and my iniquity I have not hidden. I said, "I will confess my transgressions to the Lord," and You forgave the iniquity of my sin. (Psalm 32:5)

Confess any personal sins which the Holy Spirit may bring to your mind.

3. Affirmation: As you agree with the will of God, voice your affirmation of His word:

I have Your commandments and when I keep them, it shows I love You. And if I love You, Lord Jesus, I will be loved by Your Father, and You will love me and manifest Yourself to me. (John 14:21)

4. Requests: As you make your requests known to the Lord, include:

- The Lord's leading in your life
- Opportunities for personal evangelism
- Your prayer list, the concerns of your heart, and today's activities

5. Closing Prayer: Finally, offer this closing prayer to the Lord:

Now may the God of hope fill me with all joy and peace in believing, that I may abound in hope by the power of the Holy Spirit. (Romans 15:13)

Memory Verse: No servant can serve two masters; for either he will hate the one and love the other, or else he will be loyal to the one and despise the other. You cannot serve God and mammon.

Luke 16:13
Stewardship Theme

DECEMBER 12

READING

The passage for today centers on condemnation of false teachers. Beware of false teachers whose lives deny their faith and who will be judged by God.

Read 1 Peter 2.

REFLECTING

False teachers are viewed gravely in the Scripture. Perhaps the most scathing rebukes and most unthinkable punishment are articulated against these "wolves in sheep's clothing." Why is it that they are dealt with so harshly? Because while refusing salvation themselves, they also keep others from it. They not only follow the path to destruction, but they also lead others to follow with them. It is like a drowning man who not only refuses to accept a lifesaver, but also insists on drowning someone else with him. Such cancerous deception must not be allowed to continue, but must be cut out in order to save lives. We must take great care in the accuracy of our own teaching and shun those who do not.

RESPONDING

1. Praise: Let us praise our God in these words:

Give to the Lord, O kindred of the peoples, . . . Give to the Lord the glory due His name; bring an offering, and come before Him. Oh, worship the Lord in the beauty of holiness! (1 Chronicles 16:28-29)

I will praise the Lord according to His righteousness, and will sing praise to the name of the Lord Most High. (Psalm 7:17)

Now offer to the Lord your personal praise and thanksgiving.

2. Confession: Pray this confession to the Lord as you seek to keep your life free from sin and in fellowship with Him:

O Lord, You blot out my transgressions for Your own sake; and You will not remember my sins. (Isaiah 43:25)

Confess any personal sins which the Holy Spirit brings to your mind.

3. Affirmation: As you agree with God's will, voice your affirmation of His word:

The Spirit also helps me in weaknesses. For I do not know what I should pray for as I ought, but the Spirit Himself makes intercession for me with groanings which cannot be uttered. (Romans 8:26)

4. Requests: As you make your requests known to the Lord, include:

- Love for the lost
- The work of missions in Africa
- Your prayer list, the concerns of your heart, and today's activities

5. Closing Prayer: Finally, offer this closing prayer to the Lord:

Now to You who are able to establish us according to the gospel and preaching of Jesus Christ—to You, alone wise, be glory through Jesus Christ forever. Amen. (Romans 16:25-27)

Memory Verse: No servant can serve two masters; for either he will hate the one and love the other, or else he will be loyal to the one and despise the other. You cannot serve God and mammon.

Luke 16:13
Stewardship Theme

READING

The passage for today centers on the Day of the Lord. In the last time, people will scoff at the Day of the Lord, but we ought to purify ourselves for it.

Read 1 Peter 3.

REFLECTING

No one thinks the world will last forever. If nothing happens before, eventually the hydrogen in the sun will burn out, and the sun will grow cold, destroying the earth in the process. So how will the earth end? Is this the picture of the end times? No. The Bible tells us that the day will come when the heavens and the earth will go up in a universal ball of fire. A new heaven and a new earth will then be created. It may not happen soon, but it will happen. No one knows the time. But, since all of us must face "the end" sometime, Peter writes that as we look forward to these things, we should accept salvation through the Lord for ourselves and direct others to do the same.

RESPONDING

1. Praise: The Lord is worthy to receive our praise because of all that He has done for us:

Tremble before Him, all the earth. The world also is firmly established, it shall not be moved. Let the heavens rejoice, and let the earth be glad. . . . Oh, give thanks to the Lord, for He is good! For His mercy endures forever. . . . Blessed be the Lord God of Israel from everlasting to everlasting! (1 Chronicles 16:30-31, 34, 36)

Now offer to the Lord your personal praise and thanksgiving.

2. Confession: Pray this confession to the Lord as you seek to keep your life free from sin and in fellowship with Him:

You have blotted out, like a thick cloud, my transgressions, and like a cloud, my sins. I will return to You, for You have redeemed me. (Isaiah 44:22)

Confess any personal sins which the Holy Spirit brings to your mind.

3. Affirmation: As you agree with God's will, voice your affirmation of His word:

If I keep Your commandments, O Lord, I will abide in Your love, just as You have kept Your Father's commandments and abide in His love. (John 15:10)

4. Requests: As you make your requests known to the Lord, include:

- Faithfulness with your talents
- Your state and local leaders and affairs
- Your prayer list, the concerns of your heart, and today's activities

5. Closing Prayer: Finally, offer this closing prayer to the Lord:

The grace of the Lord Jesus Christ, and the love of God, and the communion of the Holy Spirit be with us all. Amen. (2 Corinthians 13:14)

Memory Verse: No servant can serve two masters; for either he will hate the one and love the other, or else he will be loyal to the one and despise the other. You cannot serve God and mammon.

Luke 16:13
Stewardship Theme

DECEMBER 14

READING

The passage for today centers on conditions for fellowship. If we walk in the light, we have fellowship with God.

Read 1 John 1.

REFLECTING

Truth about sin is a difficult thing to keep balanced in our minds. On the one hand, we know that we shouldn't sin. It's wrong. We should never take sinning lightly. On the other hand, we all sin. It's unavoidable. John writes, "If we say we have no sin, we deceive ourselves" (verse 8). Therefore, God had to make provision for us to be in fellowship with Him. If we confess our sins, He will forgive us. When we sin, we can accept God's forgiveness and restoration to fellowship. We need not berate ourselves endlessly or do a form of penance by trying to feel bad long enough to help pay for the sin. Only the blood of Christ can pay for our sin. And only confession can bring restoration to fellowship with God.

RESPONDING

1. Praise: The Lord forgives and restores us to fellowship, and in fellowship we can praise Him:

Because Your lovingkindness is better than life, My lips shall praise You. Thus will I bless You while I live; I will lift up my hands in Your name. . . . When I remember You on my bed, I meditate on You in the night watches. Because You have been my help, therefore in the shadow of Your wings I will rejoice. (Psalm 63:3-5, 7)

Pause for personal praise and thanksgiving.

2. Confession: Pray this confession to the Lord as you seek to keep your life free from sin and in fellowship with Him:

O God, You know my foolishness; and my sins are not hidden from You. Let not those who wait for You, O Lord God of hosts, be ashamed because of me. (Psalm 69:5-6)

Confess any personal sins which the Holy Spirit may bring to your mind.

3. Affirmation: As you agree with the will of God, voice your affirmation of His word:

You, O Lord, are the portion of my inheritance and my cup; You maintain my lot. The lines have fallen to me in pleasant places; Yes, I have a good inheritance. (Psalm 16:5-6)

4. Requests: As you make your requests known to the Lord, pray for:

- Strength for obedience
- International students in America
- Your prayer list, the concerns of your heart, and today's activities

5. Closing Prayer: Finally, offer this closing prayer to the Lord:

Now to You who are able to do exceedingly abundantly above all that I ask or think, according to the power that works in me, to You be glory in the Church by Christ Jesus throughout all ages, world without end. Amen. (Ephesians 3:20-21)

Memory Verse: No servant can serve two masters; for either he will hate the one and love the other, or else he will be loyal to the one and despise the other. You cannot serve God and mammon.

Luke 16:13
Stewardship Theme

READING

The passage for today centers on marks of fellowship. If we keep His commandments and love our brothers, we walk in fellowship.
Read 1 John 2.

REFLECTING

It is sometimes difficult to know if we are in fellowship with the Lord. In error, we tend to rely on our feelings to gauge our relationship with Him. If we "feel" spiritual one day, we think we are in fellowship with Him. If, on another day, we don't "feel" spiritual, we assume we are not in fellowship. This is unhelpful because it becomes a self-fulfilling prophecy. Because we don't "feel" spiritual on a given day, we are more prone to "act" unspiritually. We don't feel well, and we tend to give into sin more readily. John helps us with this. He describes fellowship for us. If we are keeping His commandments, and if we are loving our brother, we are in fellowship, whether we "feel" in fellowship or not. Don't let your feelings encourage you to sin.

RESPONDING

1. Praise: We can walk in fellowship with the Lord, and praise Him, regardless of how we "feel":

I will love You, O Lord, my strength. The Lord is my Rock and my fortress and my deliverer; my God, my strength, in whom I will trust; my shield and the horn of my salvation, my stronghold. I call upon the Lord, who is worthy to be praised; so shall I be saved from my enemies. . . . The Lord lives! Blessed be my Rock! Let the God of my salvation be exalted. (Psalm 18:1-3, 46)

Pause for personal praise and thanksgiving.

2. Confession: Pray this confession to the Lord as you seek to keep your life free from sin:

Good and upright is the Lord; therefore He teaches sinners in the way. The humble He guides in justice, and the humble He teaches His way. . . . For Your name's sake, O Lord, pardon my iniquity, for it is great. (Psalm 25:8-9, 11)

Confess any personal sins which the Holy Spirit brings to your mind.

3. Affirmation: Now pause to pray this affirmation to the Lord:

You are the living bread which came down from heaven. If I eat of this bread, I will live forever; and the bread that You shall give is Your flesh, which You shall give for the life of the world. (John 6:51)

4. Requests: As you make your requests known to the Lord, include:

- Your "daily bread"
- Christian education institutions
- Your prayer list, the concerns of your heart, and today's activities

5. Closing Prayer: Finally, offer this closing prayer to the Lord:

Now may You, the God of peace, sanctify me completely, and may my whole spirit, soul, and body be preserved blameless at the coming of my Lord Jesus Christ. (1 Thessalonians 5:23)

Memory Verse: No servant can serve two masters; for either he will hate the one and love the other, or else he will be loyal to the one and despise the other. You cannot serve God and mammon.
Luke 16:13
Stewardship Theme

DECEMBER 16

READING

The passage for today centers on the practice of righteousness. Those who say they love God must manifest it by loving their brothers in Christ.

Read 1 John 3.

REFLECTING

The final test of Christian character is action, not words. It is not what you say that determines your life message, but what you do. John writes, "let us not love in word or in tongue, but in deed and in truth."

Consistency is one of the great challenges of the Christian walk. Whenever our actions do not match our words, the message of our actions always overrides the message of our words. Therein lies the basis for one of the most consistent complaints against Christianity over the ages: hypocrisy.

Take stock, not merely of your words, but of your actions. If you indeed are the only Bible some people will ever read, how accurate a picture do they get of the Lord?

RESPONDING

1. Praise: Though we are not always consistent in our Christian walk, we can praise the Lord that He is always consistent with us:

Be glad in the Lord and rejoice, you righteous; and shout for joy, all you upright in heart! (Psalm 32:11)

Rejoice in the Lord, O you righteous! For praise from the upright is beautiful. Praise the Lord with the harp; make melody to Him with an instrument of ten strings. (Psalm 33:1-2)

Pause for personal praise and thanksgiving.

2. Confession: Pray this confession to the Lord as you seek to keep your life free from sin and in fellowship with Him:

Sing praise to the Lord, you saints of His, and give thanks at the remembrance of His holy name. For His anger is but for a moment, His favor is for a lifetime; weeping may endure for a night, but joy comes in the morning. (Psalm 30:4-5)

Confess any personal sins which the Holy Spirit brings to your mind.

3. Affirmation: Now pause to pray this affirmation to the Lord:

O God, You are Spirit, and I must worship in spirit and truth. (John 4:24)

4. Requests: As you make your requests known to the Lord, include:

- Passion for moral excellence
- Needs of personal friends
- Your prayer list, the concerns of your heart, and today's activities

5. Closing Prayer: Finally, offer this closing prayer to the Lord:

Now may the Lord Jesus Christ Himself, and You, my God and Father, who have loved me and given me everlasting consolation and good hope by grace, comfort my heart and establish me in every good word and work. (2 Thessalonians 2:16-17)

Memory Verse: No servant can serve two masters; for either he will hate the one and love the other, or else he will be loyal to the one and despise the other. You cannot serve God and mammon.

Luke 16:13
Stewardship Theme

READING

The passage for today centers on testing the spirits. Anyone who does not claim that Jesus is the son of God come in the flesh is not of God. Read 1 John 4.

REFLECTING

Whenever you are uncertain about someone's teaching or some organization's teaching, find out what they believe about Jesus. Several flags must wave conspicuously and unambiguously from their mainsail.

First, Jesus is the Son of God, the second Person of the Trinity. Second, He came in the flesh, incarnate as Jesus of Nazareth. Third, He died for our sins and was resurrected from the dead. Fourth, His death provided atonement for our sins; the only way of salvation is by grace through faith in Him.

If these teachings are not clear and at the forefront of a group's message, be cautious. Do not believe everything someone says. Test everyone with these tests to see if they are from God.

RESPONDING

1. Praise: Praise the Lord for all that He has done in providing for our salvation:

O Lord, our Lord, How excellent is Your name in all the earth, You who set Your glory above the heavens! . . . When I consider Your heavens, the work of Your fingers . . . what is man that You are mindful of him, and the son of man that You visit him? O Lord, our Lord, How majestic is Your name in all the earth! (Psalm 8:1, 3-4, 9)

Pause for personal praise and thanksgiving.

2. Confession: Pray this confession to the Lord as you seek to keep your life free from sin and in fellowship with Him:

I acknowledged my sin to You, and my iniquity I have not hidden. I said, "I will confess my transgressions to the Lord," And You forgave the iniquity of my sin. (Psalm 32:3, 5)

Confess any personal sins which the Holy Spirit brings to your mind.

3. Affirmation: Now pause to pray this affirmation to the Lord:

You, O Lord, will keep me in perfect peace, when my mind is stayed on You, because I trust in You. (Isaiah 26:3)

4. Requests: As you make your requests known to the Lord, include:

- Wisdom in decision making
- Opportunities to serve the Lord
- Your prayer list, the concerns of your heart, and today's activities

5. Closing Prayer: Finally, offer this closing prayer to the Lord:

Now to You, the King eternal, immortal, invisible, to God who alone is wise, be honor and glory forever and ever. Amen. (1 Timothy 1:17)

Memory Verse: And my God shall supply all your need according to His riches in glory by Christ Jesus.
Philippians 4:19
Stewardship Theme

DECEMBER 18

READING

The passage for today centers on the power of faith. Faith is the fundamental principle in overcoming the world and giving us eternal life.

Read 1 John 5.

REFLECTING

John writes, "Who is the one who overcomes the world, but he who believes that Jesus is the Son of God?" Faith is the victory that has overcome the world.

John wants us to have assurance of our salvation. So, further, he writes, "And this is the testimony: that God has given us eternal life, and this life is in His Son. He who has the Son has life; he who does not have the Son of God does not have life. These things I have written to you who believe in the name of the Son of God, that you may know that you have eternal life . . . ." Faith is the victory that overcomes the world.

If you believe in Jesus as your personal savior, you have the Son of God, and you have eternal life.

RESPONDING

1. Praise: Thank the Lord that He has given us eternal life in Christ, and praise Him for that assurance:

Both riches and honor come from You, and You reign over all. In Your hand is power and might; in Your hand it is to make great and to give strength to all. Now therefore, our God, we thank You and praise Your glorious name. (1 Chronicles 29:12-13)

Pause for personal praise and thanksgiving.

2. Confession: Pray this confession to the Lord as you seek to keep your life free from sin and in fellowship with Him:

The righteous cry out and the Lord hears, and delivers them out of all their troubles. The Lord is near to those who have a broken heart, and saves such as have a contrite spirit. (Psalm 34:17-18)

Confess any personal sins which the Holy Spirit brings to your mind.

3. Affirmation: Now pause to pray this affirmation to the Lord:

I know whom I have believed and I am persuaded that You, O Lord, are able to keep what I have entrusted to You until that day. (2 Timothy 1:12)

4. Requests: As you make your requests known to the Lord, include:

- Victory over temptation
- The work of missions in North and South America
- Your prayer list, the concerns of your heart, and today's activities

5. Closing Prayer: Finally, offer this closing prayer to the Lord:

You who are the blessed and only Potentate, the King of kings and Lord of lords, who alone have immortality, dwelling in unapproachable light, whom no man has seen or can see, to You be honor and everlasting power. Amen. (1 Timothy 6:15-16)

Memory Verse: And my God shall supply all your need according to His riches in glory by Christ Jesus.
Philippians 4:19
Stewardship Theme

READING

The passage for today centers on the doctrine of false teachers. False teachers do not confess Jesus Christ as God incarnate.

Read 2 John.

REFLECTING

The Bible teaches that Christians are to be tolerant, understanding, and compassionate. We are to go out of our way to be kind and loving to others; we are to love our neighbor as ourselves. If so, then how should we act toward false teachers who subvert our faith? The Bible also teaches that, while we should not be unkind, we should have no fellowship with them. The surest way to prevent the spread of a disease is to avoid contact with the germs. John writes, "If anyone comes to you and does not bring this doctrine [salvation in Christ], do not receive him into your house nor greet him; for he who greets him shares in his evil deeds" (verses 10-11).

RESPONDING

1. Praise: Offer your praise to the Lord in these passages as you fellowship with Him:

Blessed be the name of God forever and ever, for wisdom and might are His. . . . He gives wisdom to the wise and knowledge to those who have understanding. He reveals deep and secret things; He knows what is in the darkness, and light dwells with Him. (Daniel 2:20-22)

Now offer to the Lord your personal praise and thanksgiving.

2. Confession: Pray this confession to the Lord as you seek to keep your life free from sin and in fellowship with Him:

You will again have compassion on us, and will subdue our iniquities. You will cast all our sins into the depths of the sea. (Micah 7:19)

Confess any personal sins which the Holy Spirit brings to your mind.

3. Affirmation: As you agree with God's will, voice your affirmation of His word:

For I did not receive the spirit of bondage again to fear, but I received the Spirit of adoption by whom I cry out, "Abba, Father." (Romans 8:15)

4. Requests: As you make your requests known to the Lord, include:

- Love for your family
- Revival among Christians in America
- Your prayer list, the concerns of your heart, and today's activities

5. Closing Prayer: Finally, offer this closing prayer to the Lord:

Make me complete in every good work to do Your will, working in me what is well pleasing in Your sight, through Jesus Christ, to whom be glory forever and ever. Amen. (Hebrews 13:20-21)

Memory Verse: And my God shall supply all your need according to His riches in glory by Christ Jesus.
Philippians 4:19
Stewardship Theme

DECEMBER 20

READING

The passage for today centers on personal encouragement. John praises and encourages Gaius for his "witness of love before the church."

Read 3 John.

REFLECTING

Affirmation is a powerful force for good in the Christian life. We all long to be affirmed for who we are and what we are doing. Everyone can be built up with an encouraging word. We all like to hear, "Good job!" In essence, that is what John writes in his third epistle. He affirms Gaius in several areas: for his knowledge of truth, for his walking in the truth of that knowledge, for offering hospitality to fellow Christians and to strangers, and for helping support traveling missionaries. Good job, Gaius!

RESPONDING

1. Praise: As you continue your time with the Lord, affirm His good deeds as you offer Him your praise through His word:

I will praise You, Lord, with my whole heart; I will tell of all Your marvelous works. I will be glad and rejoice in You; I will sing praise to Your name, O Most High. . . . The Lord also will be a refuge for the oppressed, a refuge in times of trouble. And those who know Your name will put their trust in You; for You, Lord have not forsaken those who seek You. (Psalm 9:1-2, 9-10)

Now offer to the Lord your personal praise and thanksgiving.

2. Confession: Pray this confession to the Lord as you seek to keep your life free from sin and in fellowship with Him:

For a mere moment You have forsaken me, but with great mercies You will gather me. With a little wrath You hid Your face from me for a moment; but with everlasting kindness You will have mercy on me. (Isaiah 54:7-8)

Confess any personal sins which the Holy Spirit brings to your mind.

3. Affirmation: As you agree with God's will, voice your affirmation of His word:

You, O Lord, are Spirit, and I must worship You in spirit and truth. (John 4:24)

4. Requests: As you make your requests known to the Lord, include:

- Faithfulness with your treasures
- The Great Commission
- Your prayer list, the concerns of your heart, and today's activities

5. Closing Prayer: Finally, offer this closing prayer to the Lord:

May You, the God of grace, who called me to Your eternal glory by Christ Jesus, after I have suffered a while, perfect, establish, strengthen, and settle me. To You be the glory and the dominion forever and ever. Amen. (1 Peter 5:10-11)

Memory Verse: And my God shall supply all your need according to His riches in glory by Christ Jesus.
Philippians 4:19
Stewardship Theme

DECEMBER 21

READING

The passage for today centers on fighting for the faith. Jude is to contend earnestly for the faith against false teachers.

Read Jude.

REFLECTING

False teachers were a major problem in the early church, and many of the epistles deal with them. Jude offers scathing rebuke and warning to false teachers, but in addition, he offers insight on how we can protect ourselves from them. In verses 20-21, he uses four phrases which are instructive: (1) "building yourselves up"—studying, growing spiritually, doing things to encourage your spiritual growth; (2) "praying"—cultivating a healthy prayer life; (3) "keep yourselves in the love of God"—monitoring your lifestyle, guarding against sin; (4) "looking for the mercy of our Lord Jesus Christ unto eternal life"—cultivating an eternal perspective on life and evaluating our present circumstances in light of our eternal destiny.

RESPONDING

1. Praise: Thank the Lord that He is truth, and praise Him that He leads the willing heart to know truth:

Bless the Lord, O my soul! O Lord my God, You are very great: You are clothed with honor and majesty, who cover Yourself with light as with a garment, who stretch out the heavens like a curtain. . . . May the glory of the Lord endure forever; may the Lord rejoice in His works. . . . Bless the Lord, O my soul! Praise the Lord! (Psalm 104:1-2, 31, 35)

Take a moment to offer the Lord your personal praise and thanksgiving.

2. Confession: Pray this confession to the Lord as you seek to keep your life free from sin and in fellowship with Him:

O Lord, You do not have as great delight in burnt offerings and sacrifices as in our obeying Your voice. Behold, to obey is better than sacrifice, and to heed than the fat of rams. (1 Samuel 15:22)

Confess any personal sins which the Holy Spirit may bring to your mind.

3. Affirmation: As you agree with the will of God, voice your affirmation of His word:

You, Lord Jesus, are the light of the world. If I follow You, I shall not walk in darkness, but have the light of life. (John 8:12)

4. Requests: As you make your requests known to the Lord, include:

- Spiritual insight
- Campus ministries
- Your prayer list, the concerns of your heart, and today's activities

5. Closing Prayer: Finally, offer this closing prayer to the Lord:

May I grow in the grace and knowledge of our Lord and Savior Jesus Christ. To Him be the glory both now and forever. Amen. (2 Peter 3:18)

Memory Verse: And my God shall supply all your need according to His riches in glory by Christ Jesus.
Philippians 4:19
Stewardship Theme

DECEMBER 22

READING

The passage for today centers on the revelation of Christ. Jesus is seen in a vision as a glorious, overpowering, heavenly being.

Read Revelation 1.

REFLECTING

When Jesus came to earth the first time 2,000 years ago, He came in poverty, humility, and obscurity. He willingly allowed men to victimize Him and apparently triumph over Him. This is not at all a complete picture of who Jesus is. In coming to earth, Jesus left a state of glory and power, clothed Himself in humanity, and veiled His divine appearance. Revelation, however, gives us a better picture of who He really is. His head and hair are brilliant white, like a lightening bolt, His eyes glowing, like fire. His feet are the color of highly polished brass, His voice thunderous, like a waterfall. With such picturesque language, we may not know exactly how He looks, but the effect is dramatic. John falls down as dead. It gives us a better picture of who Jesus really is.

RESPONDING

1. Praise: Offer the Lord your praise that in His power and glory, He still loves us:

O Lord, how manifold are Your works! In wisdom You have made them all. The earth is full of Your possessions. . . . I will sing praise to my God while I have my being. May my meditation be sweet to Him; I will be glad in the Lord. (Psalm 104:24, 33, 34)

Take a moment to offer the Lord your personal praise and thanksgiving.

2. Confession: Pray this confession to the Lord as you seek to keep your life free from sin and in fellowship with Him:

I have sinned greatly in what I have done; but now, I pray, O Lord, take away the iniquity of Your servant, for I have done very foolishly. (2 Samuel 24:10)

Confess any personal sins which the Holy Spirit may bring to your mind.

3. Affirmation: As you agree with the will of God, voice your affirmation of His word:

Now faith is the substance of things hoped for, the evidence of things not seen. (Hebrews 11:1)

4. Requests: As you make your requests known to the Lord, include:

* Desire to be like Christ

* Needs in inner cities

* Your prayer list, the concerns of your heart, and today's activities

5. Closing Prayer: Finally, offer this closing prayer to the Lord:

Blessing and honor and glory and power be to You who sit on the throne, and to You, Lord, forever and ever! (Revelation 5:13)

Memory Verse: And my God shall supply all your need according to His riches in glory by Christ Jesus.
Philippians 4:19
Stewardship Theme

READING

The passage for today centers on messages to the churches. Jesus gives prophetic messages to four churches: Ephesus, Smyrna, Pergamos, and Thyatira.

Read Revelation 2.

REFLECTING

Jesus commends the church at Ephesus for all the good work which they have done. Nevertheless, he cautions them for having left their first love. Unless they repent and take care of top priorities, they will experience the chastening of God.

To Smyrna, Jesus offers encouragement in the face of impending persecution. "Be faithful unto death, and I will give you the crown of life."

To the church at Pergamos, He speaks warning. They hold fast to the name of Christ, but at the same time tolerate evil and sin in their midst. The same is true of the church at Thyatira. Unless they repent, Jesus warns that He will judge them quickly and severely.

RESPONDING

1. Praise: The Lord does not leave us to ourselves, but leads us into truth, and so we praise Him:

Oh, give thanks to the Lord! Call upon His name; make known His deeds among the peoples. Sing to Him, sing psalms to Him; talk of all His wondrous works. Glory in His holy name; let the hearts of those rejoice who seek the Lord. Seek the Lord and His strength; seek His face evermore. (Psalm 105:1-4)

Take a moment to offer the Lord your personal praise and thanksgiving.

2. Confession: Pray this confession to the Lord as you seek to keep your life free from sin and in fellowship with Him:

O my God, I am too ashamed and humiliated to lift up my face to You, my God; for my iniquities have risen higher than my head, and my guilt has grown up to the heavens. (Ezra 9:6)

Confess any personal sins which the Holy Spirit may bring to your mind.

3. Affirmation: As you agree with the will of God, voice your affirmation of His word:

For by grace I have been saved through faith, and that faith is not from myself; it is Your gift, O God, not of my works, lest I should boast. For I am Your workmanship, created in Christ Jesus for good works, which You prepared beforehand that I should walk in them. (Ephesians 2:8-10)

4. Requests: As you make your requests known to the Lord, include:

- Personal witness for Christ
- Local churches around the nation
- Your prayer list, the concerns of your heart, and today's activities

5. Closing Prayer: Finally, offer this closing prayer to the Lord:

Amen! Blessing and glory and wisdom, thanksgiving and honor and power and might, be to You, God, forever and ever. Amen. (Revelation 7:12)

Memory Verse: And my God shall supply all your need according to His riches in glory by Christ Jesus.
Philippians 4:19
Stewardship Theme

DECEMBER 24

READING

The passage for today centers on Jesus' prophetic messages to three additional churches: Sardis, Philadelphia, and Laodicea.

Read Revelation 3.

REFLECTING

To the Church at Sardis, Jesus offers a scathing rebuke. He calls them "dead," and warns them to recall their initial response to the gospel and repent. Some, even in Sardis, have not defiled themselves, and those Jesus commends.

Jesus commends Philadelphia for having kept His command to persevere, and because of that, He will keep them from the hour of trial which will come upon the whole world.

Perhaps the most frightening message goes to the church at Laodicea. They are wealthy and complacent. Jesus urges them to repent. Because their works are neither hot nor cold, but lukewarm, Jesus says He will spew them out of His mouth.

RESPONDING

1. Praise: Thank the Lord that He cares enough not to let us drift, and praise Him for His correction:

Praise the Lord! Oh, give thanks to the Lord, for He is good! For His mercy endures forever. Who can utter the mighty acts of the Lord? Or can declare all His praise? . . . Blessed be the Lord . . . from everlasting to everlasting! And let all the people say, "Amen!" Praise the Lord! (Psalm 106:1-2, 48)

Take a moment to offer the Lord your personal praise and thanksgiving.

2. Confession: Pray this confession to the Lord as you seek to keep your life free from sin and in fellowship with Him:

O Lord, do not rebuke me in Your anger, nor chasten me in Your hot displeasure. Have mercy on me, O Lord, for I am weak; O Lord, heal me, for . . . my soul also is greatly troubled. (Psalm 6:1-3)

Confess any personal sins which the Holy Spirit may bring to your mind.

3. Affirmation: As you agree with the will of God, voice your affirmation of His word:

If I love You, Lord Jesus, I will keep Your word; and Your Father will love me, and You and Your Father will come to me and make Your home with me. (John 14:23)

4. Requests: As you make your requests known to the Lord, include:

- An eternal perspective
- Needs of work or school mates
- Your prayer list, the concerns of your heart, and today's activities

5. Closing Prayer: Finally, offer this closing prayer to the Lord:

I will wait on You, the Lord; I will be of good courage, and You shall strengthen my heart; I will wait on You! (Psalm 27:14)

Memory Verse: Let your conduct be without covetousness, and be content with such things as you have. For He Himself has said, "I will never leave you nor forsake you."

Hebrews 13:5
Stewardship Theme

DECEMBER 25

READING

The passage for today centers on the heavenly throne. John describes an astounding vision of the throne of God in heaven.

Read Revelation 4.

REFLECTING

At Christmas, our thoughts are on Jesus' birth, focusing on His humanity. By radical contrast, today we see the throne room of heaven and the surroundings, which magnify His deity. In the center is a throne, behind which an emerald-colored rainbow arises. Dignitaries are seated around the throne in white robes with gold appointments. The floor of the massive room is like crystal. Unusual looking creatures give verbal praise to God constantly, and the dignitaries form a celestial choir, worshiping and praising God. This is the normal abode of Jesus. This is the world of which He is a part and from which He came. Revelation pictures Jesus' majesty and grandeur.

RESPONDING

1. Praise: Praise the Lord that He was willing to become what we are, that we could become what He is:

O God, my heart is steadfast; I will sing and give praise. . . . I will awaken the dawn. I will praise You, O Lord, among the peoples, and I will sing praises to You among the nations. For Your mercy is great above the heavens, and Your truth reaches to the clouds. Be exalted, O God, above the heavens, and Your glory above all the earth. (Psalm 108:1, 3-5)

Take a moment to offer the Lord your personal praise and thanksgiving.

2. Confession: Pray this confession to the Lord as you seek to keep your life free from sin and in fellowship with Him:

Can I understand my errors? Cleanse me from secret faults, O Lord. Keep me back from presumptuous sins; let them not have dominion over me. Then I shall be blameless, and I shall be innocent of great transgression. (Psalm 19:12-13)

Confess any personal sins which the Holy Spirit may bring to your mind.

3. Affirmation: As you agree with the will of God, voice your affirmation of His word:

For You, Lord Jesus, were a Child born to us, a Son given to us; and the government will be upon Your shoulder. And Your name will be called Wonderful, Counselor, Mighty God, Everlasting Father, Prince of Peace. (Isaiah 9:6)

4. Requests: As you make your requests known to the Lord, include:

• Personal discipline

• Christians worldwide who are persecuted for their faith

• Your prayer list, the concerns of your heart, and today's activities

5. Closing Prayer: Finally, offer this closing prayer to the Lord:

Show me the path of life; in Your presence is fullness of joy; at Your right hand are pleasures forevermore. (Psalm 16:11)

Memory Verse: Let your conduct be without covetousness, and be content with such things as you have. For He Himself has said, "I will never leave you nor forsake you."

Hebrews 13:5
Stewardship Theme

DECEMBER 26

READING

The passage for today centers on the Lamb of God. Jesus, the Lamb of God, is seen as the focal point of worship in heaven.

Read Revelation 5.

REFLECTING

Into the scene of unspeakable glory in the throne room of heaven enters Jesus, the Lamb of God. In a symbolic reenactment of His death and resurrection to provide atonement for the sins of mankind, Jesus captures the imagination of all heaven. The throne room erupts in praise and adulation to the Son of God and Savior of the world. More than one hundred million angels break into songs of praise. They sing the song of the ages: "Blessing and honor and glory and power to Him who sits on the throne, and to the Lamb, forever and ever!" (verse 13). This worship scene is, can be, and should be repeated thousands of times both here on earth and forever more by angels and men alike.

RESPONDING

1. Praise: In the eyes of God, it is wisdom to praise Him for who He is and what He has done for us:

O God, You are my God; early will I seek You; My soul thirsts for You, my flesh longs for You in a dry and weary land where there is no water. So I have looked for You in the sanctuary, to see Your power and Your glory. (Psalm 63:1-2)

Pause for personal praise and thanksgiving.

2. Confession: Pray this confession to the Lord as you seek to keep your life free from sin and in fellowship with Him:

Bless the Lord, O my soul; and all that is within me, bless His holy name! Bless the Lord, O my soul, and forget not all His benefits: who forgives all your iniquities. (Psalm 103:1-3)

Confess any personal sins which the Holy Spirit brings to mind.

3. Affirmation: Now pause to pray this affirmation to the Lord:

I may come to You, O Lord, weary and heavy laden, and You will give me rest. I may take Your yoke upon me, and learn from You, for You are gentle and lowly in heart, and I shall find rest for my soul. For Your yoke is easy, and Your burden is light. (Matthew 11:28-30)

4. Requests: As you make your requests known to the Lord, include:

- Love for the Lord
- The work of missions in the Middle East, Australia, and the Islands
- Your prayer list, the concerns of your heart, and today's activities

5. Closing Prayer: Finally, offer this closing prayer to the Lord:

Save Your people, and bless Your inheritance; shepherd us also, and bear us up forever. (Psalm 28:9)

Memory Verse: Let your conduct be without covetousness, and be content with such things as you have. For He Himself has said, "I will never leave you nor forsake you."

Hebrews 13:5
Stewardship Theme

READING

The passage for today centers on the judgment of God. John begins a description of the judgment of the earth, which continues in following chapters.

Read Revelation 15.

REFLECTING

One of the sobering realities of the Scripture is the prophecy of judgment on mankind at the end of time. God has chosen to put into language the truth of coming judgment that is graphic enough for us to grasp the point. While theologians debate timetables and exact meanings, they all agree on one thing: judgment is a central feature of the end times. While the depiction of judgment in Revelation is shrouded in symbolism and mystery, it is clear that it is paralyzingly unpleasant. But these descriptions are not given at random or without purpose. Accounts of judgment are accompanied by warnings to men to take heed and prepare themselves to meet the Lord.

RESPONDING

1. Praise: Worship the Lord by offering Him your praise in spirit and in truth:

Be merciful to me, O God, be merciful to me! For my soul trusts in You; and in the shadow of Your wings I make my refuge, until these calamities have passed by. . . . I will praise You, O Lord, among the peoples; I will sing to You among the nations. For Your mercy reaches unto the heavens, and Your truth unto the clouds. Be exalted, O God, above the heavens; let Your glory be above all the earth. (Psalm 57:1, 9-11)

Pause for personal praise and thanksgiving.

2. Confession: Pray this confession to the Lord as you seek to keep your life free from sin and in fellowship with Him:

Deliver me from bloodguiltiness, O God, the God of my salvation. And my tongue shall sing aloud of Your righteousness. O Lord, open my lips, and my mouth shall show forth Your praise. (Psalm 51:14-15)

Confess any personal sins which the Holy Spirit brings to your mind.

3. Affirmation: Now pause to pray this affirmation to the Lord:

You, Lord Jesus, are the Way, the Truth, and the Life. I come to the Father only through You. (John 14:6)

4. Requests: As you make your requests known to the Lord, include:

- Faithfulness in sharing Christ
- The Lord's work in national and world affairs
- Your prayer list, the concerns of your heart, and today's activities
- Whatever else is on your heart

5. Closing Prayer: Finally, offer this closing prayer to the Lord:

You, the Lord, will command Your lovingkindness in the daytime, and in the night Your song shall be with me—a prayer to You, the God of my life. (Psalm 42:8)

Memory Verse: Let your conduct be without covetousness, and be content with such things as you have. For He Himself has said, "I will never leave you nor forsake you."

Hebrews 13:5
Stewardship Theme

DECEMBER 28

READING

The passage for today centers on the second coming of Christ. John describes heaven being opened and Jesus returning to earth as a conquering King.

Read Revelation 19.

REFLECTING

Apocalypse: "The revelation of a violent struggle in which evil will be destroyed"—Webster. The second coming of Christ is apocalypse fulfilled. While the symbolism of the language makes it difficult to ascertain exactly how events will unfold, it is clear that when Jesus returns again, it will be to confront evil and destroy it. The heavens split, and Jesus descends upon the armies of the earth which have gathered in opposition to His return. On His robe is written "King of kings, and Lord of lords." In contrast to his role in coming as Savior of man, He now comes as King of Creation. Whereas once he made himself subject to men, now all men will become subject to Him. History will end, and eternity begin.

RESPONDING

1. Praise: The Lord is coming again, and we praise Him that we can look forward to His appearing:

Inasmuch as there is none like You, O Lord (You are great, and Your name is great in might), who would not fear You, O King of the nations? For this is Your rightful due, for among all the wise men of the nations, and in all their kingdoms, there is none like You. . . . The Lord is the true God; He is the living God and the everlasting King. (Jeremiah 16:6-7, 10)

Take a moment to offer the Lord your personal praise and thanksgiving.

2. Confession: Pray this confession to the Lord as you seek to keep your life free from sin and in fellowship with Him:

O Lord, You blot out my transgressions for Your own sake; and You will not remember my sins. (Isaiah 43:25)

Confess any personal sins which the Holy Spirit may bring to your mind.

3. Affirmation: As you agree with the will of God, voice your affirmation of His word:

My eye has not seen, nor my ear heard, nor have entered into my heart the things which You, O God, have prepared for me who loves You. (1 Corinthians 2:9)

4. Requests: As you make your requests known to the Lord, include:

- Compassion for others
- Missions in America
- Your prayer list, the concerns of your heart, and today's activities

5. Closing Prayer: Finally, offer this closing prayer to the Lord:

Blessed are You, the Lord, forevermore! Amen and amen. (Psalm 89:52)

Memory Verse: Let your conduct be without covetousness, and be content with such things as you have. For He Himself has said, "I will never leave you nor forsake you."
Hebrews 13:5
Stewardship Theme

READING

The passage for today centers on Satan's destiny. After leading a final rebellion, Satan is confined forever. Read Revelation 20.

REFLECTING

Satan is not taken seriously by society as a whole. Because of excesses of the past, in which witches were burned at the stake, and because of our present anti-supernatural mindset, Satan is joked about, scoffed at, and discounted. Yet from Genesis to Revelation, Satan is taken seriously, and is a force to be reckoned with. As part of the culmination of the end times, He is confronted, conquered, and confined. Satan is a deceiver and a destroyer. He deceives in order to destroy. Yet, in the end, he is defeated, and his reign of terror on earth is ended. "And the devil, who deceived them was cast into the lake of fire and brimstone . . . ."

RESPONDING

1. Praise: Because the Lord's victory over Satan is certain, we can rejoice and praise Him confidently:

Great and marvelous are Your works, Lord God Almighty! Just and true are Your ways, O King of the saints! Who shall not fear You, O Lord, and glorify Your name? For You alone are holy. For all nations shall come and worship before You, for Your judgments have been manifested. (Revelation 15:3-4)

Take a moment to offer the Lord your personal praise and thanksgiving.

2. Confession: Pray this confession to the Lord as you seek to keep your life free from sin and in fellowship with Him:

Bless the Lord, O my soul; and all that is within me, bless His holy name! Bless the Lord, O my soul, and forget not all His benefits: who forgives all my iniquities. (Psalm 103:1-3)

Confess any personal sins which the Holy Spirit may bring to your mind.

3. Affirmation: As you agree with the will of God, voice your affirmation of His word:

If I believe on the Lord Jesus Christ, I will be saved. (Acts 16:31)

4. Requests: As you make your requests known to the Lord, include:

- Personal spiritual growth
- Military ministries
- Your prayer list, the concerns of your heart, and today's activities

5. Closing Prayer: Finally, offer this closing prayer to the Lord:

Glory to You in the highest, and on earth peace, good will toward men! (Luke 2:14)

Memory Verse: Let your conduct be without covetousness, and be content with such things as you have. For He Himself has said, "I will never leave you nor forsake you."

Hebrews 13:5

Stewardship Theme

DECEMBER 30

READING

The passage for today centers on the new heaven and earth. The old heaven and earth are replaced with glorious new ones.

Read Revelation 21.

REFLECTING

In the new heaven and new earth, the distance between God and man will be removed. In the Old Testament, the glory of God was displayed, but men were not able to look on it. The glory of God, symbolized as a brilliant light, inhabited the inner room of the tabernacle and temple, but was unseen by the eyes of men. In the New Testament, men were able to approach Jesus, but His glory was not seen, being veiled by His human form. In the new heaven and new earth, the glory of God will not be veiled, and we shall be able to behold it. The distance will be removed, and we will fellowship with God. "The tabernacle of God is with men, and He will dwell with them, and they shall be His people, and God Himself will be with them and be their God."

RESPONDING

1. Praise: We have such a glorious home and future with the Lord, we can begin now to praise Him eternally:

Who is like You, O Lord, among the gods? Who is like You, glorious in holiness, fearful in praises, doing wonders? (Exodus 15:11)

Therefore You are great, O Lord God. For there is none like You, nor is there any God besides You, according to all that we have heard with our ears. (2 Samuel 7:22)

Take a moment to offer the Lord your personal praise and thanksgiving.

2. Confession: Pray this confession to the Lord as you seek to keep your life free from sin and in fellowship with Him:

You have not dealt with me according to my sins, nor punished me according to my iniquities. For as the heavens are high above the earth, so great is Your mercy toward those who fear You; as far as the east is from the west, so far have You removed our transgressions from us. (Psalm 103:10-12)

Confess any personal sins which the Holy Spirit may bring to your mind.

3. Affirmation: As you agree with the will of God, voice your affirmation of His word:

You did not spare Your own Son, but delivered Him up for me; how shall You not with Him also freely give me all things. (Romans 8:32)

4. Requests: As you make your requests known to the Lord, include:

- Fruit of the Spirit in your life
- The ministry of Christian literature
- Your prayer list, the concerns of your heart, and today's activities

5. Closing Prayer: Finally, offer this closing prayer to the Lord:

Grace, mercy, and peace from You, the Father, and the Lord Jesus Christ our Savior. (Titus 1:4)

Memory Verse: Let your conduct be without covetousness, and be content with such things as you have. For He Himself has said, "I will never leave you nor forsake you."

Hebrews 13:5
Stewardship Theme

READING

The passage for today centers on the final message. After completing the description of heaven, Jesus reaffirms his second coming and encourages us to be ready.

Read Revelation 22.

REFLECTING

Looking forward to the Messiah, Isaiah writes, "Ho! everyone who thirsts, come to the waters; and you who have no money, come, buy and eat. Yes, come, buy wine and milk without money and without price. Why do you spend money for what is not bread and your wages for what does not satisfy? Listen diligently to Me, and eat what is good, and let your soul delight itself in abundance" (55:1-2). Then John, looking back to the Messiah, picks up the same theme: ". . . the Spirit and the bride say, 'Come!' And let him who hears say, 'Come!' And let him who thirsts come. And whoever desires, let him take the water of life freely."

RESPONDING

1. Praise: Praise the Lord for His salvation which He offers us freely in Christ:

You are the Rock, Your work is perfect; for all Your ways are justice, a God of truth and without injustice; righteous and upright are You. (Deuteronomy 32:4)

The Lord lives! Blessed be my Rock! Let God be exalted, the Rock of my salvation! (2 Samuel 22:47)

Take a moment to offer the Lord your personal praise and thanksgiving.

2. Confession: Pray this confession to the Lord as you seek to keep your life free from sin and in fellowship with Him:

Out of the depths I have cried to You, O Lord. . . . If You, Lord, should mark iniquities, O Lord, who could stand? But there is forgiveness with You, that You may be feared. (Psalm 130:1,3-4)

Confess any personal sins which the Holy Spirit may bring to your mind.

3. Affirmation: As you agree with the will of God, voice your affirmation of His word:

You will keep me in perfect peace, my mind is stayed on You, because I trust in You. (Isaiah 26:3)

4. Requests: As you make your requests known to the Lord, include:

- Boldness in living for Christ
- God's blessing on America
- Your prayer list, the concerns of your heart, and today's activities

5. Closing Prayer: Finally, offer this closing prayer to the Lord:

Be glad in the Lord and rejoice, you righteous; and shout for joy, all you upright in heart! (Psalm 32:11)

Memory Verse: Let your conduct be without covetousness, and be content with such things as you have. For He Himself has said, "I will never leave you nor forsake you."

Hebrews 13:5
Stewardship Theme